THE BLENDING AMERICAN

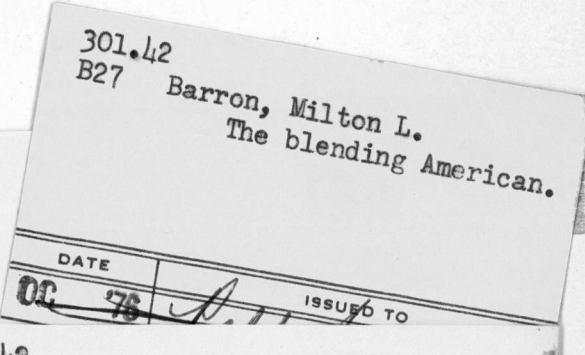

THE
BLENDING
AMERICAN
Patterns of
Intermarriage

Edited by MILTON L. BARRON

Chicago: Quadrangle Books, 1972

THE BLENDING AMERICAN. Copyright © 1972 by Milton L. Barron.
All rights reserved, including the right to reproduce this book
or portions thereof in any form. For information, address:
Quadrangle Books, Inc., 12 East Delaware Place, Chicago 60611.
Manufactured in the United States of America. Published
simultaneously in Canada by Burns and MacEachern Ltd., Toronto.

Library of Congress Catalog Card Number: 78–182502

International Standard Book Number: 0–8129–0234–3

In memory of a most
unusual mother-in-law
Ray Cogan

PREFACE

This is the first comprehensive anthology on the various aspects of intermarriage but it does not represent my first intensive reading in the literature nor the research experience that is the foundation for so much of what we know about the problem. Three decades ago, having completed the course requirements for the Ph.D. in sociology at Yale, I left New Haven and returned to the smaller but equally heterogeneous city nearby where I had been born and raised. My mentors and I were convinced that the important work of such pioneer social science researchers and writers on intermarriage as Adams in Hawaii, Wessel in Woonsocket, and Kennedy in New Haven still left many basic questions unanswered. Perhaps in the compact "human zoo" of my home town a modest research contribution could be made. The smallest in area of Connecticut's 169 townships, it was so richly endowed ethnically that one could identify no less than thirty-two immigrant nationalities and all the major racial and religious components of American society. I spent a year there, gathering and analyzing the data which ultimately were incorporated in my doctoral dissertation, *Intermarriage in a New England Industrial Community*. In the intervening years since its publication under the title *People Who Intermarry,* I have developed several other research, teaching, and publishing interests, but I have lost none of my original curiosity and fascination for the topic, its patterns, and its social ramifications.

Like many other sociologists, I still find in intermarriage literature a bountiful source for understanding the tenacity of ethnic groups, social distance between groups, social equality and inequality, and many aspects of acculturation and assimilation in multigroup societies. Especially noteworthy are the ambivalent attitudes toward intermarriage held by Americans, giving rise to the same dilemma in a single dimension that has been characteristic of American ethnic intergroup relations in general. Almost two centuries ago, for example, the immigrant farmer Jean de Crèvecoeur wrote in admiration of "the American, this new man" as "that strange mixture of blood which you will find in no other country." Much later, and in an even more positive vein, William Jennings Bryan and Israel Zangwill saw intermarriage as the ultimate solution for traditional intergroup hostilities transplanted from the old world. It would produce a homogenized American type which would combine all the virtues of its ingredient ethnic groups. On the other hand, many American laymen have come to view intermarriage as a threat, creating more social problems than it could ever possibly solve. To them it undermines such basic social values as ethnic identity, homogeneity, and group survival. In their judgment it enhances the already ominous indicators of American marriage and family disorganization, particularly the high divorce rate.

This is a strategic time for an intermarriage anthology like *The Blending American*. In the first place, American society is now experiencing the influx of the third generation, the native-born children of native-born parents. These are the grandchildren of the foreign born who comprised the first generation from the heavy "new" immigration that came out of central, southern, and eastern Europe during the years 1880–1930. Unlike their foreign-born grandparents and their second-generation (or native-born of foreign-born) parents, third-generation Americans are not considered "foreign stock." Theoretically, they are sufficiently distant from old world cultural influences to break away at will from the ingroup ties that promote ethnic inmarriage. One would expect, in other words, a population "implosion" within a large range of American society, as expressed by a significantly higher rate of intermarriage on the part of the third generation than in the case of their grandparents and parents. In the second place, opportunities for ethnic intergroup contact culminating in intermarriage have increased immeasurably since World War II, and not the least significant of these has been a consequence of the large movement into higher education. Whereas heretofore college training was available primarily for the children of the privileged classes and white Anglo-Saxon Protestants, and one could thereby expect that during the crucial premarital years people would ordinarily meet their "own kind," today the typical college population is ethnically mixed. There is considerably less assurance now that a son or daughter will meet and fall in love with a classmate of the same race, religion, or nationality. Finally, as a reflection of these and similar social trends, intermarriage literature, both fictional and scientific, has proliferated during the past generation, but nowhere is there a satisfactory volume that samples and coordinates the various major findings and interpretations.

The Blending American represents an effort to achieve this sampling and coordination of the social scientific, especially sociological, literature on intermarriage. Subject to the very practical limitations in book size, I have tried to bring together the most representative thought and research on American intermarriage. When confronted by a difficult choice, I resolved the dilemma by selecting the shorter or more recent essay over the lengthier and more dated competitor. Reluctantly I omitted many equally valuable readings; but they may be pursued independently by the reader who turns to the bibliography at the end of the book.

The introductory part offers three comprehensive perspectives on intermarriage: the first on definition of terms, the second on the factual and theoretical relationships between intermarriage and the social structure, and the last on the scope of research findings in recent decades. Part Two of the book comprises an historical essay on institutional control of intermarriage by the church and state. In Part Three, the questions of measuring intermarriage rates and an appraisal of intermarriage research until mid-century are presented. Part Four explores new research on racial intermarriage and representative nationality intermarriage studies on the West Coast and the East Coast. Part Five is on religious intermarriage, the most thoroughly studied of all ethnic patterns, neither as infrequent as racial intermarriage nor as commonplace as nationality intermarriage. Finally, in Part Six, the spectrum of postmarital consequences of intermarriage is considered, with special emphasis upon the husband-wife relationship and the impact on children.

I am naturally very grateful and acknowledge in the pages that follow my obligations to the authors and publishers on whose previous labor I have so heavily relied. For whatever unintended misuse I may have made of their efforts, I assume an editor's usual role of exclusive responsibility.

Dobbs Ferry, New York   MILTON L. BARRON
Fall 1971

ACKNOWLEDGMENTS

For their kind and gracious permission to reprint the copyrighted materials in this volume, I wish to thank the following publications, scholarly organizations, and publishers: American Jewish Committee (*Commentary* and the *American Jewish Year Book*), American Sociological Association (*American Sociological Review*), Beacon Press, Doubleday, *Jewish Journal of Sociology,* National Council on Family Relations (*Journal of Marriage and the Family*), the *New York Times Magazine, Psychiatry,* the Ronald Press, Syracuse University Press, Thomas Yoseloff (subsidiary of A. S. Barnes and Company), University Extension of the University of California at Berkeley, the University of Chicago Press (the *American Journal of Sociology*), and the University of North Carolina Press (*Social Forces*).

To the following authors of the articles, essays, and excerpts of monographs which appear here, most of whom are my professional colleagues in sociology, I extend my deep appreciation and gratitude: Kenneth E. Barber, Louis A. Berman, Paul H. Besanceney, John Biesanz, Eleanor S. Boll, James H. S. Bossard (deceased), John H. Burma, Harold T. Christensen, Sydney H. Croog, Joseph P. Fitzpatrick, William Barry Furlong, Richard Goldhurst, Albert I. Gordon, Andrew M. Greeley, Bernard Lazerwitz, Robert K. Merton, Erich Rosenthal, Luke M. Smith (deceased), Anselm L. Strauss, James E. Teele, John L. Thomas, and Clark E. Vincent.

To my temporary colleagues at Fresno State College where I spent the sabbatical year of 1969–70, especially Professor William C. Beatty, Jr., chairman, and Margaret Cheatham, departmental secretary, I owe many thanks for providing me with comfortable quarters on a beautiful California campus and for their encouragement and assistance in preparing the first draft of this book for publication. As usual, my wife's advice and patience were indispensable in helping me throughout the entire project.

CONTENTS

What, then, is the American, this new man?
He is neither an European nor the descendant
of an European; hence that strange mixture of
blood, which you will find in no other country.
I could point out to you a family whose
grandfather was an Englishman, whose wife
was Dutch, whose son married a French
woman, and whose present four sons have
now four wives of different nations.

> —JEAN DE CRÈVECOEUR,
> *Letters from an American Farmer,*
> London, 1782

THE BLENDING AMERICAN

PART ONE

Introduction to Intermarriage

Intermarriage, the term most generally used to refer to the crossing of ethnic lines in marital selection, has never satisfied the rigorous demands of conceptual purists in sociology. Obviously, something is conspicuous by its absence, making it an awkward term. If the prefix "inter" means "between," then we have a right to ask: Between whom does the marriage in question take place, other than the implied heterosexual couple? The same criticism may be leveled against the counterpart term—inmarriage. If the prefix "in" is used with the meaning of "inside" or "within," then within or inside of whom does the marriage occur?

Many years ago some scholars suggested the adoption of the neologisms "heterogamy" and "homogamy," preceded by whatever descriptive ethnic term—racial, religious, or nationality—was appropriate. But these and other proposed semantic solutions have never received widespread favor. We must reluctantly accept the fact that intermarriage, and to a lesser degree, "mixed" marriage, predominate in popular usage. The most realistic approach is to understand how these terms are used by examining the context of their usage.

One of the best of the infrequent formal analyses of terminology on the subject was prepared by the late Albert I. Gordon for his book *Intermarriage: Interfaith, Interracial, Interethnic*. In the excerpt that follows, he has provided us not only with a widely accepted set of definitions of terms, but also with the basis for his expectation that an increase in the rate of intermarriage is likely in the immediate future of American society.

INTERMARRIAGE:
WHAT IT IS*

Albert I. Gordon

The term "intermarriage" is generally applied to those married persons whose religious, racial or ethnic background is or was different from each other's, either prior to or after their marriage. Even if the marriage partners differ from each other in only one of these three categories, they may be said to be intermarried. For example, a Catholic married to a Jew is intermarried. This is true, also, of a Protestant married to a Catholic or of a Negro married to a white person. Interethnic marriages involving persons of the same religion and color but differing with respect to national and cultural backgrounds are also said to be intermarriages. An Irish Catholic married to an Italian Catholic is a party to an interethnic marriage. Although we are less inclined to regard the marriage of an Episcopalian to a Baptist as an intermarriage, it may technically be described in these same terms. If one of the parties to the marriage has not formally converted to the faith of the other, such a marriage is more properly termed a "mixed marriage." We shall use the term "mixed marriage" to describe only those marriages in which separate religious ideologies are maintained by the parties subsequent to their marriage.

To be more specific, an interfaith marriage is one in which the parties to the marriage were born or reared in families, each of which has identified with a different religion. If, prior to or following the marriage, the parties continue to identify with their separate religions, they are not only intermarried but are parties to a "mixed marriage" as well. If both parties formally accept the same religion even though they are intermarried, they are nevertheless of the same religious persuasion and hence no longer "mixed."

We shall refer to an "interethnic" marriage as one in which

*Excerpt of Chapter 1 of Albert I. Gordon, *Intermarriage: Interfaith, Interracial, Interethnic* (Boston, Beacon Press, 1964), pp. 1–5. Reprinted by permission of the Beacon Press, copyright © 1964, by Albert I. Gordon.

each of the parties to the marriage was reared in a cultural and nationality environment which differs from that of the other. Thus, an Irish Catholic differs in many ethnic characteristics from an Italian Catholic; a German Jew differs in the same respects from a Russian or Polish Jew. It should be noted that in both cases the religion of the parties is the same. . . .

Interracial marriages are those in which the parties to the marriage belong to different races. . . . Hence, even though a Negro Protestant may marry a white Protestant, their marriage will correctly be regarded as "interracial." . . .

Interfaith marriages are said to occur rather frequently in the United States, but interethnic marriages are, by far, the most common. Racial intermarriages occur least frequently of any of these three types. . . . There are indications that the rate of increase in the three major forms of intermarriage will grow in the years ahead. The reasons may be outlined as follows:

In 1961, for example, there were 2,040 colleges in the United States. Where in 1900 only 4 per cent of the college-age group attended colleges and universities, the college attendance in 1956 was 35 per cent of this age group. . . . Eighty to 90 per cent of high-school graduates in some areas of this country now go to our colleges and universities. . . . There has been an increase of 61.2 per cent in college, university and professional school attendance since 1950. . . . The number is increasing annually. Seven million college and university students are projected by 1970. The high birth rate of the 1940's is thus reflected as is the tendency to regard a college or university degree as indispensable in contemporary American society. . . .

The attitudes of American young people, particularly those who are college and university students, has markedly changed with respect to intermarriage. The social controls of parents, family and organized religion that exerted influence upon our youth prior to World War II have lessened in influence and importance. The reduction of religious denominationalism, so good from one point of view, is nevertheless deleterious and damaging to the survival of Church and Synagogue. The lowering of barriers of race and religion in most fraternities and sororities has increased the opportunities for social intercourse among our college youth. These changes in attitude do not necessarily mean that these young people will, in all certainty, intermarry. There is a vast difference between a person's *attitude* and his ultimate *action*. He may be influenced by many factors that presently fail to impress him. His early religious training; the response to parents, to priest, rabbi or minister in the moment of decision; his knowledge of his own cultural tradition—among other factors— may, as he gets older, tend to sway him from an earlier attitude. The liberalism of an earlier age may give way to a greater conservatism at a later age. Hence, it is hardly likely that every liberal attitude of our college youth will later be translated into a liberal action such as intermarriage is supposed by some to be. . . .

The likelihood that religious, ethnic or racial differences will exist between people who come into contact with each other within the next generation means, too, the further likelihood that more marriages will end in divorce, annulment or separation. For reasons which to date have not been fully explained, the number of divorces and separations between intermarried couples in the past decade has been two to three times as high as those divorces and separations involving persons of the same religion. . . .

It is my hypothesis, supported particularly by a study of attitudes of college and university students in forty schools throughout the nation, in addition to a review of the literature on the subject that:

(1) There will be an increase in all forms of intermarriage— interfaith, interethnic, interracial—with the greatest increase occurring in the area of interethnic marriages, the next greatest in that of different religions and the lowest among different racial groups.

(2) This increase will take place because, in addition to the general factors making for intermarriage, changes have occurred and are occurring within four special areas: (*a*) The number and per cent of young people attending colleges and universities are rapidly increasing. The propinquity resulting therefrom; the increasing similarity of backgrounds, with the consequent reduction in differences along ethnic, educational, economic and national lines; the elimination of sectarianism and denominationalism in state-operated colleges and universities and in private, church-founded schools tends to make cultural homogeneity more likely. (*b*) The elimination of religious differences and distinctions, in schools and out, the ecumenical trends in our society and the indifference to religion generally, tend to minimize the importance

of those distinctions that in former years played a major role in separating and dividing men into distinctive groups. (*c*) The official change in status of colored nations, their recognition by the United Nations and the greater number of their citizens traveling throughout the world (including the United States) and attending our universities and colleges; the lowering of color bars that formerly separated men and women of different races; the increasing number of Negroes who are attending institutions of higher learning; the Supreme Court's decision of 1954, officially outlawing segregation in the schools—all these seem to assure a slow, but definite, increase in racial mixtures. (*d*) The general decrease in parental authority, and the weakening of family ties which is apparent in our day, as well as the attitude of an increasing number of parents who are less militant and more permissive than formerly with respect to intermarriage in any of its forms . . . are consistent with the other patterns. . . . Aware of this and other changes, young people of college and university age are more likely to intermarry in the decades ahead.

Editor's note

To round out Gordon's discussion, it must be pointed out that sociologists and others who have studied and written about the problem of intermarriage do not always agree with him or each other in terminology or definition. Roman Catholic scholars and some Jewish scholars, for example, refer to religious intermarriage as being synonymous with "mixed marriage." On the other hand, some sociologists use the term "mixed marriage" indiscriminately to mean any form of intermarriage: racial, ethnic, as well as religious. Another consideration is in connection with the various refinements in the Roman Catholic definition of religiously "mixed marriage." For their purposes, Catholic authorities have found that a general definition is inadequate. They have devised the four following variations:

1. *Mixed marriage.* This designates a marriage between a Catholic and a non-Catholic who does not subsequently become converted to Catholicism. Two subtypes are: (*a*) *Mixta religio,* a "mixed marriage" in which the non-Catholic was validly baptized, and (*b*) *Disparitas cultus,* a "mixed marriage" in which the non-Catholic was not validly baptized.

2. *Mixed convert marriage.* This specifies a "mixed marriage" between a Catholic and a non-Catholic who subsequently becomes converted to Catholicism.

3. *Invalid mixed marriage.* This refers to a marriage between a Catholic and a non-Catholic before a non-Catholic clergyman or a civil official.

4. *Validated mixed marriage.* Reference here is to a marriage between a Catholic and a non-Catholic which, originally invalid, has been later validated by a priest.

The following selection, originally published in 1941, the oldest contribution to this volume, was written by one of the most distinguished sociologists of our time, an articulate and influential spokesman for the so-called "structural-functional" approach in sociology. In "Intermarriage and the Social Structure," Merton points out that, from a standpoint of functionalism, rates and patterns of inter-marriage are understandable only if one takes into consideration the cultural orientations and the system of social stratification in our society. The social structure comple-ments a personal interaction such as marriage, or, as he puts it, the two phenomena are "mutually implicative." Among the social variables affecting intermarriage incidence and direction are group size, sex ratio, age composition, and degree and kind of intergroup contacts. With special reference to the caste system involving blacks and whites, he shows how structural and functional elements in American society explain the taboo against racial inter-marriage that has been such a pronounced feature through-out most of American history.

INTERMARRIAGE AND THE SOCIAL STRUCTURE: FACT AND THEORY*

Robert K. Merton

The paradox is now fully established that the utmost abstractions are the true weapon with which to control our thought of concrete fact.
— A. N. WHITEHEAD

Intermarriage is a concrete action involving numerous facets, the more dramatic of which have been accorded considerable attention by students of interpersonal relations. The dramatic, however, is not always the theoretically significant; human interest and scientific relevance do not invariably coincide. Among the more prosy aspects of intermarriage is the role of the social structure. Rates and patterns of intermarriage are closely related to cultural orientations, standardized distributions of income and symbols of status. The conflicts and accommodations of mates from socially disparate groups are partly understandable in terms of this environing structure. A provisional theory of structural components in intermarriage, then, can contribute to the analysis of interpersonal relations although, as Sapir has noted, the sociological abstractions refer to consistencies in cultural definitions rather than to the actions of particular persons. The theory of social structure complements the theory of personal interaction; from a functional standpoint, regularities in the two spheres are mutually implicative.

No society lacks a system of marriage. In no society is the selection of a marriage partner unregulated and indiscriminate. The choice, whether by the contractants themselves or by other delegated persons or groups, is subject to regulation by diffuse cultural controls and sometimes by specific social agencies. These regulations vary in many respects: in the degree of control—per-

*Originally published in *Psychiatry*, Vol. 4, No. 3 (August 1941), pp. 361–74. Reprinted by special permission of the William Alanson White Psychiatric Foundation, Inc. Copyright © by the Foundation.

mission, preference, prescription, proscription; in the social statuses which are thus categorized—for example, kinship, race, class and religion; in the sanctions attached to the regulations; in the machinery for carrying the rules into effect; in the degree to which the rules are effective. All this can be said with some assurance but there still remains the problem of systematizing these types of variation into some comprehensible order. To assume that the variations are random is to provide a spurious solution of the problem by abandoning it. The apparent chaos must be shaped into a determinable order. The task of organizing these data has of course long since been taken up. Such concepts as endogamy, exogamy, preferential mating; as caste, class and estate; and a host of interrelated concepts reflect preliminary victories of an attack upon the problem. In this paper we seek to extend these conceptual formulations by suggesting some means for their further integration in the field of intermarriage.

Speaking literally, all marriage is intermarriage in the sense that the contractants derive from different social groups of one sort or another. This follows immediately from the universal incest taboo which forbids marriage at least between members of the same elementary family unit and derivatively restricts marriage to members of different family groups. Marriage contractants invariably[1] come from different elementary family groups; often from different locality, occupational, political, nationality groups; and at times from different religious and linguistic groups, races and castes. Thus, if the term intermarriage is used to denote all marriage between persons of *any* different groups whatsoever, without any further specification of the groups involved, it becomes virtually synonymous with the term marriage and may well be eliminated. In other words, differences in group-affiliation of the contractants may occur, but if these affiliations—for example, political, neighborhood, social clubs—are not defined as relevant to the selection of a spouse, then the case is one of marriage, not intermarriage. The fact is, however, that certain types of marriage are sufficiently distinctive with respect to the group-affiliations of the contractants as to mark them off as a special category. Intermarriage, then, will be defined as *marriage of persons deriving from those different in-groups and out-groups other than the family which are culturally conceived as relevant to the choice of a spouse.* Thus, a given marriage may be, within one

RULES GOVERNING CHOICE OF SPOUSE

PRACTICES IN CHOICE OF SPOUSE	In-Group Marriage Prescribed = Out-Group Marriage Proscribed		In-Group Marriage Proscribed = Out-Group Marriage Prescribed
Conformity to Rule: Agathogamy[2]	Endogamy	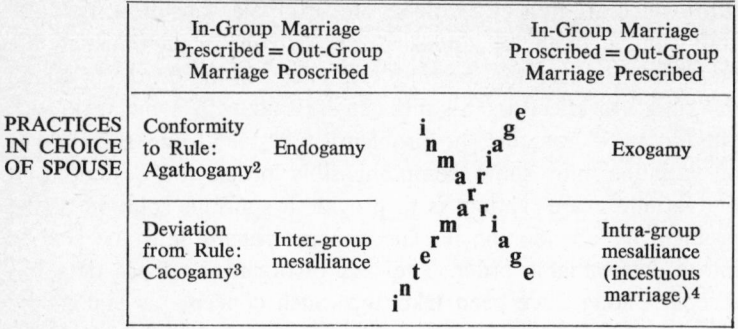	Exogamy
Deviation from Rule: Cacogamy[3]	Inter-group mesalliance		Intra-group mesalliance (incestuous marriage)[4]

frame of reference—for example, the caste—in-marriage, and within another frame of reference—for example, social class—intermarriage. The distinction is analytical.

The standardized rules of intermarriage range from prescription, and social approval, to proscription, and social disapproval. These polar extremes give rise to two distinguishable types of intermarriage: the first, representing conformity to the rules, called *exogamy:* the second, involving prohibited deviations from the rules, may be called *cacogamy.* Prescribed marriage with*in* a specified group is, of course, *endogamy.* The combination of *rules* requiring or forbidding in-marriage and of *practices,* which may or may not conform to the rules, thus generates four type-cases of marriage. These are set forth in the above table.

This set of distinctions may help to eliminate that theoretical confusion in interpretations of intermarriage which stems from the failure to distinguish clearly between the two levels of rules and practices. Marriages which are superficially similar should not be classified as though they were significantly alike. Thus, marriages between persons with grandparents of different nationalities are often categorized as internationality marriage even in those cases where there is no consciousness by the contractants or the community of such group "affiliation" and, more importantly, even where there are no norms in the law or mores prescribing, preferring or proscribing such marriages. Cases such as these are not profitably classified as intermarriage since the ultimate group origins of the contractants are not culturally defined as relevant to the choice of a spouse. They are socially and culturally in-marriages, not intermarriages. The failure to discriminate between norms and practices also obscures the necessary distinction between those intermarriages which are approved and those disapproved by the community. Clearly, cacogamous intermarriages which repudiate social norms are not to be classified with exogamous marriages which represent conformity to these norms. The confusion here lies in not discriminating between significantly different types of marriage just as in the previous instance it lies in discriminating between essentially similar types. Our fourfold table provides a ready guide for the avoidance of such errors.[5]

The distinction between norms and practices of mate-selection is further necessary because practices are influenced not only by the rules but also by certain *conditions* which facilitate or hinder conformity to the rules. In other words, the actual practices are resultants of the norms *and* specifiable conditions of group life. Among the non-normative conditions affecting actual rates of in- and out-marriage are size of groups, sex composition, age composition and degree of contact between members of different groups. These conditions, it will be noted, are not directly matters of standardized attitudes, sentiment or cultural definitions although they are interdependent with normative factors. Norms may affect the degree and type of social contact; as embodied in immigration laws, for example, they may influence the size of nationality groups and indirectly even their sex and age composition. But the conditions may best be treated as largely independent factors in the selection of mates, quite apart from the cultural norms. As Romanzo Adams has indicated in this connection, "the larger the group the higher the percentage of in-marriage, irrespective of any sentiment relative thereto."[6] Likewise, a radical disproportion in the sex ratio, as in the case of Chinese and Filipinos in this country, exerts a pressure for out-marriage. These pressures may be more than counterbalanced by in-group sentiments but analytically it is necessary to recognize their significance. Comparisons between rates of intermarriage in different populations should take account of the relative numbers of potential in-group mates, as affected by size, sex and age composition, territorial distribution and technologically determined opportunities for contact. Norms and actual frequencies of intermarriage, then, are not to be confused.

When, with a changing social structure, the functional significance of certain norms governing choice of a spouse diminishes, the antagonism toward violations and finally the norms themselves will tend to disappear. When the in- and out-groups are in fact progressing toward social and cultural assimilation; when pathways for group consolidation are established; when a considerable part of the population is alienated from traditional group distinctions; when social mobility is notably high; when physical and cultural marks of group distinction have largely disappeared and group "differences" persist merely as a matter of purely technical definition—as, for example, with the third generation of native-born white Americans—then a state of affairs is reached where the quadrisyllable, "intermarriage," is whittled down to a bisyllable, "marriage." The groups previously defined as severally endogamous become redefined as jointly endogamous; the circle of permissible mates is enlarged and the change in social organization is registered by newly modified norms concerning the selection of marriage partners.

Intermarriage whether permitted or tabooed does not occur at random but according to more or less clearly describable patterns. Two of these patterns may be selected for special attention. The first may be called *hypergamy,* a term which we adapt from its usage in connection with the Hindu caste system to denote institutionalized or non-institutionalized patterns of intermarriage wherein the female marries into a higher social stratum, in a system of caste, class or estate—*Stände*. We may introduce the term *hypogamy* to denote the pattern wherein the female marries into a lower social stratum. *Institutionalized* hypergamy or hypogamy denotes those instances where the practice conforms to a norm contained in the law or mores; *non-institutionalized* hypergamy or hypogamy denotes statistical uniformities of a hypergamous or hypogamous nature which are not, however, explicitly governed by a norm. Thus, Hindu hypergamy is an institutionalized pattern; American caste-hypogamy, a non-institutionalized pattern or a statistical uniformity but not a normatively prescribed arrangement.

We have now reviewed certain types of regulations and practices in the field of intermarriage. We have distinguished between endogamous and exogamous norms; between prescription, proscription, preference and permission; between agathogamy, or conformity to rules, and cacogamy, or nonconformity; between hypergamy and hypogamy; between institutionalized and non-institutionalized practices. It is suggested that these conceptual distinctions provide a framework for the observation and arrangement of relevant intermarriage data. In other words, one of the more general theses of this paper is that an explicit conceptual outfit, a part of theory, is necessary even for fruitful discoveries of fact. It is our second general thesis that much of the available statistical materials on intermarriage are of relatively little value because the fact-finders, so-called, have not assembled and classified *relevant* facts and that this inadequacy is tied up with their neglect of a coherent theoretical system in terms of which relevance of facts might be determined.[7] Studies of intermarriage which are concerned simply with "the facts" may incidentally be of some use for the scientific study of the subject but only when they tacitly relate to a system of theory. A science without a matrix of logically inter-related propositions is a contradiction in terms. A canvass of empirical studies of intermarriage suggests that these views need to be labored for the "factual materials" are often discrete, scattered and arranged in what seems to be a wholly private and unusable fashion.

NEGRO—WHITE INTERMARRIAGE

A survey of the scanty statistical materials on Negro-white intermarriage in the United States will illustrate the basis for this judgment. The relations of "fact" and "theory" will be further instanced by setting forth a theoretically oriented taxonomy for the fruitful classification of such data. Accordingly, although our general categories apply to other types of intermarriage as well, the rest of our discussion will be devoted to the caste-class aspects of Negro-white intermarriage in this country. To refer to these cases merely as "interracial marriage" is an insufficiently analytic statement of a complex kind of event. It fails to bring out the fact that such intermarriage involves intercaste, and sometimes interclass, as well as interracial marriage. Furthermore, it does not direct attention to the racial, caste and class origins of each of the marriage contractants. Yet, there are significant sex differentials in the rate of Negro-white intermarriage. These interracial marriages, then, must be resolved into their elements, of which we shall attend to three: the caste, class and sex of each contractant. A classification of these attributes suggests categories in which statistical data on Negro-white intermarriage might profitably be arranged and provides a benchmark for evaluating the available data. The *logically possible* combinations of the three attributes give rise to eight types of Negroes and whites who may enter into marriage.

	Racial caste	Social[8] class	Sex
A.	Negro	lower class	female
B.	White	lower class	female
C.	Negro	upper class	female
D.	White	upper class	female
E.	Negro	lower class	male
F.	White	lower class	male
G.	Negro	upper class	male
H.	White	upper class	male

These eight types of potential mates may be arranged into sixteen logically possible marriage pairs, which are readily classifiable into four major categories: those which conform to norms of both caste and class endogamy; those which involve caste endogamy and interclass marriage; those which involve class endogamy and intercaste marriage; those which deviate from norms of both caste and class endogamy.

I
Caste and class endogamy

1. AE
2. BF
3. CG
4. DH

II
Caste endogamy
Interclass marriage

5. AG—class hypergamy
6. BH—class hypergamy
7. CE—class hypogamy
8. DF—class hypogamy

III
Intercaste marriage
Class endogamy

9. AF—caste hypergamy
10. BE—caste hypogamy
11. CH—caste hypergamy
12. DG—caste hypogamy

IV
Intercaste marriage
Interclass marriage

13. AH—caste and class hypergamy
14. BG—caste hypogamy; class hypergamy
15. CF—caste hypergamy; class hypogamy
16. DE—caste and class hypogamy

Although these sixteen pairings are logically possible, it is evident that they are not, in fact, equally probable. At this juncture the proper procedure would be, of course, to determine the relative frequency with which these possible combinations actually occur in order to test theoretically derived hypotheses concerning the selection of marriage-partners.[9] Significantly, this cannot be done for the available statistical series do not include the necessary data, possibly because the empiricism of "fact-finders" included no canons of theoretical relevance. The statistical data will be briefly reported and the rest of our discussion will be devoted to an interpretation which these data are not altogether adequate to sustain. It should be noted, however, that our hypotheses are such that they are clearly subject to confirmation or refutation when the relevant facts have been assembled.

In view of the fact that Negro-white intermarriage has been forbidden by law in thirty states and condemned by the mores throughout the nation, it is scarcely surprising that such marriages seldom occur. Reuter's estimate of "perhaps less than one hundred per year"[10] since the Emancipation may be a slight understatement, but as the scattered statistics in the table below indicate, the figure is not appreciably higher. Moreover, there is no tendency for this negligible rate to increase.

This low rate of intermarriage is not particularly problematical; it simply reflects a high degree of conformity to strongly entrenched norms. In view of the vigorous taboos on intercaste marriage, we expect that most marriages in this country will be caste-endogamous—categories I and II. What is problematical, what

NEGRO-WHITE INTERMARRIAGE

	Negro males-White females		White males-Negro females		Total	
	Per cent[11]	No.	Per cent[11]	No.	Per cent[11]	No.
New York City, 1908–12[12]..	1.78		.44		1.08	
New York State, 1919–29[13].	2.92		1.00		1.95	
Rhode Island, 1881–93[14]....		51		7		58
Michigan, 1874–93[14].......		93		18		111
Connecticut, 1883–94[14].....		..		..		75
Boston, 1855–90[14].........		..		..		624
Boston, 1900–07[15].........		203		19		222
Massachusetts, 1900[16]......		43		10		53

does require generalized explanation, is the presence of these endogamous norms. Three related problems require consideration. First, what are the structural and functional bases[17] of the current norms governing Negro-white intermarriage? Second, what are the putative sources of deviations from these norms? Finally, how can we account for the prevalently caste-hypogamous pattern of these deviations?

Although the taboos on Negro-white intermarriage are primarily a matter of caste, as distinct from social class, the class affiliations of potential interracial spouses are not altogether irrelevant. In our open-class system, the preferred type of marriage, so far as *both* partners are concerned, is class endogamy. However, this norm is flexible and anything but rigorous for reasons which derive from the class structure itself and from other aspects of the culture. In a mobile social system, it is of course advantageous to marry a person of high class position. Interclass marriage has an acknowledged place as a means of consolidating class-gains within a structure which contains mobility as a primary aspiration. Thus, despite preferential class endogamy, we should expect relatively frequent interclass unions. Paradoxically, this pattern is supported by the prevalent *romantic complex* which emphasizes the dominant importance of "love" rather than utilitarian calculations in choosing a marriage-partner. Romance is presumably blind to class differences. The marriage of the heiress and the chauffeur, the wealthy scion and the shop-girl, when love conquers all, are enshrined in our folklore, our folksongs and drama. The romantic complex is largely but not wholly integrated with preferential class endogamy. Unless closely restricted by the prior importance of class-endogamous preference, romanticism interferes with the smooth functioning of the regulations regarding choice of a spouse; it makes for some instability and lack of consensus in appraising certain interclass marriages which may be disapproved in terms of the endogamous norms but praised in terms of romanticism. Such lack of consensus also derives in part from our *democratic creed* which officially denies strict class lines and thus subverts the effectiveness of preferential class endogamy. These interdependent definitions—preferential class endogamy, on one hand, and romantic and democratic values, on the other— prevent class endogamy from being a stable, unchallenged norm in our society. It is a tendency, not a strict uniformity. We expect the majority of marriages to occur within a social class, if only for reasons of mutual accessibility and participation in common social groups by members of the same class, but the norm is sufficiently flexible to allow frequent interclass unions. Class endogamy is loosely preferential, not prescriptive.

Insofar as Negro-white intermarriage is a matter of social class, that is, insofar as we may temporarily abstract from other considerations affecting such intermarriage, a loose class endogamy with some interclass marriage is to be expected. Of course, it is abundantly clear that Negro-white marriage in our society is *not simply* a matter of the class affiliation of the contractants, but this is no reason for assuming that the class positions of the mates are wholly irrelevant to the probability of certain types of pairing. The class origins of spouses in interracial cacogamy are distinctly relevant to patterns of such intermarriage.[18] However, considerations of social class are supplemented by the norms of caste which prescribe, not merely prefer, endogamy.

In our racial-caste system,[19] the taboos on intermarriage are not materially counteracted by the influences of romanticism and the democratic creed. The romantic complex operates largely with*in* the confines of a caste and, when it fails to do so, it is more than outweighed by caste controls. Moreover, in a racial-caste structure, the criteria of pulchritude are commonly derived from the physical traits characteristic of the dominant caste, so that even in these terms, lower-caste members will usually be deemed "unattractive." These derived aesthetic criteria thus minimize one possible source of deviation from the endogamous norm. Another such potential source, the democratic creed, has been largely accommodated to the caste structure so that its "subversive" influence with respect to the non-democratic caste system is negligible.[20] In other words, although the caste structure is not integrated with the democratic and romantic values, it persists by being largely insulated from the application of criteria contained in these value-systems. Conflict arising from this lack of integration is minimized by segmentation of attitudes and rationalization: democratic and romantic criteria are largely restricted to intracaste evaluations and elaborate explanations account for the necessity, justice and desirability of doing so. Intercaste marriage is not granted even qualified approval as subserving the function of social mobility for mobility is ruled out by the very nature of caste structure. Finally, the contacts between members of different racial castes are regulated by codes of racial etiquette so that there are few opportunities for relationships not involving considerable social distance. This in turn largely prevents the type of contact which might result in marriage.

Thus, various characteristics of the social and cultural structure support the prevalent code of racial-caste endogamy in the United

States. But all this does not account for the existence of such endogamy. What, then, are the structural and functional bases of racial-caste endogamy?

Endogamy is a device which serves to maintain social prerogatives and immunities within a social group.[21] It helps prevent the diffusion of power, authority and preferred status to persons who are not affiliated with a dominant group. It serves further to accentuate and symbolize the "reality" of the group by setting it off against other discriminable social units. Endogamy serves as an isolation[22] and exclusion device, with the function of increasing group solidarity and supporting the social structure by helping to fix social distances which obtain between groups. All this is not meant to imply that endogamy was deliberately instituted for these purposes; this is a description in functional, not necessarily purposive, terms.

Facts which apparently controvert this functional account seem, upon analysis, to lend it further support. Thus, in American society where the class structure involves preferential rather than prescriptive endogamy, interclass marriage acts as a means of social mobility. When groups are relatively permeable, when new class status may be attained through socially recognized achievements, the endogamous norms are sufficiently relaxed to be integrated with mobility. Contrariwise, in a caste system with unbridgeable gaps between strata where individual mobility is the rare exception, the endogamous norms are rigid. This interpretation is consistent with historical changes in endogamous norms. It appears that notable increases in group consciousness and solidarity involve a tightening of endogamous prescriptions. The Nazi taboo on interracial and interreligious marriage is a case in point.

The structural basis for endogamous rules may be seen by examining their bearing upon the conjugal family units themselves. Endogamy ensures to a certain extent that the marriage contractants will have a rough similarity of cultural background inasmuch as they have been socialized in groups with similar cultures.[23] A universe of discourse common to the contractants lessens the likelihood of intra-familial conflict deriving from different sets of values of the spouses. Moreover, by precluding diverse group loyalties of the mates, the conjugal unit is integrated with the larger social structure. Both class and caste endogamy prevent that familial instability which occurs when children identify themselves with the upper-status parent and condemn the lower-status parent in terms of the cultural values which they have assimilated. This potential split of loyalties becomes especially disruptive within a racial-caste system where the child's animosity may be directed against himself as well as the lower-caste parent who bears the invidious racial marks. This interpretation in terms of the functions of endogamy for the conjugal family unit may account in part for the widespread tendency to conceive of the conjugal unit as involving equality of status in the framework of stratification.[24]

A further structural basis for the taboo on intercaste marriage is found in the effect of such marriage upon the network of social relationships in which the contractants are implicated. Marriage introduces the mates into a new set of kinship relations. Kinship relatives, with exceptions such as mother-in-law avoidances which are not relevant here, are culturally defined as standing in a relation involving ready social accessibility.[25] Cacogamous intercaste marriage introduces an abrupt breach into this network of social relations for with it comes a conflict between the superordinate-subordinate relations deriving from status differences of the new-made kin and the mutual accessibility in terms of equality deriving from the kinship structure. Nor does the conflict cease at this point. Each of the persons in the new kinship group is normally embedded in a matrix of friendships and cliques. Usually, such friendship groupings are, apart from age and sex differences, potentially accessible to one another.[26] Intermarriage between persons of radically different social status thus conflicts with the existing organization of cliques and friendship groups involving the spouses and their kin. Rules of avoidance or social distance and rules of accessibility are brought into open conflict. The taboo on such intermarriage may be construed as a defensive arrangement for restricting the incidence of such conflicts. A cross-caste mésalliance would entail a considerable readjustment of established systems of social relationships which, since they are affectively significant, are most resistant to abrupt and profound alterations. Intercaste marriage is thus seen to involve not only an internally contradictory relationship between the spouses but to influence directly an elaborate network of social relations ramifying through the immediate families, the extended kinship group and their friends. Viewed in such a context, the profound emotional resistance to racial-caste intermarriage becomes largely comprehensible. These outbursts of moral indignation are defensive devices which stabilize the existing organization of interpersonal relations and groups.

In a society where certain types of intermarriage are forbidden, several alternative adjustments by cacogamous pairs are possible. The relative frequency of these attempted adjustments depends at least in part on the larger social organization. In any case, the "adjustment" will involve the rupture of some social systems involving the offending pair. In a society such as our own, with its pattern of virtual independence of conjugal groups and with high rates of geographic mobility, ostracism of the offending couple involves a minimum of social readjustment, particularly should the pair leave the immediate community. Such ostracism, when the marriage provoking it is not widely known, *approximates*—though it is not affectively identical with—a recognized cultural pattern in which new conjugal pairs maintain relatively few active relations with their families of orientation and their native community. If the cacogamous pair leaves the local community, the families of orientation are *publicly* little more depleted than if the departure were in response to economic opportunities elsewhere. A highly mobile, segmented society, then, to this extent minimizes the disturbing influences of cacogamy upon the local community and affords somewhat more loopholes for such irregular unions.

In the case of intercaste mésalliances, however, the problem is not solved by such makeshift "escapes" to another community, for here the problem of establishing new social relationships is encountered. This problem becomes almost insuperable in cases of racial-caste intermarriage where ineffaceable physical badges of affiliation with different castes bar the way to a reintegration of the conjugal pair with new social groups. Similarly, when status differences are correlated with marked cultural differences leading to high visibility of another kind, flight from the native community fails to solve the problem. Under these conditions, new relationships can no more satisfactorily be established than the old relationships could be maintained. In cases of intermarriage where both physical and cultural visibility are absent, the temporarily atomized pair may gear into a satisfactory set of new social relationships as a conventional family group. But all such adjustments by the deviant pair which, in the optimum case, may attain some measure of personal success are still at the expense of the social relationships which have been sloughed off by ostracism and mobility. Successful evasions indicate loopholes in the structure of community control, not modifications of the marriage structure. Hence, although a segmented, mobile society may reduce the animus directed toward certain types of cacogamy, it is functionally necessary to maintain such effective antagonism if the going arrangement of social relationships is not to be endangered.[27] Metaphorically, intercaste marriage may be viewed as a catalyst which activates and intensifies group consciousness. It symbolizes the repudiation of standardized cultural values which have been defined as sacrosanct and inviolable. A cultural axiom is being challenged. Cultural orientations are, by virtue of this challenge, presumably no longer secure. The response is immediate and familiar. The violation is intensely condemned; the nonconformists are stigmatized; the cultural norms are reaffirmed. All this has little of design, of the predetermined plan. It resembles rather the automatic, the prompt trigger-like response ensured by socialization and rooted in sentiment. The pattern is an integrated arrangement of action, sentiment and reaction serving to order social relationships. It may suggest a premeditated structure but it is more nearly reminiscent of the ordered integration of reflexive behavior. The crisis arouses self-consciousness; in this instance, consciousness of self as a member of the in-group.

THE PATTERN OF CASTE HYPOGAMY

Structural and functional elements, then, would appear to account for the prohibition of racial-caste intermarriage in our society. The taboo appears to be largely supported by the standardized sentiments of both Negroes and whites and, consequently, the rate of intermarriage continues to be low. But what of the intermarriages which do occur, in spite of the taboo? The most striking uniformity in the statistics of Negro-white intermarriage is the non-institutional pattern of caste hypogamy, *i.e.*, marriage between white females and Negro males. In our samples, such pairings are from three to ten times as frequent as the Negro female–white male combination. This uniformity has often been remarked by students of the subject. Even the collection of mixed marriages assembled from cases "personally known" to a group of students consists of 18 caste-hypogamous unions to seven hypergamous unions.[28] What is the basis of this uniformity?

The hypogamous pattern is clearly not attributable to non-normative conditions affecting intermarriage. There is no significantly unbalanced sex ratio among either the Negro or white populations which can be taken to account for this pattern.[29] Similarly, neither the etiquette of race relations nor sheer propinquity would make for more frequent contacts between white females and Negro males than between Negro females and white males.[30] We may entertain the hypothesis that hypogamy is understandable in terms of the social structure; a view which is not invariably shared by other students of the subject. Thus, Baber raises the question in these non-structural, individualistic terms: "Surely there is no more stigma attached to the white man who marries a Negro woman than to the white woman who marries a Negro. Is color difference in the mate less repulsive to the white woman than to the white man?"[31] This way of posing the problem illustrates the necessity of systematic theory if empirical data are to be made intelligible. An *ad hoc* common sense hypothesis such as Baber's contains no reference to social structure and ignores the fact that most illicit miscegenation involves Negro women and white men. "Repulsiveness" is not a datum; it is a cultural artifact requiring sociological analysis.

Dealing with this same general question, Park asserts that hypergamy is "one principle which seems to have been everywhere operative in determining the amount of miscegenation." It appears to be true that intercaste sex relations largely involve upper-caste males and lower-caste females, but clearly "hypergamy," which denotes a form of *marriage,* is far from universal. Park further holds that hypergamy "seems to be a principle in human nature . . . . which operates spontaneously."[32] A third hypothesis holds that "the disposition of men to go abroad for wives and of women to welcome these roving strangers is probably part of original nature. Human beings are naturally exogamous." Here again, certain abstract characteristics are attributed to human nature as such and, in contrast to Park's usual analytical insight, with no regard for the role of social organization. How would one test the hypothesis that exogamy is fixed in original nature? What theoretical or factual basis exists for this hypothesis? In any case, these gratuitous assumptions do not clarify the prevalently hypogamous pattern of Negro-white intermarriage.

Donald Young[33] and Kingsley Davis[19] have severally advanced hypotheses which may be elaborated to account for the relative frequencies of the logically possible pairings of Negroes and whites. Inasmuch as the statistics show a marked predominance of caste-hypogamy, we know that most of the actual intercaste pairings are contained among the following types: Numbers 10 BE; 12 DG; 14 BG; 16 DE. It is suggested that the frequencies of these pairings may be interpreted within the context of the generalized scheme shown on page 28.

Limitations of space and the absence of sufficient concrete data prevent a detailed analysis of the multiple structural factors involved in patterns of interstratum marriage. The general lines of analysis may be briefly illustrated. In our twofold racial-caste and open-class structure, all Negro-white marriages are cacogamous, that is, they deviate from endogamous norms and are attended by the sanctions of ostracism and the ascription of lower-caste status to offspring. Within such a context, it is likely that pairing Number 10 will be found among the pariahs of the society, among those persons who have become, as it were, "cultural aliens" denying the legitimacy of much of the social structure in which they occupy disadvantaged positions.[34] Interracial cacogamy is, in this instance, simply a special case of the larger repudiation of cultural means and goals. There is little in the way of mutual socioeconomic compensation between the cross-caste mates. This particular pairing, however, would not be expected to occur any more frequently than its complementary hypergamous type, Number 9, involving a lower class Negro female and a lower class white male. Concubinage, rather than marriage, would be the probable type of durable sex relationship in these cases.

Type Number 12, when it occurs, will also not involve mutual compensation with respect to socioeconomic position, since here the class positions of the upper-class mates are roughly equal. The relation is asymmetrical inasmuch as the Negro male does not compensate for the upper-caste status of his wife. Such marriages would be expected to occur among "emancipated" persons, so-called radicals, who repudiate legitimacy of caste distinctions. The sole formal difference between types Numbers 10 and 12, then, is that in the former the contractants are disadvantaged persons who relinquish social norms because of the ineffectiveness of their efforts to gear into the social structure and achieve a "respectable" status, whereas in the latter type, the contractants enjoy eminently satisfactory status as judged by conventional standards but have become alienated from the values, institutional ideologies and organization of the caste system.[37]

VARIABLES IN THE ANALYSIS OF INTERMARRIAGE BETWEEN PERSONS FROM DIFFERENT SOCIAL STRATA

I. *The System of Stratification*

A. Open-class
B. Estate or *Stände*
C. Caste
   1. Racial
   2. Non-racial

these may be combined in concrete social systems: racial caste-and-class in United States; estate-and-class in England, Prussia—especially 18th to 19th centuries

II. *Bases of Ascribed or Achieved Status in the System of Stratification*[35]

A. Membership in a kinship unit
B. Personal qualities—including race
C. Achievements
D. Possessions
E. Authority
F. Power

III. *Types of Intermarriage*

A. Exogamy—agathogamous intermarriage
   1. Compensatory[36]
     a. hypergamy
     b. hypogamy
   2. Non-Compensatory
     a. hypergamy
     b. hypogamy

institutionalized or non-institutionalized

B. Intergroup mésalliance— cacogamous intermarriage
   1. Compensatory
     a. hypergamy
     b. hypogamy
   2. Non-compensatory
     a. hypergamy
     b. hypogamy

IV. *Status of Children of Cross-Stratum Marriage*

A. Matrilineal
B. Patrilineal
C. Positional (that is, status of either upper-stratum or lower-stratum parent)

V. *Status of Conjugal Pair*

A. Same as prior status of husband
B. Same as prior status of wife
C. Same as prior status of upper-stratum spouse
D. Same as prior status of lower-stratum spouse
E. Status of pariahs, outcaste, déclassé

We should expect pairing Number 14—lower class white woman and upper class Negro man—to occur most frequently for it involves a reciprocal compensatory situation in which the Negro male "exchanges" his higher economic position for the white female's higher caste status.[38] This does not at all imply that the "exchange" is necessarily the result of an explicit utilitarian calculus in which the contractants deliberately weigh the economic and social returns to be gained from the marriage. The event may be experienced by them as simply an affectional relationship, but this psychic reaction is manifestly structured by the social organization. A comparable reciprocity pattern often emerges even more clearly in hypergamous unions in caste or estate systems of stratification. In the Hindu caste system, for example, the bride's family "have to pay for marrying her to a man above her in rank, whilst they also desire to make a show of wealth as a set-off to the bridegroom's social advantages."[39] In an estate-system where titles descend patrilineally, the hypergamous exchange of wealth for noble status is often quite explicit, as in the patterns involving American heiresses and foreign nobles since the middle of the last century. Thus, the marriage settlement between Consuelo Vanderbilt and His Grace the ninth Duke of Marlborough was set forth in an official document in which the Duke was guaranteed for life the income from $2,500,000 of Beech Creek Railway stock.

Among the hypogamous pairings, type Number 16 would, on our hypothesis, occur least frequently. Here *both* the class and caste positions of the white female are superior to that of the Negro male, and there is no element of social or economic compensation involved. Such a marriage abjures all social and cultural considerations and for this compound deviation from class-and-caste standards it would be most difficult to find culturally acceptable motivation. It is consistent with our interpretation that the upper class white woman in a union of this sort, reported by Baber, believed that her Negro husband is "the only man who can satisfy her sexually."[40]

This brief canvass of types of caste hypogamy is avowedly hypothetical, but it involves theoretically derived hypotheses which lend themselves to empirical confirmation or refutation. Furthermore, it sets forth the particular attributes which must be included in future statistical and case materials in order to test this interpretation. Baber has apparently made a step in this direction. However, the available data are too unsystematic and fragmentary to provide an adequate test although, so far as they go, they are consistent with our analysis. Thus, Reuter observes that uniformly in intercaste marriages the Negro "groom is of some importance and the white bride a woman of the lower class."[41]

We have yet to examine the structural bases for the greater frequency of caste-hypogamy as compared to caste-hypergamy in our society. Two aspects of the roles ascribed to males and females appear to be primarily relevant. The latitude permitted women to seek an occupational career has increased greatly but it does not approximate that accorded men. Moreover, even in the most "emancipated" circles the status of a conjugal unit is primarily that of the male head of the family. The standardized case is one in which the social rank of the female is largely derivative from that of her husband or, prior to social adulthood, her father. In a society where this is the case, intra-familial conflict often occurs when the wife has outdistanced her husband in the occupational sphere since feminine careers are hedged about by conceptions of the impropriety of competition between husband and wife. Occupational achievement is still considered the usual if not the exclusive prerogative of the male, despite the larger participation of women in economic and public life. The male is "the provider," the chief source of economic status. The second difference in sex roles is contained in the prevalent code of sex morality wherein, despite some slight modifications, the female of the species is more circumscribed in the range of allowable activity. Moreover, it is commonly considered more appropriate that sex relations be initiated by the male; that the male will propose and the female dispose; and that the male will seek out the female, for examples. These definitions are not unchallenged but they exercise a discernible control.

Given these differences in role-definitions, then, an upper-caste male, by virtue of his sex role, may more properly make advances than an upper-caste female and, secondly, he may more readily flout the caste taboos, by virtue of his upper-caste status, than a lower-caste male may dare. In short, the sex morality supports sex advances by the male; the caste morality more easily enables the dominant upper-caste member to initiate cross-caste sexual overtures. Thus, the individuals who incorporate the "male-attribute" and the "upper-caste attribute," that is, white males, may more readily initiate cross-caste sexual relations than either the white female, who lacks the male prerogative, or the Negro male, who lacks the upper-caste prerogative. This enables us to see structural sources of the fact that most intercaste *sex relations*—not marriages—are between white men and Negro women.

It remains to be seen, then, why the durable relationships between white men and Negro women are usually extramarital. Once again, sex roles and the caste-and-class structure would appear to account for the facts. Given the dominance of the white male with his relative immunity from active retaliation by the lower-caste male, there is no pressure to legitimize his liaison by marriage. Concubinage and transient sex relations are less burdensome and less damaging to his status, since these may be more easily kept secret and, even if discovered, are less subject to violent condemnation by fellow caste-members, since they do not imply equality of the sex partners. Furthermore, as Davis has suggested, the marriage of a lower class white male with a wealthy Negro woman is less likely than the complementary hypogamous pairing in view of the standardized role of the male as "economic provider."

We may tentatively conclude that most cross-caste sex relations will be clandestine and illicit. Within a racial-caste structure, the non-institutionalized statistical pattern of the few intermarriages which do occur will be largely hypogamous. In a nonracial caste structure, as in India, the institutionalized pattern of hypergamy may be interpreted as a system manifesting the prerogatives of upper-caste males who thus have *legitimate* access to women of their own caste *and* to women of the immediately inferior sub-caste. In a racial-caste structure, the institution of hypergamy is not probable because the ambiguous position of cross-caste offspring would introduce an instability in the caste system by eventually eliminating the identification of race and caste.[42]

The classification and interpretation presented in this paper are highly provisional and rudimentary: the one needing to be further tested for convenience, the other requiring a larger body of systematically collated data than is yet at hand. The random collection of facts will not lead to further understanding of the phenomenon of intermarriage; the collection of facts in terms of our conceptual framework may do so. Confirmed by whatever relevant facts are available, our interpretation enjoys a measure of plausibility; consistent with a wider body of theory which in turn is supported by systematic empirical inquiry, it may lay claim to a further degree of validity; stated in such terms as to be testable by freshly accumulated facts, it is, at the very least, open to further confirmation or disconfirmation.

NOTES

1. "Invariably" on the basis of a study of 220 societies by George P. Murdock, "Sex Mores and Social Structure," an unpublished paper presented at the annual meetings of the American Sociological Society, 29 December 1940. "All societies prohibit sexual intercourse and marriage between mother and son, father and daughter, and brother and sister. Our 220 cases reveal no genuine exception to any of these three universal incest taboos. To be sure, in two instances brother-sister marriages are customary in the royal family, and in one case a paramount chief may marry his own daughter, but in all three societies such incestuous unions are rigorously forbidden to the rest of the population and special factors explain their occurrence among the chosen few of highest status." Ralph Linton, *The Study of Man*; New York, Appleton-Century, 1936 (ix and 503 pp.); p. 125, holds that "the prohibition of marriage between mother and son is the only one universally present." Whether occasional exceptions to this taboo are "genuine" or not, the approximation to universality is not questioned.

2. *Agathogamy:* marriage which conforms to the norms governing selection of a spouse. From *agathos* = good, virtuous + *gamos* = marriage. At present there is no word to denote that class of marriages which conform to these norms. Agathogamy is intended to fill this gap.

3. *Cacogamy:* marriage which involves tabooed deviations from the norms governing selection of a spouse. From *kakos* = bad + *gamos* = marriage.

4. Incestuous marriages are often termed *inter*marriage. This would appear to be an instance of the rhetorical fallacy of catachresis, in which one term is wrongly put for another. Its source is possibly the following. In lay language, the term intermarriage commonly denotes those marriages which *deviate* from *endogamous* norms. This attribute of *non-conformity and group disapproval* has come to be the identifying characteristic of intermarriage. Hence, incestuous marriage—surely at the polar extreme from inter- (group) marriage—which is also commonly *condemned*, comes mistakenly to be assimilated to the category of intermarriage, which is interpreted as tabooed marriage. This usage is misleading for analytical purposes and should be dropped from the sociological if not the folk lexicon.

5. It will be noted, however, that this classification is not exhaustive for it does not distinguish between permissive, preferential and assortative mating. Uniform patterns of mate-selection and the standardized ratings of potential spouses constitute a familiar phenomenon in many societies. Both preferential mating, which occurs in accordance with definite rules setting forth the particular statuses from which the spouse is to be selected, and assortative mating, which involves selection on the basis of more diffuse cultural values, are contained within the foregoing categories. Rules of preferential marriage simply specify in more detail the status attributes of the potential spouse; assortative mating is also usually within the normative framework—that is, agathogamous. A more detailed analysis would follow through the special features of preferential marriage but this problem is not wholly relevant here.

6. Romanzo Adams, *Interracial Marriage in Hawaii*; New York, Macmillan, 1937 (xvii and 353 pp.); p. 191—Adams has an excellent discussion of the problem of distinguishing between practices and norms in the field of intermarriage.

7. In this general connection, reference is made to Talcott Parsons, "The

Role of Theory in Social Research," *Amer. Sociological Rev.* (1938), 3:13–20.

8. The evident simplification involved in dealing with only two social classes, loosely termed "upper" and "lower," is not of crucial importance at this point. Consideration of further class differentiation would serve only to multiply the possible types of mates without materially affecting the analysis. This twofold class distinction is advisedly a first approximation designed to indicate the general lines of the classification.

9. For the logic of this procedure, consult Paul F. Lazarsfeld, "Some Remarks on the Typological Procedure in Social Research," *Zeitschr. f. Sozial-forschung* (1937), 6:119–139; Carl G. Hempel and Paul Oppenheim, *Der Typusbegriff im Lichte der neuen Logik*; Leiden, A. W. Sijthoff, 1936 (viii and 130 pp.); in particular, pp. 44–101. For other samples of this procedure, consider Robert K. Merton, "Social Structure and Anomie," *Amer. Sociological Rev.* (1938), 3:672–682; Karl Menger, "An Exact Theory of Social Groups and Relations," *Amer. J. Sociol.* (1938), 43:790–798; George A. Lundberg, *Foundations of Sociology;* New York, Macmillan, 1939 (556 pp.); pp. 353 and 372–373.

10. Edward Byron Reuter, *The American Race Problem*; New York, Crowell, 1938 (xiii and 430 pp.); p. 143.

11. These are percentages of "all Negro marriages."

12. Julius Drachsler, *Intermarriage in New York City*; New York, Columbia University Press, 1921 (204 pp.); p. 50.

13. J. V. De Porte, "Marriages in the State of New York with Special Reference to Nativity," *Human Biology* (1931), 3:376–396; in particular, p. 393. These figures are exclusive of New York City.

14. Frederick L. Hoffman, *Race Traits and Tendencies of the American Negro*; New York, Macmillan, 1896 (x and 329 pp.); pp. 198–200.

15. Gilbert T. Stephenson, *Race Distinctions in American Law;* New York and London, D. Appleton, 1910 (xiv and 388 pp.); p. 98. . . . Alfred H. Stone, *Studies in the American Race Problem;* New York, Doubleday Page, 1908 (xxii and 555 pp.); p. 62, reports that 13.6 per cent of all Negro marriages in Boston, 1900–04, were intermarriages with whites. Although Edward Byron Reuter, *The Mulatto in the United States;* Boston, Badger, 1918 (417 pp.); p. 136, quotes this percentage, it appears to be implausibly high and Stone's original sources should be re-checked.

16. Reference footnote 15, *Studies in the American Race Problem,* p. 62. This refers to 37 Massachusetts towns and cities.

17. We are primarily concerned with the generalized, not the historical, bases of these norms. A full analysis would deal with the historical or diachronic as well as the structural-functional or synchronic elements involved. The two approaches are readily integrated in this case.

18. In fact, Miller goes so far as to say that the objection to Negro-white intermarriage is "merely a class objection and strong as it is, it is no stronger than has prevailed between clearly defined classes within the same race." H. A. Miller, "Race and Class Parallelism," *The Annals* (1923), 140:3–4. This view attaches too much weight to class whereas others have completely ignored this element in interracial cacogamy.

19. Kingsley Davis has distinguished between racial castes, nonracial castes and noncaste systems of race relations. He indicates that the differences lead to different types of regulation of intermarriage. "Inter-

marriage in Caste Societies," *Amer. Anthrop.* (1941), 43:376–395. The nature of my extensive debt to Davis' analysis will be evident to those who consult his excellent paper. Despite some differences in terminology, our substantial agreement on certain independently conceived classifications and interpretations may be held to enhance the cogency of both papers. The convergence of independent researches toward common conclusions is, after all, a significant test of reliability. This applies particularly to the following items: conformity to and deviations from norms of mate-selection-agathogamy and cacogamy; ascription to endogamy of the function of making for cultural compatibility of spouses; ascription to the taboo on cacogamy of the function of precluding disruption of the matrix of kinship and other interpersonal relations in which the spouses are embedded; the concept of compensatory intermarriage.

20. Robert K. Merton, "Fact and Factitiousness in Ethnic Opinionnaires," *Amer. Sociological Rev.* (1940), 5:13–28; in particular, pp. 23–28.

21. Reference footnote 1; Linton, p. 204.

22. [E. T.] Hiller has introduced the useful term, *isolation device*, to denote arrangements and symbols which mark off in-groups from out-groups. His usage may be profitably modified to this extent: *isolation devices* are those employed by subordinate groups for this function; *exclusion devices,* those employed by dominant groups. E. T. Hiller, *Principles of Sociology;* New York, Harpers, 1933 (xix and 661 pp.); pp. 24 and 325.

23. Kingsley Davis—Reference footnote 19—properly stresses the importance of this fact.

24. Kingsley Davis, "The Forms of Illegitimacy," *Social Forces* (1939), 18:85–87; Talcott Parsons, "An Analytical Approach to the Theory of Social Stratification," *Amer. J. Sociol.* (1940), 45:841–862; in particular, p. 850. These two papers may be profitably read in conjunction with the present study since they all involve the same general theoretical system.

25. Reference footnote 24; Davis, p. 86.

26. To be sure, friendship groupings are often confined to a single sex and a single generation, but this limits rather than eliminates the potential accessibility of friends and kin of members of the group.

27. This functional statement does *not* imply a value-judgment favoring or rejecting the current social arrangements. Only a perversion of functional analysis systematically results in rationalizations of the *status quo* in various areas of social life.

28. Ray E. Baber, "A Study of 325 Mixed Marriages," *Amer. Sociological Rev.* (1937), 2:705–716. Reference is also made to Baber, *Marriage and the Family;* New York, McGraw-Hill, 1939 (656 pp.); pp. 163–173.

29. Consult, for example, relevant data presented by Oliver C. Cox, "Sex Ratio and Marital Status Among Negroes," *Amer. Sociological Rev.* (1940), 5:937–947.

30. If at all involved, the contrary is more probable since Negro females and white males are more likely to have sustained contacts than are the complementary pairs, in view of the fact that the ratio of Negro women to Negro men engaged in domestic and personal service is about 4 to 1. [It should be added, however, that this disproportion did not obtain prior to 1910, the period to which all but one of our statistics of Negro-white intermarriage refer. Consult Abram L. Harris and Sterling D. Spero, "Negro Problem," *Encyclopedia of*

the Social Sciences; New York, Macmillan, 1937, 11:342; Elizabeth R. Haynes, "Negroes in Domestic Service in the United States," *J. Negro History* (1923), 8:384–442; in particular, pp. 386–393.] In any event, such contacts scarcely serve to account for the caste-hypogamous pattern, in view of the social distance deriving from both caste and class differences.

31. Reference footnote 28; "A Study of 325 Mixed Marriages," p. 706.

32. Robert E. Park, "Race Relations and Certain Frontiers," E. B. Reuter [ed.], *Race and Culture Contacts;* New York, McGraw-Hill, 1934 (261 pp.); in particular, pp. 80–81. Park's essay contains an excellent summary of comparative materials on interracial marriage.

33. Donald Young, *American Minority Peoples;* New York, Harpers, 1932 (xv and 621 pp.); p. 409.

34. For an account of the structural sources of the cultural alien, see Robert K. Merton, "Social Structure and Anomie," *Amer. Sociological Rev.* (1938), 3:672–682.

35. For a discussion of these bases of differential valuation, consider Parsons, reference footnote 24.

36. Ernst Kohn-Bramstedt, *Aristocracy and the Middle-Classes in Germany;* London, P. S. King, 1937 (xii and 362 pp.); p. 244, properly stresses the importance of social or economic compensation in cacogamous intermarriage.

37. One of the cases reported by Baber appears to fall more or less in this category. The white woman "was very well educated, a member of Phi Beta Kappa, and from a highly respected family." The Negro male, evidently highly mobile within the class system, was a law student who came of a poor family. "They were both radicals . . . ." Reference footnote 28; Baber, p. 708. The distinction between the personality types in pairings Numbers 10 and 12 corresponds to those established by Merton as "retreatism" and "rebellion." Reference footnote 34; p. 676.

38. This is the special case of hypogamy with which Kingsley Davis was primarily concerned in which the dual caste-class structure "makes it economically profitable for some white women to marry some Negro males." Reference footnote 19.

39. E. A. H. Blunt, *The Caste System of Northern India;* London, Oxford University Press, 1931 (vii and 374 pp.); p. 70.

40. Reference footnote 28; p. 708. "She comes of an excellent family and is well educated, while he is ignorant and of very poor family stock."

41. Reference footnote 15; Reuter, p. 138. Reuter cites Hoffman's study of 57 mixed unions which were predominantly between members of the lower classes of both castes—pairing No. 10—and included a generous proportion of criminals and prostitutes. This again concurs with our analysis but since Hoffman does not indicate the basis on which he selected his cases, his study cannot be accorded much weight. Only 23 of Hoffman's cases were actual marriages. Although Reuter refers to Hoffman's canvass as a "careful investigation," it should be noted that Hoffman gives only the following indication of the source of his information and the basis of selection of cases: "I have been able during a number of years to collect information of a fairly reliable character in regard to 37 mixed relations. . . ." Reference footnote 14; p. 204. In view of Hoffman's bias and naiveté in other respects, there is no reason to assume that this sample was representative.

42. Consult the article by Davis for a comparative analysis. Reference footnote 19.

The final essay in this introductory section is meant to answer four broad questions on intermarriage, leaving more detailed research findings and theoretical discussions of their significance to the subsequent sections. First, we want to know why American society is such a strategic locus for the social scientific study of intermarriage. Second, we ask how one can account for the inefficacy and virtual breakdown of the controls of intermarriage by institutional mechanisms in the church and state. Third, we are curious about the major social variables associated with the rising incidence of intermarriage in American society. Finally, our concern is with the key marital and familial consequences of intermarriage as revealed by the fragmentary research on these questions.

INTERGROUP ASPECTS OF CHOOSING A MATE*

Milton L. Barron

In the study of intergroup relations it is axiomatic that whenever and wherever two or more races, religious groups or nationalities establish prolonged contact, even under the conditions of intense animosity and great social distance inferred in the confrontations between conquerors and the vanquished during postwar occupations, there will inevitably be some miscegenation,[1] and, as tension lessens and status differences are reduced, a modest incidence of intermarriage.[2] Because the latter, intermarriage, calls for many

36

of the same official and ceremonial sanctions and regulations—
engagement, announcement, license, wedding, witnesses, etc.—as
does intragroup marriage, thereby lending itself to systematic
study, whereas miscegenation is by its very nature furtive and
difficult to observe, our knowledge about one is clearly more reliable than that of the other.

SOCIAL SCIENTIFIC APPROACH TO INTERMARRIAGE

In two respects, from a social scientific point of view, American
society has long been an enviable locus—some have thought of
it as almost ideal—for the study of intermarriage. First, its population, comprised of the descendants of a variety of European and
Asiatic immigrant groups, Negroes predominantly derived from
the west coast of Africa, and an indigenous Indian population,
is unusually heterogeneous in all ethnic respects. In all likelihood
it is the most varied of all western and industrial societies at the
present time with the possible exception of the Soviet Union. If
we consider only those that have experienced acute discrimination, the so-called minorities, the best estimate is that they amount
to approximately 40 per cent of the total American population.
Roman Catholics,[3] the largest single American ethnic minority,
comprise slightly more than 21 per cent; Negroes, the second
largest minority, make up almost 11 per cent; and Jews account
for about 3 per cent. In subsequent, declining order of proportionate size in the general population, there are also substantial
numbers of Southwestern Spanish Americans, Mexicans, Indians,
foreign-born Balkans, Puerto Ricans, whites from Central and
South America and the West Indies, Japanese, Chinese, Mennonites, and minor Asiatic groups.[4] To assume that the remaining
60 per cent of the American population, the ethnic non-minorities,
are homogeneous is to ignore the variation in their national origins
and the fact that they contribute the greater part of the 256 identifiable religious denominations and sects in our society at the
present time.

Secondly, from the very beginning the spectrum of relations between American groups has ranged all the way from genocidal
hostility at one extreme,[5] discouraging all intermarriage, to intergroup indifference that encouraged intermarriage without hin-
drance. However, it has been the broad middle ground of

accommodative tolerance, or what the great pioneer American sociologist, William Graham Sumner, called "antagonistic cooperation" that has characterized intergroup relations in most times and places in American society. In this middle range, the intermarriage pattern as expected is neither sporadic nor voluminous, but nonetheless noticeable. A recognition of this pattern was achieved almost two hundred years ago. At that time, a French aristocrat who had become an American immigrant farmer could write about the emerging new American as follows:[6]

What, then, is the American, this new man? He is neither a European nor the descendant of a European; hence that strange mixture of blood, which you will find in no other country. I could point out to you a family whose grandfather was an Englishman, whose wife was Dutch, whose son married a French woman, and whose present four sons have now four wives of different nations.

There is one other word concerning the social scientific approach to intermarriage. Many, if not most, of the consumers of intermarriage literature produced by sociologists and other social scientists fall into two polarized camps. One group comprises the alarmists and purists who hope to find a battle plan for combatting intermarriage. The other group is made up of assimilationists searching for some indication in intermarriage of a panacea for the problems of intergroup relations. The social scientific approach is usually disappointing to both partisan camps. In the first instance, the scientist's position is that intermarriage in itself need not be an authentic threat to an ethnic group's values of homogeneity, identity, and survival, even though some of the social forces that induce intermarriage are undoubtedly not in the best interests of the group's perpetuation. Recognizing that no one takes pride in noting that his own group prefers outsiders for marriage partners, the scientist is still obliged to point out that in an open society a person has an undeniable right to free marital choice. Berman, a clinical psychologist and authority on Jewish-Gentile intermarriage, put it this way:[7]

An open society where ethnic boundaries survive because they serve the people's need for variety, for belongingness, for continuity, for identity, for authenticity; where ethnic boundaries are not prison walls; where (for example) those Jews who would rather be Gentiles and those Gentiles who would rather be Jews are equally free to cross the boundary and find a more congenial ethnic home—that, in this writer's opinion, is a good society.

In the second instance, the scientific perspective disappoints the assimilationists whose viewpoints happen to be second only to cultural pluralists among members of academic communities. This is because the literature informs them that intermarriage does not have a one-to-one relationship with assimilation, nor is intermarriage free of the symptoms usually associated with social disorganization and abnormal psychology. Rather than functioning as a panacea for the problems of prejudice and discrimination in intergroup relations, intermarriage may actually bring forth a new set of problems focussing on "marginal man" and his ambiguity and alienation in group identification.

INEFFICACY AND BREAKDOWN OF INTERMARRIAGE CONTROLS

All records show that in every society, historical or contemporary, primitive or modern, cultural restrictions are designed to limit the possible marriage partners available to any person. Among the many restrictions, endogamy or inmarriage is basic and universal, for it defines the social groups outside of which marriage is either prohibited or to be avoided. In most societies, endogamy is applicable with respect to race, religion, and, to a lesser extent, nationality background. To frustrate intermarriage along these lines, societies have devised many types of informal taboos and controls, including gossip, ridicule, and family sanctions. But the two social institutions that typically establish formal, explicit control-systems against intermarriage are organized religion and government. The former has generally worked, first of all, to check religious intermarriage. Where this has proved to be impractical, the second line of defense by the Church is to control intermarriage in the sense of reducing to a minimum the consequential loss to the group. The latter in many multigroup societies has enacted laws principally to prohibit racial intermarriage, and in those instances where there is an Established Church, to reenforce the restrictions and sanctions against religious intermarriage as well.

However it is no exaggeration to say that the larger cultural configuration regulating marriage and the family in western, urban, and industrial societies on the whole, and American society in particular, have made these normative restrictions against intermarriage ineffective during the decade of the 1960's. In fact, it appears to be tantamount to a virtual breakdown of institutional controls. Many sociologists now go so far as to claim that in American society, with few exceptions, no institutional controls or edicts—whether they be familial, religious or governmental—can prevent two adult people of the opposite sex from marrying if they so insist. Traits of American culture that have led to this pattern of inefficacy and breakdown of intermarriage controls begin with the high priority in the system of American values placed upon marriage itself. Marriage is such a dominant goal for Americans that they have actually become the most marrying people in the Western world. Since 1890 it has been noticeable that they have married in steadily increasing proportions and at earlier ages. This in turn is related to another cultural generalization about American marriage, namely, that its major purpose is now personal happiness, not family service and the perpetuation of the group. Concomitants of this emphasis on happiness in marriage and de-emphasis on the social obligations of the marital couple are lower birth rates and higher divorce rates. It follows from all this that the American family has become conjugal-centered, built around the married pair and nuclear or segregative from other kin and relatives who count for less than they do in a consanguineal family structure. Horizontal (or spatial) and vertical (or socioeconomic) mobility encourage this reduction in size and the inward orientation of family life. Mobility of this kind in turn influences courtship and marriage patterns in the direction of personal affection and choice, one aspect of which is intermarriage.

The two most prominent expressions of the deterioration of institutional controls of intermarriage occurred in 1966 and 1967, one involving the Roman Catholic approach to religious inter-marriage, and the other having to do with state prohibitions against racial intermarriage. As a concession to the realities of modern conditions[8] and the new ecumenical movement, the Vatican in March 1966 gave Catholic bishops the right to eliminate the requirement for a written pledge by the non-Catholic partner and to refer to Rome for a ruling on any strong objections advanced by the non-Catholic partner to other aspects of the Catholic system of control. It also gave permission to Protestant ministers to speak and pray at a religious intermarriage in a Catholic Church with the consent of the bishop and provided the event does not "shock the faithful." A year later, in February 1967, the Vatican went still further by its recognition of the validity of intermarriages between Catholics and members of the Orthodox Church performed by an Orthodox priest. This concession of validity means that the marriage ceremony at which an Orthodox priest officiates is considered as binding and sacramental as one performed by a Catholic priest and that it bars the Catholic partner from contracting a second marriage while his or her first spouse is alive. Nor are Catholics who marry outside their Church any longer considered separated from Catholicism. But none of these concessions changed either the Catholic insistence that both partners to a religious intermarriage agree to raise their children as Catholics or the Catholic position that Catholics who marry outside the Church are guilty of a "grave sin of disobedience." By April 1970, Pope Paul VI felt compelled to make even further concessions, allowing local bishops to permit a mixed marriage without performance by a priest and permitting the non-Catholic not to promise Catholic rearing of the children.

In June 1967, the Supreme Court of the United States ruled unanimously that the sixteen states that still outlawed racial intermarriages could no longer do so under the Constitution. Prepared by then Chief Justice Earl Warren, the opinion stressed that "we have consistently denied the constitutionality of measures which restrict the rights of citizens on account of race. There can be no doubt that restricting the freedom to marry solely because of racial classifications violates the central meaning of the Constitution's equal protection clause."

SOCIAL PATTERNS IN THE RISING INCIDENCE OF INTERMARRIAGE

It is not surprising, therefore, that a generally consistent finding is that intermarriage rates of all kinds are increasing in American society. The prevailing pattern is that racial intermarriage occurs least frequently, religious intermarriage more frequently, and nationality intermarriage the most of all. Most scholars and researchers concentrate their attention on religious intermarriage because racial intermarriage on the one hand is still a relatively rare phenomenon despite signs of upward dynamics, and nationality intermarriage on the other hand has become so commonplace as to be considered almost normal rather than norm-violating

behavior in many communities. Consequently religious intermarriage has become the only expression of intermarriage worthy
of study for practical purposes.

Virtually everything we know in a systematic way about the
characteristics and patterns of people who intermarry is derived
from studies in small communities conducted by independent researchers. This in itself invites, methodologically speaking, a distorted view of intermarriage. The reason is implicit in the sociological truism that the percentage of intermarriage increases as
the proportion of the group in the community decreases. That is,
the smaller an ethnic group relative to the surrounding population, the greater will be the proportion of its members who contract intermarriage with non-members of the group. The Jewish
case is a good example. The fewer the Jews relative to the Gentile
population in the larger community, the higher will be the rate
of Jewish intermarriage. Therefore, to depend on a perspective
of Jewish intermarriage through the study of social settings where
Jews are few (merely because it is more convenient for a single
researcher) rather than to study the phenomenon in dense and
complex concentrations of Jewish population such as the Northeast where more than half of American Jews are believed to
reside, is to distort the impression of Jewish participation in intermarriage.

The only nationwide factual information on intermarriage was
obtained in the 1957 Current Population Survey conducted by
the United States Census Bureau. Obviously even this has diminished in validity with the passing of each succeeding year. On
the basis of its voluntary but representative sample of American
households, the Bureau determined that 7.2 per cent of existing
marriages in which at least one marital partner was Jewish had a
Gentile spouse, whereas 8.6 per cent of existing Protestant marriages and 21.5 per cent of those involving Catholics were denominational intermarriages.

In 1968, eleven years after the Census Bureau's nationwide
study, the National Opinion Research Center collected information on the original as distinguished from the present religious
denominations of both the respondents who were 1961 college
graduates and their spouses. It showed virtually no difference between the intermarriage rates for young college alumni in 1968
and the general American population in 1957. It should be noted

that the 1957 rates are *cumulative* rates of all living generations in that they tell us the ratios of all the intermarried households to the inmarried households. They are not to be confused with the rates *currently* characteristic of the newlywed generation.

There is very little risk in estimating significantly higher percentages for all three religious groups today. The reason is that intermarriage tends to increase by generations, with the most noticeable increase in the third generation or the native-born of native-born parents. Now that the foreign stock (that is, the foreign-born and the native-born of foreign-born parents) is not replenishing itself by immigration, the years since 1957 obviously have propelled Americans further in the direction of the impact of advanced generations. In the case of the Jews, for example, while the cumulative rate of intermarriage may be about 7 per cent, the current rate is estimated to be as high as 25 per cent.

Spatial and social mobility are also associated with higher intermarriage rates, while immobility in both respects correlates with lower rates. Accordingly, when we find that the more orthodox and conservative branches of a religious group are less mobile than its progressive and liberal wings, we have a right to expect a relatively new community will be actually dominated by those who are most amenable to intermarriage, whereas a relatively stable community is more resistant to the practice. In an even broader sense, one can say that intermarriage has a high instrumental value for those who are so mobile that they feel "out of step" with their ethnic group-of-origin.

College life, too, favors intermarriage, with the graduate school experience serving especially effectively as a predisposing factor. Those who choose the new, salaried professions such as college teaching, engineering, architecture, and journalism are also more likely to intermarry than are those who continue in their parents' traditional, independent businesses, occupations, and professions. In some ethnic groups those who intermarry typically report having had loose and inconsistent family ties to the extent it is possible to generalize that most of them never acquired a secure feeling of family identification.

Unconventional types—actors, musicians, and writers—are likewise prone to intermarry. A sex-bias in the practice takes the form of a preponderance of minority-group husbands married to dominant-group wives.[9] Researchers for the most part explain this in terms of the minority male's culturally defined sex-role permitting him to offset his ethnic disadvantage by implementing the masculine advantage of taking the initiative. What needs to be brought out, however, is that minority-group wives are appearing in increasing frequency in intermarriage roles as they gain in mobility, freedom, and sexual equality with each succeeding generation.

A finding of a few studies is that those who are the youngest in the family have the highest intermarriage rate, the only child occupies the middle range of rates, and the eldest child has the lowest rate. Some utilize the ideas of Alfred Adler and his followers concerning possible differences in personality development and socialization to explain these differences in intermarriage tendencies. But if these Adlerian ideas seem farfetched, one may merely adapt the generational explanation on a small scale to comprehend the pattern.

Another interesting set of variables significantly associated with religious intermarriage concerns age and previous marital experience. Those who intermarry tend to do so at a later age than do those who inmarry, and there is some evidence they are more likely to have been previously married than in the case of their inmarrying counterparts. One interpretation of the greater maturity of intermarrying persons is that it indicates their reluctance to violate the taboo against intermarriage. For such persons, after several marriageable years have passed and no ingroup mate has been found, the taboo presumably loses its potency. As for the pattern of previous marriages among those who intermarry, some scholars claim that divorced and widowed people turn to intermarriage after unsuccessful marriages inside their groups in the first instance and a relative scarcity of eligible endogamous mates as one advances in years in the second place. What this explanation overlooks is that for both older people and those trying second marriages (who, of course, are also likely to be older than those never previously married) there are opportunities to intermarry denied those who are younger and maritally inexperienced. There are fewer inhibitions as well. That is, mobility and death may have removed their parents' conservative influence, and greater sterility that accompanies age may have absolved them from much of the anxiety about their prospective children's ethnic identity. This freedom from the social control exercised by preceding and succeeding generations deserves some credit theoretically for the higher age and previous marital experience of people who inter-marry.

CONSEQUENCES OF INTERMARRIAGE

The evidence that removes much of this from the level of sheer speculation or theory is to be found in the actual comparative rates of childlessness and divorce. People who intermarry are indeed more frequently infertile or without offspring entirely. Re-enforced in their marital status by fewer supportive social pres-sures from parents, children, other relatives, and friends, they more readily turn to divorce after (as well as before) their inter-marriages than in the case of those who have married within the group. An early study of over 13,000 families in a suburb of Washington, D.C., showed a divorce and separation rate of 6.4 per cent for Catholics, 6.8 per cent for Protestants, and 4.6 per cent for Jews. But the rate of divorce and separation for Catholic-Protestant intermarriages was 15.2 per cent. A decade later, a similar study in Michigan of over 4000 cases found a divorce rate of 4.4 per cent for Catholics, 6.0 per cent for Protestants, and 5.2 per cent for Jews. For the Catholic-Protestant intermarriages, the rate was 14.1 per cent.[10] Where one party, however, had con-verted to the religion of the other, the divorce rate was reduced by one-fourth from 14.1 per cent to 10.7 per cent, with no sig-nificant difference attached to the direction in which the conver-sion went.

In a recently conducted study in Indiana,[11] of all couples mar-ried in 1960 and divorced during the next five years, Catholics and Jews had divorce rates 79 per cent and 69 per cent below the state average respectively. But intermarrying Catholics had a di-vorce and annulment rate five times as high as those who had married within the group, and for intermarrying Jews the rate was six times as high as for inmarrying Jews. Since Protestants had a much higher divorce rate than Jews and Catholics to begin with, the increase in divorce rates for intermarrying Protestants was understandably not as impressive in comparison with their in-marrying co-religionists.

Divorce is admittedly not a direct and reliable measure of marital unhappiness, but there is more than one basis for conjecture sociologically, as we have already seen, that if two couples suffer with equal intensity in their marital relations, the intermarried couple would more likely resort to divorce, desertion, or separation than the endogamous couple. The question persists nevertheless: is there actually more unhappiness in one marriage pattern than in the other? The writer, Albert Memmi, discoursing autobiographically on his own intermarriage experience, answers the question as follows: "I have had to conclude that mixed marriage is no solution. . . . It was experience that convinced me of this, and not only my own. I have witnessed many dramas in which this conjugal difficulty was the basis of all conjugal difficulties. On the other hand, I have almost never seen a mixed marriage alter an oppressed condition and very rarely have I seen it subjectively help someone."[12] In stark contrast to this stands an earlier autobiographical account by David Daiches, the Scottish-born literary critic and professor of English literature.[13] Son of a prominent rabbi, Daiches wrote of his intermarriage: "And let me at this point give the lie direct to those who claim that intermarriage never works. I write within a month of our eighteenth wedding anniversary, and I know of no marriage which has been as consistently and mutually rewarding as ours. . . ."

NEW PATTERNS: ECUMENICAL INTERMARRIAGES AND THE UNMARRIED MARRIEDS

The style of intermarriage changes in conformity with the dynamics of intergroup relations and culture. It is now almost commonplace, for example, to announce a religious intermarriage ceremony as having been officiated jointly by the clergy representing the different faiths. The new sexual morality of our times offers an alternative to those who might otherwise find a formal intermarriage too difficult to undertake. "Living together" as "unmarried marrieds" no longer violates the mores and invites the severe sanctions characteristic of an earlier era. Although we have no empirical evidence of the extent to which ethnically heterogeneous couples resort to this practice as a way of avoiding the difficulties of intermarriage, it is reasonable to anticipate that systematic research will uncover a not inconsiderable incidence.

CONCLUSION

Relying mainly on data gathered in small-scale and local studies, and on clinical evidence, social scientists have gradually and painstakingly enhanced our understanding of the processes and problems of intermarriage in American society. The problem, however, is that our references and sources are not sufficiently representative with regard to answering adequately and reliably all key questions concerning the causes, patterns, and consequences of intermarriage. Until social scientists are fully supported in their long overdue study of a nationwide cross-sectional survey of the behavior, we shall have no alternative but to continue to rely upon the same fragmented and uneven data to provide us with the tentative explanations and solutions that will placate our curiosity and anxieties about intermarriage.

NOTES

1. Informal and illicit physical interbreeding between the dominant group's males and minority's females.
2. Formal and legally-sanctioned marriage across racial, religious, or nationality lines.
3. Exclusive of those enumerated here as belonging to specified racial and nationality groups.
4. Including Filipinos, Koreans, and others.
5. One motto suggested normatively that the best Indian was a dead Indian.
6. Jean de Crèvecoeur, *Letters from an American Farmer*, London, 1782.
7. Louis A. Berman, *Jews and Intermarriage: A Study in Personality and Culture*, New York, Thomas Yoseloff, 1968.
8. After a restatement of the Catholic view on the undesirability of marriages between Catholics and non-Catholics, Christians or non-Christians, the instruction issued by the Holy Congregation for the Doctrine of the Faith stated further: "It cannot however be denied that the characteristic conditions of our time, which have rapidly brought about radical changes in social and family life, make more difficult than in the past the observance of canonical regulations regarding mixed marriages."
9. An outstanding exception to this pattern is the case of Japanese intermarriages. For reasons that are not yet sociologically understood, the present pattern is that of non-Japanese husbands married to Japanese wives. But John Tinker's study of Fresno County, California, shows that in the mid–1960's this pattern all but disappeared. See his "Intermarriage and Ethnic Boundaries," unpublished manuscript.
10. The number of Jewish-Gentile intermarriages in both studies were so small that no divorce figures were given.

11. Indiana and Iowa are the two states that list religious affiliation at the time of marriage and divorce, thereby permitting the study of intermarriage through marriage licenses and records. A detailed analysis of the data in both states reveals that the effects of previous marital statuses are uneven. Previous widowhood strongly encourages subsequent ingroup marriage. Previous divorce, on the other hand, leads to so much subsequent intermarriage as to compel consideration that it is a leading force in the etiology of religious intermarriage. See Erich Rosenthal, "Divorce and Religious Intermarriage: The Effect of Previous Marital Status Upon Subsequent Marital Behavior," *Journal of Marriage and the Family,* August 1970, Vol. 32, No. 3, pp. 435–40.

12. *Liberation of the Jew,* New York, Orion Press, 1966.

13. *Two Worlds: A Jewish Childhood in Edinburgh,* New York, Harcourt Brace, 1954.

PART TWO

Institutional Control

How is intermarriage controlled in multigroup societies, and what are the mechanisms of institutional control? How effective are these controls in a society such as our own? As the following essay brings out in considerable detail, the two social institutions that have developed explicit and formal control-systems are organized religion and the state. In the case of the former in western societies, control measures have been generally restricted to confining people's marital selections within the boundaries of religious endogamy. Where there have been "established" churches, effective reenforcement has obviously been secured from the state. However, with the separation of church and state during the past two centuries and the alternative of civil marriage outside the church, clerical controls have tended to be seriously weakened. On the other hand, the state in many societies has enacted laws primarily directed against racial and nationality intermarriages.

With special reference to American society, we shall see how both systems of institutional control have been undermined in recent years to the point where some scholars now describe the situation as one of a virtual breakdown of the efficacy of formal control.

THE CHURCH, THE STATE
AND INTERMARRIAGE*

Milton L. Barron

Endogamy or inmarriage is customary in most societies with respect to societal units such as nationality, religious group, and race. Intermarriage, on the other hand, is generally norm-violating and, like other forms of variant practices, it is often tabooed by the society. It is self-evident that there is no real need for explicitly formulated rules forbidding intermarriage in societies that are homogeneous and geographically isolated. Only when groups are in contact and intermarriage is a potential or an actual alternative to inmarriage does a system of formal control develop to supplement the mores of endogamy in each group.

As Romanzo Adams generalized: "If society wishes to prevent the intermarriage of men and women . . . it must resort to some sort of social control—public opinion, religious doctrine and ritual, or legal prohibition or all together." Bernhard Stern maintains that the rules prohibiting intermarriage are constantly changing in their direction and intensity and the sanctions against such practice range from ridicule and scorn to ostracism and death. Although there is no evidence that any modern society applies the death penalty to intermarried people, severe measures are not unknown. For example, during World War II, nine Dutch churches vigorously protested to the Netherland Reichscommissar against a Nazi-imposed decree for the sterilization of male members of "mixed marriages" between Jews and Gentiles.

The two social institutions which have formulated systems to control intermarriage are the Church and the State. The former has generally tabooed religious intermarriage. The latter in many societies has enacted laws prohibiting racial and nationality intermarriages, and, at times, religious intermarriages. It is appropri-

---

*Revision of Chapter 3 of Milton L. Barron, *People Who Intermarry* (Syracuse: Syracuse University Press, 1946), pp. 21–59. Reprinted by permission of Syracuse University Press, copyright © 1946. Most footnotes omitted.

ate that an analysis of these systems of institutional control and an evaluation of their effectiveness historically be presented.

ECCLESIASTICAL CONTROL

In societies where religious ritual and ceremony give significant sanction to marriage and where the interest of the group is oriented around sectarian beliefs, religious differences interfere with free intermarriage. Religious sects demand unreserved loyalty and their emotional appeals for group cohesion develop attitudes of zealous exclusion in the marriage relation with members of other sects. The antagonisms against intermarriage are intensified if the religious leaders are seeking to counteract the assimilation process concomitant with religious tolerance or if there has been a tradition of embittered conflict between the religious groups involved.[1]

Jewish Regulation of Religious Intermarriage. The Jews are the logical choice for an introduction to the history of ecclesiastical control of intermarriage. This is so not only because of their chronological position, but also by reason of their characterization as a socio-religious group with unusually marked inmarriage tendencies. A migrating people from the earliest period in their history, the Jews constantly faced the problem of preserving their identity and their religious beliefs when confronted with prolonged contact with other peoples. It was recognized by Jewish leadership that marriage with non-Jews endangered the religion of Israel. Consequently, intermarriage was tabooed.

Biblical literature contains many explicit statements forbidding the practice. The first one is expressed in Deuteronomy as follows:

When the Lord thy God shall bring thee into the land whither thou goest to possess it, and shall cast out many nations before thee . . . thou shalt make no covenant with them . . . neither shalt thou make marriages with them; thy daughter thou shalt not give unto his son, nor his daughter shalt thou take unto thy son. For he will turn away thy son from following Me that they may serve other gods; so will the anger of the Lord be kindled against thee and He will destroy thee quickly.

The contagious "nations" with whom intermarriage was prohibited were initially limited to seven in number—the Hittites, Girgashites, Amorites, Canaanites, Perizzites, Hivites, and Jebusites.

Despite this interdiction and any others that may have been formulated previously, intermarriages were probably quite common in the early period of Jewish history. Many of the patriarchs had Gentile wives and they were undoubtedly imitated by their followers. Furthermore, Jews were permitted to marry Gentile women captured in warfare, provided the women shaved their heads, pared their finger nails, and mourned for their parents for a full month.

The incidence of religious intermarriage by the Jews during their Babylonian captivity, 586–516 B.C., indicates that the extant prohibitions were largely ineffective. Ezra noted that "the holy seed have mingled themselves with the people of those lands" and Malachi deplored the tendency of Jews "marrying daughters of a strange God." Accordingly the Jews were urged to abandon their Gentile wives and children. In addition, the prohibition against intermarriage was extended to include all non-Jews.

In post-Biblical times, the rabbinical authorities reaffirmed the position of Ezra and Nehemiah and forbade marriage with all Gentiles. No special provision was made concerning intermarriage with Christians, even though they were not regarded as heathens. In effect they were excluded along with other Gentiles. However, Jews were permitted to intermarry with the Gentile converts to Judaism. Punishment for transgression of the intermarriage taboo was known as *cherem*—a ban or curse imposed upon the guilty Jewish party by the religious authorities equivalent to social death or excommunication. This became the established law of the Talmud and the Rabbinical Code.

In one respect, the Talmudic law surpassed the Biblical in its opposition to religious intermarriage. It considered the practice to be invalid and stated that the contracting parties were not even obliged (from a religious standpoint) to be formally divorced in order to nullify their marriage and to separate. Talmudic authorities, such as Maimonides and the codifiers and commentators of the rabbinical law during the Middle Ages, all agreed in the condemnation of religious intermarriage.

During the first thousand years of the Christian era, Judaism and Christianity were not clearly distinguishable. Therefore intermarriage between Jews and Christians was frequent, despite prohibitive measures by both the Jewish and the Christian religious authorities. They decreased, however, with the widening breach between Christian and Jew after the Crusades. In the year 1280, the Talmudic prohibitions against intermarriage were restated in a book written by Moses Coucy who urged those Jews who had married Christians and Moslems to annul their marriages.

The effectiveness of Jewish control of intermarriage in Europe during the Middle Ages was enhanced considerably by an aversion to intermarriage among Christian authorities. Furthermore, European states endorsed the Christian Church's policy regarding religious intermarriage because "the ancient and medieval countries were churches as well as states and could not allow those to be citizens who could not be of the State religion. The isolation into which the Jews were thus cast led in the course of time to a feeling of combined contempt and terror about them among the populace. . . . The ancients already had something of this feeling, and this was intensified when the Christian Church rose into power, regarding as it did, the Jew as the arch-heretic, the Deicide, the incarnate anti-Christ." Fishberg states that there were few religious intermarriages "excepting clandestinely, among persons of different religion in medieval days, when the Church and the Synagogue had full sway over the people. Indeed, before the Church had such great power, intermarriage between Jews and Christians did take place. . . ."

Wherever the church and the state in Europe were separated and civil marriages became acceptable, the effectiveness of the Jewish as well as the Christian systems of intermarriage control declined. The first of these separations accompanied the French Revolution, and religious intermarriage received legal recognition. From France this extended to Belgium, Holland, Denmark, Great Britain, Norway, Sweden, Italy, and the United States. In Germany religious intermarriages were legalized by a law of 1875 although they had already been permitted in some of the German states before that date. In Hungary they were legalized in 1895, and in Rumania, Bulgaria, and Serbia they became permissible before the First World War. The state ban in Russia on religious intermarriage was lifted by the Revolution of 1917. In the former Russian provinces added to Poland the ban was held in force, but religious intermarriages were allowed in the Polish districts which formerly belonged to Austria, i.e., Galicia. In postwar Austria, even though an official permit was necessary for a mixed marriage, it was obtainable without difficulty. Countries where the Moslem religion prevailed continued to ban intermarriage.

As governments terminated their cooperation with the church in the prohibition of Jewish-Christian intermarriage, the actual strength of ecclesiastical control could be more clearly measured. According to Fishberg: "The clergy has been losing its influence in this respect, while the State has not been helping them, and the number of mixed marriages has been increasing among persons belonging to all creeds, including Jews." He pointed out that in Prussia following state recognition of religious intermarriage, the number of such marriages quadrupled while the number of marriages in general increased only 70 per cent. Further evidence was the fact that in the first half of the nineteenth century religious intermarriage constituted less than 3 per cent of the total number of marriages, whereas in 1911 more than one in ten marriages were religious intermarriages.

Civil recognition of religious intermarriage in France led governmental officials to ask whether or not the heretofore strict Jewish ecclesiastical stand had been modified in any way. In 1807 Napoleon I submitted a number of questions to the assembly of Jewish leaders known as the Sanhedrin regarding the status of Jews as citizens. One of the questions was as follows: "May a Jewess marry a Christian, or a Jew a Christian woman, or does the Jewish law order that the Jews should marry among themselves?" The answer given by the Sanhedrin was that ". . .marriages between Israelites and Christians when concluded in accordance with the civil code are valid, and should not be subject to rabbinical anathema (*cherem*)." It said further that the Jewish law does not say a Jewish woman cannot marry a Christian, or a Jew a Christian woman, nor that Jews can marry only among themselves. The prohibition in Jewish law, it was pointed out, applies to idolatrous peoples. Christians, however, are not to be considered idolatrous since they, like the Jews, worship the God of heaven and earth. For this reason, the Sanhedrin emphasized, intermarriages between Jews and Christians had been frequent in France, Spain, and Germany. But, the Sanhedrin added, it could not withhold the fact that the attitude of the rabbis had always been antagonistic to religious intermarriages. Furthermore, although Biblical law did not forbid the Jews to intermarry with non-Jews, marriage according to the more recent Jewish law, the Talmud, required a religious ceremony called *Kiddushim*. Whereas a certain benediction is pronounced during the ceremony and whereas this ceremony cannot be performed unless both parties are Jews, marriage between a Jew and a Christian could not be considered religiously valid.

It is likely that this evasive position taken by the Sanhedrin was influenced by a consideration of the government's liberal tendencies and the consequences that a more conservative statement might have for the Jews in the Napoleonic states. The fact that laymen as well as rabbis were members of the Sanhedrin may account for the concession that a religious intermarriage was to be considered legally, if not religiously, valid. Significant too is the fact that the Orthodox Jews did not accept the Sanhedrin's statement as an expression of their own position. On the other hand, the Reform Synagogue of Germany took an even more liberal stand than that of the French Sanhedrin. At a rabbinical conference in Braunschweig in the year 1844, the German reform rabbinate at first intended merely to endorse the declaration of the Sanhedrin. Instead they resolved "that the intermarriage of Jews with adherents of any of the monotheistic religions is not forbidden, provided that the parents are permitted by the law of the State to bring up the offspring of such marriage in the Jewish faith." One of the rabbis at the conference made a motion to add the words: "and the rabbi is permitted to solemnize them." His amendment, however, was tabled.

The decision of these Reform rabbis at Braunschweig was strongly opposed, not only by the rabbis of Conservative Judaism, but also by some other Reform rabbis. A motion made at the Augsburg Conference of rabbis held shortly thereafter to endorse the resolution of the Braunschweig Conference was voted down. Moreover, Rabbi Ludwig Philippson, the author of the Braunschweig declaration, subsequently changed his views and declared himself against religious intermarriage of any kind. The following quotation from one of his works indicates how his attitude changed:

Religion must pronounce against mixed marriages. It has been said that such marriages will contribute toward the promotion of tolerance and toward bringing the different religions nearer to each other. But, on the other hand, it must be conceded that they contribute as well toward the weakening of true religiousness and sincerity in matters of faith. It is certainly our duty to widen the sway of tolerance so that it may rule over all classes and individuals, however they may differ in regard to creed and religious life. But this duty is not done by merely levelling the religious ground in order to gain a little more space for the dominion of tolerance. Therefore, little as any true friend of religion and humanity could wish that religion should stand between those who sincerely love and cling to each other, deeply as it must pain him to grieve such persons, still, from the standpoint of religion and of a sincere religious life, he cannot but disapprove of mixed marriages.

In 1869, Rabbis Aub and Geiger, members of a committee appointed by the first Reform Jewish Conference at Leipzig, also expressed this viewpoint. They said that harmony could not be expected to be present in a marriage in which the parties were affiliated with widely divergent religious groups such as Christians and Jews. Experience, the two rabbis observed, demonstrates that only in the rarest cases of such religious intermarriage can domestic life be conducted and children be raised according to the requirements of Judaism. They also pointed out that Judaism is the religion of a minority group. If religious intermarriages prevailed, the religion's existence would be endangered.

In England, the orthodox rabbinate, like those in other countries, did not tolerate religious intermarriage except when the Gentile party was converted to Judaism prior to the marriage ceremony. Conversion usually included circumcision if the Gentile was male, and the ritual bath in the case of a Gentile female. The English Reform Jews were also opposed to the practice. Claude Montefiore, a Reform Jewish leader speaking on the principles of religious reform, said: "We agree with our orthodox brethren in rejecting and deprecating intermarriage, for the simple and adequate reason that only by this means can Judaism as a distinct and separate religion be preserved."

France in the nineteenth century had only an Orthodox Jewish synagogue which, of course, opposed religious intermarriage despite the declaration of the Sanhedrin. Nevertheless, the number of religious intermarriages in France was large, and after the final act separating the church and state in 1905, a Reform Synagogue was founded in Paris which permitted "mixed marriages."

In the United States, Orthodox and Conservative rabbis have opposed religious intermarriage as firmly as their European counterparts. But the American rabbis who followed the German Reform movement were lenient in this matter for many years.

Some actually officiated at the ceremonies of Jewish-Gentile inter-marriages. Dr. Emil G. Hirsch, one of the leading Reform rabbis in the United States, stated in 1909 that intermarriage was in-evitable under existing conditions of easily established social relationships between Jews and Gentiles. He said that he could not agree with the opinion of some rabbis that religious intermar-riages would destroy Judaism, for Judaism to him was a philos-ophy of life and an interpretation of history which could survive without an ethnic foundation.

When the number of religious intermarriages by Reform Jews in the United States increased sharply in the latter half of the nineteenth century, a conservative attitude developed among sev-eral rabbis. Rabbi Isaac Wise, outstanding in the Reform move-ment, explained this changing viewpoint in a public lecture, en-titled "Intermarriage," that he delivered in 1883. Among other things, he criticized the position that rabbis should officiate at religious intermarriages in which both parties were religiously lax:

It might be urged that there are thousands and tens of thousands of individuals in this country who profess no religion at all; hence they are free of those prejudices. Why should any rabbi refuse to solemnize in behalf of Judaism the marriage of such irreligious parties whose parents happened to be Jewish on one side and Christian on the other, if no existing law restrains him? . . .To this might be re-plied: Because the parties are irreligious; or because such solemniza-tion would be a mere mockery to persons who profess no religion; and no rabbi will abuse the authority vested in him to perform the task of a lower magistrate; no rabbi has the right to act the part of an ordinary stage actor—to go through a performance and pronounce formulas and benedictions to parties who believe in neither, and can-not consider themselves benefited by either, as the next justice of the peace can declare them man and wife without any performance or benediction.

Rabbi Wise concluded his lecture with the suggestion that the question of religious intermarriage be decided, in connection with the problem of proselytism, by a Jewish synod.

At their conference held in New York City in 1909, the Cen-tral Conference of American Rabbis, the professional association of Reform Jewish clergymen, took up the question. Although many present agreed with Rabbi Wise in his disapproval of inter-marriage as an assimilation-related process, only the following relatively mild resolution was passed by a large majority:

Resolved, that the Central Conference of American Rabbis declare that mixed marriages are contrary to the tradition of the Jewish religion and should therefore be discouraged by the American rabbinate.

An amendment to the effect that a rabbi "ought not to officiate" at a mixed marriage was lost when put to a vote. The chief reason for the failure of this stronger position to take hold was alleged to be the general acknowledgment that if a rabbi refused to officiate, the couple would probably go to a Christian minister. The majority also agreed that each prospective case of intermarriage should be judged on its own merits and that the rabbi should not be tied down by any stringent or arbitrary rules of procedure.

The manner in which American Reform rabbis actually proceeded in cases of religious intermarriage was not determined until 1937. In that year a questionnaire was sent to all members of the Central Conference who were active in the ministry. Of the rabbis who replied, 54.5 per cent said that they did not perform intermarriages and that they favored the enactment of a rule forbidding rabbinic participation in intermarriage ceremonies; 21.25 per cent replied that they officiated at intermarriages but required the couples to promise either that the children be brought up as Jews, or that the couples join a Jewish congregation, or both. The latter group of rabbis indicated their opposition to any rule forbidding participation by rabbis in religious intermarriages. A smaller group, 12.5 per cent, stated that while they themselves did not officiate at intermarriages, they were not opposed to other rabbis acting differently. Seven per cent answered that they did officiate at intermarriages, that they exacted no promises, and that they wanted no rule against rabbis officiating. Finally, there were 4.5 per cent who replied that while they themselves performed intermarriage ceremonies and exacted a promise, they were not opposed to a rule forbidding rabbis to officiate. The significant fact derived from these percentages is that approximately two-thirds of the Reform rabbis admitted they did not officiate at religious intermarriages, whereas only a minority, or one-third, reported they did—and this despite the declared liberal position of Reform Judaism.

Another concrete indication of the trend toward conservatism among Reform Jewish clergymen in the matter of religious intermarriage is the treatment of the subject in textbooks for Jewish youth who attend Reform Sunday schools. One such textbook propagandizes as follows to discourage the practice:

1. Jewish-Gentile romances often lead to tragic results such as suicide.
2. The majority of Gentile college students at times have been opposed to intermarriage with Jews.
3. Jews who intermarry are generally lost to Judaism.

Jewish opposition to religious intermarriage is purported to have a strong foothold in the mores of the people as well as in the sacred documents and dictates of the clerical hierarchy. Regarding cases of Jews marrying Gentiles, one sociologist noted:

Those that do occur are subject to considerable disfavor. . . .This tradition is so strong that it is mentioned in the wills of parents, urging the children not to marry out of the fold. A generation or two ago among many Jews, a father would say Kaddish (a prayer for the dead) over the child who was intermarried, as if he had died. Intermarriage was an unforgivable sin, more sinister and dangerous than religious apostasy, and was never to be condoned on grounds of love or any other basis. Reform Jews, and even apostates, are scarcely less uncompromising in their demand for a rigid enforcement of the rule of endogamy. Many Jewish writers, in fact, refer to intermarriage as "exogamy."[2]

Yet the efficacy of Jewish control of religious intermarriage, both ecclesiastical and lay, has been far from foolproof. Religious authorities became powerless to prevent Jews from marrying Gentiles from the moment various states gave official recognition to such intermarriages. We may conclude our survey of Jewish control policy with the following realistic observation by Fishberg many years ago, an observation that still holds in our time:

Just as they find that it is practically impossible for the majority of the Jews to obey the Sabbath in a country where the majority of the population rests on Sunday, and they therefore have Sunday services in their temples; just as they find that dietary laws cannot be observed by Jews who come in intimate social contact with their Christian neighbors, in just the same manner they acknowledge that social intimacy must often result in intermarriage.[3]

The Development of Roman Catholic Regulation of Religious Intermarriage. It is the belief of Claris E. Silcox and Galen M. Fisher, two expert students of religious intergroup relations in Canada and the United States, that among early Christian ecclesiastics, "the recognition of the manifold complications of marriages involving mixed religions or disparities of cult were inherited, at least in part, from the Jewish people." The New Testament contains no clearly stated prohibition against religious intermarriage except that a Christian should not marry a heathen. This is explained in part by the fact that it would have been impossible to forbid Christians from marrying non-Christians at the time of the Holy Apostles and for many years thereafter because Christians were few in number. The absence of ecclesiastical control of religious intermarriage during the early period of Christianity is also explained by the Church's desire to use "mixed marriage" as a means of proselytism. Only when the Church's success in propagating Christianity was beyond doubt did it feel sufficiently secure to prohibit intermarriage.

Ecclesiastical control did not commence at Rome, but rather it began to appear at various widely diffused centers of early Christianity. Sooner or later, prohibitions were published against Christian intermarriage, not only with "heathens" or "pagans" but also with those regarded as heretics, such as Jews and, subsequently, Protestants. In the Roman Catholic Church prohibitions against intermarriage with "heathens" precede all other prohibitions. The Council of Elvira in the fourth century forbade Christian parents to permit their daughters to marry such people, warning them that the penalty for disobedience would be excommunication. The Council of Chalcedon in 451 extended the list of ineligible marriage mates by legislating against the intermarriage of Catholics with all non-Catholics—namely, heretics, Jews and pagans.

Special attention was next paid to the Jews. The French Council of Orleans in 538 and the Spanish Council of Toledo in 589 declared themselves opposed to intermarriage between Christians and Jews. They were followed by the Council of Rome in 743 under Pope Zachary which pronounced anathema against any Christian who gave his daughter in marriage to a Jew. The same penalty was in store for a widow who married a Jew. No dispensation from these prohibitions was given by any of the councils. Support came from Emperors Constantius, Theodosius, and Justinian who issued strongly worded warnings against Christian-Jewish intermarriages.

With the diffusion of Christianity throughout Europe, the Roman Catholic Church intensified its drive against such intermarriages. From the fifth until the thirteenth century, councils of the Catholic Church issued no less than fourteen decrees, all of which prohibited Catholic-Jewish intermarriage. According to the historian Salo Baron, these numerous pronouncements, many of them reiterations of former decrees by the same councils, were due to the realization by Catholic authorities that Jews were culturally secure and frequently economically superior to the mass of the Christian population in the Middle Ages. They felt that intermarriage with Jews would result more frequently in the conversion of Christians to Judaism than in the baptism of Jews. More recently, especially since the nineteenth century, the authorities learned that the situation was actually the opposite. Conversions to Christianity, as a result of religious intermarriage, far outnumbered those to Judaism, and the children of intermarried couples were even more frequently raised as Christians. Consequently, the Church relaxed its opposition to intermarriage between Christians and Jews with the realization that it was less endangered.

The activities of the Catholic Church to control intermarriage with Jews as early as the medieval period may have included more than the issuance of decrees. It has been claimed that the reason Pope Innocent III, in 1215, ordered Jews to wear a special kind of clothing was his determination to keep Jews apart from Christians and thus prevent intermarriages between them.

Along with the Jews, the Catholic Church next decided to exclude Moslems from intermarriage with Christians. What were the ecclesiastical reasons? The Jews had allegedly been hostile to the early Christian Church, but the Moslems were presumably a far greater menace. Repeatedly they jeopardized the Christian countries of Europe, having taken a large slice when they occupied Constantinople in 1453. It is not surprising, therefore, that the Church entertained the conviction that, as a rule, there was more danger to the faith of the Catholic marrying a Moslem than in marrying other unbaptized persons.

When in the sixteenth century, Protestantism developed in many parts of Europe, particularly in the northern and western areas of the continent, and contact between Catholics and Protestants became frequent and menacing from the Catholic point of view, Catholic synods and councils as well as the Pope added the new heretics to their list of those with whom intermarriage was forbidden. Nevertheless, the subsequent loss to the Catholic Church resulting from Protestant-Catholic intermarriage was alarming, both on the part of Catholic participants and the children of such marriages. In an attempt to prevent such losses, the Council of Trent, 1545–1563 A.D., enacted an impediment of clandestinity which held that intermarriages between Catholics and non-Catholics were "null and void" unless each couple went to the Catholic party's parish priest or another priest delegated by him for the marriage ceremony. Marriages otherwise contracted were "clandestine" marriages. When it became apparent that the Church could not enforce this legislation in predominantly Protestant countries, Pope Benedict XIV in 1741 issued a declaration to the effect that religious intermarriage would be valid in Holland and Belgium provided they were in conformity with the civil laws of those countries. A further concession was made by Pope Pius VI who allowed religious intermarriage to take place in Austria provided no religious rites were used in the ceremony and the public banns were omitted. These two provisions were supposed to show the reluctance of the Church to sanction intermarriage. Similar concessions were made later in other countries of Europe.

Catholic attempts to prevent religious intermarriage were compromised and weakened in other respects as well. The civil laws of some European countries demanded that the male children born of religious intermarriages should follow the religion of their father and the females that of the mother. The popes obviously could not sanction such legislation, but they had no alternative other than to permit parish priests to officiate at intermarriages contracted under those terms. Another Catholic handicap lay in the fact that, in some localities, non-Catholic clergymen were simultaneously civil magistrates and the laws of the land required their officiating at all marriages. This led to a declaration by Pope Pius IX in 1864 that, under such a condition, the Catholic party to a religious intermarriage would be permitted to have a ceremony performed by a non-Catholic minister. But this ceremony would be considered merely the legal one from the Catholic perspective. A second or religious ceremony under Catholic auspices was to be required either before or after the non-Catholic one.

Intermarriage with Protestants continued to occur frequently, despite repeated statements and warnings by popes, bishops, and lesser Catholic authorities that they "must be entirely avoided," were "unlawful," "strictly forbidden," "wholly pernicious," and "detestable." In the year 1922 the German bishops in a joint pastoral letter stated that, according to their statistics, more Catholics were lost to the Church annually through "mixed marriages" than were gained by all the missionary activity of the Church. Ostensibly, the Catholic system of control—especially that concerning intermarriage with Protestants—was grossly inadequate. But despite the greater loss because of intermarriage with Protestants than with any other religious group, Catholic ecclesiastical policy has actually reflected an out-group preference by Catholic laymen for Protestants and other baptized Christians over non-Christians. Christians who are non-Catholic are, from the Catholic point of view, "heretics," but if they were baptized properly, Catholics have conceded that at least they are Christians. On this basis the Catholic Church has regarded intermarriage with them as being less of a violation of the integrity of the Catholic in-group than is intermarriage with "infidels" such as the Jews and Moslems. The Church has expressed these preferences by differentiating between marriages of Catholics to non-Catholic Christians who have been validly baptized, called *mixta religio,* from marriages of Catholics to non-Christians, termed *disparitas cultus.*

The Catholic scale of preference goes even further. Among the least preferred group, the "infidels," a Reform Jew has been considered more desirable in religious intermarriage than is an Orthodox Jew. Permission to marry the former has been easier to obtain from Catholic authorities than in the case of the latter who may be expected to adhere to minutely detailed Jewish traditional observances.

Essentially, there have been two reasons given by Catholic ecclesiastics for their disapproval of religious intermarriage. One is that they have feared culture conflict, "the absence of intimate union and mutual harmony between husband and wife." The second is that they have wished to avoid a loss to the Catholic Church as a consequence of "perversion" of the Catholic party or offspring.

With the revision of its Code of Canon Law in 1918, the Catholic Church attempted to control these conflicts and membership losses by detailed and explicitly formulated rules of procedure for both priests and laymen. First, priests were instructed to "use every endeavor to deter the faithful from contracting mixed marriages." It was tacitly recognized by Catholic authorities, however, that when a prospective intermarriage was brought to the attention of the Catholic parish priest, little could be done to dissuade the couple. The Catholic priest was therefore advised to be prepared for what was likely to be inevitable. He was to concentrate his attention on minimizing loss to the Church. The following "manual" of procedure was suggested for the use of priests:[4]

Even under these trying circumstances, the usual affability and courtesy must not desert us. It will not help matters to visit our severest displeasure on the offenders, for such an attitude may only serve to force them into a more regrettable course of action. The non-Catholic party in particular should be treated with the utmost kindness and consideration. If this is done, a real opportunity may be created and a convert may be won to the Church. Harshness, on the other hand, will spoil everything. In the great majority of cases, the non-Catholic party is not animated by any hostility toward the Church, and will gladly listen to good counsel if it is imparted in a tactful manner. If it is gently hinted that the prospects for future domestic happiness and peace will be brighter and that the necessary dispensation can be obtained more easily on condition that the non-Catholic consents to familiarize himself or herself with the doctrines of the Church, the latter rarely will manifest any reluctance to undergo the required instruction. . . .Manifestly not too much can be expected of the personal fervor of the non-Catholic. His interest in the matter is slight, and his visits to the rectory for instruction may be nothing more than a concession made to the kindness and urbanity of the priest. . . . At all events he must be treated with unfailing and uniform kindness, and his flagging enthusiasm must be buoyed up if necessary. In this manner we may succeed in making a convert; but, whatever may be the outcome, nothing will be lost. For if the non-Catholic party does not enter the fold, at least he will gain a better appreciation of the Church, and the danger of perversion on the part of the Catholic will be lessened.

The Catholic layman who has planned to intermarry may have been given a similarly detailed manual of procedure, such as the following:[5]

The least you can do is to impress upon the Protestant party that if he will not agree to the Catholic education of the children, you will decline the marriage. If he answers that you have agreed already that the children should be educated Protestants, tell him that to keep this promise would be sinful for you. . . . If the other party says he thinks as much of his religion as you do of yours, and you cannot expect of him that which you would not consent to yourself, you may answer that it is not at all the same case. The Protestant may yield rather than the Catholic because the children who participate in the Catholic Church get all the benefits which can be found amongst believing Protestants . . . but the Catholics have got many things which have been set aside by the so-called reformers. . . .

If the Protestant party insists upon the Protestant education of the children, you have no choice but to withdraw from the engagement if you do not want to forsake your faith. You dare not even agree to the proposal often made by Protestants, that the boys should follow the religion of their father and the girls that of the mother. It would be like a woman with twins who nourishes the one and lets the other starve. She is the murderess of the soul of the child whose faith perishes. . . .

Certain formal requirements have had to be fulfilled before the Catholic Church would allow a Catholic and a non-Catholic to be married by a Catholic priest. A waiver or "dispensation" to forego the religious difference between the two parties has been required from the Catholic hierarchy. The dispensation has been awarded only if there were "just and grave causes," among which the application form for dispensation has listed the following:

1. The community in which the Catholic resides contains a small Catholic population, thereby restricting the choice of a marriage partner.
2. The Catholic party is a spinster and her chances of securing a Catholic husband are slight.
3. The Catholic party is a poor widow who needs someone to support her.
4. There is a strong suspicion that the two parties have had sexual relations and "if they do not marry, worse things might happen."
5. Indeed, "worse things have happened and the woman is pregnant."
6. The couple will probably be married by a Protestant minister or by a civil magistrate if the Catholic dispensation is not granted.

Another Catholic requirement for dispensation has been that certain promises be made in writing by both the Catholic and the non-Catholic. Although they have not been considered to be binding in a legal sense, these promises have been believed to exercise some moral restraint on the partners in the marriage. The non-Catholic has been asked to promise that the Catholic party would be permitted to practice Catholicism. Both persons have had to promise that all children resulting from the marriage would be brought up as Catholics. The Catholic party has promised to try to bring the non-Catholic mate into Catholicism if this was not accomplished before the ceremony. Finally, both Catholic and non-Catholic have promised that no marriage ceremony other than that to be performed by the Catholic priest would take place.

In many Catholic dioceses it has also been required that the non-Catholic take at least six instructions from the pastor in Catholic doctrine and the duties of married life. Sometimes the Catholic party has been advised to attend these instructions. Another requirement has pertained to the actual marriage ceremony. According to traditional Catholic ecclesiastical law, religious rites are prohibited in an intermarriage ceremony and the banns must be omitted. Furthermore, the ceremony takes place either behind the rail in church or outside the church, but in the rectory.

In order to enforce the promises regarding uninterrupted allegiance by the Catholic party to Catholicism and Catholic training for all children born to the intermarried couple, the Catholic Church authorities in 1932 issued a letter, listing the punishments for violation. These included religious annulment of the marriage, exclusion from participation in church activities, denial of a church burial, and, in some cases, public excommunication. In 1943 an article entitled "Non-Catholic Clergyman Opposes Mixed Marriage" appeared in the official publication of the Roman Catholic Diocese of Brooklyn, one of the largest dioceses in terms of population in the United States. It represented an innovation in Catholic efforts to discourage and control religious intermarriage by demonstrating to Catholics that non-Catholics as well as Catholic clergymen disapprove of the practice. The article stated that a Toronto Protestant minister "warned against the dangers of mixed marriages" in a sermon he had preached in the Fairlawn United Church there. The clergyman said:

In the crisis of family life, people face the deepest mysteries of life. Sustenance from superhuman sources is needed. It is not easy to meet such crises in fellowship while the parents are unable to share in common worship and hope. Give earnest consideration to the complications involved in mixed marriages, remembering that unless the common ground is found before marriage, difficulties will accumulate afterwards.

Perhaps the best indication of the continuing failure of the Catholic system to check what it has considered to be the undesirable results of religious intermarriage is the fact that a large percentage of "invalid" religious intermarriages have been noted in recent Catholic surveys. The term "invalid mixed marriage" is defined by Catholics as marriage by a Catholic and a non-Catholic before a non-Catholic minister or a civil official.

As a concession to the realities of modern conditions and the new ecumenical movement, the Vatican in March 1966 gave Catholic bishops the right to eliminate the requirement for a written pledge by the non-Catholic partner and to refer to Rome for ruling on any strong objections advanced by the non-Catholic partner to other aspects of the Catholic system of control. It also gave permission to Protestant ministers to speak and pray at a religious intermarriage in a Catholic Church with the permission of the bishop, provided the event did not "shock the faithful." A year later, in February 1967, the Vatican went further and recognized the validity of marriages between Catholics and members of the Eastern Orthodox Church performed by an Orthodox priest. This concession of validity means that the marriage ceremony performed by an Orthodox priest is now considered as binding and sacramental as one performed by a Catholic priest and that a Catholic partner is barred from contracting a second marriage while the first spouse is living. Furthermore, Catholics who marry outside the church are no longer considered excommunicated. However, none of these concessions in 1966 and 1967 changed the Catholic position that Catholics who married outside the Church's jurisdiction were guilty of a "grave sin of disobedience," or the Catholic insistence that both partners to a religious intermarriage had to agree to the education of their children as Catholics.

By April 1970, the Catholic Church felt compelled to make even more concessions. Pope Paul VI decreed relaxation of Roman Catholic policy regarding mixed marriage while upholding the Church's basic opposition to the practice.

In a papal letter allowing local bishops to permit a mixed marriage to be performed without a priest, Pope Paul also lifted the requirement that the non-Catholic partner promise to allow the children to be reared in the Roman Catholic Church. But in another key passage, the papal letter stated that a Catholic marrying a non-Catholic must promise "to do all in his power" to have the children reared as Catholics. This qualifying phrase did not exist in previous Church rules and recognized problems that might be faced by the Catholic party. The Pope noted that mixed marriages involving Roman Catholics were inevitable and were increasing in a world of greater mobility and contact and, in the final analysis, the Church had to recognize man's "natural right to marry and beget children."

Protestant Regulation of Religious Intermarriage. When the Church of England seceded from the Roman Catholic Church, it continued to adhere to the mother church's policy regarding religious difference as an impediment to marriage. Religious intermarriages were prohibited and annulled when Jews and Moslems were the other parties. In 1647, "papists" or Roman Catholics were added to the list of "idolaters" with whom marriage was forbidden. Since then, the regulation of religious intermarriage in the United Kingdom has been related to the existence of civil marriage. During the Commonwealth, marriages were purely civil for they were performed by justices of the peace. A law of Charles II pronounced these marriages as valid without any religious solemnization.

The Marriage Act of 1753 completely reorganized the English law of marriage. Its purpose was to end "clandestine" marriages. The act provided that all marriages, except those of Jews and Quakers, "should be null and void to all intents and purposes" unless they had been celebrated by a priest in orders according to the Anglican liturgy, and after banns had been published in the parish church or in a public chapel. A special license from the Archbishop of Canterbury would be acceptable also in place of the publication of banns. This law recognized marriage as a religious institution only, placing it directly under the authority of the Church, requiring a religious ceremony for a marriage to be valid. In turn, it aroused the protests of members of other religious denominations who objected to being married in an Anglican Church and by an Anglican clergyman.

In 1836 a new law was passed which is still in effect. It introduced once again the purely civil marriage. The marriages of members of the Church of England were unaffected except by the added requirement of civil registry. Dissenters from the Church were permitted to celebrate their marriages in their own chapels. Those who rejected a religious ceremony were permitted to contract a valid marriage before the registrar.

With the exception of some small sects such as the Mennonites who excommunicate any member marrying a non-Mennonite, American Protestants have no formal system of controlling religious intermarriage. Three reasons for this policy are a feeling that religion is essentially a personal matter, and that consequently the rights of individual consciences must be respected, whatever the social dangers in such intermarriages may be; a sense, on the part of Protestant ministers, that they are, in officiating at a marriage ceremony, civil authorities as well as ecclesiastical authorities—probably due to the hangover from the peculiar function of clergymen of the Established Church in England in this connection; and a desire, on an occasion which ought to be associated with all the sanction that a religious rite can give to it, not to withhold a religious ceremony from those who seek to be married, thus compelling them to consider marriage purely as a civil contract.

Protestant clergymen, however, generally object to religious intermarriage. For example, a special commission of the Presbyterian Church in the United States concerned with marriage, divorce, and remarriage, presented to the General Assembly in 1930 the following recommendation:

We recommend as consonant with the religious temper of our day that there be stricken from our confession of faith the following words: "And therefore such as profess the true reformed religion should not marry with infidels, papists, and other idolaters. . . ."
The Commission feels that caution enough is given candidates for matrimony in this section: "It is lawful for all sorts of people to marry who are able with judgment to give their consent; yet it is the duty of Christians to marry only in the Lord," without adding the second sentence, which we recommend for elision, and which we believe adds no weight to the caution, but does add a means of offense.

Although the purpose of this proposal was merely to moderate the language expressing disapproval of religious intermarriage, the General Assembly voted it down.

When the Roman Catholic Church increased its restrictions against religious intermarriage in 1932, Protestant authorities countered with a stronger position of their own. Shortly after the Catholic declaration that year, the Committee on Marriage and the Home of the Federal Council of Churches of Christ announced that "where intolerable conditions are imposed . . . persons contemplating a mixed marriage should be advised not to enter it." The "intolerable conditions" referred to the promises required by Catholic authorities that the children born of intermarriages be raised as Catholics and that the Catholic party encourage the non-Catholic to convert to Catholicism. The committee explained its stand as follows:

Religion is a basic interest in human life, and differences in religion, if these are fundamental, may strain a marriage to the point of breaking, especially where they are aggravated by ecclesiastical interference. No religious body which confesses itself Christian can tolerate the imposition upon one of its own members the requirements of another religious body by which the religious scruples of that member are aroused, or action repugnant to reason and conscience is forced upon him by an authority which he does not acknowledge.

For example, if one of the partners to a mixed marriage submits to the dictation of such an authority and promises that his children will be brought up in a faith which he does not share, reason and conscience are offended, the seeds of future discord are sowed at the very outset of married life, and the prospect of true marriage, with true conjunction of mind and soul, becomes remote. Of if either partner enters upon the union as a propagandist, determined through the intimacies of marriage to subvert the religious faith of the other, disaster is imminent.

The committee advised persons of different Protestant sects who planned to intermarry that they should reach agreement with their partners to attend one or the other of their churches, or a third church if necessary, and that their children should be raised in the chosen church.

In May 1940, the *Messenger,* a religious publication of the Lutheran Church, published an editorial specifically warning against intermarriage with Roman Catholics, as follows:

We should continually pray and do all that we can to strengthen our young people, that they may not be blinded by the glamour of unthinking affection, and consequently become unequally yoked together with a Catholic husband or wife, for these marriages generally are disastrous. There are some exceptions it is true, but they help only to prove the general rule that mixed marriages with Roman Catholics fall short of the attainment of full marital happiness.

In summary, nothing seems more obvious than the fact that the Catholic stance regarding religious intermarriage, especially before the Catholic Church began to make significant concessions in the decade of the 1960's, provoked hostile Protestant responses and became an important bone of contention in the relations between the two groups. To Silcox and Fisher, religious intermarriage had already surpassed the birth control controversy as "the 'hottest spot' in anti-Catholic feeling on the part of Protestants." After Pope Paul's new ruling on mixed marriages in April 1970, the Lutheran World Federation quickly responded with an expression of satisfaction but said that it failed to solve some fundamental issues. A statement issued by the Lutheran General Secretary in Geneva said:

We are pleased by the noticeable effort to alleviate the distress and problems in mixed marriages through new directives. In spite of a certain moderation which seems to apply especially on the pastoral level, it is our impression that there are fundamental issues still not solved. This is particularly true with regard to the continuing obligation to educate the children of a mixed marriage in the Catholic faith and to the fundamental necessity to meet canonical requirements for a valid marriage.

Greek Orthodox Regulation of Religious Intermarriage. The Greek Orthodox Church is opposed to the intermarriage of Orthodox and non-Orthodox individuals. But by making distinctions among the non-Orthodox and ranking them in terms of an order of affinity to itself, the Orthodox Church's policy resembles the Roman Catholic system of out-group preference. Intermarriage with *schismatici,* or those who differ from the beliefs and practices of the Greek Orthodox in minor points only, is viewed as less objectionable than intermarriage with *haeretici,* or those who differ in fundamental doctrine. Also like the Roman Catholic Church, Greek Orthodoxy in Europe asked that children resulting from the marriage of Orthodox and non-Orthodox be raised in the Orthodox religion. These regulations of religious intermarriage were supported in Czarist Russia, Greece, and Serbia where Eastern Orthodoxy in one form or another was the state religion and the government accordingly adopted the ecclesiastical restrictions.

In America, on the other hand, it is only considered advisable, not mandatory, that the offspring of intermarriage be baptized in the Orthodox Church. Furthermore, the Church in the United

States does not proselytize among the non-Orthodox parties to intermarriage. According to an informant priest of the Church, it advises people to remain in their own faith because experience has indicated that "a good Methodist is better than a poor Greek Orthodox." In the last analysis, Orthodoxy is primarily interested in retaining its own people.

Churches and Racial Intermarriage. There are no ecclesiastical laws prohibiting racial intermarriage. Nevertheless, clergymen have been known to refuse to marry couples who have differed racially, even in jurisdictions where racial intermarriage has been legal. One of the most notorious cases occurred in Rockville, Connecticut, in 1928 when a Mayflower descendant, granddaughter of a Confederate general, and a Negro laborer took out a marriage license. All the Christian clergy in the community, in defense of the mores opposed to intermarriage of this type, refused to perform the ceremony, leaving the couple no recourse except to have a civil ceremony.

GOVERNMENTAL CONTROL

Unlike the churches which have sought to control and prevent religious intermarriage only, various governments at different times and in different societies have attempted to check nationality and religious as well as racial intermarriage, their major concern.

Nationality Intermarriage. The only state in the western world which forbade intermarriage on the basis of nationality was Rome. The Roman citizen could legally marry other Roman citizens and aliens who, either individually or collectively, had been granted the privilege of intermarriage with Romans. Privileged aliens consisted of inhabitants of colonies established by Rome elsewhere in Italy. In 212 A.D. when all free subjects of the Roman Empire were granted full Roman citizenship, the range of legal inmarriage was extended accordingly.

Religious Intermarriage. In societies where the religion of the majority of the population has been officially recognized as the state religion, the government has often supported the Church in its endeavors to control and prevent religious intermarriage.

The Roman Emperor Constantine prohibited intermarriage between Christians and Jews in 339 A.D., and in 388 A.D. a statute was enacted which stated that such intermarriages were adulterous. Predominantly Protestant countries have also had state control of religious intermarriage. North Ireland in 1697 passed a law which forbade the intermarriage of affluent Protestants with "Papists." It stated that a Protestant who either owned or was heir to property valued at five hundred or more pounds could not marry a Catholic. The penalty for infraction of this law was forfeiture of all property. This has been interpreted as a law revealing the economic factor underlying many prohibitions against intermarriage, "usually concealed by the overtone of rationalization." The government of North Ireland next turned its attention to Catholic priests in its efforts to thwart religious intermarriage. In 1725 a law was passed making it a felony for a priest to officiate at such an occasion. Twenty years later a new law subjected those who performed "mixed" marriages to capital punishment.

Some Protestant-dominated countries have legislated to counter the Catholic rule that intermarrying couples promise to raise their children as Catholics. The Prussian government in 1825 decreed that all children born of religious intermarriages should be brought up in the religion of the father or, at least, in the religion he saw fit to choose for them. The law forbade priests to exact any promise from persons about to intermarry regarding the religious affiliation of their forthcoming children. This precipitated a controversy between the government and the Catholic bishops of the Rhine province and Westphalia.

Austria in 1868 passed a similar law. It provided that the parents could make any arrangement they pleased about the religious upbringing of their children. In the absence of any such arrangement the boys should be brought up in the religion of their father and the girls in the religion of their mother. Every person above the age of fourteen could have the right to choose his or her own religion independently.

Intermarriage with Jews was forbidden by civil law as well as by ecclesiastical law in many European countries. In Czarist Russia and the former Austrian empire—the two states in which more than half of all Jews in the world lived in the nineteenth century—intermarriage between Jew and Christian could not take place unless the Jew was first baptized. In the case of Austria, one or both of the parties had to declare himself or herself a "freethinker."

With the separation of church and state in Europe and the establishment of civil marriage, one after another of the governments recognized and permitted religious intermarriage despite the protests of the several churches. Civil impediments to marriage based upon the religious affiliation of one of the parties were abolished. However, a few European states did not abandon control. Poland, for example, continued to prohibit intermarriage between Christians and Jews until its conquest by Germany in 1940. The Polish government also required that the male children of intermarriage involving Catholics and Protestants follow the father's religion and the female children follow that of the mother. Yugoslavia and Lithuania before the Second World War, like Poland, also prohibited intermarriage between Christians and Jews.

The revival of state control of religious intermarriage in European countries began in Germany in the autumn of 1935 when the Nuremberg laws were enacted. The prohibition of intermarriage under these laws was based upon alleged blood or hereditary differences rather than religious differences. Marriages between Jews and "Aryan" Germans were forbidden "for the protection of German blood and German honor." According to the same laws, marriages were also prohibited between Jews and Jewish "mongrels" having only one Jewish grandparent. The Germans and Jewish "mongrels" having one Jewish grandparent could not contract marriage with Jewish "mongrels" having two Jewish grandparents without the consent of the Minister of the Interior and the assistant of the Fuehrer or the officer appointed by him. Marriages also could not take place between two Jewish "mongrels" each of whom had only one Jewish grandparent. However, these so-called quarter-Jews could marry "Aryans" in order that "their absorption into the German people may be hastened." Italy adopted a version of this German Nazi system of control in 1938 to indicate its basic orientation with the Third Reich even though racism, of which this type of law was but one expression, was not as pronounced in Italy as it had been for many years in Germany. The Nuremberg laws were extended in the wake of the German conquest of other European countries after 1939.

In the United States, civil law sanctions all religious intermarriages and does not recognize annulment of some such marriages by the Catholic Church. In the Canadian province of Quebec, the civil courts support the Catholic procedure of control to a certain extent. If a Catholic and a non-Catholic are married by a non-Catholic clergyman and the Catholic party later decides to dissolve the marriage, the Catholic authorities will annul the marriage and the civil courts will do likewise. The basis for this is that no Catholic in Quebec has a civil right to contract a marriage with a non-Catholic before a non-Catholic clergyman.

Racial Intermarriage. The first American governmental edict to attempt to deter racial intermarriage was enacted during the colonial period in 1661. The General Assembly of the colony of Maryland, reflecting the attitude of the dominant white caste, deplored the fact that there were many cases of intermarriage between white female servants and Negro slaves. It legislated, therefore, that if any free-born white woman intermarried with a Negro slave, she would be compelled to serve her husband's master as long as the slave lived. Children of all these intermarriages would also be slaves, and those born of racial intermarriages that had occurred before the law was passed were to remain with their parents' master until they reached thirty years of age. A new Maryland law in 1681 provided that any free-born white woman who married a Negro slave with the permission of the latter's master could retain her freedom, and her children would also be free. However, the master or mistress of the intermarried slave and the clergyman who had officiated at such a ceremony were to be penalized by a fine. This law was an attempt to make more effective the deterrence of racial intermarriage by shifting the sanctions to those allegedly responsible for the behavior of slaves.

Some of the other colonies also legislated against Negro-white intermarriage. North Carolina in 1715 provided for a heavy fine and a period of servitude for any white who married a Negro, and a fifty pound fine for the officiating clergyman. Massachusetts in 1705 and Pennsylvania in 1725 passed similar legislation.

The practice of enacting legislation against racial intermarriage continued after the American colonies achieved their independence. By the end of the 1940's there were laws in thirty states prohibiting one or more forms, such as Negro-white, Indian-Caucasoid, Oriental-European, etc. The states so legislating were Alabama, Arizona, Arkansas, California, Colorado, Delaware, Florida, Georgia, Idaho, Indiana, Kentucky, Louisiana, Maryland, Mississippi, Missouri, Montana, Nebraska, Nevada, North Carolina, North Dakota, Oklahoma, Oregon, South Carolina, South Dakota, Tennessee, Texas, Utah, Virginia, West Virginia, and Wyoming. Six of these states considered the prohibition so fundamental that the laws were made part of their state constitutions. Edward B. Reuter, in noting the lack of such legislation elsewhere, cautioned against the presumption that this should be taken as evidence that such marriages were approved or even that there was a popular indifference to them. The absence of such legislation was rather the expression of the fact that Negroes and Orientals were such a negligible part of the population of several states and intermarriages were so few that the question could be ignored. Moreover, the absence of this kind of legislation was a source of some pride and it gave a certain feeling of self-righteousness that was luxuriously pleasing.

It is also noteworthy that in the legislatures of several of the states that never passed laws against intermarriage, bills were actually introduced at one time or another. In some cases they were actually introduced several times. This happened in Wisconsin, Massachusetts, Connecticut, Washington, Kansas, Minnesota, Iowa, Illinois, Michigan, Ohio, Pennsylvania, and New York. Bills were also introduced in Congress to make racial intermarriage unlawful in the District of Columbia.

A clear-cut regional pattern was discernible in the distribution of racial intermarriage laws among the states. All southern and some western states legislated against Negro-white intermarriage, whereas those west of the Mississippi River, especially on the West Coast, had a virtual monopoly on the legal prohibition of intermarriage between white or European with Mongoloid or Asiatic peoples. East of the Mississippi only Virginia, Georgia, and the state of Mississippi legally opposed Mongoloid-white intermarriage.

Chester G. Vernier, one of the most highly regarded specialists in American marriage and family law, analyzed the geographic distribution of racial intermarriage statutes as follows:

The chief basis of such legislation is doubtless the social problem raised by the presence of minority racial groups, and by the existence of a varying degree of race prejudice. In states where the racial minority is large, the social problem and the prejudice are apt to be of proportionate importance. Other factors, such as the social and economic history and development of a state, also exert a definite influence in creating racial prejudice and discrimination, one logical result of which is legislation prohibiting miscegenation.

This applied to the southern states. As for the states west of the Mississippi, Vernier claimed that

the legislation is motivated by the presence of Mongolians in sufficiently large numbers to interfere seriously with the social and economic structure, as well as by a seemingly inherent prejudice against the yellow race, and by a vigorous opposition to their intermarriage with whites. In the states of the Middle West, South and East the problem is practically nonexistent and it is therefore easy to understand why intermarriage is not prohibited.

Illinois, Ohio, and New York were the only states with high proportions of non-whites that did not have intermarriage laws. One of these, Ohio, and the states of Maine, Massachusetts, and Michigan once had statutes prohibiting racial intermarriage which were later repealed. In 1927 and 1928 Senator Cole Blease and Representative Allard H. Gasque of South Carolina collaborated with Senator Caraway of Arkansas in an unsuccessful attempt to have a racial intermarriage law passed for the District of Columbia. At the same time, the Ku Klux Klan and other conservative organizations and individuals were active in introducing similar bills in the legislatures of Connecticut, Maine, Massachusetts, Michigan, New Jersey, and Rhode Island. All such attempts died in committee discussions because of the strong opposition of liberal representatives.

The successfully enacted statutes were, on the whole, nebulous and disagreed with each other in their definitions of the "colored" people with whom intermarriage was forbidden. They differed too in the penalties for violations, although here the range of variation was less than in other respects. Of the states which prohibited Negro-white intermarriage, seventeen used general terms for the former besides "Negro," and these included "mulatto," "black race," and "of African descent." Five states applied the prohibition to Negroes with one-sixth or more of so-called Negro "blood"; six states applied it to those having one-eighth or more of such ancestry; one to people having one-fourth or more; and one to persons having one-sixteenth or more of Negro heritage.

Two states—Georgia and South Carolina—prohibited the inter-marriage of "mestizos" and whites. Five states—Arizona, North Carolina, South Carolina, Oregon, and Virginia—did not allow Indian-white intermarriage. Three states—Louisiana, Oklahoma, and North Carolina—forbade Indian-Negro intermarriage. The motive for the last type of legal prohibition at first seems to be beyond comprehension inasmuch as intermarriage between two ethnic minority groups could not have been of much concern to the dominant whites in the state legislatures. However, reason-able explanations have been offered for two of the three laws. In the case of Oklahoma, the enactment was alleged to have been passed in order to prevent Negroes from sharing the wealth of those Indians who owned oil lands. If there was to be any money gained by racial intermarriage with Indians, the whites wanted to be the sole beneficiaries. In the case of North Carolina, the law was believed to be connected with a legend that the Cherokee Indians of Robeson County had mixed with whites and were therefore "part-white" in ancestry. Indian-Negro intermar-riage would also be white-Negro intermarriage. One version of the legend is as follows:

In 1585, the date of the first attempt by Englishmen to colonize the New World, there was an island off the coast of North Carolina called Croatoan. By the shifting of the sands, it is now probably a part of Hatteras or Ocracoke Island. In 1587, a colony of one hundred and seventy-seven persons under John White was landed by Sir Walter Raleigh on this island. Here, the same year, was born Virginia Dare, granddaughter of John White and the first child of English parents born in America. Later, part of the colonists under White had to go back to England to seek further aid. By agreement, those left behind were to go over to the friendly Croatoan Indians if they needed succor. When Governor White returned many months later, he found the settlement deserted and carved upon a tree nearby the single word "Croatoan." This supposedly meant that the colonists had gone over to the Croatoans. For some unexplained reason, the party under White never went in search of their lost brethren. Not a word more has ever been heard of Virginia Dare and the others. A tradition says that they went over to the Croatoans and eventually became absorbed into that tribe. Credence is given this by the fact that there are many Croatoan Indians—now called Croatans—with light complexion and blue eyes. Recently a considerable body of mixed-blood Indians in Robeson County, North Carolina, have laid claim to descent from this lost colony, and the State has officially recognized them under a separate name as the "Croatan Indians."[6]

Fifteen states prohibited intermarriage between whites and "Mongolians," some of them defining the latter as Chinese, Japanese, Malayans, Koreans, and even "persons of Kanaka blood." The last group to be added to the category of "colored" peoples with whom whites were legally forbidden to intermarry were the Filipinos. In California many protests had been made against Filipino-white marriages. The argument had been that the Filipinos actually were "Mongolians," a group tabooed by California law as marriage partners with "Caucasians." Those unwilling to accept this position had insisted that in fact the Filipinos were Malayan, or Spanish-American, or Anglo-Saxon culturally. They had also pointed out that the California law was not applicable to Filipinos for there was none of this group here at the time the law was enacted. All doubts about the intent of California law in this respect were dispelled in 1933 when a new statute explicitly stated that Filipino-white intermarriages were prohibited. Subsequently, other states interpreted their statutes to include Filipinos among the "colored" peoples with whom whites could not intermarry.

What sanctions were there in store for violations of all these legal prohibitions against racial intermarriage? Twenty-six of the states' laws pronounced the intermarriage null and void, and almost all of them provided penalties of imprisonment or fines, or both, for each party. Many also penalized those who issued marriage licenses for, or who officiated at, racial intermarriages. In Indiana, "counseling or assisting in such amalgamation" was punishable by a fine ranging from as little as one hundred dollars to as much as a thousand dollars. Mississippi provided that "any person, firm or corporation who shall be guilty of printing, publishing or circulating printed, typewritten or written matter urging or presenting for public acceptance or general information, arguments or suggestions in favor of social equality or of intermarriage between whites and Negroes, shall be guilty of a misdemeanor and subject to a fine not exceeding $500 or imprisonment not exceeding six months or both fine and imprisonment in the discretion of the court."

Some states, like Georgia, could not enforce their statutes prohibiting racial intermarriage because there had been no appropriations for that purpose. Others, however, were strict in their law enforcement. During World War II, a Louisiana appellate court, for example, held invalid a marriage between a so-called white man and a woman whose only known Negro ancestor was a great-great grandmother.

The lack of restrictive legislation of this type in the remaining states and the District of Columbia did not necessarily mean complete freedom to cross racial lines in search of marriage partners. Quasi-legal devices to frustrate them were in abundance. In states where there were no such statutes, judges often refused to issue licenses to racially differentiated couples. In the western state of Washington the county auditor whose task it was to determine the mental competence of applicants for marriage licenses often used this power to deny licenses to prospective racial intermarriages. In at least one other state, New Jersey, mental "tests" were also used to prevent such marriages.

After the adoption of the Fourteenth Amendment to the Constitution, the question arose whether or not state laws against intermarriage denied to "colored" peoples the equality guaranteed them by the amendment. Several cases testing the constitutionality of these laws came before the state courts and invariably, until 1947, they were held valid. The decisions in almost all cases were based upon the ground that there was no discrimination since the laws applied equally to both whites and non-whites. Furthermore the courts held that although marriage is a civil contract, it is one over which the state may exercise control with regard to the granting of permission to enter the contract. The following opinion of an Alabama court in 1877 in the case of *Green* v. *the State* was typical of many:

And there are (we presume) but few localities anywhere in the United States, in which the conviction has not obtained, and been approved by minds the most sedate, that the law should absolutely frustrate and prevent the growth of any desire or idea of such an alliance. . . . Manifestly, it is for the peace and happiness of the black race, as well as of the white, that such laws should exist. And surely there can not be any tyranny or injustice in requiring both alike, to form this union with those of their own race only, whom God hath joined together by indelible peculiarities, which declare that He has made the two races distinct.

Besides this theological rationalization upholding the legal taboo, the pseudo-scientific argument that racial intermarriage brings about physical abnormalities in the offspring was also used by legislatures and courts in their laws and decisions against the practice. Yet it has been apparent for a long time that legislation and court decisions have not been very effective, for it is axiomatic that no governmental edict in an "open" society can stop a marriage if a couple is highly motivated to marry. By way of illustration, one can cite an authority on the subject who noted that the California law of 1933 forbidding Filipino-white intermarriages had not succeeded in preventing them "despite the adverse socio-legal attitudes toward such unions. . . ." Not only did Filipinos continue to intermarry with whites inside California in a surreptitious manner, but they also circumvented the law by going to Oregon, New Mexico, Utah, and Idaho—states that lacked prohibitive laws.

Edward Reuter once stated that laws prohibiting racial intermarriage are only as effective as the mores of which they are a formal expression. He believed that the legislation itself probably had no effect at all upon the rates. He also pointed out that in the colonial period the intermarriage laws were largely ineffectual because they could not prevent miscegenation. The best evidence that laws against racial intermarriage have served to control little, if any, of the practice is gained from a comparison of rates in states where it has been legal with those where it has been illegal. In both instances there is little intermarriage. For example, New York State in 1929 had only 2.7 per cent of its Negro grooms and 0.8 per cent of its Negro brides legally marrying whites, and "statistics in this state running back to 1916 indicate little trend in this respect." In Los Angeles, California, on the other hand, for the decade beginning in 1924 and ending in 1933, the rate for illegal racial intermarriages was not significantly lower. Of the total of 4885 marriages by Negroes during that period, only 1.1 per cent were racial intermarriages.

The first indication of the ultimate declaration in 1967 by the United States Supreme Court that such laws are invalid and unconstitutional came in 1948 in the state of California. The previous year a Negro man and a white woman, having been refused a marriage license, challenged the prohibition in court. On October 1, 1948, California's law against racial intermarriage was ruled unconstitutional by the State Supreme Court in a four to three decision. It was the first time that any tribunal in the United States, state or federal, had declared such a law invalid. The court ordered the Los Angeles County Clerk to issue a marriage license to the interracial couple. But legislators in favor of the old prohibition were not ready to concede defeat, for in May, 1951, the California State Senate defied the State Supreme Court and voted by a large majority to keep on the statute books the law forbidding marriages of whites with those of other races. Furthermore, it voted to postpone indefinitely any consideration of a State Assembly bill that would have stricken the ban from the law. While California's judges appeared to be more liberal than its legislators, the reverse seemed to be the case elsewhere. By 1966, as a result of acts of repeal, only nineteen states—the seventeen southern and border states and Indiana and Wyoming—continued to have laws against racial intermarriage. In view of the fact that at one time or another, thirty-eight states had such laws, this represented a 50 per cent decline. But in 1966 the state of Virginia's Supreme Court of Appeals, confronted with the case of an interracial couple who had been married in 1958 in Washington, D.C., upheld unanimously the state's ban on racial intermarriages.

Later that year, the United States Supreme Court granted the appeal of the couple and agreed to decide whether state laws prohibiting racial intermarriages were in fact unconstitutional as claimed by the plaintiffs, Richard P. Loving, the white husband, and Mildred Loving, his part-Negro and part-Indian wife. Although it had long since struck down all other types of laws that created discriminatory racial classifications, the highest court in the land had not yet ruled directly on intermarriage laws. On June 12, 1967, the Supreme Court ruled unanimously that states cannot outlaw racial intermarriage, thereby voiding Virginia's and the fifteen other remaining states' statutes on the subject. In the decision which he delivered, Chief Justice Earl Warren said: "We have consistently denied the constitutionality of measures which restrict the rights of citizens on account of race. There can be no doubt that restricting the freedom to marry solely because of racial classification violates the central meaning of the Constitution's equal protection clause." In writing the opinion that struck down the last category of segregation laws—those requiring racial separation in marriage—Chief Justice Warren completed the process that he had set in motion with his opinion in 1954 that declared segregation in public schools to be unconstitutional.

CONCLUSION

Underlying all varieties of institutional control of intermarriage there appears to be one basic element: the desire for group survival. Even when the institution has relented, such as the church's toleration of religious intermarriage, the conditional requirements have not infrequently been conversion of the out-group individual, with particular emphasis on the affiliation of all children resulting from the intermarriage.

The factor of group preservation has become evident too in the cases of groups such as the Reform Jews and those Protestants whose intermarriage policies were relatively liberal or permissive initially. Reactionary tendencies that developed in the leadership of both groups were based upon the realization that their earlier laissez-faire approach was inimical to the existence of their respective ingroups.

Careful study of the development and efficacy of institutional control demonstrates that no intermarriage can be stopped in a society such as our own if the couple is sufficiently motivated to resist the formal and informal pressures directed against them. It now appears quite certain that nationality groups are less able to withstand the forces of intermarriage than are religious and racial groups. Most types of ethnic groups are still more anxious that their women marry within the group than that their men so conform, but even this seems to be ineffectual. The end of all governmental control of racial intermarriage in the United States and the retreat of the Roman Catholic Church from its traditional highly rigid stance regarding religious intermarriage suggest most clearly that if groups feel threatened by the onslaught of intermarriage, they will have to develop new and more effective mechanisms and sanctions to overcome the powerful forces that make for intergroup and marital convergence in contemporary multigroup societies.

NOTES

1. Bernhard Stern, "Intermarriage," *Encyclopedia of the Social Sciences,* Vol. 8, p. 152.
2. J. O. Hertzler, "The Sociology of Anti-Semitism Through History," Isacque Graeber and Steuart Henderson Britt, eds., *Jews in a Gentile World,* Macmillan (1942), p. 79.
3. Maurice Fishberg, *The Jews: A Study of Race and Environment,* 1911, p. 224.

4. Charles Bruehl, "Pastoralia, Way of Approach," *Homiletic and Pastoral Review,* Vol. 30 (May 1930), pp. 799–800.
5. Allan Stolz, *Mixed Marriage: The Forbidden Fruit for Catholics,* translated from the German by Monsignor H. Cluever, 1938, pp. 16–17.
6. Gilbert T. Stephenson, *Race Distinctions in American Law* (New York: D. Appleton and Co., 1910), pp. 90–91.

PART THREE

Dimensions of Intermarriage

To students and laymen alike, few aspects of intermarriage are more interesting than its dimensions, especially
its incidence and dynamics. How much intermarriage is
there at a given time? Is it increasing or decreasing? Do
some ethnic groups intermarry more than others? Is there
a discernible differential participation by sex?

Unfortunately, answers to these and related dimensional
questions are handicapped by a lack of consensus even with
regard to the meaning of "rate" of intermarriage, the
basic tool in the measurement of the phenomenon. Sociologists such as Besanceney and Rodman, both of whom
have made special studies of the problem, tell us that the
difficulty here is the tendency to use two different systems
of calculating rates indiscriminately: the intermarriage rate
for marrying *couples* and the intermarriage rate for
marrying *individuals*. In the first instance, rate refers to
the percentage of marriages that are intermarriages of all
cases of marriages involving people in a specific ethnic
group. The second usage of rate refers to the percentage of
marrying individuals in a given ethnic group who enter
into intermarriage. This can be illustrated by the performance of a fictitious group, the "Danireans." In a given
year, there are six Danirean inmarriages and four Danirean–
non-Danirean intermarriages. Some researchers would
report this as an intermarriage rate of 40 per cent because
four of the ten marriages involving Danireans were intermarriages. But others at the same time would call it an
intermarriage rate of 25 per cent because four Danireans
out of sixteen intermarried.

One can deduce from this example that it is essential to
indicate which of the two systems of calculating rates is
actually being employed in a given research project and to
make sure that the same system is applied in making
comparisons between two or more research reports. The

formula proposed by Rodman in transforming one rate system into the other is as follows: If x is the intermarriage rate for marriages, and y is the intermarriage rate for individuals, then the former can be transformed into the latter by the equation that $y = \dfrac{100x}{200-x}$. The inverse of this equation is what one follows for transforming the intermarriage rate for individuals into the intermarriage rate for marriages, namely, $x = \dfrac{200y}{100+y}$. It is noteworthy, however, that this distinction between the two systems of calculating rates is necessary only with reference to the performance of a given ethnic group. When reference is made to the total marrying population within a society, there is no difference between the two calculating systems. This can be seen by re-using the illustration of the Danireans. The four intermarriages out of ten marriages produce a rate of 40 per cent, and the total of eight intermarrying individuals (four Danireans and four non-Danireans) out of twenty marrying individuals also produces a rate of 40 per cent.

Still other traps built into the discussion and analysis of intermarriage rates call for caution on the part of the student and the general reader. Where Protestants are considered collectively as members of a single religious category, their intermarriage rates will appear to be lower than that of Roman Catholics, but where each Protestant denomination is considered separately, the rate may be higher. Furthermore, rates of religious intermarriage based on marriage records tend to exclude from consideration those cases in which conversion took place prior to the marriage. If the rates are based upon a household survey (as was true of the 1957 "Current Population Survey" by the Census Bureau which revealed that the cumulative intermarriage rate for marriages—not individuals—was 21.5 per cent for Catholics, 8.6 per cent for Protestants collectively, and 7.2 per cent for Jews), cases are excluded in which conversion occurred after as well as before the marriage—that is, prior to the survey. Both types of exclusion of conversion cases obviously afford a conservative view of the rate of intermarriage.

These and other important considerations in reporting the rates of intermarriage are taken up by Besanceney in the short essay that follows.

ON REPORTING RATES OF INTERMARRIAGE*

Paul H. Besanceney

After reviewing all of the available literature on mate selection, particularly on intermarriage, and after conducting a lengthy secondary analysis of survey data from the University of Michigan's Detroit Area Study, the writer believes that several points should be put into writing in regard to the reporting and interpreting of rates of intermarriage. They are, in brief: (1) Let rates based on marriages always be distinguished from rates based on individuals. (2) Let group size be acknowledged as operating through mathematical necessity when it is found to be inversely related to intermarriage rates. (3) One should recognize inevitable differences between ethnic and religious intermarriage rates in evaluating the "triple melting pot" hypothesis. (4) When possible, let the ratio of a group's actual rate of intermarriage to its "expected" intermarriage rate be reported.

THE BASIS FOR COMPUTING RATES

The first point can be disposed of rather quickly. Although most published rates of intermarriage are based on the total num-

*American Journal of Sociology, Vol. 70, No. 6 (May 1965), pp. 717–21. Copyright 1965 by the University of Chicago. Reprinted by permission of the University of Chicago Press.

ber of a group's marriages, it sometimes happens that these are misinterpreted as though they were based on the number of individuals marrying.[1] For example, in a combined sample of 1,470 marriages of whites in the Detroit area, the writer found that interfaith marriages constituted 36 per cent of all marriages involving Protestants and 41 per cent of all marriages involving Catholics.[2] It would be false to conclude from this that 36 per cent of married Protestants and 41 per cent of married Catholics are in mixed marriages. Actually, the rates based on married *individuals* show that 22 per cent of married Protestants and 26 per cent of married Catholics in the Detroit area have intermarried. To understand this, one need only recognize that the 599 *unmixed* Protestant marriages in our combined sample involve twice that number of Protestants, whereas the 336 *mixed* marriages of Protestants involve just 336 Protestants. Similarly, the 343 Catholics in *mixed* marriages (compared to the Catholics in the 495 *unmixed* marriages) comprise just 26 per cent of all married Catholics—considerably lower than the 41 per cent mixed-marriage rate for white Catholics in the Detroit area. In the former percentage we are talking about individuals; in the latter, about marriages. Researchers could forestall some misinterpretations by others if they chose to report both types of percentages.

SIZE OF GROUP AS A FACTOR

The second point concerns the size of a group as a factor in its rate of intermarriage. Barron long ago made the observation that "the larger the group, the lower its rate."[3] Thomas specified the size of the group as one of the factors influencing Catholic intermarriage rates. He showed by many illustrations from the *Official Catholic Directory* that the highest rates occur in dioceses where Catholics have the smallest representation in the population.[4] Others have observed the same. However, the generalization has been tested most extensively in Canada, where religious affiliation is recorded in the national census and in marriage license applications. A study by Locke *et al.* showed a perfect negative rank-order correlation in 1951 between rates of Catholic intermarriage and the Catholic percentages of the local population in the ten provinces of Canada. The relationship for Anglicans in Canada was said to be "much less striking."[5]

It seems to the present writer that we should recognize this generalization based on the size of the group to be not so much a sociological as a mathematical explanation of the differences in rates of intermarriage. To be specific on this point, the smaller the group relative to the total population, the faster its rate goes up with each intermarriage; it can quickly reach a *real* upper limit of a 100 per cent intermarriage rate. A majority group, on the other hand, will find not only that its intermarriage rate goes up more slowly, but that it can never reach a *real* limit of 100 per cent simply because there are not enough mates available outside its group. Therefore, to compare marriage rates without this fact in mind is misleading.[6]

THE "TRIPLE MELTING POT" HYPOTHESIS

We may profitably apply this observation to the "triple melting pot" hypothesis proposed by Ruby Jo Reeves Kennedy some years ago.[7] Based on data covering many decades in New Haven, Connecticut, the hypothesis proposed that ethnic lines were being crossed repeatedly in the United States while people continued to marry within their own religious groups, that is, within the three major religious groups in our country. The point made just above is pertinent here. Since a religious group is larger than any of the ethnic groups that constitute it, we must expect that these ethnic intermarriage rates will be larger than the corresponding religious intermarriage rates—from mathematical necessity.

Furthermore, the fact that identification with a religious denomination is at least in some degree a voluntary association makes it inappropriate to compare rates of religious intermarriage with those of ethnic intermarriage, since the latter are based on an ascribed status. No matter how one is asked to identify his ethnic origins (e.g., by the question, "What is the original nationality of your family on your father's side"), the answer is determined by birth and not by personal choice. On the other hand, we know that husband and wife frequently state that they have the same religious preference even though one of them has converted. Lenski discovered in his sample that "one fifth of the now homogeneous marriages had been contracted by persons raised in different faiths."[8] Similarly, the present writer found in a somewhat larger sample that *three out of five* marriages involving partners raised in different faiths became homogeneous marriages through the conversion of one or the other.[9] When rates of religious intermarriage are based on *present* religious preferences, these facts are hidden and the rates of intermarriage appear to be small.

At least these two facts, therefore, indicate to this writer that the "triple melting pot" hypothesis is not a good substitute for Zangwill's original image of a "single melting pot." Granted that rates of ethnic intermarriage are usually reported to be larger than those of religious intermarriage, a closer examination of the bases for such computations will frequently show that these two types of rates are not truly comparable.

RATIO OF ACTUAL TO "EXPECTED" RATES

To return to the problem of the size of a group as a factor in its rate of intermarriage, we believe that, in a national report for 1957, Glick used an effective way of avoiding misconceptions.[10] By also computing the "expected" percentage of intermarriage if the members of each group had married randomly, he arrived at the *ratio* of actual to expected mixed marriages for each religious group. Table 1 presents the findings of our Detroit study after the manner Glick used. We noted above the actual intermarriage rates for Protestants (36 per cent) and Catholics (41 per cent).[11] Let us now observe that the "expected" intermarriage rate would be 68 per cent for Protestants and 73 per cent for Catholics, if they had chosen their marriage partners randomly among whites in the Detroit area. To compute the "expected" rate of religious intermarriage, one must know the frequency distribution of the relevant religious groups in the population. A sample of the Detroit area from the Detroit Area Study, 1954–59, included 3,789 Protestants, 3,307 Catholics, and 642 others, in addition to the Negro denominations.[12] One then uses these totals as marginals in a χ^2 table and makes the calculations shown below Table 1 in order to arrive at the expected rate of intermarriage. The writer believes that he has replicated Glick's statistic reported in the article already cited, although the latter did not give the details of his procedure.[13]

The Catholic and Protestant populations are more nearly equal in the Detroit area than they are in the country as a whole. Nevertheless, the Catholic population is smaller. Computing the ratio

TABLE 1

Actual Intermarriage Rates (per 100 Marriages) and Intermarriage Rates "Expected" if Husbands and Wives Were Distributed at Random, for Marriages of Protestants and Catholics in the Detroit Area, 1955, 1958, and 1959

Early Religion of Husband and Wife	Married Couples		"Expected" Per Cent if Random Inter-Marriage	Ratio of Actual to "Expected" Mixed Marriages
	Actual No.	Actual Per Cent		
One or both Protestant	935	100	100	
Protestant:				
Protestant	599	64	32	
Catholic or other	336	36	68*	.53
One or both Catholic	838	100	100	
Catholic:				
Catholic	495	59	27	
Protestant or other	343	41	73	.56

*As an example for the reader's guidance, the following are the calculations used to determine the expected intermarriage rate for white Protestants in the Detroit area:

Religion of Wives	Religion of Husbands		
	Protestant	Other	All
Protestant	928	967	1,895
Other	967	1,008	1,975
All	1,895	1,975	3,870

$$1,895 \times 1,895 \div 3,870 = 928$$

Marriages of Protestants:

$$928$$
$$967$$
$$967$$
$$\overline{}$$
$$2,862$$

$$928 \div 2,862 = .32$$
$$1.00 - .32 = .68$$

of actual to expected mixed marriages for the two groups has the effect of narrowing the differences between the measures of their intermarriage behavior. The five-point difference in the actual percentages is reduced to a three-point difference in the ratios. This is the adjustment for the "size of group" factor which the writer believes is needed before comparing intermarriage rates for different groups and different localities.

The ratio of actual to expected mixed marriages reported by Glick for Protestants was .19; for Catholics it was .26. Our ratios are .53 and .56, respectively. Why so much larger? The reason is that our ratios are based on *early* religious preferences and therefore include many marriages that are *now* religiously homogeneous because of the conversion of one partner or the other. Glick's ratios are based on marriages which are *now* mixed, but do not include as "mixed" those marriage partners who were brought up in different religions. If we consider only the *present* religious preference of the respondents and their spouses in our data, as Glick did for the national data, then the ratio computed by the method described above becomes the same for both white Protestants and white Catholics in Detroit: .22. This is certainly comparable to the ratios that Glick computed from the national data.

CONCLUSIONS

We here recommend that in reporting rates of intermarriage researchers (1) indicate rates based both on marriages and on individuals; (2) acknowledge group size as a factor that operates at least partly through mathematical necessity; (3) avoid the "triple melting pot" hypothesis because ethnic and religious intermarriage rates are basically not comparable in such fashion; (4) adjust rates, if possible, to a group's "expected" intermarriage rate.

NOTES

1. Two instances of this error are criticized in the following: Loren E. Chancellor and Thomas P. Monahan, "Religious Preference and Interreligious Mixtures in Marriages and Divorces in Iowa," *American Journal of Sociology*, LXI (1955), 233–39; Paul H. Besanceney, "Unbroken Protestant-Catholic Marriages among Whites in the Detroit Area," *American Catholic Sociological Review*, XXIII (1962), 3–20.
2. The chances are 95 out of 100 that each of these percentages is accurate for the population within four points. See Paul H. Besanceney, "Factors Associated with Protestant-Catholic Marriages in the Detroit Area: A Problem in Social Control" (unpublished Ph.D. dissertation, Michigan State University, 1963), p. 214.

3. Milton L. Barron, *People Who Intermarry: Intermarriage in a New England Industrial Community* (Syracuse, N.Y.: Syracuse University Press, 1946), p. 191.
4. John L. Thomas, "The Factor of Religion in the Selection of Marriage Mates," *American Sociological Review,* XVI (1951), 489. See also Lee G. Burchinal and Loren E. Chancellor, "Catholics, Urbanism, and Mixed-Catholic Marriage Rates," *Social Problems,* IX (1962), 363.
5. Harvey J. Locke, George Sabagh, and Mary M. Thomas, "Interfaith Marriages," *Social Problems,* IV (1957), 331. For rural-urban differences in this matter see Victor J. Traynor, "Urban and Rural Mixed Marriages," *Social Order,* VI (1956), 155.
6. Apart from the problem of sociological analysis, there is great practical importance in this matter. A small group may be faced with extinction through intermarriage with other members of the general population in a given locality. There seems to be a gravitation to the patterns of behavior of the majority in any community, with the result that the children of an intermarriage (other things being equal) will probably be drawn to affiliation with the majority. Hence, in a practical sense, a high rate of intermarriage for a small group is a threat to survival.
7. Ruby Jo Reeves Kennedy, "Single or Triple Melting Pot? Intermarriage Trends in New Haven, 1870–1940," *American Journal of Sociology,* XLIX (1944), 331–39. See also her "Single or Triple Melting Pot? Intermarriage in New Haven, 1870–1950," *American Journal of Sociology,* LVIII (1952), 56–59.
8. Gerhard Lenski, *The Religious Factor: A Sociological Study of Religion's Impact on Politics, Economics, and Family Life* (Garden City, N.Y.: Doubleday & Co., Inc., 1961), p. 49.
9. Besanceney, *op. cit.,* p. 218.
10. Paul C. Glick, "Intermarriage and Fertility Patterns among Persons in Major Religious Groups," *Eugenics Quarterly,* VII (1960), 31–38.
11. Permission to use the data on which these rates are based was obtained from Ronald Freedman, then chairman of the Executive Committee of the Detroit Area Study, University of Michigan, and from at least one of the faculty participants responsible for each of the annual studies used. The present writer accepts full responsibility, of course, for interpretations in this paper.
12. Albert J. Mayer and Harry Sharp, "Religious Preference and Worldly Success," *American Sociological Review,* XXVII (1962), 221.
13. After this paper had been written, Paul Glick confirmed in private correspondence that the writer had correctly interpreted the methodology he had used for computing this ratio.

As one examines the sociological research on the dimensions of intermarriage in American society, the literature seems to fall into two broad and "natural" chronological sequences. The first comprises research during the period from the end of World War I until the post–World War II era, a time span of approximately thirty years. Reflecting such social conditions as an apparently unyielding caste line separating Blacks from whites, and a very large recent immigrant or foreign stock from non-Protestant Europe still stratified economically and socially from old or earlier arriving Protestant groups, research on intermarriage showed that it was taking place most often between nationality groups, less often between religious groups, and least of all between racial groups. The culminating study was in New Haven, Connecticut, where Ruby Jo Reeves Kennedy detected an intermarriage pattern of selection which she conceptualized as the "triple melting-pot."

The etiology or causal factors inducing this and other patterns of intermarriage incidence and selection was another research concern during this period until midcentury. Finally, research explored the marital consequences of intermarriage as compared with inmarriage in terms of such criteria as divorce, desertion, and separation, and the familial consequences in terms of size and ethnic identification of the family.

The following appraisal of research during this initial period indicates many important gaps that remained for investigation by the next generation of researchers from midcentury until the present time. It also emphasizes the inconsistency found among Americans between conservative attitudes toward intermarriage on the one hand, and activities promoting social and cultural conditions favoring intermarriage, on the other.

AN APPRAISAL OF
RESEARCH
UNTIL MIDCENTURY*

Milton L. Barron

Periodically since the end of World War I, American sociologists and their academic cousins, the demographers, have been exhorting each other to engage in research on a neglected aspect of human relations—intermarriage. In a multigroup society like the United States, they have maintained, the study of intermarriage may provide a precise, quantitative measurement of such vital and related sociological questions as the process of assimilation, the degree of internal cohesion in individual racial, religious and ethnic groups and the extent of social distance between groups of these types.

But there have been other reasons for the attraction of social scientists to the analysis of intermarriage. Of interest to them is the considerable number of American people who have not adopted Israel Zangwill's romantic notion[1] that America is God's crucible, that the new society's complex ingredients should blend eventually by intermarriage into a race of supermen, combining the virtues of all races, creeds and nationalities. Indeed, many Americans today look upon the practice as a threat to their social values and way of life rather than as a panacea for their tensions in intergroup relations. For example, Gunnar Myrdal[2] found that most Southern whites place the taboo on racial intermarriage in the highest rank among the various parts of their concern about the maintenance of the status quo between themselves and Negroes. Roman Catholic spokesmen in this country continually deplore "mixed marriage" with non-Catholics, and Protestant clerics are becoming increasingly vociferous not only in opposing such marriages but also in pointing to the Roman Catholic policy

*Originally entitled "Research on Intermarriage: A Survey of Accomplishments and Prospects," *The American Journal of Sociology*, Vol. 57, No. 3 (November 1951), pp. 249–55. Copyright © 1951 by the University of Chicago. Reprinted by permission of the University of Chicago Press.

therein as an important issue in the struggle for power between the Catholic Church and other religious groups. Perhaps the best indication of Jewish anxiety about the "problem" is its popularity as a theme in plays and novels by and about Jews, especially and possibly significantly in terms of causation—in times of social disorganization as during World Wars I and II. Ever since the astonishing response to Anne Nichols' comedy about Abraham Levy's marriage to Rose Mary Murphy during the armistice of the First World War[3] there has been a steady procession of other works, some of them more prominent than others.[4]

Sociologists may well ask themselves why so many Americans consider intermarriage to be a social problem. A tentative answer is that the practice is a grave threat to the people's values of identity, homogeneity and survival. As one writer sees the menace in operation with reference to Jews: "The one great factor, making for group survival, is the ability to keep offspring within the group. As between two or more groups, intermarriage is forever a source of danger to the less favorably situated group, since the younger generation is usually anxious to escape the inherited hardship. The severance of relations favorable to exogamous marriage thus becomes the desideratum of every minority. . . ."[5] Not infrequently the problem-mentality of those resistant to the practice, especially clergymen, is expressed in terms of "culture conflict," a concept borrowed from the social scientists. Intermarriage, it is maintained, should be avoided because conflict almost invariably results between culturally disparate mates and harmfully affects their children. The validity of this claim will be weighed in a subsequent section of this article. At this point it is appropriate to suggest that there are two flaws in such a rationalization for resistance. First, there are occasionally only nominal differences at the most between intermarrying mates. Secondly, important cultural differences often stratify husbands and wives, let us say, of the very same religious affiliation. Yet few priests, ministers and rabbis preach caution or refuse to officiate at such technically non-mixed marriages.

What have American sociologists and demographers learned about intermarriage? Their research findings may be organized and summarized as follows:

1. *Causal factors.* What are the social and psychological forces which induce intermarriage? Studies in New York City, Los

Angeles, Burlington, Woonsocket, New Haven and Derby[6] have shown that an unbalanced sex ratio and numerically small representation lead some groups into considerable incidence of intermarriage. But even more important, in contrast to the theme of "America divided" expressed by most writers on intergroup relations, is that in this immigrant-receiving society our heterogeneous groups have developed cultural similarities and social proximity to a surprising extent. For example, residential propinquity, a well-known factor in courtship, not only because of the premarital contacts facilitated but also because of the economic and cultural similarities implied, is found to be an important correlate of intermarriages as well as inmarriages. Our communities' ecological areas are not always homogeneous with regard to race, religion and nationality.

Premarital studies also indicate that young people of diverse groups are led into marital ties through economic propinquity and similarity, both occupational and spatial; by close association and common experiences in the amount, type and locale of education; and by recreational contacts. Indeed, the high degree of similarity in economic and educational status of those who intermarry lends support to the prediction of the ultimate emergence of clearly defined ingroups and "consciousness of kind" along these lines.

Religious and racial intermarriages also occur today because of the inefficacy of institutional control by church and state. Historical as well as contemporary evidence demonstrates that churches and synagogues cannot effectively curb religious intermarriage in societies where church and state are separate and civil marriage, accordingly, is an alternative to a clerical ceremony. As far as racial intermarriage is concerned, the point is perhaps best made by way of illustration. There were cases of such marriage in California long before October 1, 1948, the date when that state's law prohibiting the practice was ruled unconstitutional by a decision of the State Supreme Court. In short, easy social contact and a cultural common denominator negate much of the prohibitive impact of institutional control.

But that is not all. Sociologists also have several hypotheses to explain why intermarriage occurs which need to be tested in future empirical studies. They propose that post-adolescence and the premarital years constitute an age of rebellion against the more conservative values of parents, which, coupled with the conflict between generations and the emancipation from family control brought on by extramural and secular experiences in education and the economy, are conducive to intermarriage. For many young Americans the cultural relativity with which they are indoctrinated in the public school system and the psychological association which they develop between the intermarriage taboo and "backwardness" are also conceivably significant in this context. A likely explanation is to be had too in the individualistic choice of a marriage partner embedded in the "romantic complex" of American culture. And lastly, one must consider the roles of self-hatred among many members of minority groups and the drive toward upward social mobility, both of which may find expression in marriage outside the group.

2. *Patterns.* A second type of research activity has centered upon patterns of incidence and selection. Which groups tend to intermarry more than others? Which groups are selected most frequently by other groups? And what are the dynamics or trends of incidence and selection in intermarriage over the years? Sociologists who pose these questions in their community studies generally find that intermarriage occurs most often between nationality groups, less often between religious groups and least between racially defined groups. This, of course, is not only useful in terms of evaluating the relative cohesive strength of group types, but it is suggestive of possible realignments in the structure of American society.

Unquestionably the most valuable sociological study in this connection was made by Ruby Jo Kennedy in New Haven.[7] Marriage records in that community for 1870, 1900, 1930 and 1940 were analyzed, and over each time interval there was found to be an increase in the percentage of those intermarrying from most— *but not all*—groups. The proportion of Protestants intermarrying with non-Protestants and Roman Catholics with non-Catholics, for example, declined slightly over the last measured decade. This is more important than it may seem to the casual observer, largely because it disrupts the armchair, speculative idea that intermarriage relentlessly increases in the dimension of time in a smooth, unbroken pattern. It supports the contention that no mystical force pushes any aspect of intergroup relations in a single direction.

The most interesting pattern discovered by Dr. Kennedy is rhetorically mentioned in the title of her article. Negro-white intermarriages in New Haven have been practically nonexistent on the one hand. Ethnic groups, on the other hand, have intermarried at a very high rate, but not indiscriminately. Rather they have tended to intermarry within the confines of the apparently hardening lines of religion. Catholic nationalities have intermarried with other Catholics; Protestants have chosen other Protestants; and Jews, probably in large part because their religious and ethnic characteristics coincide, have married Jews. Thus we have had the pattern of the "triple melting-pot."

The need for further research on this aspect of intermarriage is obvious. The communities studied so far have been few in number, mostly concentrated on the eastern seaboard. It is important that we get a more adequate regional coverage. Second, many more studies are needed on the dynamics of intermarriage. Are second and third generation Americans intermarrying more than their first generation parents and grandparents elsewhere than New Haven? Third, studies of intermarriage incidence and selection must keep within reasonable distance of the ever-changing calendar. It is absurd in terms of time as well as place to assert that "Americans intermarry" according to a pattern of a triple melting-pot when all we really know is that residents of one community, New Haven, were demonstrating such a pattern more than ten years ago.

3. *Consequences*. The third and last major kind of research on intermarriage has dealt with the consequences of the practice in family life. How do intermarried mates and their children fare in numerical size, personality development and interpersonal relations, religious affiliation and participation, and success or failure as measured by the criteria of divorce, desertion and separation?

The fragmentary research of this sort so far has been concerned mainly with religious intermarriage and will be summarized below. First, one should be reminded that such research has been challenged by the vested interest, social myopia and wishful thinking of many laymen. To be sure, few racists and fundamentalist zealots now argue against intermarriage on the grounds of detrimental biological consequences. But there are numerous people who insist on a consequence of overwhelming doom for those who intermarry in social and cultural matters. For example, at the annual conference of the Rabbinical Council of America in January, 1950, Rabbi Israel Tabak of Baltimore, then president of the Council, contended that such marriages are 90 per cent unsuccessful and that they "undermine the stability of the home, increase the number of unhappy marriages and bring children into the world with a rift in their souls which can never be healed."[8]

Very unusual and seemingly more objective and realistic is a recent statement by another rabbi. "There are many Jews who . . . deprecate mixed marriage on simple practical grounds. Marriage, they argue, involves at best many problems and difficulties. Why complicate it still more? Why enter on a union with a reduced chance of success? This would be an impressive argument if we should show that a majority, or even a dangerously high percentage, of intermarriages are failures. We do not, in fact, have reliable statistics; nor do we have a satisfactory way of measuring success in marriage. . . . Everyone knows of successful intermarriages, and they are not so rare as to be labeled exceptions."[9]

Another preliminary to the results of empirical studies concerning intermarriage consequences is in order; that is the review of relevant theory formulated by specialists in the field of marriage and the family. For the most part they have assumed that extreme differences in background should foster marital discord rather than rapport. They have suggested, for instance, that the element of mixture is a focal point for conflict in some cases of intermarriage in that it becomes the scapegoat for tensions which originate elsewhere in the marital relationship; it is an easy substitute explanation for a couple's poor adjustment in, let us say, financial affairs. At the same time, however, the theorists have maintained that the consequences of any marriage depend upon the total situation, and not merely upon the fact of mixture. That is, a marriage's inner solidarity is affected not only by its various parts but also by the influences of those with whom the couple has had and continues to have social ties. Theoretically, no type of marriage contains within itself the germs of its own inevitable failure. Success or failure depends upon total adjustment rather than upon the mere elements of difference.

Accompanying this theory pertinent to the husband-wife relationship in intermarriage, there is the theory regarding the children of such marriage. Most prevalent is the notion that lack of adequate identification and the status of marginality and outcast are the burdens they must bear. At least one sociologist has specu-lated that in order to avoid the situation, one adjustment prob-ably at work in society is the greater exercise of birth control so that the number of children born of such marriages is less than the number born of "pure marriages."[10] For those religiously intermarried couples who do have children there are known to be several alternative adjustments. An early European practice sanc-tioned by law in some countries and transplanted informally to the United States is for the boys to follow the religion of the father and the girls that of the mother. Another practice is for all members of the family—parents as well as children—to assume the religious affiliation of one of the parents. Still another is for one parent and all the children to join one denomination while the other parent remains in his own. Next is the "compromise" alternative, that is, the parents become members of a neutral re-ligious body like the Universalists or Unitarians and raise their children accordingly. Idealists try one of two other alternatives: either the children are exposed to both of the parents' divergent faiths, or they plan to allow their children to make up their own minds when they reach the age of discretion.

Occasionally the problem of religious identification of children of intermarriages comes before the courts, and in two cases im-portant precedents may have been established. A test case in Texas was concerned with the legal validity of that part of the Roman Catholic Ante-Nuptial Contract and Promises signed by the non-Catholic in a "mixed marriage" which states "that all children, both boys and girls, that may be born of this union shall be baptized and educated solely in the faith of the Roman Catholic Church, even in the event of the death of my Catholic consort. In case of dispute, I furthermore, hereby fully agree that the cus-tody of the children shall be given to such guardians as to as-sure the faithful execution of this covenant and promise." The decision in court was that the promises signed are not valid in law; they are only binding in "good faith."

The second case was in New Jersey and dealt with the ques-tion of the religious affiliation of children of "mixed marriages" in the event of a divorce. The mother, a Jew, had married and divorced a Roman Catholic. There were two children of the mar-riage, a 10-year-old son and a 5½-year-old daughter. The mother insisted on raising them as Jews, and the father insisted on his religion. The Court of Errors and Appeals decided in the mother's favor after the father had contended that the right to control religious training is vested exclusively in the father. The court, rejecting this, cited the state law that each parent has an equal right in the matter, and noted that in the divorce case the custody of the children had been awarded to the mother. Therefore she had the right to raise the children in the religion she saw fit.

What systematic and empirical data has sociological research uncovered about the consequences of intermarriage? The most fruitful study so far was conducted by Judson T. Landis at Michigan State College.[11] For three years Dr. Landis had collected information on their parents' marriages from the students in marriage lecture sections, such as age when married, occupation, education, religion, present marital status, whether either parent changed his or her religious faith at or after marriage, which parent took the responsibility for providing religious training, how much conflict over religion had been evident to the children, and the eventual faith taken by the children, the students themselves.[12]

Of the 4,108 families whose histories were thus analyzed, it was discovered that almost two-thirds of the parents had inmarried as Protestants, 573 families had parents inmarried as Catholics, and in 346 cases there had been intermarriage between Catholics on the one hand and 305 Protestants and 41 persons of no religious faith on the other. In 192 of these 346 intermarriages, each spouse retained his or her own religious affiliation after the marriage; in 113 of the cases either the Catholic or the Protestant changed to the faith of the other.

What about the comparable divorce rates of the inmarrying and intermarrying parents?[13] The rates were lowest in non-mixed Catholic marriages; next came non-mixed Protestant marriages; higher were the rates in Catholic-Protestant intermarriages, and the highest of all was the percentage of divorce in marriages involving a partner with no religious faith. Analysis showed that the Catholic-Protestant intermarriages had a better chance to avoid divorce when one mate—particularly the Protestant wife or the Catholic husband—changed to the faith of the other mate. Further analysis showed that it made a difference to the divorce rate whether the mother was Catholic or Protestant in the intermarriage. There were three times as many divorces in intermarriages between a Catholic man and a Protestant woman as there were in cases in which the husband was Protestant and the wife Catholic.

Landis' explanation for this significant differential is that fewer factors make for tension in intermarriages in which the mother is Catholic. This is because the mother-role and Roman Catholicism are more likely to be "constants" or inflexible; the father-role and Protestantism, on the other hand, are more likely to be "variables" or flexible. Consider, for example, the serious question about the religious training of the children. "In the American home," Landis observes, "the mother is more likely to be a church member and is more apt to take the responsibility for the religious instruction of the children. When a man who has no faith or is a Protestant is married to a Catholic woman, he signs the ante-nuptial agreement and does not find it difficult to abide by the agreement when his children are born. He expects his wife to be responsible for their religious training. There is then no great cause for conflict in this type of mixed marriage. If the mother is Protestant the marriage seems to have many more serious problems. The Protestant mother has agreed that the children will be baptized Catholic, and yet she can hardly bring up her children in a faith which she herself does not accept. Since the major responsibility for religious training falls upon her, she will probably bring the children up in the only faith she knows and believes in. This means that the agreement made before marriage must be scrapped. The Catholic husband is more apt to be a church member than the Protestant husband who marries a Catholic. It may be quite a blow to him to find that his wife will not have the children baptized into his faith. Conflict results since many Catholic fathers cannot give up without a struggle. The Catholic father not only has his own conscience to live with but he is also constantly aware of the attitude of his church and of his family when they see his children being brought up in the Protestant faith."

How were the children of Landis' study actually brought up? First, the data showed that Elmer's previously mentioned theory of intermarriage adjustment by limitation of offspring is substantiated. The students whose parents had intermarried had fewer brothers and sisters than those whose parents were non-mixed. Catholic women married to Protestants had had 2.2 children; Protestant women married to Catholics, 1.9; both Catholics, 3.6; and both Protestants, 2.7. The most common tendency was for the children, especially daughters, to follow the faith of the mother, this being the case for approximately 75 per cent of the girls as compared with 65 per cent of the boys. This is consistent with the students' description of the parental responsibility for religious training in their homes. The most frequent policy was that "mother took all responsibility for the religious training"; the second in frequency was that "our parents told us about both faiths but let us decide for ourselves when we were old enough."

Conspicuous by their absence in Landis' study as well as in other studies are data about the consequences of Jewish-Gentile intermarriages. However, before we can rest assured about the adequacy of our knowledge about the consequences of the inter-marriage process, sociologists must also meet the challenge to do more research on a larger sampling of socioeconomic groups in our society than that implied in the college level. They must pursue studies of intermarriage among those people who are childless; they need to interview intermarried subjects in order to check on their statistical analyses. More needs to be known, too, of the degree or lack of acceptability of intermarried couples by the individual's family of orientation. Other studies should be made of inmarriages and intermarriages which have not ended in divorce or separation in order that we may determine success or failure in terms of other meaningful standards. And there is a call for research on intermarriages between members of different Protestant denominations and sects, in which cases the problems of adjustment may often be as great as those between the major religious affiliations of Catholic, Protestant and Jew.

One final task confronts American sociologists. It is to bring to the attention of laymen the inconsistency of their conservative attitudes toward intermarriage on the one hand with their activities on the other hand in creating social and cultural conditions favoring intermarriage. Sending children to public schools and to centres of higher education away from home, the struggle against restrictive covenants, job discrimination and quota systems, participation in interfaith activity are but a few practices which lead inevitably to intergroup contacts that sometimes become love and intermarriage. The recognition of this dilemma is a fundamental beginning to any intelligent approach to the problem.

NOTES

1. *The Melting Pot* (New York: Macmillan, 1909).
2. *An American Dilemma* (New York: Harper and Bros., 1944), pp. 60–61.
3. *Abie's Irish Rose* (New York: Samuel French, 1924) was the stage play. In 1927 it was published as a novel by Harper. Subsequently it became a movie film, and more recently it has been a radio serial presented weekly by one of the major broadcasting networks.
4. Some of the better known novels dealing with Jewish-Gentile inter-marriage have been Gwethalyn Graham, *Earth and High Heaven* (Philadelphia: Lippincott, 1944); Sholem Asch, *East River* (New York: Putnam, 1946); Norman Katkov, *Eagle at My Eyes* (New York: Doubleday, 1948); and Myron Brinig, *Footsteps on the Stair* (New York: Rinehart, 1950).
5. Julius A. Leibert, "Somatic Jews," *Liberal Judaism,* XIII (December, 1945), 56–60.
6. See M. L. Barron, *People Who Intermarry* (Syracuse: Syracuse University Press, 1946).
7. "Single or Triple Melting Pot? Intermarriage Trends in New Haven," *American Journal of Sociology,* XLIX (January, 1944), 331–39.
8. *New York Times,* January 31, 1950.
9. Bernard J. Bamberger, "Plain Talk About Intermarriage," *The Reconstructionist,* XV (December, 1949), 10–14.
10. M. C. Elmer, *The Sociology of the Family* (Boston: Ginn and Co., 1945), p. 195.
11. See "Marriages of Mixed and Non-Mixed Religious Faith," *American Sociological Review,* XIV, No. 3 (June 1949), 401–07.
12. The study's significance has two restrictions. It does not reflect a cross section of the American population, but rather it represents the background of young people in college in the Midwest. Secondly, because of the method used in collecting the data, the results shed light only upon intermarriages in which there are children. A study of child-less intermarriages would probably show different results.
13. Professor Landis acknowledges that the divorce rate is not an accurate index of marital success or failure. This may be illustrated by low divorce rates in cases where the wife is Roman Catholic and yet the situation is unhappy for her. Inasmuch as three out of four divorces are granted to women in the United States, a devout but unhappy Roman Catholic wife cannot take the initiative toward divorce, whereas most unhappy Protestant wives are free from any dogmatic restrictions to do so.

PART FOUR

Recent Research on Racial and Nationality Intermarriage

World War II and its aftermath in American society brought increasing opportunities for interracial contact in urban education, employment, leisure-time activities, the struggle for civil rights and social equality, and, to a certain extent, housing. An inevitable concomitant, reenforced by the repeal of many state laws prohibiting racial intermarriage and the climactic decision by the Supreme Court of the United States in 1967 that the sixteen remaining state laws against racial intermarriage were unconstitutional, has been an increase in the incidence of Negro-white intermarriages. But does the Census Bureau finding that there are two-and-a-half times as many of these intermarriages recorded now as there were in the prewar years really mean a corresponding increase in the rate of racial intermarriage, or is the figure spurious? And what is the social significance of racial intermarriage in contemporary society? What kinds of social problems do interracial couples and their children confront in their interaction with blacks and whites? Does intermarriage lead to a life of being "banished from the white world and ignored in the black one"? What have been the consequences of the black separatism movement since the 1960's for racial intermarriages? These and related questions are taken up by William Barry Furlong in the following review of recent research accompanied by an account of his own informal interviews with racially intermarried people and their children.

INTERRACIAL MARRIAGE
IS A SOMETIME THING*

William Barry Furlong

The U.S. Supreme Court recently declared invalid the antimiscegenation laws in Virginia. Stanley Kramer's latest movie, "Guess Who's Coming to Dinner," and Gore Vidal's recent play, "Weekend," deal with interracial couples. The daughter of Dean Rusk, the Secretary of State, has married a Negro, and the daughter of Senator Edward W. Brooke, a Negro whose wife is white, plans to marry a white man.

Clearly interracial marriage is in a kind of vogue, though it is hardly the racial amalgamation that Arnold Toynbee once saw as one of the two routes to world peace (the other, which holds out about the same hope, was world government). More interracial marriages are recorded today than in the past—according to census figures, 2.5 times as many as in the nineteen-thirties. But the figures may be misleading; the increase may be the result of the population growth, of a more widespread willingness to acknowledge an interracial marriage—a willingness that may diminish with the rise of black separatism—or of more thorough record-keeping by the Census Bureau. The 1960 census turned up 51,409 Negro-white couples. That was 0.12 per cent of all the married couples in the country. Roughly the same percentage was found in a survey by the Department of Health, Education and Welfare on marriages performed in 32 states in 1963. However, the experts agree that, because of flaws in the reporting technique or less than representative samples, both studies may have underestimated the number of interracial unions.

There is a singularity to each of those marriages, though some are more singular than others. No one couple reflects all the woes and worries of marriage across racial lines, but there are some representative reactions and problems. Here are the thoughts of a few of the people who have been through it:

A white social worker married to a pretty Negro girl: "I think at first there's a feeling of pride for the white person—that you've brought somebody into the world, that you've given her a chance that she wouldn't have had otherwise." Her rejoinder: "Dear, don't you think at first you were trying too hard to impress Negroes with how liberal you were?"

A blonde woman married to a half-Negro truck driver: "At times my mother has said, 'Don't stop in this weekend. So-and-so is coming to visit, and what they don't know won't hurt them.' And when our daughter was born and turned out to be quite light, she said, 'Better not have any more. Don't press your luck.' "

The half-Negro truck driver, whose mother was Italian and whose father was black: "I treated my father like a dog—I resented him so much because he was black. It took me a long time to admit it, but I'm as prejudiced as the next man. Now I'm passing as white; no one at work knows I'm Negro. Why shouldn't I, if that's how life is better for me? I had to spend a lot of time with a psychiatrist before I realized what a great guy my father was. He came from the South with no education, moved into an Italian neighborhood and proved himself, taught himself math and English, moved up to foreman. Now when I go back to the old neighborhood, everybody tells me what a great guy he was. I know that, too, now. But he's dead now, and he'll never know how I love him."

A Negro postal worker just over 40 and a white woman a few years younger might represent the fairly typical interracial couple. They have been married for 20 years—and isolated for about as long. In the most middling of middle-class circumstances, they live on the second floor of a two-flat house in Hyde Park–Kenwood, an integrated neighborhood near the University of Chicago. It was a step up for him; he grew up in one of those tormented slums in which the sun always seems strained through a brassy haze and the houses are filled with the sweet smell of rotting wood. "I can still remember the stairways," he says. "The smell, the garbage, the way the wood was worn by all those feet all those years." You could almost sense his toes wriggling in his shoes, still feeling the scalloped stairways bleached at the edge by wear. For his wife, the move to Hyde Park–Kenwood was lateral. She came from a middle-class neighborhood on the South Side, an area of six-flats and an occasional bungalow behind a patch of creeping bent where the kids were forbidden to play for fear of "bruising" the grass.

Their early years were spent in worlds apart: she knew no Negroes and he no whites. He won a parochial fame in the ghetto as a high-school athlete and that brought him a football scholarship to college. Then he fell sick and couldn't play, so the college canceled his scholarship. He returned to Chicago just after World War II and went to work in the "car barns," the maintenance sheds for the transit system, at night. On his lunch break each night, he went to a soda fountain where she happened to work and ordered three milk shakes. "Nothing else," she remembers, "just three milk shakes. He always had a book to read. Paperback. He'd just sit there and drink his milk shakes and read his book and never raise his eyes." She thought he didn't notice her.

The sickness had left him underweight, he says, and he thought the milk shakes were a good remedy. He also thought he should be quiet and keep his eyes down; this was white man's territory. But he did notice her: "She was a well-girdled girl. I remember wondering why a girl like that—with the way she looked and the way she moved—why she wore a girdle." In those days and in that neighborhood a teen-age girl wore a girdle not to shape her figure so much as to help preserve her chastity. It was a warning to the bolder young men that they would have a struggle on their hands.

In those days, too, the great migration of poor Negroes from the South was beginning to engulf Chicago. Housing patterns began to shift, and soon the neighborhood around the soda fountain was showing the first faint signs of "changing." "My father wanted me to quit the job," the housewife remembers, "but you know how kids are. The money looked good and I was having fun." The ex–football player changed with the neighborhood: he lifted his eyes a little and began a careful give-and-take with the girl behind the counter. One night she was quite nervous, and he noticed a gang of boys from *his* neighborhood looking at her in a way that he didn't like. "They were smartin' off," he says, "but I could see what was on their minds." He ordered more milk shakes and lingered over them until closing time. Then he stood under a streetlamp and read his book until she came out.

It was half a block to the street-car stop and she would have to wait at least 15 minutes, so he made an excuse to say hello and suggested that they walk to the car stop together. It was very difficult for him, he remembers; he is not an outgoing man. But the gang was waiting down the street in a car and he felt he should protect the girl. The gang made no move when the couple passed. At the street-car stop he made a sudden decision and got on behind her. But then he didn't know whether to pay her fare—does a black boy do that with a white girl?—or to sit beside her. He did neither. When she was getting off she paused—just slowed down, really—beside his seat and said, "Thank you."

Though he lost his job at the car barns because he had not returned to work that night, every night for a week he waited at the soda fountain until closing time because the gang was still hanging around. If the girl left with friends he disappeared into the shadows. If she left alone he fell into step beside her. Soon it became a habit, something he looked forward to; and soon she made it a point to leave alone. The progression thereafter was natural: he paid her fare on the street-car, he sat beside her, and soon he got off and walked her home.

They found, as young people do, that they had a lot in common, and they imagined that the similarities outnumbered the differences. They also found that they were being thrown together by outside pressures. "Somebody saw him walking home with me one night—a Negro with a white girl—and in those days you didn't do that, not in our neighborhood." So the talk began going around, and the more it went around the more defiant she felt. Talk was going around in his neighborhood, too. "Your people get to thinkin' you're a little uppity," he says. The gossip forced them together.

So they got married. Nothing big; in fact, nothing at all—a City Hall wedding. Her family—like the average white one in such circumstances—didn't acknowledge the marriage. They feel she's living in sin because she didn't get married in church; they also feel that she's living in sin with a *nigger*. That disgraced the whole family. "I just dropped off the edge of the earth as far as they were concerned," she says.

Her brothers and sisters married and moved to a newer Chicago neighborhood or to the suburbs. Her mother is living with one of her sisters in the suburbs. "I've never gone out to see her; she's not interested. She's got plenty of other grandchildren, none of them niggers." She read of her father's death in the newspaper. "I went to the church and sat in the back. I thought I could get in and out without anybody seeing me. You know, go a little late, leave a little early."

At first, she and her husband made a decision typical of interracial couples: to have no children. "We thought it would be too hard on them," she says. "And we had each other—sort of the two of us against the world." They also faced typical problems of the Negro-white couple. All of their relatives and friends had suddenly disappeared, and it was difficult to find new friends, black or white. They were reluctant to face the humiliation of travel together, even in the North. Both met people at work, but—again, typically—they hid from their co-workers the interracial character of their marriage. "The kind of relationships you have at work," she says, "if there's a party and you're a young girl you don't want to show up with a husband who's a black man."

Their solution was night school. "We both had this thing about education, that it would help us. Well, it's not us that has to be educated. It's the rest of the world." They enrolled at a junior college and happily mapped out their whole future together, right through graduate school. "We had some pretty grand plans," she says.

When the second semester began, however, they registered individually, not as man and wife. "It was too hard, everybody was staring at us because we sat next to each other and talked as if we *knew* each other." For almost three years, they pretended in class to be strangers. "Then we asked what was happening to us. We were spending half our nights in a place where we felt uncomfortable just saying hello to each other." They dropped out with a handful of credits and not much in the way of pleasant associations.

It took time, but they gradually adjusted to their twilight world. Like most interracial couples, they suffered the inequities visited upon Negroes in search of adequate housing—higher rents and the constant threat of rejection by real-estate salesmen who want to sell or rent only to whites. But they found an apartment in an integrated neighborhood. "It's not as good as Lake Meadows"—a newer high-rise development in which many interracial couples live—"but it suits us," he says.

He did well in his job, eventually becoming a supervisor. Some of his progress he probably owes to his Government employment. Dr. Robert E. T. Roberts, a Chicago sociologist who has devoted almost 30 years to the study of interracial marriages, says that in one 36-member group he questioned only eight were employed in private enterprise. Four worked for the Government, 12 were self-employed and 12 were unemployed or retired. Dr. Roberts points out that marriage to a Negro may mean the end of advancement for a white man in the business world, and a girl who is the product of a mixed marriage adds: "A young man with talent and ambition is going to think twice—maybe five or six times—before he marries a Negro girl because he knows that's the end of his high ambitions." In the view of Dr. Roberts, the effect of interracial marriage on business advancement is one of the reasons that the male partner in such a union has historically tended to be the Negro.

The postal worker and his wife built a little nest egg and decided that children might help fill the vague, indefinable gap in their lives. They have two now, one colored, one virtually white. "I suppose it might be hard in some neighborhoods, being a white woman with a colored baby," she says. "You might not want to take him out walking or go to the park or even go shopping with him, there'd be so many tongues wagging." But it's not so bad in their neighborhood. "You go to the Co-op"—the local supermarket—"and you see a lot of mixtures there. You begin to realize just how many mixed marriages there are, Saturday mornings at the Co-op."

They are reluctant to think too deeply about the future of the children. "It'll be all right for the boy," says the father. "He can choose the black world, whatever that's going to be 10 or 15 years from now. But the girl, she'll be torn." She's light enough to go into the white world, but "she'll *know* she's been brought up a Negro. That makes a difference—it's like a secret you dread having." His somber looks grow heavier. "She's a good little girl; I don't think she'll want to turn her back on her daddy and what he is. But what if she falls in love with a white boy and they want to get married and she doesn't tell him—she'll always be worried about what color children she'll have."

He is not quite defeated, but neither does he have the soaring ambitions of youth. He still loves to read and takes refuge in his books. One wall in the front room of their apartment is lined with books. "I don't have a really *fine* mind," he says with just a touch of firmness in his husky voice. "But I know it's not a mind to be ashamed of."

His wife is, perhaps, more obviously alienated; it is usually the white partner who suffers more. She has lost her family, her friends, the social position and middle-class home in which she grew up—even her religion, though she still goes to church regularly. There is no place she belongs: the white community has banished her to the ghetto, and the ghetto refuses to accept her. "There are two classes of people who can't stand mixed marriages," says the white wife of another Negro. "They are colored women and white men." Negro women resent the loss of one of their men and the implication that white women are superior to them; the white men resent the supposed degradation of white womanhood. Even in her own neighborhood, an integrated area, the postal worker's wife feels left out. The neighborhood is academically oriented, and she says that she never really went to college—"just junior college at night, *nothing*."

She is back in school at night, not for college credit but for the "culture courses"—art appreciation, music appreciation, drama, literature. This is her separate world: "Nobody knows about me down there. They accept you for what you are." Her husband has noticed a change in her. "She's spruced up a little more, she has something to look forward to every week."

He does not give voice to the fear that she finds people "down there" more attractive than he is. He knows that she has her problems, but he talks about them in general terms: "I imagine there are a lot of housewives out in the suburbs who are trying to find their way, too." He realizes that he's growing inward as she struggles to move outward. But instead of trying to hold things together, he has prepared for the ultimate separation; although he is only in his 40's, he talks of death. When their first child was born, he insured his own life heavily—he knows that if he dies, his wife will not easily find another husband, particularly a white husband. "Not with a black boy for a son, she won't." And he can't quite see her marrying another Negro, as many such white widows do, for fear that it would only add to her problems. He regards her with an enormous fondness and he appreciates how much he's complicated her life. "If I go first," he says, "maybe she'll be able to go back to her church." He pauses. "And maybe even her family."

Some interracial couples insist that they have not experienced the quiet, smoldering desperation that has been the lot of the postal worker and his wife. Edwin C. (Bill) Berry, for instance, contends that the partners in an interracial marriage suffer no indignities except those heaped upon Negroes in general. Berry is a slim, spare man with gray hair, penetrating eyes and an air of muted humor. He has worked for the Urban League in various cities for 31 years, for the last 10 as executive director in Chicago. "I didn't marry a white woman," he says, "I married my wife. Races don't get married; only people do. I didn't marry the white race. I married Betsy Berry and all the problems that come with this particular woman."

Despite his contention that their marriage of 10 years is normal, the Berrys were opposed by in-laws on both sides, and the wedding took place in Milwaukee, not Chicago. When a Chicago newspaper discovered their plans, Berry arranged to have the paper omit any mention of the interracial aspect of their marriage. Instead, the paper printed a picture of Betsy that made the point more subtly.

The Berrys are not uneasy about "the stare," the look that annoys most interracial couples when they appear in public. "If somebody stares at us, I wave and say hello. I don't know if they know me or not." They did not travel together in the South until recently, but they have now visited Atlanta and Miami, and they are not sure that a venture into Mississippi would be altogether intolerable. "We didn't see any signs of hostility that we might not have seen in New York City," he says.

Berry is equally sanguine about the place of the child of an interracial marriage. He and Betsy have no children of their own, but they have raised his son by an earlier marriage. Berry deplores the notion that interracial marriage is necessarily bad for the child. "What's so bad?" he asks. "Look, my boy was a little brown boy. Now there are several ways he can get to be a little brown boy. One way is for brown and brown to marry. Another way is for black and white to marry. So the boy turns out brown. Society doesn't know how he got that way." But certain segments of society—the child's neighborhood, his church, and his school—invariably do know how he got that way and direct at him an attention that is not given others.

Berry concedes that he knows of an interracial marriage in which the husband is terribly tormented. "But all his life he wanted to punish himself," Berry says, "and he thought that by marrying a Negro he would *really* be punished." Some psychiatrists agree that an interracial marriage may be motivated by the desire for punishment. One of them calls such a union "the exquisite torment," and Dr. Thomas L. Brayboy, a New York psychiatrist who has treated many partners in interracial marriages, suggests that the ultimate motive is often a feeling of guilt over the white man's treatment of the Negro.

A spirit of rebellion is also common among the partners in interracial marriages, Dr. Brayboy says. "They make use of the unique opportunity that socially opposed interracial sex offers for acting out their hostility toward parents or society. It was their desire for revenge, not love, that brought them together." Dr. Roberts, who concedes drily that "romantic love occurs occasionally in any society," adds that the Establishment's reaction to interracial courtship and marriage may add a certain urgency to the relationship: "To lose all for love, to voluntarily suffer disgrace and humiliation for a loved one, is very much in keeping with the romantic ideal."

The experts also say that the myth that Negroes offer more satisfaction in sexual relations may encourage some interracial marriages. "Sex—whether in mind or in fact—is certainly a conspicuous factor," says one psychiatrist, "but it works both ways." The belief in greater sexual prowess may impel some whites to marry Negroes, he explains, but it also produces in some white men a fear of inadequacy that is "one of the basic drives underlying racial antagonism in our society." Love, sex, rebellion, or the desire for punishment can, of course, be a motive for any kind of marriage. "The primary difference in interracial situations," Dr. Brayboy says, "is that the broader social problem accentuates the neurotic potential."

One might consider a marriage that is both interracial and interreligious to be loaded with neurotic potential. Diane and Steve Cohen, an uncommonly intelligent young couple, illustrate some of the problems and some of the solutions in this kind of union. Diane is the daughter of Earl Dickerson, one of the richest Negroes in America. She and Steve met while studying for their master's degrees at the University of Chicago. Diane had been married—to a Negro—and had a son, Steven, now 10 years old. Steve, her present husband, is an Orthodox Jew. "It wasn't that

Diane was a Negro that upset my family," he says. "They would have been upset by my marrying anybody who wasn't Jewish." Diane became a convert to Judaism and she and Steve are raising their son, Joshua, as a Jew. Diane's first son is being raised as a Christian.

One of their first problems after their marriage five and a half years ago was the attitude of Steve's father, who had many stereotypes about Negroes. "He'd ask us to dinner and have watermelon *just* for me," says Diane with more wonder than rancor. "Or he'd ask—seriously—if I ate anything besides fried chicken."

"He liked to believe—as I suppose most fathers would in the same circumstances—that, as the white relative in the union, he was bringing a little bit the better to the situation," says Steve. "Then, bit by bit, he discovered that Diane's father has many of the things that most people covet in life—great wealth and high status in the community. Eventually, I noticed that he was bragging just a little bit that his son was married to the daughter of Earl Dickerson."

Joshua, it turned out, has his own insight into color. One day when he was three years old, an insurance man visiting the family asked Joshua what color he was. Joshua didn't hesitate. "Beige," he said. And so the world looks to Joshua Cohen. His mother is beige and a Negro; his father is beige and a white man. There are no simple blacks and whites to Joshua.

The Cohen family is not only black and white but also Christian and Jewish. Young Steve Cohen, the non-Jew in the family, might be expected to have some difficulty in identifying. One day while he was out playing touch football in the neighborhood, one of the other youngsters dropped a forward pass. The leader of his team became enraged and shouted the worst names he knew: "You dirty Jew! You filthy kike!"

One of the kids happened to remember Steve Cohen. "Say," he said, "you're not *Jewish,* are you?"

"At that moment," says the elder Steve Cohen, "he was. He had complete identification with his family."

The history of opposition to interracial unions stretches back to Biblical times. In Numbers, XII, 1, there is a suggestion of the ferment raised against Moses for his interracial marriage: "And Miriam and Aaron spake against Moses because of the Ethiopian woman whom he had married." In "Othello," Iago foreshadows the antagonism of Desdemona's family to her marriage to the Moor, described as "thick-lips," when he warns her father:

> Even now, now, very now,
>   an old black ram
> Is tupping your white ewe.
>   Arise, arise!
> Awake the snorting
>   citizens with the bell,
> Or else the devil will make
>   a grandsire of you.

Thus, while marriage between the races and social opposition to it are not new, there have been changes. Dr. Roberts, who in his investigations has interviewed more than 500 interracial couples, some of whom were married as early as 1882, sees a social evolution.

In earlier times, encounters between the races were most likely to take place at work, he says, whereas today they are likely to occur in schools or social movements. Just before and after the turn of the century these encounters tended to bring together Negro men and white immigrant girls. They were thrown together in menial jobs in the mansions of the rich or in businesses that demanded unskilled help. Dr. Roberts has uncovered "at least a dozen" interracial marriages that developed in a hotel in Milwaukee where Negro men worked as porters and waiters and white immigrant girls worked as pantrygirls and chambermaids. The girls frequently came from cultures in northern Europe in which there was no conspicuous prejudice against the Negro, and they were so new to this country that they didn't understand how deep was the antagonism between the races in the United States. Immigration was restricted in the nineteen-twenties, reducing the number of foreign girls who might marry Negro men. After World War I there was a tendency for white girls to take the jobs once held by Negro men—waiting on tables in restaurants, for example—and for Negro girls to take the jobs once held by white immigrant girls. Thus the opportunity for encounters between the Negro male and white immigrant female was reduced.

During World War II, American Negroes met foreign white girls who lacked the strong prejudices of their counterparts in the United States. When the soldiers came home, society began to change: leisure time was increased and television arrived, bringing with it a new prominence for entertainers, many of whom—Sammy Davis Jr., Harry Belafonte, Lena Horne, Pearl Bailey, and Eartha Kitt, among them—married across racial lines. There were other changes as well.

"In the nineteen-twenties and before," Dr. Roberts says, "you rarely—I might almost say you never—saw a marriage between a Negro and a Jew." This was because endogamy—the custom or requirement of marrying only within one's tribe, caste, or social system—is strongest among Jews. After World War II, there was a lessening of endogamy among Jews and there were more opportunities for social encounters between Negroes and Jews or other potential "high-status" whites as more Negroes entered college. The number of Jewish-Negro marriages increased.

Dr. Roberts says that an influx of Negroes into colleges in the postwar period created interracial unions entirely different from those of the late Victorian era. He believes that the percentage of interracial marriages involving partners who have had some college education has increased 10 or 15 times over the level of the nineteen-twenties. In a study of 22 interracial couples in New York, the median schooling was 16.5 years—somewhat above the average for married people in general.

"Before World War I," says Dr. Roberts, "children of interracial marriage were likely to know as many white people as Negroes. Then in the nineteen-thirties I found they were likely to know Negroes only—they seemed to know Negroes 99 per cent of the time. Now it's changing back—the kids are likely to know whites about as often as Negroes."

Before World War I, interracial couples frequently lived in predominantly white neighborhoods, if only because the vast Negro ghettos had not been formed. In 1910, for instance, only 2 per cent of the population of Chicago was Negro and some 24 per cent of the Negro population of the city lived in neighborhoods that were 95 per cent white. But the ghettos began forming swiftly after World War I, and by 1929 interracial couples were forced more and more deeply into the ghettos.

In recent years, interracial couples have been moving out of the ghettos into integrated neighborhoods—sometimes even into the suburbs. Not long ago, Dr. Roberts made a search of two large ghetto areas in Chicago and found among almost a quarter-million people only 15 interracial marriages. "In Hyde Park–Kenwood, you might find five or ten marriages in a single block," he says.

The interracial marriage has tended to involve a Negro man much more often than a white man. Of the first 188 couples Dr. Roberts interviewed, 147, or 78 per cent, involved Negro husbands. There were, as we have seen, economic reasons (the penalties fell more heavily on the white man) and social reasons (encounters were more likely between Negro men and white women). But as the social situation changed, so did the economic structure.

The white husband in an interracial marriage today enjoys a choice of occupations not available in the past. It is unlikely that any such man will become head of A.T.&T. or I.B.M., but he might rise high in government or academic life; he might enter the professions or find a rewarding niche in those fast-expanding areas in which his marital status would not be a matter of vast concern—in the entertainment industry, for instance, or in editorial work.

Dr. Roberts contends that the percentage of white men entering interracial marriages is increasing, and the figures of the Census Bureau support him. The bureau's 1950 figures indicate that 44 per cent of the husbands in interracial marriages were white; its 1960 figures indicate that slightly more than half the husbands were white.

Yet another change that affects the interracial couple is the rise of the black-separatist movement. The Black Power advocates are beginning to bring some pressure on the many "public-status" Negroes who are married to white women—such men as Bill Berry, James Farmer, once national director of CORE, and Senator Brooke of Massachusetts—in an effort to cut them off from the civil rights movement.

In a San Francisco speech in April, Cassius Clay, after explaining that he did not wish to offend the integrated couples in his audience, said: "We believe mixed marriages should be prohibited."

None of the major speakers at the innumerable Black Power rallies in Harlem these days ever appear with their white wives, and the subject of interracial marriage is rarely mentioned at the

meetings. There seems to be a tacit agreement among black sep-
aratists that nothing will be said about those who married whites
before the movement became popular. Nonetheless, some of the
militants—notably LeRoi Jones, the playwright—have divorced
their white wives and married Negroes, and the leaders seem to
realize that they would jeopardize their positions by dating or
marrying white women.

It has become popular in some parts of the black community
to observe that the modern Negro who is attracted to white girls
is forced to "sneak around like the old master snuck around" in
the South when he hoped to dally in the slave quarters. The number of visible Negro-white relationships in Harlem has diminished,
and the bonds between black men and black women have grown
stronger. It used to be said that Negro mothers told their daughters
that black men would do nothing for them, and black girls now
say they were forced to go to white men because Negro men
couldn't or wouldn't protect them. As the black woman turns back
to the black man, she is putting great pressure on him to shun
the white woman. Black Power militants are even taking the
process one step further: they are ignoring average Negro girls
in favor of those who have "gone natural"—who wear their hair
African-style and prefer African print dresses and jewelry. H. Rap
Brown's wife "went natural" about a month after she began dating him, and others have followed.

In a less formal way, the Black Power adherents are offering a
challenge to the offspring of interracial marriages. "It comes up
all the time in conversation," says the attractive young daughter
of a white mother and a Negro father. She is brown-skinned but
dates young men of both races. "It would be a shame to cut out
one entire race," she says with a smile. "Think of all the fun I'd
miss."

But her militant friends deplore her lack of commitment. "Oh,
so you're going 'unblack,' too," said one such friend not long
ago. "No," she replied. "But if I do what you want or what the
other side wants, I'm going to have to deny the existence of my
mother or my father. I'm not going to do that, for you or anybody else." Her attitude, she says, "is to pick issues. I won't pick
sides."

On the West Coast of the mainland of American society, the county of Los Angeles with its large and ethnically heterogeneous urban population has offered a succession of sociologists one of their richest resources for the study of intermarriage incidence and its dynamics, and for the detection of some of the most significant social variables associated with the phenomenon. One of the more fruitful studies during the past decade was conducted by John H. Burma, who examined the records of marriage licenses in the county during the eleven consecutive years from 1948 to 1959. Identifying over 3,200 racial and nationality intermarriages out of a total of more than 375,000 marriages during this period, he observed a pattern of considerable increase over the years. While Negro-white and Filipino-white intermarriages were the most common, he found that the smaller groups in Los Angeles intermarried proportionately far more than did the larger groups. Burma also noted that intermarriage occurred within the framework of cultural similarity, that the age of those who intermarried tended to be higher than of those who did not except in the instances where intermarrying persons had parents who had also intermarried, and that a divorced status (except for whites) was more likely for the intermarried subjects in comparison with those who married inside their groups.

INTERETHNIC MARRIAGE IN
LOS ANGELES, 1948–1959*

John H. Burma

All major groups in the United States today—racial, religious, or
ethnic—look with favor on homogeneous marriage and definite
disfavor on intermarriage. Thus, all intermarriage is relatively
rare. In the most extreme situations, such as New York, Los
Angeles, Chicago, and Philadelphia, probably no more than one
in two hundred marriages has been interethnic in the sense of
involving the marriage of Negroes, Filipinos, Chinese, Japanese,
or Indians with Mexicans or Anglos. At the other extreme the
number is zero. Various meritorious attempts have been made to
study interracial marriages on the mainland of the United States,
but with a few brilliant exceptions they usually have resulted in
reports valid only for a particular group in a particular city or
county at a particular date. Because of the difficulty of securing
data, most researchers have had to content themselves with a few
years and a few dozen or a few hundred cases. Examples include
studies by Baber, Barron, Catapusan, Davis and Gardner, Drake
and Cayton, Golden, Klineberg, Lawrence, Risdon, McWilliams,
Rogers, Schuyler, and Smith.

The present report suffers from these same difficulties, but
through the special cooperation of the County Clerk of Los Angeles County and of the Ford Foundation, it suffers somewhat
less. That is, it covers eleven consecutive years, over 375,000
total marriages and well over 3,200 mixed marriages in a county
having a sizeable number of each racial group. The term "mixed
marriage" as used here needs special definition immediately, for
it has a special meaning: "marriage" actually refers to taking out
a marriage license, not the true marriage itself, on which the
gathering of data was prohibitive in both time and money. It further was found that to refer to "couples who have taken out a
marriage license, but who may not have married" was impossibly

*Social Forces, Vol. 42 (December 1963), pp. 156–65. Reprinted by per-
mission of the University of North Carolina Press.

wordy and cumbersome, so "married" was substituted. In Los Angeles County about 5 per cent of marriage licenses applied for are not used within the time span of their validity, but there is no information on whether interethnic couples are more or less likely than others to let their licenses lapse. "Interethnic intermarriage" is used to mean cases in which an Anglo or Mexican married either a Negro, Filipino, Japanese, Chinese, or Indian or member of another non-European racial-ethnic group.

A number of possible theoretical hypotheses are available and will be mentioned, but this particular paper is concerned more with reporting facts and analyzing them than in deriving or proving theories, which will be done in a later paper.

The data presented here have several inherent limitations. They are based solely on marriage license applications, and such applications contain only very limited information about the persons applying for the license. Further, this study is based on three separate projects of data-gathering, which unfortunately were not always fully comparable. The first of these studies is based on photostatic copies of raw data gathered by the office of the Los Angeles County Clerk for its own internal purposes. This office was interested only in names, race, age, and sex, so this was all of the data available. To secure something of a control group the author himself gathered comparable data from an equal interval sample of interethnic marriages. This phase of data gathering produced the reports on the years 1948–1954. These data were reported in part previously.[1] The second data-gathering period covered the years 1955–57, and consists essentially of slightly different raw data made available by the office of the County Clerk of Los Angeles County and gathered by that office for its own purposes, but without the evidence of surnames of those married. Again, control data were gathered, under the author's direction, for a regular interval-sample of interethnic marriages. Finally, when the California legislature in 1959 forbade asking the race of applicants for marriage licenses, the author secured financial assistance from the Ford Foundation to hire a direct study of the County Clerk's files for 1958 and 1959. Therefore for these two final years all the types of data used were gathered again.

Until November of 1948 the laws of the state of California prohibited the legal intermarriage of whites with persons of any other race. Some intermarriages did occur through the falsification of racial data, but little is known of the number of such cases. Panunzio reports for the years 1924–33, for Los Angeles County, "some" Mexicans marrying Asiatics; seven Anglo and Japanese marriages; possibly 85 Filipino and Anglo marriages (then legal); one Chinese and Anglo; 38 Indian and Anglo or Mexican marriages; and five Negro marriages with Anglos or Mexicans.[2] When the California miscegenation law was held unconstitutional, the earlier marriage license forms requiring a statement of race continued in use, with some registrars, at least in Los Angeles County, refusing to accept marriage licenses unless the section on race was filled out with some accuracy. By "some accuracy" is meant that the registrars looked at the words on the application, looked at the persons, and if no discrepancy readily was observable, they accepted the application. It must be remarked that some registrars accepted applications with "races" such as "Korean," "Samoan," or "Guamanian," but in general there was considerable uniformity. As a sidelight, the author did hear a couple threaten the County Clerk with suit because he refused to accept "human race" as a satisfactory description. By observation it appeared both persons in the dispute were clearly Caucasoid.

From 1948 through 1957 this study offers no information on the intermarriage of whites and American Indians. The County Clerk's office was not interested in these marriages and did not gather these data. The author was interested, but did not have the staff to go back and recheck all the records for this single item. When more staff was available to study the licenses for 1958 and 1959, white-Indian and Indian-white marriages were included as an index of what presumably had been happening in the recent past. For the same reason divorce data also were gathered only for these final two years. No data of any kind were gathered after September 18, 1959, for on that date a new law made it illegal to ask race or color on marriage licenses.

Table 1 shows the total number of marriage licenses taken out by interracial couples for the two months of 1948 in which this was legal, and for twelve months of each succeeding year until 1959. For 1959, the figure is prorated for a full twelve months so that the final year will be comparable to the other years. It is to be noted that the number of interracial marriages immediately after the old law was declared unconstitutional[3] was small. Certainly there was no "rush" of interracial couples clamoring to

TABLE 1

Interracial Marriages in Los Angeles County, 1948–59

Year	Total Marriages	Interracial Marriages	Interracial Marriages per 1,000 Marriages
1948 (2 mo.)	5,376	28	5.2
1949	31,779	187	5.8
1950	31,915	168	5.3
1951	29,459	187	6.4
1952	30,178	171	5.7
1953	31,980	197	6.2
1954	32,095	238	7.4
1955	33,996	264	7.8
1956	36,365	268	7.4
1957	38,333	346	9.1
1958	37,700	465	12.3
1959	39,300	631*	16.1*
		3,150	

*In the 8½ months of 1959 in which race could be recorded, there were 447 intermarriages, which were prorated to 631 for twelve months and 16.1 per 1000 per year. The twelve year total also includes this proration.

marry, nor was there any significant increase during the next several years. During the middle years of the study an increase does become apparent, assuming very significant proportions in 1958 and 1959. Even though the numbers remain small, any rate which triples in eleven years is showing significant increase. Even at its highest the rate is small but since some 7 per cent of Los Angeles County population is non-white, the rate conceivably could be eight to ten times as great as it actually is. On the other hand, this is a high rate compared to most of the remainder of the nation where the rate is practically zero.

As was previously mentioned, it is quite significant that there was no rush to intermarry when intermarriage was legalized; it was not until 1954 that any sizeable increases are seen. The 1957–59 period, however, shows by far the most rapid rate of increase found in any study with which the author is familiar. The total number of marriages increased by approximately 22 per cent, from 1953 to 1959; the number of intermarriages for the same period increased approximately 220 per cent. As far as these data are concerned, there can be no question of the recent "snowballing" characteristic of these marriages. There is no way of determining whether this "snowball" trend is continuing, since the new law which forbids asking race on licenses effectively prevents any count. What is clear is that the intermarriage rate per 1,000 marriages in Los Angeles County is now about triple what it was in the early years of the period studied. This is a minimum count too, for it does not include marriages between American Indians and any other group, marriages between two ethnic groups where neither is white (e.g., Chinese-Filipino), or the Mexican-Anglo or Anglo-Mexican marriages, some of which may well have included persons of primarily Indian descent.

It can be seen from Table 2 that the white and Negro groups contain more women than men, and that all other groups contain a preponderance of men. If nothing more than sheer numbers were involved, and if all men and women in each group would marry within that group if it were physically possible to do so, then white men would marry only white women and Negro men would marry only Negro women. There would be an excess of both white and Negro women, however, available to marry into other groups. All Japanese, Chinese, Filipino, Indian, and Other women would marry within their respective groups, although there would be excess males in each group to marry the excess white and Negro women. According to this hypothesis the largest number of intermarriages would be Filipino-white, then Chinese-white, Other-white, Japanese-white, and Indian-white in that

TABLE 2

Population of Los Angeles County, by Races, by Sex
with Sex Ratios and Sex Differentials, 1960*

Race	Male	Female	Excess		Sex Ratio
White	2,656,627	2,797,239	F +	140,612	95
Negro	222,731	238,815	F +	16,084	93
Japanese	38,998	38,316	M +	682	102
Chinese	10,836	8,450	M +	2,386	128
Filipino	7,696	4,426	M +	3,270	174
Indian	4,139	3,970	M +	169	104
Other	3,620	2,908	M +	712	128

*Adapted from U.S. Bureau of Census, *U.S. Census of Population*: 1960 *General Population Characteristics, California*. Final Report P.C. (1)-6B Table 28 (Washington, D.C.: U.S. Government Printing Office, 1961).

order. There would be no intermarriages involving white or Negro males or of females of any but these two groups, and Negro females would intermarry like white females except on a one to nine ratio. This is what Panunzio meant when he said that sex distribution was a primary factor producing or preventing inter-marriage.[4]

Observation of Table 3 indicates how fallacious is the above theory and how obvious it is that sheer numbers do not explain the incidence of intermarriage. Negro males, despite having the largest proportion of excess females, out-marry by three and three-quarter times their populational expectancy. White males, despite the excess of white females, make up over one-third of all out-marrying males.

While these data do not explain why out-marriages occur, they do make it clear that sex ratios are not very significant causal factors in such marriages. Take for example Filipino men; the figures would indicate that about one in eleven Filipino males in Los Angeles County contracted an interethnic marriage during the 1948–59 period. Even this high proportion is a great understate-ment, however, due to those previously and continuingly married, and those too young to marry. It is more likely that one in every three or four Filipino males marrying during this period did not marry a Filipino woman. That about two-thirds of these men married Mexican American women is not surprising in view of the color homogamy and the fact that a large number of Filipinos

TABLE 3

Percentage of Males and Females of Selected Groups, Los Angeles County, 1960; Percentage of Males and Females Intermarrying, 1948–59, and Index of Proportion of Each in the Population and Intermarriages

	MALES		FEMALES	
GROUP	Per Cent of total population	Per Cent of total population intermarrying	Per Cent of total population	Per Cent of total population intermarrying
White	87.51	35.98	90.61	63.98
Negro	7.33	27.60	7.73	10.12
Japanese	1.29	7.02	1.24	13.42
Chinese	.36	5.83	.27	4.94
Filipino	.31	23.95	.14	7.50

in the United States speak Spanish. These data bear out Panunzio's theory that when people do marry outside their own group, culture homogeneity in the main determines the selection. Filipino females, whom one would expect to be the most sought after of all groups by the Filipino males, nevertheless out-marry proportionally far more than any other group of females. Although the data are not fully complete, these Filipino girls seem well below the average age, were mostly born in America, and are very disproportionately themselves actually Filipino-white products of mixed marriages.

As for the almost 400 Japanese females who married white men, there is no obvious explanation in the data. Once the author, in common with other sociologists interested in this field, explained the first out-marriages of Japanese girls in terms of the shortage of Japanese males due to high casualties during World War II and the marriage of Nisei soldiers to Japanese girls during the occupation of Japan. These factors may have accounted for some early intermarriages, but in no way do they shed light on the large number of these marriages during the last three years of this study, the girls being much too young to have married veterans. Since during the same period some 200 Japanese males married white females, this earlier explanation must be discarded, preferably in favor of a sociocultural one.

That some 170 Chinese males married white females is arithmetically reasonable, but that nearly 150 Chinese females married white males is arithmetically so improbable that one has no alternative but to assume that other factors are involved. Although the data give no causal inferences, it is the author's opinion that assimilation, decreasing social distance, improved social status of minorities, and decreasing intolerance are likely to be found among the causal factors for all intermarrying groups. For the smaller groups not yet mentioned the samples are not large enough to draw any conclusions other than the obvious one that their intermarriages, as much as or more than those of the larger groups, have made significant increases in the last few years, quite possibly for the same reasons. At the very most, only about 40 per cent of intermarriages could be accounted for on the basis of sex ratio imbalances.

Whatever the causal factors, Table 3 and Table 4 show that the probability that any given member of the smaller groups will intermarry is much greater than the probability that any given member of the white group will intermarry. Comparison with Table 2 shows that size of group is a much more predictive factor than sex ratio. For example, white females are found to make up 58 per cent of the women intermarrying and in this sense are more likely to be involved in intermarrying than any other females. On the other hand, in Los Angeles there are far more white females than any other group, and it is only sheer numbers which make the probability of their appearance seem high. Ac-

TABLE 4

Percentage of Males and Females in the Total Population, 1960, and Percentage in Total Intermarriages, for Selected Groups, Los Angeles County, 1948–59

GROUP	MALE			FEMALE		
	Per Cent in Total Pop.	Per Cent in Inter-marriage	Index	Per Cent in Total Pop.	Per Cent in Inter-marriage	Index
White	90.2	42.0	.47	90.4	58.0	.64
Negro	7.6	21.5	2.83	7.7	6.5	.84
Japanese	1.3	7.4	5.70	1.2	12.6	10.50
Chinese	.4	4.2	10.50	.3	4.4	14.66
Filipino	.3	13.7	45.67	.1	8.1	81.00
Indian	.1	3.8	38.00	.1	4.0	40.00
Other	.1	7.4	74.00	.1	6.4	64.00

tually, the probability that a random white female will intermarry is far less than the probability that a random Filipino female will intermarry. For any group the formula of per cent of intermarriages divided by the per cent of population gives the measure of probability of intermarriage for a person within that group. For white females this index is only .64, but for Filipino females the same index is 81.00; thus a Filipino female is over 125 times as likely to intermarry as is a white female.

Whether we consider the whole period or the last two years it is clear that proportionately white males, despite bulking large in total numbers, are individually the least likely to intermarry, with white women next and Negro women next. All other categories have much higher indices. No specific populational figures are available for Hawaiians or Koreans, but it's clear their rates also are high. That these variations are significant cannot be doubted when we see that for the total period, for example, the probability that a Filipino male will intermarry is almost 450 times as great as the probability of a white male intermarrying. Only among Negroes was the probability of male intermarriage significantly higher than that of female intermarriage and only among Japanese was there a consistent tendency for females to outmarry considerably more than males.

Using the supplementary and admittedly inadequate base of two years, as seen in Table 5, one observes that there was a sizeable number of white-Indian and Indian-white intermarriages (there were less than 20,000 Indians in all of California in 1950), and that there was little difference in the number of males and females intermarrying from this group. Because of the definitions used, whites were involved in 100 per cent of the intermarriages counted, and 25 per cent of these whites were Mexican Americans. Negroes were involved in 34 per cent of the cases; Filipino Americans in 29 per cent; Japanese Americans in 18 per cent; Chinese Americans in 11 per cent; and Other groups in 8 per cent.

During the period studied there was a significant increase not only in total intermarriages but also in every individual category. Comparing the 1949–50 average with the 1958–59 average we find that while total marriages were up 21 per cent, total intermarriages were up 210 per cent. Marriages involving Filipinos and whites increased by 65 per cent; those involving Chinese and whites increased by 122 per cent; those involving Negroes and whites increased by 235 per cent; those involving Japanese and whites increased 525 per cent; and those involving Other groups and whites increased 1840 per cent. While these trends are clear, it would be dangerous to extrapolate them beyond the immediate future.

Although all data are not presented here, it has been computed that Mexican Americans are about three times more likely to outmarry than are Anglos. In the case of intermarriages involving Negro men, the incidence of Mexican American females is about 328 per cent of arithmetic expectancy; with Chinese males it is about 300 per cent of expectancy; with Japanese males it is about 328 per cent of expectancy; and with Filipino males it is about 827 per cent of expectancy.

In the cases involving white men, the incidence of Mexican American females is about 31 per cent of expectancy; in the cases of Chinese females it is about 141 per cent of expectancy; for Japanese females it is about 119 per cent of expectancy; and for Filipino females it is about 336 per cent of expectancy. The disproportionate numbers of Filipino and Mexican intermarriages would seem to confirm Panunzio's theory of the significance of cultural similarity in intermarriage. Thus, Mexican American females are more likely to intermarry than are either Anglo females or Mexican American males, and the latter are more likely to intermarry than are Anglo males. One might hypothesize on this evidence that the social distance between Mexican Americans and the other ethnic groups studied is less than between Anglos and the other ethnic groups. The 1958–59 evidence would indicate that social distance is less between Anglos and Mexican Americans than between Anglos and any of the other groups. In general one might hypothesize that the Anglos felt least social distance between themselves and Mexican Americans, then Filipinos, then Chinese, then Japanese, and felt the greatest social distance between themselves and Negroes. Dynamically, the interpretation may be made that while the social distance between whites and the other groups is decreasing in all cases, it is decreasing more rapidly between whites and Negroes and Filipinos (and about at the same rate). While this social distance hypothesis does not clash with the data (and in fact is supported by the large proportion of marriages between Mexican Americans and Filipinos), it would be a serious oversimplification to assign a monistic cause to any large social phenomenon.

One type of information which is both useful and available from marriage license applications is the age of the applicant. In order both to compare each of the groups and also to show any trends which might be occurring, the reporting is in terms of the median age for 1951–53 and for 1957–59. As a base from which to compare other groups, it should be noted that our sample of males in the white-white marriages had a median age of about 24.5 for the early period and 25 for the later period. Our sample of males in the Negro-Negro marriages had a median age of about 28 for this earlier period and about 25.5 for the later period.

The oldest group of males was in the Filipino-white marriages; for the earlier period their median age was about 41, but by the later period it had declined to about 28 which, as will be seen, is not far different from the ages of other intermarrying males during that period. We interpret this change (the largest in any group) as being due to the earlier period containing a significant number of the "wave" of Filipinos who came here 25 to 35 years ago. By the later period, most of these persons who ever were going to marry had done so, and most later marriages were by younger Filipinos who were second generation, and fewer in number. What influence, if any, a differential divorce and remarriage rate might have on ages will be explored later in this paper.

Our next oldest group of males, also significantly above the average in age, was the white males marrying Negro females. This group had a median age of 36.7 during the earlier period, which dropped to 32.8 during the later period. Also older were the Chinese males marrying white females who in the earlier period had a median age of 36.3 and of 27.7 in the later period. Like the Filipino males, it is probable that some of the differential is due to marriage of the first generation persons in the earlier period and not in the later period. The Negro males who marry white women are slightly older than the Negro-Negro average in both time periods. Anglo males who marry Japanese, Filipino, or Chinese women are about average age, and are significantly younger than Anglo males marrying Negro females. As a total group, intermarrying males are somewhat older than intramarrying males.

Intermarrying females are somewhat older than intramarrying females. For the earlier period of this study, the median age of females in white-white marriages was 23; for the later period it was 21.5 years. In Negro-Negro marriages the median ages were 27 and 23 respectively. In the first period the two oldest groups were Anglo females marrying Chinese or Filipinos and Negro females marrying Anglo males; all three were significantly beyond the median age for white brides. The Filipino girls who married Anglo men were the youngest of all—just under 23 for the earlier period and just under 22 for the later period. In the later period, all female median ages were lower, with the Anglo women marrying Negroes or Chinese being the oldest, closely followed by the Japanese women marrying Anglo men.

The groom-bride age differential in the early period for white-white marriages was 1.5 years; for Negro-Negro marriages it was 1 year. In the later period it was 3.5 for white-white and 2.5 for Negro-Negro. In the early period the median age differential between Filipino males and their white brides was 12 years; for Anglo males with Negro brides it was 6.7 years. Even though the white brides of Chinese males were the oldest group in the early period, they were almost six years younger than their husbands. The Japanese brides who in the earlier period married white grooms were the only group whose median age was older than their husbands' (1.3 years). In the second period this group's median age was 1.3 years below that of their husbands, and still the nearest to equal of any group.

It would be realistic to hypothesize that some of the persons entering mixed marriages would be themselves the products of mixed marriages, and such was found to be the case. A separate study of the 1952–57 data found that marriages of persons identifiable as such (an obvious under-count since no Negro-white mixtures were included) were approximately 10 per cent of the total for that period. Significantly, the number increased from under 7 per cent for the first two years to over 12 per cent for the last two years. Roughly two-thirds were intermarriages of Anglos with persons of mixed Filipino-Anglo ancestry. The remaining one-third were fairly evenly divided between Japanese-white, Chinese-white, and Other-white mixtures. A significant age differential also existed for this intermixed group; they were the youngest of all, and were the only group with any sizeable number of 18-year-old grooms or 16–17-year-old brides. The median age for the "mixed" grooms of Anglo brides was 22, the mode was only 18; the median age for Anglo grooms of "mixed" brides was 23, the mode was 18. For the "mixed" brides of Anglo grooms, the median age and mode both were 20; for the Anglo brides of "mixed" grooms the median age was 19 and the mode was 18. Should one present the hypothesis that "mixed" children leave their parental homes to set up their own homes earlier than is true of Anglo and Negro children, the data would not contradict such an hypothesis.

In summary as regards age: (1) for the male groups, median age decreased between the earlier and the later periods studied, but tended to remain higher than for intramarriages; (2) for the earlier period males in the Filipino-Anglo, Anglo-Negro, and Chinese-Anglo intermarriages were the oldest; Anglo males marrying Japanese or Filipino females were the youngest; (3) there was much less age range in the later period, but most intermarrying males were two or three years older than the intramarrying males; only in Anglo-Filipino marriages was the male median lower than in Anglo-Anglo marriages; (4) for the female groups median age decreased between the earlier and the later periods, but tended to remain higher than for intramarriages; (5) in the earlier period women in the Chinese-Anglo, Anglo-Negro, and Filipino-

TABLE 5
Intermarriage by Ethnic Classification and Sex
1958–59

Classification	Total Number	Per Cent of Total
Negro-white	256	21.5
Filipino-white ...	163	13.7
White-Japanese ..	150	12.6
White-Filipino ...	96	8.1
Japanese-white ..	88	7.4
White-Negro	77	6.5
Hawaiian-white ..	63	5.3
White-Chinese ...	52	4.4
Chinese-white ...	50	4.2
White-Indian	48	4.0
White-Hawaiian ..	47	4.0
Indian-white	45	3.8
White-Korean ...	11	1.0
Korean-white	7	.6
Other	36	3.0
Total	1,189	100.1
Anglo-Mexican ..	1,433	
Mexican-Anglo ...	1,226	

TABLE 6

Intermarriage by Racial Classification and Sex, 1948–59

Classification	1948	1949	1950	1951	1952	1953	1954	1955	1956	1957	1958	1959	Total	Per Cent of Total
Negro-White	6	43	30	50	45	53	61	84	77	95	111	145	800	25.4
Negro-Anglo	4	32	19	38	33	34	52	—	—	—	93	121	426	
Negro-Mexican	2	11	11	12	12	19	9	—	—	—	18	24	118	
Filipino-White	14	74	69	69	59	50	56	53	42	63	76	87	712	22.6
Filipino-Anglo	12	39	33	37	34	31	32	—	—	—	65	56	339	
Filipino-Mexican	2	35	36	32	25	19	24	—	—	—	11	31	215	
White-Japanese	3	12	12	16	13	20	29	37	45	57	65	85	394	12.5
Anglo-Japanese	3	11	10	16	11	18	25	—	—	—	60	78	232	
Mexican-Japanese	0	1	2	0	2	2	4	—	—	—	5	7	23	
White-Negro	0	10	16	12	13	25	30	23	27	34	35	42	267	8.5
Anglo-Negro	0	10	11	10	10	16	23	—	—	—	31	34	145	
Mexican-Negro	0	0	5	2	3	9	7	—	—	—	4	8	38	
White-Filipino	0	10	9	12	11	12	14	12	22	22	41	55	220	7.0
Anglo-Filipino	0	6	4	9	9	10	12	—	—	—	33	45	128	
Mexican-Filipino	0	4	5	3	2	2	2	—	—	—	8	10	36	
Japanese-White	1	8	6	10	11	14	10	18	14	26	30	58	206	6.3
Japanese-Anglo	1	5	6	6	10	12	7	—	—	—	24	44	115	
Japanese-Mexican	0	3	0	4	1	2	3	—	—	—	6	14	33	
Chinese-White	3	19	11	9	5	8	21	12	16	17	25	25	171	5.4
Chinese-Anglo	2	11	10	6	5	7	15	—	—	—	23	23	101	
Chinese-Mexican	1	8	1	3	0	1	6	—	—	—	2	2	25	

													Total	%
White-Chinese	1	6	10	5	10	11	11	13	13	13	18	34	145	4.6
Anglo-Chinese	1	5	10	5	9	11	9	—	—	—	16	31	77	
Mexican-Chinese	0	1	0	0	1	0	2	—	—	—	2	3	9	
Hawaiian-White	0	0	0	0	0	1	0	0	3	7	26	37	74	2.3
White-Hawaiian	0	0	0	0	0	0	0	0	0	0	15	32	47	1.5
White-Korean	0	2	4	2	1	2	0	6	2	6	4	7	36	1.1
Korean-White	0	0	0	0	0	0	0	0	0	0	3	4	7	
Other	0	3	1	2	3	1	6	6	7	6	18	18	71	2.2
Total	28	187	168	187	171	197	238	264	268	346	467	629	3,150	

Note: 1948 was not prorated to 12 months because no legal intermarriages took place before its last two months and 1959 was prorated to 12 months because intermarriages did continue through the remaining three and a half months of the year. Data on Mexican surnames are not available for 1955–57, so the "total" for that group represents 1948–54 plus 1958–59 with no prorating except 1959.

Anglo marriages were the oldest; Filipino women marrying Anglo males were the youngest; (6) in the later period there was less age differential, but with the same older and younger groups; (7) in both periods intermarrying females tended to be one to three years older than intramarrying females; (8) the youngest of all groups were the products of mixed marriages who themselves were intermarrying; (9) median age differential between husbands and wives was significantly greater in intermarriages than in intramarriages.

Tables 5 and 6 present data concerning which ethnic groups marry which and by what sex. In each case the group written first represents the male partner in the marriage. Thus "Negro-white" is to be interpreted as Negro male marrying white female. "Korean," "Hawaiian," "Filipino" are not included as the author's analysis of race, but because they were accepted as "race" by the Los Angeles Marriage Bureau; they are reproduced for the light they shed on intermarriage, not for their anthropological authenticity. The marked increase in 1958–59 in "other" marriages is only partly real. In analyzing the prior data the author arbitrarily assigned one ethnic group (by father's classification) to cases of mixed-parentage persons. The author failed to tell the persons hired to gather the 1958–59 data to do this and it was only after all data were gathered that this oversight was discovered. Thus most of the increase in "other" consists of mixed-parentage cases. The term "Mexican" refers to a Caucasian with a Mexican name, without reference to where the person was born; similarly "Anglo" is used to refer to any Caucasian who does not have a Mexican name. The form in which the author received the 1955–57 data made it impossible to determine surnames in the same fashion as 1948–54 and 1958–59. This explains incomplete tables and why the Anglo and Mexican totals do not equal the grand total for any category.

It would be nice if marriage license data could tell us whether the applicants lived happily ever after. Unfortunately, they cannot; but they can tell us whether or not the persons being married have previously been divorced. Table 7 and Table 8 present information which, in summary, shows that intermarriages involving Negroes are most likely to include previously divorced persons, the odds being about even that one of the parties has previously been divorced, and it being twice as likely that a person involved in a marriage between a white and a Negro has been married at least twice before than if the intermarriage was between any other groups. Most other intermarriages are less likely to involve divorced persons than are regular white-white marriages. Other than Negro-Negro intramarriages, all other intramarriages are very significantly less likely to include divorced persons.

In intermarriages the percentage of divorced white women by group of the groom is approximately: white 20 per cent; Mexican 20 per cent; Japanese 20 per cent; Filipino 13 per cent; Chinese 16 per cent; and Negroes 40 per cent.

In summary, this study indicates that in Los Angeles intermarriages are increasing significantly: the largest number of marriages include whites and Negroes, but proportionately the smaller groups intermarry tremendously more than the larger groups; some evidence of intermarriage by cultural homogamy exists; intermarried couples are on the average somewhat older than persons intra-

TABLE 7

Previous Divorces per 1,000 for Mixed and Non-mixed Marriages, with White-White as Index, Los Angeles County, 1958–59

Classification	Divorces per 1,000 Marriages White-White as Index
White-Negro	158
Negro-White	146
Negro-Negro	127
Chinese-White	102
White-White	100
Filipino-White	98
Hawaiian-White	92
Anglo-Mexican	87
Mexican-Anglo	82
White-Japanese	75
White-Chinese	74
Japanese-White	72
White-Filipino	69
White-Hawaiian	68
Indian-White	53
Mexican-Mexican	50
Filipino-Filipino	45
Other	37
Korean-Korean	37
White-Indian	34
Chinese-Chinese	14
Japanese-Japanese	13
Indian-Indian	12

TABLE 8

Percentage, by Groups, of Divorced and Never Divorced Couples, 1958–59

	Intramarriage								
	A-A	M-M	N-N	F-F	J-J	C-C	I-I	K-K	Other
ND	72	82	60	86	95	94	94	88	76
D-ND	6	6	8	4	2	2	2	0	6
ND-D	7	6	10	4	2	3	2	0	11
D-D	7	3	10	4	2	0	2	5	3
EDMI	8	3	12	2	2	1	0	7	4

	Intermarriage											
	A-M	A-N	A-F	A-J	A-C	A-I	M-A	F-A	N-A	J-A	C-A	I-A
ND	70	52	72	67	69	79	75	66	50	70	59	81
D-ND ..	9	15	6	13	12	3	5	8	9	9	10	6
ND-D ..	8	2	13	12	12	5	7	12	12	11	15	6
D-D ...	7	10	5	4	2	8	5	3	13	4	5	3
EDMI ..	6	21	5	4	5	5	7	11	15	6	10	3

KEY

A—Anglo	ND—No divorces
M—Mexican	D-ND—Male divorced, female not divorced
N—Negro	ND-D—Male not divorced, female divorced
F—Filipino	D-D—Both divorced
J—Japanese	EDMI—Either divorced more than once
C—Chinese	
I—Indian	
K—Korean	

marrying, except if they themselves are the products of intermarriage; and, except for whites, in most cases there was a greater likelihood that one party had been divorced previously than in comparable intramarriages.

NOTES

1. John H. Burma, "Research Note on the Measurement of Interracial Marriage," *American Journal of Sociology,* Vol. 57, No. 6 (May 1952), pp. 587–589.
2. Constantine Panunzio, "Intermarriage in Los Angeles, 1924–33," *American Journal of Sociology,* Vol. 47, No. 5 (March 1942), pp. 690–701.
3. The winning argument came when two Catholics, one Negro and one white, declared that their religious freedom was hampered by the law; they could receive all the sacraments except that of marriage, which was being unconstitutionally denied them by the law.
4. Constantine Panunzio, *op. cit.,* p. 690.

On the East Coast, New York City's Puerto Ricans are the most recent of the large ethnic groups to have arrived on the mainland. Concentrated mostly in the first and second generations, they afford sociologists the opportunity to determine how their intermarriage, as an indicator of the acceptance of newcomers by the more established host ethnic groups, compares with the performance of comparable groups of southern and eastern European newcomers at the turn of the twentieth century. Joseph P. Fitzpatrick, a sociologist specializing in the problems of Puerto Rican migrants, reports in the last essay of this section on his study of Puerto Rican intermarriage, based on all marriages in New York City in 1949 and 1959 in which one partner was either first or second generation Puerto Rican. His findings show quite clearly that intermarriage by Puerto Ricans increased significantly by generation in both of the years studied. Indeed the increase in rate by the second generation over the first was just as great as that found in the earliest studies of intermarriage by all immigrant groups in New York City during the years 1908–12.

INTERMARRIAGE OF PUERTO RICANS
IN NEW YORK CITY[1]*

Joseph P. Fitzpatrick

According to the 1960 Census of Population,[2] there were 612,574 Puerto Ricans living in the city of New York; 429,710 (70 per cent) of these had been born in Puerto Rico; 182,864 (30

*The American Journal of Sociology, Vol. 71, No. 4 (January 1966), pp. 395–406. Reprinted by permission of the University of Chicago Press.

per cent) had been born in New York of Puerto Rican parentage. The question is frequently raised about the assimilation of the Puerto Ricans into the New York community: how rapidly are they becoming assimilated; is their assimilation more rapid or less rapid than that of immigrant groups which came to the city at an earlier date? The present study is an effort to determine the rate of assimilation[3] on the basis of marriage behavior. It indicates that assimilation is proceeding rapidly.

In every study of cultural assimilation, the factor of marriage is of central importance. A high rate of intermarriage of members of one ethnic group with another is generally accepted as a reliable index of cultural assimilation. Ruby Jo Reeves used intermarriage as the crucial sign of assimilation and found that ethnic groups were intermarrying with other ethnic groups, but within the three major faiths of Protestant, Catholic, Jewish.[4] Will Herberg accepts this same position.[5] John Thomas questions the fact that marriages take place this way within religious groups. He finds interreligious marriage not only extensive, but increasing.[6] These three studies are all concerned with the factor of intermarriage, especially interreligious marriage, in the process of assimilation.[7]

This study, therefore, seeks to determine the rate of assimilation among Puerto Ricans on the basis of the extent of in-group versus out-group marriage. The simple hypothesis is that a high level of out-group marriage reflects a high level of assimilation. The phenomenon of out-group marriage will be examined in relation to generation, occupational status, age, and type of marriage ceremony.[8]

The best known earlier study of this kind was one published by Julius Drachsler[9] in 1921, analyzing the rates of intermarriage of immigrants in New York City from 1908–12. Drachsler found a rate of out-group marriage of 11 per cent among first-generation immigrants, and a tripling in the rate of out-group marriage among second-generation immigrants, namely 32 per cent.[10] Drachsler analyzed three hypotheses offered to explain this intermarriage: (1) the sex ratio, the preponderance of the number of marriageable men over the number of marriageable women; (2) a rise in economic status which places people of different nationality groups (especially women) in closer contact with the out-group; and (3) the breakdown of the cohesive ethnic group. Drachsler discounts hypotheses (1) and (2) and accepts hypothesis (3) as the only reasonable explanation for the high rate of intermarriage in the second generation. In other words, intermarriage is an index of cultural assimilation or integration.

In the present study, every marriage in the city of New York of a first- or second-generation Puerto Rican in the years 1949 and 1959 was reviewed, and all relevant data were gathered from the marriage record. The data were as follows:

1. Place of birth of bride; of groom.
2. Age at marriage of bride; of groom.
3. Place of residence at time of marriage of bride; of groom.
4. Place of marriage; time of marriage according to month.
5. Type of ceremony: civil, Catholic, Protestant, other.
6. Color, as declared, of bride; of groom.
7. Occupation of bride; of groom.
8. Previous marriage of bride; of groom.
9. Place of birth of father and mother of bride; of groom.

On the basis of these data, first-generation Puerto Ricans (born in Puerto Rico of Puerto Rican parentage) and second-generation Puerto Ricans (born on the mainland, of Puerto Rican parentage) can be identified. Beyond the second generation, all persons are recorded as native-born of native parentage, and it is no longer possible to draw an accurate distinction between persons of different ethnic backgrounds.

In-group and out-group marriages were determined by the following criteria:

In-Group: marriage of a first- or second-generation Puerto Rican with a first- or second-generation Puerto Rican.[11]

Out-Group: marriage of a first- or second-generation Puerto Rican with a partner born on the mainland of mainland parentage; marriage with a partner foreign-born or born in the United States of foreign parents.[12]

The data on out-group marriages are presented in Table 1. The data give evidence of a significant increase in the rate of out-group marriages among second-generation Puerto Ricans, both men and women, in both 1949 and 1959. One difficulty in these comparisons is the small number of second-generation marriages in comparison to first-generation. Nevertheless, the trend over the 10-year period was consistent. And the trend indicates a significant increase in out-group marriage.

Is the increase as significant as the increase that occurred among former immigrants? In his study of immigrant marriages of 1908–12, Drachsler[13] found a rate of out-group marriage of 10.39 per cent for first-generation men, and of 10.1 per cent for first-generation women. This rate of out-group marriage was higher than the rate for first-generation Puerto Ricans in either 1949 or 1959. The data are compared in Table 1. However, the percentage increase in out-group marriage from first to second generation is almost the same for all three groups. In fact, in terms of percentage, the rate of out-group marriage among

TABLE 1

Rate of Out-Group Marriage of Puerto Ricans in New York City, 1949 and 1959, by Generation; and of All Immigrants in New York City, 1908–12

	First Generation		Second Generation		Increase in Second Generation
	Per Cent	N	Per Cent	N	Per Cent
Grooms:					
Puerto Rican, 1949 ..	5.2	3,079	28.3	378	23.1
Puerto Rican, 1959 ..	3.6	7,078	27.4	638	23.8
1908–12	10.39	64,577	32.4	12,184	22.01
Brides:					
Puerto Rican, 1949 ..	8.5	3,077	30.0	523	21.5
Puerto Rican, 1959 ..	6.0	7,257	33.1	717	27.1
1908–12	10.1	61,823	30.12	14,611	20.02

second-generation Puerto Rican women is the same in 1949 and higher in 1959 than was the rate for second-generation immigrant women in the years 1908–12; the rate among second-generation Puerto Rican men approaches the rate of out-group marriage for second-generation men, 1908–12. On the basis of this evidence, it appears that the assimilation of Puerto Ricans is advancing as fast as the assimilation of the immigrants in the 1908–12 period.[14]

In seeking to explain the great difference in out-group marriage rates between first and second generation, Drachsler first hypothesized that it was a consequence of the sex ratio. However, he found that this was not relevant.[15] Neither is it relevant to the Puerto Rican marriage. The sex ratio for all Puerto Ricans, aged 15–44, in New York City in 1949 was 82.7; in 1960 it was 91, identical with the ratio for the total population of New York State, aged 15–44. However, there was no appreciable difference in total out-group marriages among Puerto Ricans between 1949 and 1959. It is only when the first generation is distinguished from the second that the increase in out-group marriage appears as a second-generation phenomenon, nor does this have any relationship to the sex ratio. In 1949, the sex ratio showed a marked increase in the second generation (82 to 90), but there was a marked increase also in the percentage of out-group marriages. In 1959, there was little difference between the sex ratio of the first and second generation (90 to 92); yet there was a marked increase in the percentage of out-group marriages.

The second hypothesis of Drachsler was that out-group marriage increases as socioeconomic status advances. The occupational categories used by Drachsler are much different from the standard categories now used by the U.S. Census. He used five categories of occupation:

a) Highest Group: Professionals.
b) Middle Group: Persons in commerce.
c) Lower Group: Personal and domestic service; lower grades of public service.
d) Low Group: Agricultural, transportation, and navigation workers.
e) Lowest Group: The unskilled.

Drachsler combined categories (*a*) and (*b*) into one which he called "higher economic classes," and he combined (*c*), (*d*), and (*e*) into what he called "lower economic classes." When the data are presented in these categories, as in Table 2, it is evident immediately that intermarriage was a phenomenon of the higher economic classes. However, economic level was as significant for the intermarriages of the first generation as it was for the second. Since Drachsler was trying to determine the factors that accounted for an increase in intergroup marriage in the second generation, he therefore discounted economic level as a variable.[16]

In the present study, the standard occupational categories of the U.S. Census were used, and collapsed to represent three different levels:

Higher occupational level:
Professional, technical, and kindred workers.
Managers, officials, proprietors.

Middle occupational level:
Clerical, sales, and kindred workers.
Craftsmen, foremen, and kindred workers.
Lower occupational level:
Operatives and kindred workers.
Non-household service workers.
Private household workers.
Laborers.
Farm workers.

TABLE 2

Distribution of Out-Group Marriages of First- and Second-Generation
Immigrants, 1908–12, for New York City, According
to Occupation and Sex

	Men		Women	
	First Generation (Per Cent)	Second Generation (Per Cent)	First Generation (Per Cent)	Second Generation (Per Cent)
High occupational level..	63.6	72.4	45.4	75.7
Low occupational level...	36.4	27.6	54.6	24.3
Total out-group marriages	100 (2,108)	100 (1,572)	100 (2,014)	100 (1,662)

Adopted from Drachsler (see note 9 at the end of this article), p. 65. Only a
third of the marriage records reported occupation.

Marriages in which occupation was unknown were omitted. They
were too few to be significant. Data on occupation are presented
in Table 3. It is important to note two things, in contrast to
Drachsler, in evaluating the marriage according to occupational
level: (1) The occupation of the *groom* alone was used. This was
done to maintain consistency. It is also reasonable since, in the
United States, the status level of a marriage is generally determined according to the occupation of the husband. (2) The data
are presented according to the percentage in each occupational
level that married out, rather than the percentage of all out-group
marriages which took place among persons of high or low occupational status. In view of the small numbers, this was considered
a more accurate method of indicating the differences.

Two things are evident from these data: Among Puerto Rican
brides, the higher the occupational level at which they marry, the

TABLE 3

Out-Group Marriages of Puerto Ricans in New York City,
1949 and 1959, According to Occupation of Groom

Occupation Level	1949		1959	
	Per Cent	N	Per Cent	N
	Grooms			
High:				
First generation	8.7	127	8.5	212
Second generation	53.0	34	20.0	62
Middle:				
First generation	7.7	650	5.0	1,584
Second generation	26.4	106	28.7	307
Lower:				
First generation	4.3	2,182	2.6	5,133
Second generation	25.0	207	24.9	241
	Brides (According to Occupation of Groom)			
High:				
First generation	21.0	127	26.8	269
Second generation	51.2	45	55.4	83
Middle:				
First generation	12.6	673	9.6	1,706
Second generation	39.6	149	35.9	268
Lower:				
First generation	5.8	2,231	3.5	5,120
Second generation	16.6	283	26.3	319

higher the rate of out-group marriage. Although it can only be surmised from these data, it is likely that Puerto Rican women are marrying up as they marry out. On the other hand, there is no such consistent trend among the Puerto Rican grooms. There is little difference between the rate of out-group marriage among second-generation grooms of lower and middle occupational status, and, in 1959, the rate is lower for Puerto Ricans on the high occupational level than it is for those on the lower levels. Among the Puerto Rican grooms, generation, not occupational level, appears to be the significant variable in out-group marriage.

Two other types of data taken from marriage records may also be helpful in a study of the assimilation of Puerto Ricans, namely, age at marriage and type of religious ceremony. A comparison between practices on the island and practices on the mainland may indicate the extent of adaptation to mainland American patterns. Table 4 presents median age at marriage for men and women, 1950 and 1960, in Puerto Rico. It also presents median age at marriage for Puerto Ricans in New York, first and second generation, 1949 and 1959. There is no consistent pattern evident in the change in age at marriage among Puerto Ricans in Puerto Rico and in New York. The consistency appears in the tendency of second-generation Puerto Ricans in New York, both grooms and brides, to marry at an earlier age than those of the first generation. This is more evident in Table 5, which gives the percentages of Puerto Ricans marrying below age 20.[17]

TABLE 4

Median Age at Marriage for All Marriages, Puerto Rico, 1950 and 1960; and for Puerto Ricans in New York, by Generation, 1949 and 1959

	Men		Women	
	All Marriages	Out-Group Marriages	All Marriages	Out-Group Marriages
Puerto Rico (1950)	26.02	....	22.16	....
Puerto Ricans in New York City:				
1949	24.68	24.62	23.01	23.70
First generation	25.47	26.91	23.59	25.05
Second generation	21.83	22.42	19.99	21.43
Puerto Rico (1960)	23.01	....	21.75	....
Puerto Ricans in New York City:				
1959	24.23	24.49	22.85	23.7
First generation	24.33	25.62	23.00	24.4
Second generation	23.13	23.46	21.66	22.04

A number of factors enter into the tendency toward lower age at marriage for the second generation. It may simply reflect the trend toward lower age at marriage in Puerto Rico itself. However, as Mills, Senior, and Goldsen pointed out in their study of the Puerto Rican migration,[18] the migrating population is an older population than that of the island. Most migrating people are in their late teens or early twenties. There is a selective feature in economically motivated migrations, since single people are more mobile. The children of the migrants, however, being settled in the new land, are evidently tending toward the pattern of the United States of younger age at marriage.

Finally, it may be of some help to examine the factor of religion in the marriage of New York Puerto Ricans to determine

TABLE 5

Percentage of Grooms and Brides under 20 Years of Age, All Marriages,
for Puerto Rico, 1950 and 1960; for Puerto Ricans in
New York by Generation, 1949 and 1959

	Men		Women	
	All Marriages	Out-Group Marriages	All Marriages	Out-Group Marriages
Puerto Rico (1950)	6.4	....	32.1	....
Puerto Ricans in New York City:				
1949	5.7	6.3	22.0	18.1
First generation	3.7	2.3	17.9	13.1
Second generation	20.9	14.4	45.8	31.4
Puerto Rico (1960)	10.3	....	36.1	
Puerto Ricans in New York City:				....
1959	8.4	11.8	26.3	19.7
First generation	7.7	11.5	25.7	16.3
Second generation	14.8	12.7	32.1	29.2

whether evidence from this source may indicate the speed of
assimilation.[19] No one has reliable evidence of the exact number
of Puerto Ricans who profess Catholicism or Protestantism. The
overwhelming majority, probably 80–90 per cent, profess the
Roman Catholic faith, although the level of instruction in the
faith is often very limited and the practice of the faith, as in most
Latin areas, is quite different from the practice that is common in
the United States.[20] One notable contrast between Puerto Rico
and the United States mainland is in the extent of the use of the
Catholic religious ceremony at marriage. Religious marriage is
the overwhelming pattern for Catholic people in the United
States. John Thomas estimates that 80 per cent of all marriages
involving a Roman Catholic are marriages with a religious ceremony.[21]

In Puerto Rico, however, the situation is not easily determined.
The pattern differs sharply from one area of the island to another. The pattern also differs from one year to another. Table 6
presents marriages according to type of ceremony for selected
areas of Puerto Rico for 1960. It illustrates the wide differences
from one municipality to the other. Table 7 presents marriages
according to type of ceremony for 1949, 1956, and 1960, to indicate the wide fluctuations from year to year for all marriages on
the island. The percentage of Protestant marriages tends to be
reasonably consistent. Variations in the percentage of Catholic

and civil ceremonies are not easy to explain. A sharp increase in Catholic marriages may be the result of island-wide parish missions. Variation may also be due to the presence or absence of a pastor from a parish. No one seems to have a reliable explanation.

If one compares type of ceremony in all Puerto Rican marriages in New York (Table 8) with type of ceremony in Puerto Rico, a number of differences appear immediately. The percentage of civil marriages is consistently much lower in New York than in Puerto Rico. In 1949, the percentage of Protestant marriages in New York was much higher than that of the island (50 versus 14.3 per cent), whereas the percentage of Catholic marriages was much lower (27 versus 61.4 per cent). There was a considerable change in this situation in 1959: Catholic marriages had increased greatly and Protestant marriages had decreased, but the percentage for Catholic marriages still remained

TABLE 6

Type of Marriage Ceremony for Selected
Municipios of Puerto Rico

	N	Civil (Per Cent)	Catholic (Per Cent)	Protestant (Per Cent)
Aguada	206	22.6	71.4	6.0
Aguadilla	400	12.7	34.3	53.0
Barranquitas	115	31.0	69.0	0.0
Guayanilla	125	27.0	55.0	18.0
Santa Isabel	111	71.0	23.0	6.0
Total for Puerto Rico	20,580*	36.2	45.8	17.6

* A small number of other types of ceremony are included in this total.
Source: Registro Demografico, Departmento de Salud, Gobierno de Puerto Rico.

TABLE 7

Type of Marriage Ceremony for All
Marriages in Puerto Rico,
1949, 1956, 1960

	Civil (Per Cent)	Catholic (Per Cent)	Protestant (Per Cent)
1949	24.3	61.4	14.3
1956	26.5	59.5	14.0
1960	36.2	45.8	17.6

Source: Registro Demografico, Departmento de Salud, Gobierno de Puerto Rico.

TABLE 8

Type of Marriage Ceremony in All Marriages Involving
Puerto Ricans in New York City, 1949 and 1959

	N*	Civil (Per Cent)	Catholic (Per Cent)	Protestant (Per Cent)
1949	4,514	20	27	50
1959	9,370	18	41	38

* A small number of other types of ceremony are included in this total.

Note.—This table includes all marriages which were omitted in Table 1.

considerably lower than that of the island, and the percentage of Protestant marriages much higher.

It is difficult to interpret the meaning of these differences in marriage practice between Puerto Rico and New York. In view of the reports referred to in footnote 20, the high percentage of Protestant marriage ceremonies does not indicate affiliation with Protestant churches; it would appear to indicate casual contact for the purpose of marriage alone. The increase in the percentage of Catholic marriages undoubtedly reflects the widespread efforts of the Catholic archdioceses of New York and Brooklyn during the 1950's to develop special programs and prepare personnel for the spiritual care of the Spanish-speaking people. Two other kinds of data were analyzed, which helped to clarify the relationship of marriage behavior to assimilation, namely: the differences between first and second generation, and data which indicated that most of the Protestant marriages were performed by Spanish-speaking ministers of Pentecostal and Evangelical sects. The data on differences between first and second generation are given in Table 9.

The low percentage of civil marriages and the consistent drop in civil marriages from first to second generation may reflect a tendency toward the preference for religious marriage ceremonies which is characteristic of the United States. What is more striking is the difference in religious ceremonies. The percentage of Catholic marriages is much higher in the second generation than the first, both for grooms and brides, and in both years; while the percentage of Protestant marriages is much lower.

More light was thrown on the significance of these differences when the Protestant ceremonies were analyzed in more detail. It

TABLE 9

Type of Ceremony in Marriages of First- and Second-Generation
Puerto Rican Grooms and Brides, New York City, 1949 and 1959

	N*	Civil (Per Cent)	Catholic (Per Cent)	Protestant (Per Cent)
1949 (Grooms):				
First generation	3,212	18.8	25.2	53.6
Second generation	418	11.5	40.4	45.5
1949 (Brides):				
First generation	3,435	20.5	24.2	52.5
Second generation	591	10.0	41.8	45.2
1959 (Grooms):				
First generation	7,316	15.8	41.6	42.0
Second generation	694	14.7	47.1	36.6
1959 (Brides):				
First generation	7,777	17.6	41.4	40.5
Second generation	793	15.1	49.2	33.9

* A small number of others are included in this total.

was possible, on the basis of the marriage record, to distinguish between ministers of Protestant denominations (Lutheran, Methodist, etc.) and ministers of Pentecostal and Evangelical sects, many of the latter being in storefront churches. Table 10 gives the data on Protestant marriage ceremonies performed by ministers of these sects. The decline in Protestant marriages was actually a decline in marriages performed by Pentecostal and Evangelical ministers. This tends to confirm the theory, widely discussed, that the storefront church and the sect are lower-class religious phenomena. People tend to abandon them as they advance socially and economically.

TABLE 10

Marriages of First- and Second-Generation Puerto
Ricans Performed by Ministers of Pentecostal and
Evangelical Sects, New York City, 1949 and
1959—Percentage of All Marriages

	Grooms	Brides
1949:		
First generation	47.2	46.2
Second generation	38.1	38.1
1959:		
First generation	38.4	37.0
Second generation	33.3	30.1

The excellent study by Sidney Mintz[22] of the conversion of a poor sugar cane worker in Puerto Rico to a Pentecostal sect proposes the theory that poor people, caught in the midst of upsetting change, uprooted from a traditional way of life, tend to seek security in the strong sense of community which is characteristic of the sect. Mintz's theory could be projected to the experience of migrating Puerto Ricans, whose traditional way of life is upset by migration rather than economic development at home. The sect would provide a means of security. A study by Thomas F. O'Dea and Renato Poblete[23] of the storefront churches among Puerto Ricans in New York supports the theory of Mintz. O'Dea and Poblete indicate that the sect has a strong attraction for the poor and underprivileged, especially in the process of transition in which they are uprooted from their native land and find themselves strangers in a strange and complicated society. The informality of the sect, the fact that all members are on the same social and economic level, the active participation in religious services, the sense of brotherhood and community which is fostered, its availability in the neighborhood, all contribute to providing for the poor and uprooted a sense of satisfaction, of belonging in a community which supports and strengthens them. However, as the migrants become more firmly established, as they find themselves more a part of the larger society and able to interact more effectively with it, they either give up the practice of religion or convert to their more traditional Catholic or established denomination.

A further analysis of the data was made to determine whether there was any relationship between type of religious ceremony and in-group versus out-group marriage. No consistencies appear. The significant variables related to type of religious ceremony are generation and year of marriage.

SUMMARY

1. There is a significant percentage increase in out-group marriage among second-generation Puerto Ricans in New York. The increase is as great for grooms and greater for brides than the increase in out-group marriage among second-generation immigrants of the period 1908–12. The number of second-generation marriages is still small relative to first-generation. But the differ-

ence is evident in both years studied and indicates a consistent trend.

2. Correlation between higher occupational status and out-group marriage is not consistent. Among grooms the significant variable is generation, not occupational level. Among brides, out-group marriage increases consistently as the occupational level of their husbands rises. This suggests that they may be marrying out in order to marry up.

3. The only significant feature of age at marriage is the change to lower age at marriage among second-generation Puerto Ricans in New York. They tend toward the young age at marriage, which is characteristic of the United States as a whole, and appears to be a trend in Puerto Rico also.

4. Civil marriage is much more common in Puerto Rico than among Puerto Ricans in New York. Protestant marriages in 1949 were much more common among Puerto Ricans in New York than in Puerto Rico. Catholic marriages increased between 1949 and 1959 in New York. There is a strong tendency for Catholic marriages to increase and Protestant marriages to decrease in the second generation in both 1949 and 1959. This appears to be related to a decline in marriages by Spanish-speaking Pentecostal and Evangelical ministers.

5. Each of the above phenomena indicates that on the basis of evidence of marriage practice, the process of assimilation to the culture of the U.S. mainland is increasing rapidly. The positive correlation of out-group marriage with second generation and with advance in occupational status, the tendency toward younger age of marriage, and the decline of interest in the Evangelical and Pentecostal sects all give evidence of the acceptance of mainland American ways.

NOTES

1. The research on which this paper is based was made possible by a grant of the Luis Ferre Foundation, Ponce, Puerto Rico.
2. U.S. Department of Commerce, *U.S. Censuses of Population and Housing: 1960* (PHC [1]–104), Part I, Table P5.
3. The term "assimilation" is used here with full awareness of its ambiguity in the literature about immigrants. It is intended in this article to indicate what S. Eisenstadt means by "social assimilation" in his book *Absorption of Immigrants* (Glencoe, Ill.: Free Press, 1955), i.e., the acceptance of the newcomers by the host society into close social interaction. It is the same concept that Milton Gordon seeks to express

in the term "structural assimilation" in contrast to "cultural assimilation," in *Assimilation in American Life* (New York: Oxford University Press, 1964), chap. ii.

4. Ruby Jo Reeves, "Single or Triple Melting Pot? Intermarriage Trends in New Haven, 1870–1940," *American Journal of Sociology*, XLIX (1944). Also "What Has Social Science To Say about Intermarriage?" in Werner J. Cahnman, *Intermarriage and Jewish Life* (New York: Herzl Press, 1963), p. 32.

5. Will Herberg, *Protestant, Catholic, Jew* (New York: Doubleday & Co., 1955), chap. iii.

6. John L. Thomas, "The Factor of Religion in the Selection of Marriage Mates," *American Sociological Review*, XVI (1951), 487–91.

7. The validity of intermarriage as an index of assimilation has been questioned by Simon Marcson, "A Theory of Intermarriage and Assimilation," *Social Forces*, XXIX (1950–51), 75–78; and by C. A. Price and J. Zubrzycki, "The Use of Intermarriage Statistics as an Index of Assimilation," *Population Studies*, XVI (1962), 58–69. Marcson argues that the significant variable in intermarriage is "class" rather than "culture," and intermarriage is an index of class similarity rather than of cultural assimilation. There is no conflict between Marcson's position and that of the present paper. Marcson uses a much more limited concept of assimilation. Price and Zubrzycki point out the difficulty of determining ethnic identity and generation accurately on the basis of marriage records. Neither problem was present in this study.

8. Data on color were taken from the marriage records, but it is so difficult to make any reliable judgment about color in the case of Puerto Ricans that any attempt to analyze its significance on this basis is useless. These difficulties are explored in detail in J. P. Fitzpatrick, "Attitudes of Puerto Ricans toward Color," *American Catholic Sociological Review*, XX (1959), 219–33. The designation of color on the marriage record is as the person himself or herself declares it. The overwhelming majority of Puerto Ricans declared themselves white. For example, the color combinations according to the marriage records are given in the table below. The significance of color in Puerto Rican marriages must be sought by another method. In the article just cited, the present author reports on a 1958 study of marriages of Puerto Ricans of noticeably different color, in which the color of each partner was identified by the priest performing the ceremony. Of 115 marriages studied, the distribution according to color combination is given below. Unfortunately, in neither case was an effort made to identify marriages of Puerto Ricans with American Negroes. The percentage would have been very small.

	1949 (N = 4,514)	1959 (N = 9,370)	1958 (N = 115)
White/white	90.25	84.83	50.4
White/brown	.35	1.99	16.5
White/colored	1.66	3.17	2.6
Brown/brown	2.37	4.14	27.0
Brown/colored	.11	2.64	3.5
Colored/colored	3.06	2.21	0.00
Other	2.20	1.12	....

("Colored," *de color,* is the term used by Puerto Ricans to designate what we call Negroes.)

9. Julius Drachsler, *Intermarriage in New York City* (New York: Columbia University Press, 1921). Studies in intermarriage have been and continue to be of great interest to sociologists. The earlier studies lacked accuracy, many of them being subject to the criticism of Price and Zubrzycki. A number of studies, other than that of Drachsler, have included New York City data. J. V. DePorte, in "Marriages in the State of New York with Special Reference to Nativity" in *Human Biology* (May, 1931), pp. 387 ff., gives general statistics on marriages between people of different nativity for the years 1916–29 but discriminates between first and second generation only for 1927–29. Only place of birth is given, such as Poland or Russia, with no indication whether the person was of German or Jewish ethnic background. Only for Italian men (1927–29) is it possible to draw an accurate conclusion about in-group, out-group marriage: 12 per cent of the first-generation Italian men married out; 37.6 per cent of second-generation men with two Italian parents; 62.7 per cent of second-generation men with one Italian parent. The rate of out-group marriage for second-generation Italian men is very high, but there is no way of determining from DePorte's data whether the out-group brides were third-generation Italians. J. H. S. Bossard, in "Nationality and Nativity as Factors in Marriage," *American Journal of Sociology,* IV (1939), 792–98, analyzes nearly 70,000 marriages in New York State (excluding New York City) for 1936. He studied the rates of intermarriage between people of different nationalities and between people of differing generations of the same nationality. Bossard acknowledges the difficulty of not being able to identify the Jews as an ethnic group (p. 795); and he does not distinguish between French and English-speaking Canadians. The most serious difficulty with Bossard's study is that many of the native-born of native parentage may be third generation of the same ethnic group as the first- or second-generation partners who marry them; Bossard's data do not permit him to identify them.

10. Drachsler, *op. cit.*, p. 35.

11. There is one difficulty in this classification. It is possible that a person mainland-born of mainland parents could be third-generation Puerto Rican. Thus the marriage would not really be an out-group marriage. This possibility is very remote. Because the Puerto Rican migration is so recent, the number of third-generation Puerto Ricans in the city is negligible. One of the difficulties of the present study is the fact that there are so few second-generation Puerto Rican marriages relative to first-generation Puerto Rican marriages.

12. Marriages of first- or second-generation Puerto Ricans with Latin Americans have been omitted entirely from these calculations on in-group and out-group marriage. In view of the cultural similarities, it did not seem correct to identify them as out-group marriages, nor did it seem correct to categorize them as in-group. Also omitted are marriages of first- or second-generation Puerto Ricans with persons whose ethnic identification could not be determined. The number of these was insignificant. However, they were retained in the calculation of "type of ceremony" in Tables 9 and 10.

13. *Op. cit.*, p. 35. It is important to note that Drachsler found a wide range between nationalities in the extent of out-group marriage. Out-group marriage was lowest among Jews; highest among northern Europeans. Drachsler found a very high rate of out-group marriage among Puerto Ricans, but their number was so small (41 men; 24 women) that they are hardly comparable to the present study. The sex ratio

was evidently an important factor since out-group marriage was twice as high for the Puerto Rican men as it was for the women (see p. 99).

14. These rates of out-group marriage are still considerably lower than those for Puerto Ricans in Hawaii. Between 1945 and 1954, 64.4 per cent of Puerto Rican marriages were out-group marriages. The sex ratio among Puerto Ricans in Hawaii in 1950 was 110, but, interestingly enough, most of the Puerto Ricans marrying out were women. The high rate of out-group marriage is attributed partly to the small number of Puerto Ricans in the total population, but more so to the general tendency of all groups to intermarry in Hawaii (C. K. Cheng and D. S. Yamamura, "Interracial Marriage and Divorce in Hawaii," *Social Forces,* XXXVI [1957], 77–84).

15. *Op. cit.,* p. 37.

16. *Op. cit.,* pp. 38–40.

17. John Burma, "Research Note on the Measurement of Interracial Marriage," *American Journal of Sociology,* LVII (1951), 249–55, gives the median age at marriage for men and women in out-group marriages in California. They tend to marry at a much later age than the population generally in the United States. No such significant difference in age at marriage is evident among Puerto Ricans in out-group marriages in New York City.

18. C. W. Mills, C. Senior, and R. Goldsen, *Puerto Rican Journey* (New York: Harper & Bros., 1950), p. 25.

19. Much of the interest of American sociologists in intermarriage is directed toward interreligious marriage. It is important to note that this present paper does not deal with that question. There was no way of determining from the marriage record whether the parties to the marriage professed to be Catholic or Protestant or Pentecostal. This paper deals only with type of ceremony.

20. Cf. J. P. Fitzpatrick, "Mexicans and Puerto Ricans Build a Bridge," *America* (Dec. 31, 1955), and "Puerto Rican Story," *America* (Sept. 3, 1960). A survey report, *Midcentury Pioneers and Protestants,* published by the Protestant Council of the City of New York (1954), estimated that 26,000 Puerto Ricans were then affiliated with Protestant work in New York City; and the number in contact with Protestant work was probably 50,000. At that time, the Puerto Rican population of New York City was estimated at 425,000. If in 1954 the estimates of the Protestant Council were accurate, it would indicate that about 12 per cent of the Puerto Ricans were in contact with Protestant work, and about 5 per cent were affiliated. The Protestant Council published a much more detailed report in 1960, *A Report on the Protestant Spanish Community in New York City.* They estimated (p. 77) a Spanish-speaking membership of 31,126 in the Protestant churches, including the Pentecostal and Evangelical sects. This would have been about 6 per cent of the Puerto Rican community. Unfortunately, no reliable estimates are available about the number of Puerto Ricans in New York who are in contact with the Catholic Church and its works.

21. *The American Catholic Family* (Englewood Cliffs, N.J.: Prentice-Hall, Inc., 1956), chap. vi.

22. Sidney Mintz, *Worker in the Cane* (New Haven, Conn.: Yale University Press, 1960).

23. "Anomie and the Quest for Community: The Development of Sects among the Puerto Ricans in New York City," *American Catholic Sociological Review,* XXI (1959), 18–36.

PART FIVE

Religious Intermarriage

In the preface of this book, it was pointed out that religious intermarriage is the most strategic and most thoroughly studied of all three ethnic patterns. Perhaps the principal reason for this centrality is that religious intermarriage is neither as rare as racial intermarriage on the one hand nor as commonplace as nationality intermarriage on the other.

Yet no systematic and nationwide data on rates of American religious intermarriage were available until the 1957 Current Population Survey of Religion conducted by the Census Bureau. Furthermore, this valuable pioneer study of a voluntary but representative sample of American households has had no follow-up. For this reason reliance on 1957 data to indicate the contemporary pattern of religious intermarriage has gradually diminishing validity with each succeeding year. However, as the following brief analysis shows, if data from the 1957 Survey are compared with findings of a 1968 study of college graduates by the National Opinion Research Center (NORC), no significant differences result. Denominational homogeneity in marriage remains characteristic of at least three-quarters of the major religious denominations in American society at the beginning of the 1970s.

RELIGIOUS INTERMARRIAGE IN A
DENOMINATIONAL SOCIETY*

Andrew M. Greeley

Data from the 1957 Current Population Survey of Religion and from the NORC study of June 1961 college graduates indicate that denominational homogeneity in marriage exists for at least three-quarters of the major religious denominations, including the various groups within Protestantism.

The United States is a denominational society, that is, a society in which membership in religious denominations plays a considerable role in determining patterns of interaction which establish the social structure. It was indeed a religiously pluralistic nation before it became a politically pluralistic one, and one of the reasons the founding fathers were constrained to keep it politically pluralistic was the denominational heterogeneity of the various liberated colonies.

While sociologists have argued about and refined considerably Will Herberg's notion of religion as a provider of "social location" in the United States, few have questioned the validity of his basic insight. This paper has two modest goals: (1) to suggest that Herberg's categories of Protestant, Catholic, and Jew are not comprehensive enough—the various denominations within the category "Protestant" still constitute important subcollectivities in the larger society; and (2) to suggest that, if denominational intermarriage is used as an indicator, there does not seem to be an appreciable decline in denominational membership.

Most research done on religious intermarriage lumps all Protestant denominations together, if only because it requires very large samples to make possible the distribution of Protestants into the various denominations. The evidence in these studies seems to indicate that Jews are the least likely to marry members of other faiths, Catholics most likely, and Protestants somewhere in between. However, the release of the tabulations of the 1957 Current

*From *American Journal of Sociology*, Vol. 75, No. 6 (May 1970), pp. 949–52. Reprinted by permission of the University of Chicago Press.

Population Survey of Religion enables us to determine rates of religious intermarriage for a number of the Protestant denominations. The first row in Table 1 provides the rather striking information that approximately four-fifths of the members of each of the four Protestant denominations are married to people whose present religious affiliation is the same as their own. Not only are Protestants married to other Protestants, as previous studies have shown, but they are married to Protestants who share the same denominational affiliation. And the ratio of mixed marriages *does not vary much across denominational lines.*

TABLE 1
Denominational Intermarriage (Per Cent)

Denominational Intermarriage	Catholic	Baptist	Lutheran	Methodist	Presbyterian	Jew
Proportion of U.S. population married to member of same denomination in 1957	88	83	81	81	81	94
Proportion of 1961 alumni married to member of same denomination in 1968	86 (1,130)	84 (355)	83 (354)	86 (712)	78 (402)	97 (353)
Proportion of alumni in which marriage took place between two people whose original denomination was the same and who currently belong to that denomination	75	35	34	30	15	94
Proportion of alumni whose original denomination has remained unchanged and whose spouse has converted to that denomination	11	14	22	16	15	2

The 1957 census data contained information for the whole population. If there had been some decline in homogeneity of denominational affiliation, one would expect to find new evidence of it among the young and the better educated. Furthermore, one would expect that the data gathered after 1957 would show such a change.

In 1968, eleven years after the national census of religion, NORC collected data on original and present religious denominations of both the respondent and spouse, as part of its ongoing study of June 1961 college graduates. The second row in Table 1 shows the proportions of the major denominations who are presently married to spouses who share the same religious affiliation. There is virtually no difference between the endogamy ratios for young college alumni in 1968 and the general population in 1957. The tendency to seek denominational homogeneity in marriage does not seem to have weakened in the slightest.

The first two rows in the table represent data indicating present denominational affiliation of both respondent and spouse, but they do not tell us whether the denominational homogeneity in marriage has been attained by marrying within one's own denomination, or by substantial conversions at the time of marriage (or at least in relation to the marriage). However, the third row in Table 1 shows the proportion of respondents who married a spouse whose original religious denomination was the same as their own, with both now practicing that religion. It becomes clear that denominational homogeneity is maintained by Catholics and Jews through the process of marrying within one's own denominational boundaries, whereas it is maintained by other religious groups largely through considerable shifting of denominational affiliations. For Catholics and Jews it is important that one marry within one's own denomination (and far more important for Jews than for Catholics). When Catholics marry into other denominations, the non-Catholic is likely to convert. Protestants may marry across denominational lines, but then denominational change occurs in order to maintain religious homogeneity in the family environment.

It also appears from the fourth row in Table 1 that those of Lutheran background are able to attract a considerable proportion of their non-Lutheran spouses to join their own Lutheran denomination; thus one-fifth of the Lutherans have married people who have converted to Lutheranism, but none of the other three major Protestant denominations seem to have any special relative strength in the game of denominational musical chairs that is required to maintain the family religious homogeneity.

We do not know, of course, whether the patterns of denominational change to maintain homogeneity observed in the college population is the same as the pattern in the more general population, since the 1957 census did not provide information about original denominational affiliation. However, further research on the subject is clearly indicated.

In summary, then, one may say that America is still very much a denominational society to the extent that denominational homogeneity in marriage exists for at least three-quarters of the major religious denominations.[1]

One may speculate that the strain toward denominational homogeneity is rooted in the American belief that religious differences between husband and wife are not good either for the marriage relationship or for the children of the marriage. This belief is probably reinforced by the fact that it is simpler and more convenient that everyone in the family belong to the same denomination. For example, one need not worry about two sets of contributions to the support of one's church. Whether the maintenance of high levels of denominational homogeneity in marriage has any specifically religious or doctrinal significance may be open to question. Nevertheless, it is still extremely important in American society that one's spouse be of the same religious denomination as oneself.

REFERENCES

Tabulations of data on the social and economic characteristics of major religious groups. In *1957 Current Population Survey of Religion.* n.d. Washington, D.C.: Government Printing Office.
Canada Year Book. 1968. Ottawa: Dominion Bureau of Statistics.

NOTES

1. Denominational homogeneity in marriage seems equally important in another denominational society, Canada. In 1967, 69 per cent of the marriages which took place in Canada were between members of the same denomination, a slight dip from the 71 per cent of 1957. It should be noted that this statistic represents homogeneity at time of marriage. Presumably some postmatrimonial conversions would push the Canadian statistic even closer to the one for the United States.

Before the Census Bureau's Current Population Survey in 1957, our knowledge of the incidence and dynamics of religious intermarriage was based largely upon community studies conducted in New Haven, first by Ruby Jo Kennedy and later by August Hollingshead. Subsequent studies elsewhere, such as that reported by John L. Thomas with special reference to Roman Catholic "mixed" marriages, have indicated that the New Haven rates were significantly lower and therefore not representative of those found in all the other communities that were studied. They have also led more easily than in the case of New Haven to predictions of indefinitely increasing rates. Finally, the more recent community studies outside New Haven have raised doubts about the validity of Kennedy and Hollingshead's theory of a "triple melting-pot" to account for their findings of a preponderance of Protestant, Catholic, and Jewish endogamy.

THE FACTOR OF RELIGION IN THE SELECTION OF MARRIAGE MATES*

John L. Thomas

This paper is concerned with the question of intermarriage between religious groups. More specifically, it will investigate the rate of intermarriage between Catholics and non-Catholics. Religion has long been recognized as a barrier to intermarriage, although the traditional assumption has been that it was only one of the factors explaining the selection of marriage mates. Recently,

American Sociological Review, Vol. 16, No. 4 (August 1951), pp. 487–92. Reprinted by permission of the American Sociological Association.

however, the theory has been advanced that religious differences function as the chief basis of assortive mating.[1] Since intermarriage is the surest means of assimilation and the most obvious indication of its occurrence, it is maintained that the classic conception of a single "melting-pot" must be abandoned and a new hypothesis of assimilation substituted for it. This is the "triple-melting-pot" theory according to which assimilation will take place within three separate "melting-pots" based on the cleavage which exists between the three major religious groups in the country, namely, Protestants, Catholics, and Jews.

Kennedy and Hollingshead arrived at this new formula of assimilation after a thorough and enlightening study of the intermarriage pattern of the citizens of New Haven, Connecticut. Kennedy summarizes her findings as follows:

We shall, in other words, be able to state that, *while strict endogamy is loosening, religious endogamy is persisting and the future cleavages will be along religious lines rather than along nationality lines as in the past.* If this is the case, then the traditional "single-melting-pot" idea must be abandoned, and a new conception, which we term the "triple-melting-pot" theory of American assimilation, will take its place as the true expression of what is happening in the various nationality groups in the United States. This is the hypothesis which we believe the present paper proves true.[2]

Hollingshead agrees with this position:

. . . in most cases, marriages across religious lines involve the mixing of ethnic stocks. This is true whether Catholics and Protestants marry, or Jews and Gentiles, because the members of each religious group came from such different parts of Europe. From the viewpoint of assimilation, marriages across religious lines are crucial if the triple melting-pot is to become a single melting-pot. But as Kennedy's and our data show, we are going to have three pots boiling merrily side by side with little fusion between them for an indefinite period.[3]

These writers have advanced a very interesting hypothesis. If it were verified for the country as a whole, it would have considerable value for predicting the rate of assimilation of our various national minorities since the religious affiliation of these groups is readily ascertainable. It shall be the purpose of this paper to test the validity of this "triple-melting-pot" hypothesis in regard to one of the major religious groups, the Roman Catholic. An adequate treatment of this highly important problem demands an answer to the following questions:

1. What is the mixed marriage rate for Catholics in the United States? For Catholics in Connecticut? Is there any evidence that the rate is increasing?
2. What are the principal factors determining the rate of mixed marriage in the various sections of the country?
3. Will Catholic marriage in the future tend toward the triple- or the single-melting-pot variety?

Before we take up these questions, a few remarks on the nature of the mixed marriage data are in order. There are fairly adequate data on all mixed marriages involving Catholics in which Catholic nuptials were held. These data are available in all chancery offices throughout the country and a reasonably accurate listing of them year by year can be found in the *Catholic Directory*.[4] There are no adequate data on the number of mixed marriages not sanctioned by Catholic nuptials. I have studied all the mixed marriages to be found in 132 parishes distributed throughout the East and Middle West. There were 29,581 mixed marriages, of which 11,710, or 39.6 per cent, were not sanctioned by Catholic nuptials. I feel that this rate is fairly representative for the section of the country covered but would hesitate to predicate the same rate for other sections of the country since my research reveals great sectional differences. However, for the purpose of testing the triple-melting-pot hypothesis, it is scarcely necessary to have accurate data on the number of mixed marriages not sanctioned by Catholic nuptials. Suffice it to say that my studies indicate there are a considerable number. Hence, if it can be shown merely from the number of mixed marriages which are sanctioned by Catholic nuptials that the triple-melting-pot hypothesis is untenable, it can be argued *a fortiori,* that if we had complete coverage on all mixed marriages, our position would be still more firmly established.

Let us turn now to the questions we posed at the beginning of this paper. What is the mixed marriage rate for Catholics in the United States? In the first place, it should be pointed out that mixed marriage rates show extreme variations from one section of the country to another. The spread is from over 70 per cent in the dioceses of Raleigh, Charleston, and Savannah-Atlanta, to less than 10 per cent for the dioceses of El Paso, Corpus Christi, and Santa Fe.[5] During the decade 1940 to 1950, mixed marriages sanctioned by Catholic nuptials approximated 30 per cent of all Catholic marriages in the United States. The rate computed from the data given in the *Catholic Directory* for 1950 is 26.2.[6] Although the listing for all dioceses is not complete, this figure may be taken as a fairly accurate picture for the present period. Complete data for the thirties are not available. However, returns from approximately half the dioceses of the country for this period reveal 912,851 Catholic marriages of which 274,000, or about 30 per cent, were mixed. It seems scarcely necessary to point out that this rate of nearly one-third, which includes only those mixed marriages sanctioned by Catholic nuptials, renders Hollingshead's hypothesis of "three pots boiling merrily side by side with little fusion between them"[7] quite untenable.

Perhaps the atypical nature of the New Haven intermarriage data can best be indicated by comparing the mixed marriage rate of New Haven Catholics with the mixed marriage rate of Catholics living in the rest of the state. According to the figures given by Kennedy,[8] the percentages of Italians, Irish, and Poles, intermarrying with British-Americans, Scandinavians, Germans, and Jews, was as follows: 1870, 4.65 per cent; 1900, 14.22 per cent; 1930, 17.95 per cent; 1940, 16.29 per cent. Hollingshead, investigating all the New Haven marriages for 1948, discovered that only 6.2 per cent of the Catholics married outside their religious group.[9] It should be pointed out that these figures apply to all intermarriages and not merely those sanctioned by Catholic nuptials. On the other hand, in the State of Connecticut, the rate for just the mixed marriages sanctioned by Catholic nuptials was 40.2 per cent of all Catholic marriages in 1949.[10] If one were to complete the data on mixed marriages by adding in all those mixed marriages not sanctioned by Catholic nuptials, the most conservative estimate would place the total rate at over 50 per cent. This indicates that the city of New Haven is not representative even of the state in which it is located in regard to its intermarriage patterns.

Is intermarriage involving Catholics increasing? Complete information for many sections of the country is lacking on this point. It is known that there was a considerable increase in mixed marriages during both World War I and World War II. Some dioceses registered an increase of from 5 to 10 per cent for mixed marriages sanctioned by Catholic nuptials alone. I have studied the records of several dioceses and have discovered a gradual but more or less constant increase from 1910 to the present. Because intermarriage rates vary so much in different sections of the country, one could venture no generalization on such an inadequate basis.

Let us take up our second major query: What are the principal factors determining the rate of mixed marriage in the various sections of the country? My studies reveal that there are three main factors influencing the rate of intermarriage: (1) the percentage of Catholics in the total population; (2) the presence of cohesive ethnic subgroups; and (3) the socioeconomic status of the Catholic population in the community. We shall treat these factors separately, although it may be difficult to determine their specific influence on intermarriage in any given community.

The proportion of Catholics in the total population greatly influences the intermarriage rates of Catholics. The scarcity of prospective marriage mates within one's own religious group leads to a high rate of intermarriage wherever ethnic and/or social status differences do not prevent occupational and social contacts. Although statistics on the Catholic population in the various dioceses are admittedly inadequate in many instances, there is sufficient information to substantiate our thesis. For example, in the dioceses of Raleigh, Charleston, Savannah-Atlanta, Nashville, and Little Rock, where the Catholic population is 2 per cent or less of the total, the mixed marriage rates are 76.3, 71.5, 70.3, 58.3, and 55.6 respectively. On the other hand, in the dioceses of El Paso, Corpus Christi, Lafayette (La.), Providence (R.I.), and Santa Fe, where the Catholic population is 50 to 70 per cent of the total, the mixed marriage rates are 8.7, 7.5, 14.2, 17.2, and 8.4 respectively. It is scarcely necessary to seek further evidence on this point but we hasten to add that the relative percentage of Catholics in the population is not the sole factor determining the rate of intermarriage as many seem to believe.

The second factor is the presence of close-knit ethnic subgroups in the community. It has long been known that ethnic groups operate as a check on intermarriage. There are many factors combining to produce this effect—fidelity to the group, social status of the ethnic minority, religion, language, and transplanted national prejudices. The important point is that it is not religion alone nor the relative number of prospective mates available in the religious group which determines the intermarriage rate. For example, the percentage of Catholics in the diocese of Amarillo,

Texas, is approximately 4.6. The intermarriage rate of Catholics is 26.9. The dioceses of St. Augustine (Florida), Lafayette (Indiana), Owensboro (Kentucky), St. Joseph (Missouri) all have approximately the same percentage of Catholics but their intermarriage rates are 47.2, 45.3, 46.2, 45.1, respectively. The reason for the difference in the mixed marriage rates is plain. The diocese of Amarillo has a large subgroup of Spanish and Mexican Catholics; the other dioceses do not have any prominent ethnic subgroup. One might compare the dioceses of San Antonio and Syracuse. Both have approximately the same percentage of Catholics (30.1 and 30.6 respectively). Their mixed marriage rates are quite different (13.8 and 26.8 respectively). San Antonio has an important ethnic subgroup which practices ingroup marriage to a high degree.

The effect of ethnic sub-groups on intermarriage rates is even more marked if one considers individual parishes. I first arrived at my conviction of their importance while making a study of intermarriage rates in different sized cities. Drawing samples from the Great Lakes and Middle West region, I studied 25 parishes in each of the following classifications: 100,000 and over, 25,000–100,000, 5,000–25,000, and 5,000 and under. Table 1 gives the result of this study. It should be pointed out that the percentages given in the table are not the mixed marriage rates but rather the

TABLE 1

Percentage of Mixed Marriages According to Size of City

Population of City	Number of Parishes	Number of Families	Percentage of Mixed Marriages
100,000 and over	25	36,353	14.9
25,000–100,000	25	15,000	24.2
5,000–25,000	25	16,624	21.4
5,000 and under	25	9,431	19.6

percentage of mixed marriages found in the parishes. Since there are a considerable number of mixed marriages which end in divorce or cease to be classified as mixed marriage through the conversion of the non-Catholic party, the percentage of mixed marriages in a parish has been found to be 5 to 10 per cent below the mixed marriage rate. As Table 1 reveals, the percentage of

mixed marriages found in cities of 100,000 and over was sur-
prisingly low. The assumption had been that the rates would increase in close relation with the size of the city. What had caused
the break at the 100,000 and over level? A more intensive comparative study of the individual parishes indicated that the major
ethnic subgroup concentrations were in the larger cities for the
territory from which we had drawn our samples. It was discovered
that those parishes in the large cities in which a prominent ethnic
group was located had relatively low percentages of mixed marriages. Hence, the conclusion that the presence of ethnic sub-
groups in the community is an important factor in determining
the rate of intermarriage.

A third factor seems to be the socioeconomic class of the
Catholic population. Intermarriage rates seem to be closely related to social class. This hypothesis is advanced tentatively since
adequate statistical support is still lacking. However, I have made
studies of several communities which furnish rather substantial
evidence that the hypothesis is well founded. For example, using
graded rental areas as a gauge of socioeconomic status, I studied
the intermarriage pattern of 51,671 families distributed in thirty
parishes of a large urban center. Table 2 gives the results of this

TABLE 2
Rental Areas and Percentage of Mixed Marriages

Rental Area	Percentage of Mixed Marriages
Lower	8.5
Mixed Lower and Middle	9.1
Middle	12.0
Mixed Middle and Upper	16.3
Upper	17.9
Suburban	19.3

study. It should be pointed out that percentages in the table are
relatively low since they record the percentage of mixed marriages
found in the parishes, not the mixed marriage rate. This study
gives every indication of a rather close relation between socioeconomic status and the intermarriage rate.

The answer to the third question posed at the beginning of this
paper implies a prediction. My studies lead me to believe that

there will be a gradual but steady increase of marriages between Catholics and non-Catholics. My prediction is based on the following points. (1) We have seen the importance of ethnic subgroups as checks on the intermarriage of group members. The decline in immigration, the horizontal and vertical mobility so characteristic of our population, and the increased cultural contacts facilitated by modern means of communication will make it increasingly difficult for these groups to maintain their isolation and ingroup loyalties. The melting-pot is a reality although the boiling process may take longer than was at first believed necessary. (2) Mixed marriages have a cumulative effect. The children of mixed marriages tend to marry those outside their religious group more often than do the offspring of ingroup marriages.[11] (3) The attitude of Catholic and Protestant young people toward mixed marriages seems increasingly tolerant. Landis reports a study of students' attitudes on marriage in which more than 50 per cent of over 2,000 students said that other things being equal they would marry into a different faith.[12] He found little difference between responses of Catholic and Protestant students. I have given the same attitude test to 224 Catholic college students in a Catholic institution and found that 33 per cent of the boys and 40 per cent of the girls would marry those of another religious group, "other things being equal." Of course, these are attitude tests and do not tell us what these young people will actually do when the occasion arrives and parental and pastoral pressure is brought to bear on them. However, the figures are indicative of an attitude which definitely does facilitate contacts leading to intermarriage. (4) It is generally agreed that the family and the church have less control than formerly over youth. Increasing individualism and the widespread acceptance of the "romantic" view of love have tended to make the choice of marriage mates a strictly personal affair.

To summarize, therefore, this paper has tried to test the validity of the triple-melting-pot hypothesis in regard to Catholics. Although complete data on all mixed marriages are not available, it was found that a consideration of only those mixed marriages which were sanctioned by Catholic nuptials raised serious doubts concerning the value of this hypothesis. The mixed marriage rate of Catholics for the past two decades has averaged 30 per cent of all Catholic marriages. There are wide variations in rates from one section of the country and the principal factors determining these differences appear to be three: (1) the relative percentage of Catholics in the total population; (2) the presence of cohesive ethnic sub-groups in the community; and (3) the socio-economic class of the Catholic population. The prediction was made that the rate of intermarriage would go on increasing gradually but constantly for some time to come.

In conclusion, I think that the data which have been presented in this paper reveal a much higher mixed marriage rate for Catholics than the formulators of the triple-melting-pot hypothesis believed. They were, perhaps, overimpressed by the low rate of intermarriage which they discovered in New Haven. As we have shown, New Haven is very atypical in this respect. It follows from our studies that religion, although important, is only one of the factors determining intermarriage rates. The single-melting-pot hypothesis is probably as valid as any hypothesis yet advanced.

NOTES

1. August B. Hollingshead, "Cultural Factors in the Selection of Marriage Mates," *American Sociological Review,* 15 (October, 1950), 619–627; Ruby Jo Reeves Kennedy, "Single or Triple Melting Pot? Intermarriage Trends in New Haven, 1870–1940," *American Journal of Sociology,* 39 (January, 1944), 331–339.
2. Kennedy, *op. cit.,* p. 332. Italics in the original.
3. Hollingshead, *op. cit.,* p. 624.
4. According to canon law, only those mixed marriages which are sanctioned by Catholic nuptials are valid. All other mixed marriages involving a Catholic are invalid according to the law of the Church.
5. A diocese is a district presided over by a bishop and generally named after the city in which his residence is located. Very few dioceses cross state lines but there may be several dioceses within the same state.
6. *The Official Catholic Directory, 1950,* New York: P. J. Kenedy & Sons, 1950. The rates computed from the *Directory* figures have been found to run slightly below the actual rates for most dioceses.
7. Hollingshead, *op. cit.,* p. 624.
8. Kennedy, *op. cit.,* p. 333.
9. Hollingshead, *op. cit.,* pp. 622–623. It is possible that the discrepancy between the data presented by Kennedy and that of Hollingshead results from the fact that Kennedy seems to have studied only the major national groups, whereas Hollingshead studied all the marriages for 1948.
10. *The Official Catholic Directory, 1950, op. cit.,* p. 379.
11. Gerald J. Schnepp, "Three Mixed Marriage Questions Answered," *Catholic World,* 156 (November 1942), 203–207.
12. Judson T. Landis and Mary G. Landis, *Building a Successful Marriage,* New York: Prentice-Hall, Inc., 1948, p. 138.

Thomas' criticisms of the conservative findings in the New Haven studies are consistent with allegations by other scholars that research of this type has tended to produce a distorted image of the phenomenon of intermarriage. According to Clark E. Vincent, for example, aspects of intermarriage ordinarily investigated are those that are bothersome to the vested interests of organized religion. Such research proceeds on the assumption that religious intermarriage is a threat to the social order. In the critique that follows, Vincent challenges the presumption that inmarriages are intrinsically less divisive than intermarriages. Furthermore, he raises doubt that etiological studies of religious intermarriage really go beyond the securing of data on the association between variables to the important concern with the actual causation of the crossing of religious lines. Finally, dissatisfied with the point of departure of most research on religious intermarriage so far, Vincent suggests new orientations for theory-building and basic research on the problem.

INTERFAITH MARRIAGES: PROBLEM OR SYMPTOM?*

Clark E. Vincent

PART I: A DEFINITION AND VALUE CONTEXTS

Robert Merton[27] has noted that all marriages represent intermarriages. The individual and social group backgrounds of every married couple reflect some differences; whether in physical con-

*Reprinted, with the permission of the author and the University Extension, University of California, Berkeley, California, from *Religion and the Face of America*, Jane C. Zahn, ed. (1959), pp. 67–87.

181

stitution, political behavior, socioeconomic status, nationality, or religious preferences and practices. (Most easily overlooked, perhaps because it is so obvious and taken for granted, is the fact that couples who do not have an intersexual marriage are generally regarded as deviants.)

This working definition that all marriages are intermarriages serves to help clarify the selectivity of our current concern over intermarriage. *Only certain types of intermarriages are viewed with concern and as social problems; namely, those intermarriages which mirror areas of prejudice and threaten vested interests in our society.* Thus, the concern over intermarriage is focused predominantly on interracial, interfaith, and international marriages. There is some interest in interclass marriages, but almost no concern manifested over interpolitical, interphysical, interregional, and rural-urban marriages.

But, you may object, the first three types of intermarriages mentioned involve differences in kind, while the latter types involve only differences in degree. And, you may ask, hasn't research shown that more marital strife results from the former than from the latter types of intermarriages? Also, you may argue, the point is circular—if the types of intermarriages we are most concerned about mirror areas of prejudice, then we should be most concerned about such intermarriages because they will result in the greatest marital strife due to the fact that they do represent areas of prejudice.

The first two of these rhetorical objections I would answer with a question, "Do we know?" *Intra*denominational marriages may represent a far greater degree of interfaith marriage than is commonly supposed. The marriage of two Presbyterians, for example, may represent as much of a difference in kind as well as in degree of interfaith marriage as does the marriage of a Roman Catholic and an Episcopalian—depending, of course, on how we define and how the parties to the marriage evaluate "religious faith." But this we will not know as long as *intra*denominational marriages are not regarded as "problems," and as long as research is subsequently focused primarily on the degree of marital discord resulting from *inter*denominational marriages.

In answer to the second rhetorical objection, we need to recognize how little we know about the phenomenon of intermarriage.

We don't know, for example, how much marital discord results when two people bring quite different physical constitutions to a marriage. Is it more or less than results when two people bring quite different religious backgrounds to a marriage? One reason why such a question is unanswerable at the present time is that interfaith marriages have an antagonist; not so with interphysiological marriages. Ministers may emphasize that marital strife can result when husband and wife attend separate churches and seek to rear their children in different faiths. But do physiologists stress that marital strife can result when the cup of physical energy and health runneth over for one spouse, but runneth dry for the other? Or when 365 nights a year the husband wants three blankets—the wife but one? And when husband wants car windows closed—wife wants them open? (To be consistent with this degree of overstatement, we should perhaps propose a basal metabolism test as part of the premarital medical examination.)

In reference to the third rhetorical objection, if the point is circular then why not enter the circle at a different point? Let's view difficulties in interfaith marriages as the symptom, religious prejudices and institutional interests as the problem. (This might stimulate the kind of creative thinking in interfaith marriages that produced heat-controlled blankets in interphysiological marriages.) If you will permit redefining the problem in this way, we might say that much of the concern over interfaith marriages is oriented to treating the symptomatic fever rather than to diagnosing and eliminating the disease.

In summary response to all three of the above rhetorical objections, may I reiterate that the interest as well as the research in intermarriage has been selective—limited primarily to those intermarriages which mirror prejudices, threaten institutional interests, and have antagonists. As a result, we have very few comparative data either on *intra*marriages in these areas of concern or on intermarriages in areas of little concern. An awareness of this selectivity in the interest and research in intermarriage is needed to furnish perspective for the research data I want to review in a moment.

Before turning to these data, however, I should like to comment very briefly on some value contrarieties which also provide perspective for viewing research on intermarriage. The following examples of contrarieties in the values by which we live are taken from Robert Lynd's more inclusive list of "outstanding assumptions in American Life."[25]

> Honesty is the best policy. *But:* Business is business, . . .
> Hard work and thrift are signs of character and the way to get ahead. *But:* No shrewd person tries to get ahead nowadays by just working hard, . . .
> Religion and the finer things of life are our ultimate values and the things all of us are really working for. *But:* A man owes it to himself and to his family to make as much money as he can.
> The family is our basic institution and the sacred core of our national life. *But:* Business is our most important institution, and, since national welfare depends upon it, other institutions must conform to its needs.
> Children are a blessing. *But:* You should not have more children than you can afford.
> Women are the finest of God's creatures. *But:* Women aren't very practical and are usually inferior to men in reasoning power and general ability.
> The American judicial system insures justice to every man, rich or poor. *But:* A man is a fool not to hire the best lawyer he can afford.

An awareness that the value systems of any society seldom represent any one harmonious whole is sometimes stated in terms of a recognized difference between what we believe and what we practice. This difference can be illustrated with reference to interfaith marriages. Shortly after the turn of this century, Israel Zangwill expressed some of the philosophy and ideology of the time in his book *The Melting Pot*,[41] which reflected the notion that this nation could become one grand, glorious, common brotherhood. People from all races, creeds, and nationalities were to be forced together in one melting pot. This was the theory which received considerable lip service. In practice or heart service, however, the contents intended for the one common melting pot were frequently placed into a series of ghetto pots. As Myrdal has noted, this difference between belief and practice represents the core of the American dilemma concerning the Negro.

To be more specific with reference to interfaith marriage, denominational spokesmen may glorify one grand melting pot and common brotherhood, but maintain that the contents of the pot should not be diluted with interfaith marriages—common brotherhood does not always include brothers-in-law.

In Judaism,[1, 2, 3, 31, 35] the stand against interfaith marriages has its roots in Old Testament writings such as Deuteronomy 7:1–4. The Jewish people were strongly advised against interfaith marriages, which at that time, and perhaps to a lesser extent today, also represented intercultural marriages. This advice is still given today—directly in official rabbinical pronouncements; indirectly in the works of novelists and playwrights (e.g., *Eagle at My Eyes, Earth and High Heaven, East River, Footsteps on the Stair, Abie's Irish Rose*).

The Roman Catholic position[4, 21, 37] against interfaith marriages has its roots in such New Testament writings as Paul's admonition to the Corinthians, "Be ye not unequally yoked together with unbelievers." The gradual codification and implementation of this position can be traced from the Council of Elvira (which at the beginning of the fourth century forbade Christian girls to marry "infidels, Jews, heretics or priests of the pagan rites") through a series of Councils and writers, to the final form given it by the Council of Trent in the middle of the sixteenth century and to the present implementation of it in the Ante-Nuptial Agreement.

Protestant pronouncements[7, 9, 13, 21, 22, 30] against interfaith marriages are usually expressed in terms of the danger of weakening the member's religious (denominational) faith, and the dangers of marital strife and divorce. These pronouncements are rarely implemented with any official procedures or codified restrictions concerning the institutional participation of members who do contract interfaith marriages. In general, formal Protestant pronouncements against interfaith marriages are quite recent and are expressed in the form of resolutions. These resolutions usually contain warnings against interfaith marriages in general, but emphasize the dangers of intermarriage with Roman Catholics in particular. The following represent a few of the church groups which within the last decade have passed resolutions containing specific warnings against contracting marriages with Roman Catholics: Presbyterian, Protestant Episcopal, Northern Baptist, Southern Baptist, and the Disciples of Christ.

If you will permit me to belabor my point a moment longer, I should like to briefly consider another area of social concern—illegitimacy. My intent is to further illustrate that an awareness of the value contrarieties by which we live is crucial if we are to understand and discuss in a meaningful manner the research and interest in interfaith marriages. I am assuming that the proportion of this group having direct emotional involvement in illegitimacy is less than the proportion having individual emotional involvement in religion. Thus, the manner in which various mores and values serve to define social problems and to limit research in such problems can perhaps be illustrated more easily and less threateningly by reference to a social problem area that is a little farther from home for most of us than is religion.

Unmarried fathers represent 50 per cent of the "cause" of illegitimacy, biologically speaking, yet there is approximately only one study of unmarried fathers for every thirty studies of unwed mothers. Why hasn't the unmarried father been studied? Primarily because research in illegitimacy has accepted the normative definition of who is the social problem—the unwed mother. It is she who, according to the double standard, has made a mistake. The male was simply proving his masculinity and playing his traditional role of pursuer. It is the unwed mother whose changing profile overtly offends and threatens our traditional sex mores. It is she for whom taxpayers support maternity homes. It is she who may need help in caring for her child or in releasing her child for adoption. Moreover, the unmarried father is protected by mores which hold an individual to be innocent until proven guilty; he bears no evidence of the illicit sexual union, while the unwed mother bears evidence that is difficult to conceal.

It is true that it is more difficult to study unmarried fathers in the population at large than to study groups of unwed mothers in maternity homes. But if the mores were different—if unmarried fathers were held equally responsible for illicit sexual unions and were made financially and legally responsible for their out-of-wedlock progeny—then unmarried fathers would come to be regarded more as a social problem, and subsequently become the subject of more research. In either case, can we really expect to understand or resolve the problem of illegitimacy as long as we study only half of the conception equation—the unwed mothers, and usually only those in maternity homes or public welfare institutions?

Similarly, can we really expect to understand the "problem" of interfaith marriages as long as we study only those types of intermarriages that have the loudest antagonists; and as long as we accept the problem as defined by interested parties? These are the kinds of questions I hope you will keep in mind in your discussions of the following research data on interfaith marriages.

PART II: FINDINGS CONCERNING INTERFAITH MARRIAGES

Extent of Interfaith Marriages. It is very difficult at the present time to ascertain the extent of interfaith marriages in this country.[3, 9, 11, 30, 40] Iowa is one of two states which require an indication of religious affiliation or preference on the marriage certificate, and Iowa has done so only since 1953. Thus, we must rely on regional and denominational studies, some of which are reviewed briefly here.

The extent of interfaith marriages among Roman Catholics has been reported by Father John L. Thomas, a Jesuit and family sociologist at St. Louis University, who has compiled data from the official *Catholic Directory* which lists interfaith marriages on an annual basis. Thomas has reported that during the decade 1940–1950, approximately 30 per cent of all *valid* Catholic marriages (those sanctioned by the Church) involved a non-Catholic.[33, 37, 38] The Catholic Bishops' Committee on Mixed Marriages has estimated that between 15 and 25 per cent of all marriages involving Catholics are invalid—those usually involving a non-Catholic and not sanctioned by the Church.[4, 33] Thus, it would appear that at least one-third of all Catholics who have married during the last two decades have contracted interfaith marriages.

A nationwide study initiated by the United Lutheran Church in America and based on a 12 per cent response from 3,319 pastors, indicated that 58 per cent of the Lutherans marrying between 1946 and 1950 had married non-Lutherans.[8, 9] Masters' theses on interfaith marriages among Mormons in Los Angeles, Oakland, and Berkeley, California, have shown the following percentages of Mormons marrying non-Mormons—20 per cent, 47 per cent, 30 per cent.[12, 13]

The above are illustrative of the types of studies and findings that provide substance for the current concern over the extent of interfaith marriages. The data from such studies also provide substance for the point previous speakers have raised concerning the degree to which the increase in church membership in this country may be a function of the *multiple* church membership of many individuals. For it has been estimated that 1 out of every

3 or 4 interfaith marriages results in one spouse changing to the other spouse's church.[8, 21, 23, 30] How many of these converted spouses are reported on the membership rolls of two or more churches?

The Trend in Interfaith Marriages. Only limited and tentative data are available on trends in interfaith marriages, but most of those that are available suggest an increase in such marriages. Father Thomas reports that there has been a gradual percentage increase in interfaith marriages among Catholics since 1910, and he predicts a gradual and steady increase in such marriages in the future. The Lutheran study referred to earlier indicates a similar trend —46 per cent of the Lutherans marrying between 1936 and 1940, but 58 per cent of the Lutherans marrying between 1946 and 1950, married non-Lutherans. The Mormon studies, completed in different cities, showed 20 per cent interfaith marriages in Los Angeles in 1937 and 47 per cent interfaith marriages in Oakland in 1955.

Patterns in Interfaith Marriage. Who married outside the church? Data in this area are also quite limited, and we shall make only brief reference to two types of findings—those on sex and socioeconomic differences. The studies referred to above on Catholics, Lutherans, and Mormons, show that about three females marry outside the church for every 2 males who do so.[8, 13, 21] Other studies have shown this pattern is reversed among Jews— about 5 males marry outside their faith for every 2 females who do so.[1, 21, 31] Such findings need to be interpreted quite cautiously, however, and need to be examined with reference to the male– female ratio within each of these religious groups.

With reference to socioeconomic differences, the data on Catholic as well as on Lutheran interfaith marriages have been interpreted to show that females who marry outside their church tend to marry above rather than below themselves socioeconomically. This tendency can be discussed with reference to several points: (a) it may be no greater than the tendency of females in the general population to marry males somewhat older, taller, better educated, etc., than themselves; (b) it may reflect what Professor Rasmussen referred to earlier as "church-hopping" or "church-shopping" as a means of social mobility; and (c) it may have relevance to the tentative findings from studies of interclass marriages,[10, 32] which suggest there is less marital strife when the wife marries above than when she marries below her own socio-economic position. (These findings on interclass marriages have also been further interpreted as being consistent with the notion that wives do most of the adjusting in marriage and the notion that wives would sooner adjust "up" than "down." Thus, marrying above themselves produces less marital friction than marrying below themselves.)

Reasons for or "Causes" of Interfaith Marriages. The research studies in this area can be grouped arbitrarily and reviewed briefly with reference to five "factors." *The first factor is the disproportionate ratio of religious groups in a given community.* Kennedy found three pots boiling merrily side-by-side, rather than one melting pot, in her studies of the New Haven community—Catholics married Catholics, Jews married Jews, and Protestants married Protestants.[16, 18] Such a finding, however, appears to be peculiar to New Haven and other communities where various religious groups are fairly well balanced, numerically. For Thomas found that in dioceses where Catholics represented about two-thirds of the total community population, less than one-fifth of the Catholics contracted interfaith marriages; but in dioceses where Catholics represented less than 5 per cent of the total community population, one-half to three-fourths of the Catholics married non-Catholics.[37, 38] The significance of this factor is also supported by data on interfaith marriage among Mormons. In 1937 Done reported that in Salt Lake City, where Mormons then represented almost three-fourths of the city's population, less than 7 per cent of Mormons married non-Mormons.[12] In 1957 Follett reported that in Oakland and Berkeley, where Mormons represented less than 5 per cent of the total community population, 47 and 30 per cent of the Mormons had married non-Mormons.[13]

A second factor is the disproportionate male–female ratios in the several social strata within *any one church.* This involves the unavailability within one's own church of those mates who have been sanctioned by mate selection mores as being desirable. In general, our society tends to sanction and encourage marriages of women to men slightly superior to them in age, education, and social status. When such men are in short supply within the women's particular church, there is an increased tendency to select partners outside the church. The Lutheran study cited earlier, for example, noted that the lower the social status of the Lutheran parish in a given community, the higher the percentage of the parish's members who marry non-Lutherans. A sizeable proportion of those who marry outside their church in such cases tend to be women who marry above their own socioeconomic status. Such findings have been interpreted as evidence that interfaith marriages represent a means of upward social mobility for women; but it needs to be kept in mind that the mate selection mores in our society tend to prescribe marriages involving some upward mobility for women—whether those marriages represent interfaith, inter-class, or rural-urban mixtures.

A third factor is our mass participation in a so-called "middle-class culture"; wherein our individual as well as group differences in values and religious beliefs tend to be minimized if not obscured by a superficial amalgamation. This factor, which may well be one of the most important in understanding the current increase in interfaith marriages, is not easily quantified. Thus, I can only make reference to some of the areas and ways in which this factor appears to be operative. Today's youth on high school and college campuses tend to use this so-called middle class as their reference group and behavior guide. The ideology and behavior patterns of this somewhat mythical reference group are disseminated to today's youth through mass media of entertainment and communication, as well as through textbooks which report findings on the mate selection patterns of primarily middle class subjects. The efforts to emulate and to be considered "middle class," combined with the considerable residential mobility and commuting distances of today's youth, tend to preclude dating couples' realistic appreciation of their differences in family and religious backgrounds. As Margaret Mead has noted, young dating couples today rarely know even a dog in common from childhood days.

This current tendency to act as if we were all very similar, and to subsequently blur individualistic and familial backgrounds, also points up the considerable evaluational task that is assigned to modern dating. In the small community and rural orientation of this country a few generations ago, the family performed many of the functions which today's dating couple perform increasingly by themselves. Yesterday, Susie's parents knew Joe's parents (on what side of the tracks they lived, if and where they attended church, and the shape and magnitude of family skeletons), and over a period of years could attempt to influence Susie's answer to Joe by imparting firsthand knowledge of his background. Today, Susie's parents usually have to rely on Joe for any information about his family background, and to hope that Susie will let them meet Joe before she gives him her answer. Thus, today's dating couple tries to accomplish during a few months or a year the evaluational tasks on which the extended family of yesterday worked for a period of years and to which the church contributed by publishing "banns."

Summarily, with reference to this third factor, the modern miracle is that there are no more interfaith marriages than there are when we consider: the "middle-class ethic" with its obscuring of origin and background as an implied test for membership; the current earlier age at marriage; the multiple tasks assigned to dating; and the tendency to replace personal religious convictions with "scientific objectivity." An even greater miracle is that today's youth are able within such contexts to choose their marital partners so well.

A fourth factor is that couples may contract interfaith marriages on the basis of nationality and cultural similarities.[1, 2, 16, 40] For example, we would expect more interfaith marriages between Lutherans and Catholics in a community composed primarily of people of German extraction than we would in a community composed of German Lutherans and Italian Catholics. This factor needs to be kept in mind not only when considering what brings together couples from different religious backgrounds, but also when considering the degree of marital strife that may be associated with interfaith marriages. Many times when we think we are talking about or studying "pitfalls" of interfaith marriages, we may really be addressing the byproducts of nationality and cultural differences.

The fifth factor represents a composite of adolescent rebellion and disaffiliation from a minority culture. Examination of this factor in the search for "causes" of interfaith marriages has been confined primarily to case history materials.[9, 29, 30, 39] The interpretations and reconstructions of the materials in these case histories frequently reflect that notion of "heads, I win; tails, you lose." When the focus is on the member of a majority culture who marries a member of a minority culture, the interpretation tends to point out how the former is using such a marriage to "act out" rebellion and resentment against parental or other superego restraints. When the focus is on the member of a minority culture who marries a member of a majority culture, the interpretation tends to point out how the former is using such a marriage to improve his or her social status. Valid as such interpretations may be in some instances, they reflect the tendency to view intermarriages in areas of prejudice as being caused by "bad" or at least negative factors. They also reflect our reluctance to admit that the contractants to interfaith and interracial marriages can be motivated positively by mutual love and respect.

Consequences of Interfaith Marriage. This is the area in which we find the greatest amount of interest, writing, and research, but probably the least complete information.[3, 19] There are two major rationales for the concern in this area. First is the membership leakage which results from interfaith marriages. Jewish writers have noted that such marriages have depleted Jewish ranks more than persecutions[2, 31, 35] The Catholic Bishops' Committee on Mixed Marriages has reported that 30 per cent of the Catholics involved in interfaith marriages are lost to the Catholic Church.[4, 33, 37] Studies of interfaith marriages involving Protestants show that between one-third and one-half of the contractants to such marriages withdraw from their original church.[9, 21, 30]

The second major rationale for the interest in the consequences of interfaith marriages is the relation of such marriages to divorce. Three studies conducted independently in different states have shown similar findings which are summarized below:[20] Bell's study of 13,528 cases was conducted in Maryland; Landis' study of 4,108 cases was conducted in Michigan; and Weeks' study of 6,548 cases was conducted in Washington.

Religious Categories	Per Cent Ending in Divorce or Separation
Both Catholic	5 per cent
Both Jewish	5 per cent
Both Protestant	8 per cent
Mixed, Catholic-Protestant	15 per cent
Both None	18 per cent

Those of you who are Protestants will undoubtedly want to point out that the "both Protestant" marriages result in more divorces and separations than the "both Catholic" or the "both Jewish" marriages, because the category of "both Protestants" probably includes many interdenominational marriages.

The limitations of using such figures as the basis of broad generalizations concerning the dangers of Catholic-Protestant intermarriages have been illustrated by Judson Landis, who was the only one of the above three researchers to explore these data further. He found that 7 per cent of the total 90 mixed marriages involving a *Catholic wife* and a *Protestant husband* ended in divorce or separation; but 21 per cent of the total 102 mixed marriages involving a *Catholic husband* and a *Protestant wife* ended in divorce or separation.

Two interpretations have been given for this difference. (a) Since approximately three-fourths of all divorce proceedings are initiated by wives, and since the Catholic Church takes a more stringent position on divorce than do most Protestant Churches, the mixed marriages involving a Catholic wife will result in fewer divorces than those involving a Protestant wife. (b) Since the Ante-Nuptial Agreement requires that the children of the marriage be reared in the Catholic faith, and since mothers tend to be more active than fathers in child rearing, the Protestant mother would find the Ante-Nuptial Agreement less palatable than would the Protestant father.

Summary Limitations of Data on Interfaith Marriage. Before leaving this all too brief sketch of some of the findings on the extent, "causes," and consequences of interfaith marriages, I should like to add a few comments concerning the limitations of such findings. These comments are not intended to imply a dismissal of such data, but to emphasize the need for humility in recognizing how little we know in this area, and the need for caution in generalizing from the exploratory data which are available.

First, it is perhaps necessary to emphasize that the statistical data on interfaith marriages and divorce show associations, not "causes." Even when those associations are higher than might occur by chance, they still do not indicate "cause" any more than a very high statistical association between storks and a high birth rate in some rural regions, and the association between no storks and the lowest birth rate in the nation in such a city as San Francisco, can be used to prove that babies are brought by storks. As noted earlier, we do not know the extent of divorce among *intra-*

denominational marriages. Nor do we know whether the divorces occurring among interfaith marriages are related primarily to religious differences or to socioeconomic, nationality, and cultural differences. Moreover, we do not have a very clear picture of the extent of divorce in the total population with which to compare the extent of divorce in interfaith marriages. In some studies each divorce involving two partners is counted as one case. In other studies each partner is counted as a separate case. Recidivists may be counted many times.

Second, may I attempt to illustrate how selective we are in viewing and using research data on interfaith marriage, by referring to a formula. . . .

$$HT + WC = IRSI; LT + EC = DRSI;$$
$$\text{and } NT + MW = NR$$

This formula stands for: "High Tide on West Coast results in Increased Rate of Sexual Intercourse; Low Tide on East Coast results in Decreased Rate of Sexual Intercourse; and No Tide in Middle West results in No Research." Since the moon controls the tide, we refer to this as the "Lunar Theory of Sexual Expression." Some of you may say that the association between the tide and the frequency of sexual intercourse is really related to nightfall. But I would argue on a logical basis that people may want to see what they are doing.

The "merits" of this theory are twofold. (a) It confuses and disorients our thinking in terms of our experiences and what we think we know. (b) Such disorientation is anxiety producing and tends, in turn, to stimulate the kind of thinking that perhaps many of us are now experiencing. Namely, rather than wait until we can check the facts on tide flow in relation to time of day and ascertain when other couples join in love-making, we quickly rearrange and select the information to fit our individual experiences and what we think we already know. . . .

PART III: WHOSE RITE AND WHO IS WRONG?

My thesis in this third part is that *many of the difficulties experienced in interfaith marriages are symptoms or manifestations of the failure of organized religion to "lose itself" as an institution.* In presenting this thesis I do not minimize that rituals, procedures, and membership criteria *now have* considerable strength and significance in the minds and emotions of church members. In fact, I think we tend grossly to underestimate just how significant the "letter and mode of the law" have become for most church members. What I should like to maximize is the need for organized religion to rediscover and emphasize the "spirit and principle of the law."

When counseling with married couples whose different religious persuasions have resulted in marital strife, I frequently find greater disagreement between them over the "letter" than over the "spirit" of their respective beliefs. A Roman Catholic and a Baptist, for example, may share a belief in the *principle* of baptism, but find an impasse in the *method* of baptism. Their respective church teachings have emphasized the *how,* the *proper age,* and the *form* to such an extent that the rite supersedes in meaning the profound principle it symbolizes.

But this is to oversimplify the issue confronting the contractants to an interfaith marriage. In church teachings, methods and procedures have a way of becoming sacred and sacerdotal. The manner in which an "I–Thou" Covenant is made has become inseparable from making such a covenant. (The bath water *is* the baby.) In fact, an improper procedure in making the covenant is usually held to invalidate the covenant. This is understandable within an institutional setting; for as a concept and a process, an "I–Thou" Covenant is both far too individual and far too universal to lend support to institutional loyalties. Thus, church teachings must rely on an implicit "I–It–Thou" Covenant—with the sacred and sacerdotal procedures prescribed by "It" (church) providing institutional loyalty and support.

It is not my intent to tread lightly on such hoary toes, for I see all too frequently their destructive imprint on the lives of couples in interfaith marriages. Such couples tend to mirror their church teachings and institutional practices when, with reference to each other's ritual in worship and form of religious commitment: they "have not charity"; they reflect a "True Believer's" guilt[15] over the proper methods for "saving" their children; and they reduce a dynamic lifetime process of religious commitment to a static once-in-a-lifetime initiatory rite.

It is not my intent to depreciate either the value of initiatory ritual in religious organizations or the variety of forms for worship; but to see them as means, not ends; and to see them as means to the individual's I–Thou commitment and as evidences of our variegated creativity in worship,[17] rather than as means to institutional growth and as tests of institutional loyalty. In this connection John MacMurray[26] has suggested that just as Jesus reminded those of His time that the Sabbath was made for man, not man for the Sabbath, so He might remind us today that the church was made for man, not man for the church. An indication of our need for such a reminder is the fact that the most frequently used measurement of "religiosity" is frequency of church attendance.

In this context, is the concern over interfaith marriages primarily a concern for the individuals involved? Or is the concern for the individual a by-product of the concern for the numerical growth of the church? Even a cursory glance at the denominational literature on the subject of interfaith marriages evinces a primary concern over the membership leakage which is believed to result from such marriages. This concern is usually stated ostensibly in terms of divorce, marital strife, lack of religious instruction for the children, etc., but figures and comments concerning the numerical loss to the church are seldom lacking.

Suppose that more complete and thorough research should show that the incidence of divorce and the amount of marital strife are as great in *intra*denominational as in *inter*denominational marriages? Would church members then be warned against marrying those of their own faith? Also, if roughly one-third of those who marry outside the church are "lost to *the* church," how many of the other two-thirds who remain in the church convert their nonmember spouse? If research should show that interfaith marriages actually augment membership goals, would such marriages continue to be discouraged and warned against?

In an effort to conclude my remarks (which is to say that the end is not yet), I should like to diagram a technique for spousal discussions. In Figure 1, the circled "H" and "W" represent a husband and a wife as measured individually by a series of pyscho-

FIGURE 1

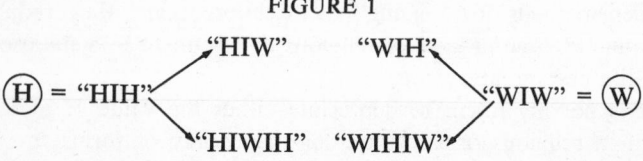

logical tests and interpreted by competent psychometricians. Few husbands and wives, however, would interact with each other on the basis of the circled H and W—which, hypothetically, is what the tests and psychometricians had measured them to be. Instead, they would more likely interact on the basis of a series of impressions:

The husband would tend to interact with his wife on the basis of:
"*H*usband's *I*mpressions of Himself as *H*usband" (HIH)
"*H*usband's *I*mpressions of *W*ife" (HIW)
"*H*usband's *I*mpressions of *W*ife's *I*mpressions of *H*usband" (HIWIH)
The wife would tend to interact with her husband on the basis of:
"*W*ife's *I*mpressions of Herself as a *W*ife" (WIW)
"*W*ife's *I*mpressions of *H*usband" (WIH)
"*W*ife's *I*mpressions of *H*usband's *I*mpressions of *W*ife" (WIHIW)

However great the difference might be between "HIW" and "WIW," for example, the impression each has of wife represents *reality* for each spouse. This is usually discussed in terms of the *selectivity* of individual perception. It is doubtful, for example, that the "same" experience, movie, book, or event, is ever experienced, seen, read, or witnessed, in exactly the same way by any two individuals. We find it understandable that the man who is hungry can usually remember more of the food items on a menu, while the man who is thirsty can usually remember more of the beverages listed on that same menu. Even such a tangible thing as a piece of chemically treated paper can taste quite differently to various people, depending on the acidic and alkaline content of the taster's saliva. One taster says the paper tastes "sweet." Another replies "bitter." Which taster is *right*? Which taste is *real*? In answer, we say both are right and real for the individual taster.

Not so in marriage and religion!! The classic spousal argument usually begins or ends in a dialogue which denies the *reality of individual impressions,* thereby forcing the participants to establish which one was right, which impression was real.

"I said this!"
"No you didn't! You said that!"
            or
"You did this! And furthermore you did it because . . . !"
"I did not! I did that! And I didn't even know . . . !"

The parties to such a dialogue may continue to believe that one of them has to be right and the other wrong, until one ends up the plaintiff and the other the defendant; for the courts, like organized religion, proceed on the premise that one has to be proven right and the other(s) proven wrong.

The concept implied by this diagram is no panacea for resolving strife in interfaith marriages in particular or in marriages in general. It is suggested only as one of many techniques by which couples may learn through years of practice to minimize the tendency to polarize every spousal disagreement, political issue, and religious belief into a black and white wrong and right side. To grant the freedom, the dignity, the creative uniqueness, and the reality of individual impressions is to enrich and better understand the universe in which we live. We accept highly individualistic fingerprint impressions as valuable identification aids; and as Dr. Roger J. Williams has shown in his work *Biochemical Individuality,* we need to accept highly individualistic physiological constitutions if we are to have healthful individuals. We resist if not deny, however, the reality of individual impressions and convictions in spousal interaction and religious beliefs.

In Western society, our religious heritage is permeated with polarization—whether in the earlier more explicit terms of people who were either among the "elect" or the "damned"; or in the current more implicit terms of the sacerdotal forms and modes of worship which are either "rite" or "wrong."[36] As long as organized religion continues to indoctrinate its members with the notion that there is only one way and one church, couples in interfaith marriages will find that loyalty to the church will preclude granting the reality of the spouse's beliefs. Differences that could enlarge and enrich their "I–Thou" commitments become stimuli for marital disharmony and threats to each other's beliefs.

Such polarization denies what is so abundantly evident in God's handiwork. How dull and uncreative, were every tree and person to have but one size; every flower and human but one color; every snowflake and child but one shape; every stimulus but one response; every painting and parable but one meaning; every bird and instrument but one pitch. What an unpicturesque and unsymphonic world! Yet organized religion would have us believe that differences, which add beauty and depth in all other areas, foretell ugliness and shallowness in interfaith marriages.

Case history materials on interfaith marriages may describe, for example, the disturbance on the part of the Protestant bride when her Catholic groom emerges from a warm bed the morning after the wedding night to attend a 6:00 A.M. Mass. Why should this disturb her? If she loves him, won't she enjoy his enjoyment of a worship experience? If she believes in God and is a worshipful person, won't she too find God and enjoy a worship experience at Mass? If he believes in God and needs to worship, won't he find God and enjoy a worship experience in her church? Is such an event in interfaith marriages disturbing primarily because the respective church teachings of the bride and groom have not given them the freedom to accept the reality of the spouse's beliefs, without thinking that to do so denies the reality of their own beliefs? Is it disturbing because the spouses' respective churches have either prohibited, or attached with guilt, attending other churches and worshiping via other forms and procedures? Is it because God and a worshipful experience can only be found in *the* right church?

Such illustrations of the difficulties in interfaith marriages can be found not only in case history materials, but also in your own experiences and those of your relatives and friends. May I suggest that in your group discussions you look at these difficulties as symptoms of a disease in organized religions? May I suggest that you focus on the disease, rather than the symptom or fever? May I suggest you leave room for those couples in interfaith marriages who may have to leave their respective churches in order to have the freedom to establish a marriage: which evinces charity and respect for the reality of individual beliefs; which is based on an appreciation if not a reverence for the creative uniqueness and variety in nature, art forms, ideologies, and religious beliefs; and which permits and encourages a lifetime pursuit and exploration of individual "I–Thou" relationships, unhampered by an "It" in the form of institutional loyalty.

NOTES

(Those marked with an asterisk * contain case histories on interfaith marriages.)
1. Barron, Milton L., "The Incidence of Jewish Intermarriage in Europe and America," *American Sociological Review,* XI (February, 1946), 6–13.

2. *Barron, Milton L., *People Who Intermarry*, Syracuse: Syracuse University Press, 1946.
3. Barron, Milton L., "Research on Intermarriage: A Survey of Accomplishments and Prospects," *American Journal of Sociology,* LVII (November, 1951), 249–255.
4. Bishops' Committee on Mixed Marriages, *A Factual Study of Mixed Marriages*, Washington, D.C.: National Catholic Welfare Conference, 1943.
5. Black, A. D., *If I Marry Outside My Religion*, New York: Public Affairs Pamphlet No. 204, 1954.
6. Blood, Robert O., *Anticipating Your Marriage*, Glencoe, Illinois: Free Press, 1955, Chapter 2.
7. Board of Social Missions of the United Lutheran Church in America, "A Study of Mixed Marriages in the United Lutheran Church in America." (See notes 8 and 9.)
8. Bossard, James H. S., and Letts, Harold C., "Mixed Marriages Involving Lutherans," *Marriage and Family Living,* XVIII (November, 1956), 308–311.
9. *Bossard, James H. S., and Boll, Eleanor Stoker, *One Marriage, Two Faiths*, New York: Ronald Press Company, 1956.
10. Brown, James S., "Social Class, Intermarriage, and Church Membership in a Kentucky Community," *American Journal of Sociology,* LVII (November, 1951), 232–242.
11. Chancellor, Loren E., and Monahan, Thomas P., "Religious Preference and Interreligious Mixtures in Marriages and Divorces in Iowa," *American Journal of Sociology,* LXI (November, 1955), 233–239.
12. Done, G. Byron, "A Study of Mormon-Gentile Intermarriages in Los Angeles," Unpublished Master's Thesis, University of Southern California, 1937.
13. Follett, Elizabeth Nicholson, "A Study of Interfaith Marriages Among Mormons in Berkeley, California," Unpublished Master's Thesis, University of California, Berkeley, 1958.
14. Freehof, Solomon B., "Report on Mixed Marriages and Intermarriage," *Yearbook,* Vol. 57, Philadelphia: Central Conference of American Rabbis, 1947.
15. Hoffer, Eric, *The True Believer*, Englewood Cliffs, N.J.: Prentice-Hall, 1953.
16. Hollingshead, August B., "Cultural Factors in the Selection of Marriage Mates," *American Sociological Review,* XV (October, 1950), 619–627.
17. James, William, *The Varieties of Religious Experience*, New York: Everyman's Library.
18. Kennedy, Ruby Jo Reeves, "Single or Triple Melting-Pot? Intermarriage Trends in New Haven, 1870–1940," *American Journal of Sociology,* XLIX (January, 1944), 331–339; and *American Journal of Sociology,* LVIII (July, 1952), 56–66.
19. Kirkpatrick, Clifford, *The Family: As Process & Institution*, New York: Ronald Press, 1955, Chapter 5 and Appendix, "Sources and Findings on Success in Marriage," 97–118; 599–624.
20. Landis, Judson T., "Marriages of Mixed and Non-Mixed Religious Faith," *American Sociological Review,* XIV (June, 1949), 401–407.
21. Landis, Judson T., and Mary G., *Building a Successful Marriage*, 3rd ed., Englewood Cliffs, N.J.: Prentice-Hall, 1958, Chapter 12, "Mixed Marriages."

22. Leiffer, Murray H., "Mixed Marriages and Church Loyalties," *Christian Century,* LXVI (January 19, 1949), 78–80.
23. Leiffer, Murray H., "Mixed Marriages and the Children," *Christian Century,* LXVI (January 26, 1949), 106–108.
24. Locke, Harvey J., "Interfaith Marriages," *Social Problems* (April, 1957), 329–333.
25. Lynd, Robert S., *Knowledge for What?* Princeton: Princeton University Press, 1948, 60–62.
26. MacMurray, John, *Reason and Emotion,* London: Faber & Faber, 1937.
27. Merton, Robert K., "Intermarriage and the Social Structure: Fact and Theory," *Psychiatry,* IV (August, 1941), 361–374.
28. Monahan, Thomas P., and Kephart, William M., "Divorce and Desertion by Religious and Mixed-Religious Groups," *American Journal of Sociology,* LIX (March, 1954), 454–465.
29. *Mudd, Emily H., *et al.* (eds.), *Marriage Counseling: A Casebook,* New York: Association Press, 1958.
30. *Pike, James A., *If You Marry Outside Your Faith,* New York: Harper & Bros., 1954.
31. Resnik, Reuben B., "Some Sociological Aspects of Intermarriage of Jew and Non-Jew," *Social Forces,* XII (October, 1933), 94–102.
32. Roth, Julius, and Peck, Robert F., "Social Class and Social Mobility Factors Related to Marital Adjustment," *American Sociological Review,* XVI (August, 1951), 478–487.
33. Schnepp, Gerald J., *Leakage from a Catholic Parish,* Washington, D.C.: Catholic University of America Press, 1942.
34. Schnepp, Gerald J., and Roberts, Louis A., "Residential Propinquity and Mate Selection on a Parish Basis," *American Journal of Sociology,* LVIII (July, 1952), 45–50.
35. Slotkin, J. S., "Jewish-Gentile Intermarriage in Chicago," *American Sociological Review,* VII (February, 1942), 34–39.
36. Taylor, Edmund, *Richer by Asia,* Boston: Houghton Mifflin Co., 1947.
37. *Thomas, John L., *The American Catholic Family,* Englewood Cliffs, N.J.: Prentice-Hall, 1956.
38. Thomas, John L., "The Factor of Religion in Selection of Marriage Mates," *American Sociological Review,* XVI (August, 1951), 487–491.
39. *Vincent, Clark E. (ed.), *Readings in Marriage Counseling,* New York: Thomas Y. Cromwell Co., 1957.
40. Williams, J. Paul, *What Americans Believe and How They Worship,* New York: Harper Bros., 1952.
41. Zangwill, Israel, *The Melting Pot,* New York: Macmillan Co., 1909.

One of the basic obstacles to empirical research on religious intermarriage in American society is that only Indiana and Iowa require a statement of religious affiliation on their marriage registration forms. The following study represents one of the first efforts to make use of the data in Indiana. Making comparisons between religious intermarriages and inmarriages in that state, Christensen and Barber found that the former were more likely to have had civil ceremonies, to involve members of religious minorities, to attract older and previously married people, to show high-status occupations, and to be residents of urban communities. By the use of the technique of record linkage, they also discovered that religious intermarriages had a higher proportion of premarital pregnancies and subsequent divorce.

INTERFAITH VERSUS INTRAFAITH MARRIAGES IN INDIANA*

Harold T. Christensen and *Kenneth E. Barber*

Though social scientists recognize religion as an important variable in human behavior, they have been handicapped in their research by the lack of nationwide statistics. America's separation-of-church-and-state tradition, laid down in the Constitution, has been strong enough up to the present to forestall all attempts to incorporate "religious affiliation" in its decennial censuses. Furthermore, with only two exceptions, and these initiated quite recently, information on religion is also missing in the vital statistics regis-

Journal of Marriage and the Family, Vol. 29, No. 3 (August 1967), pp. 461–69. Reprinted by permission.

ters of the various states. These limitations in basic source data have meant both the curtailment of quantitative research relating to religion; and, for the most part, the relegating of those studies which have occurred to small samples involving field surveys, which then cannot be considered as representative of the larger and more significant populations.

The two exceptions to the absence of religious identification in state registers are Iowa and Indiana. Iowa started collecting information concerning religious affiliation on its marriage and divorce forms in 1953. Indiana started at midyear 1959 but limited the recording to the marriage records alone and to designations of major religious categories (Protestant, Catholic, Jew, other). Analyses from the Iowa data have appeared in a series of articles by Burchinal and Chancellor.[1] This present paper is the first to exploit the Indiana data.[2]

OVERVIEW FROM EARLIER STUDIES

An excellent summary of research findings relevant to interfaith marriage has been provided by Burchinal, drawn from the works of others as well as his own.[3] A summary of his summary would include the following, considered as tentative generalizations or hypotheses which need further testing with respect to the larger society:

1. Findings vary somewhat from study to study, due probably to differences in research procedure as well as differences in the populations investigated; nevertheless, in spite of a few contradictions, suggestions of certain uniformities appear.

2. Attitudes toward interfaith dating and marriage are generally tolerant, more so for the former than the latter, however; and generally with greater tolerance shown by Catholics than Protestants (though Catholics hold more strongly to certain requirements for such marriages), by males than females, by young high-school students than the older college students, by those low on church attendance as compared with the frequent attenders, and by persons actually experiencing intimate interfaith interaction as compared with those who are not. In addition, Burchinal found inverse relationships between social status and attitudes accepting interreligious dating or marriage.

3. In practice, also, interfaith dating and marriage are high, but rates vary from group to group. Most such practices involve the Catholic-Protestant combination. Findings are unclear as to whether

interfaith liaisons are more frequent with males or females, though in the Jewish group males show the greater frequency.

4. Higher rates of interfaith marriage occur in religious groups having smallest community membership (probably the most predictive factor found), among both the very young and the older brides and grooms rather than the in-between ages, with remarriages in contrast to first marriages, with marriages involving an out-of-state bride, with marriages solemnized by civil ceremony, within communities where ethnic-group cohesiveness is low, and among couples considerably emancipated from their parents or whose parents are nonreligious.

Of even greater import than these attitudinal and behavioral factors are the possible effects that differing patterns of religious affiliation might have upon the marital outcome. It is important, in other words, to study interfaith marriage as an independent variable. Earlier studies by Bell, Weeks, and Landis[4] have attempted this and with similar results. The Landis findings may be taken to illustrate: the per cent divorced varied from 4.4 where both spouses were Catholic to 5.2 where both were Jewish, 6.0 where both were Protestant, 14.1 where one was Catholic and the other Protestant, and 17.9 where they claimed no religion. Thus, it would seem that Catholics are the least prone to divorce, that mixed-religion marriages are more hazardous by this measure than same-faith unions, and that marriages without support from the religious institutions run the greatest risk of all.

Vernon[5] has called attention to the distorted emphasis which this usual practice of comparing *failure* rates may produce. From the Landis data just cited, he pointed out that the difference between interfaith and intrafaith marriage is 200 to 300 per cent when the divorce rates are used but only about 10 per cent when the complements of the divorce rates—which give the percentages "enduring"—are compared. And he believes it is this latter, the *success* rate, that should be used for the avoidance of bias. His correction, though valuable, changes only the interpretive emphasis, not the overall research result.

Burchinal and Chancellor,[6] in their analysis of Iowa data, did compare on the basis of relative success, i.e., nondivorce or "survival rate." Survival rates for homogeneous Catholic marriages, homogeneous Protestant marriages, and interreligious marriages were found to be 96.2, 86.2, and 77.6, respectively, thus confirming the generalizations of previous studies. However, age of bride and status level of husband also were found to be associated with survival rate, both in a positive direction; and when the intrafaith-interfaith comparisons were controlled by these two variables, the differentials, though maintained in direction, were reduced in magnitude. As a matter of fact, there was the strong suggestion that these control variables influence marital survival rates more than does religious combination.

DESIGN OF THIS RESEARCH

As stated above, Indiana is the second state to ask for religious affiliation on its marriage registration forms, and even this is of recent development. The new forms were introduced late in 1959, but 1960 represents the first full year of use. Though an exploratory study was made of the 1959 data,[7] it was not published. The present analysis is based solely upon 1960 marriages except for categories involving Jewish grooms or brides, where 1961, 1962, and 1963 marriages have been added to provide larger N's (this exception does not apply to the record linkage phase of the study; see below). There were 42,043 marriages in Indiana during 1960. To these were added 581 marriages involving a Jewish person and occurring during 1961–1963, making a total of 42,624. Of these, 18,782 were discarded for one or more of the following reasons: (1) religious affiliation of one or both spouses either not given or given as other than Protestant, Catholic, or Jew; (2) data lacking on one or more other variables crucial to the analysis; (3) one or both of the spouses an out-of-state resident; and (4) one or both of the spouses a nonwhite. This left 23,842 cases of white couples who were Indiana residents and whose marriage records carried the necessary information.

The study was designed to utilize available Indiana data through both the retesting of certain relationships reported in earlier research and the exploring of new ground by means of record linkage. For the first of these goals—replication—the large 23,842 cohort was used (as shown in Table 2). The reader will note that here we are dealing with parameters and not samples, which eliminates the necessity for running tests of significance. This is a strength, which, so far as we know, is found nowhere else in studies of mixed-religious marriages except with Burchinal and Chancellor. But there is an accompanying weakness: our relatively large number of discards, with no measurable way of knowing whether this has been selective and hence biasing. Surely the decisions to eliminate nonwhite and out-of-state residents have improved the analysis by increasing homogeneity, and these cases account for nearly half the discards. But the other half, those with incomplete recordings, are of another variety. Yet, we know of no theoretical basis for assuming selectivity by religious categories in the recording of marriage data and so are inclined to assume lack of bias.

By matching marriage records with birth and divorce records, we have been able to add creatively to existing theory. Record linkage refers to the case-by-case matching of different sets of records so that individual couples can be studied over time; it has a longitudinal design, with the additional advantage of providing data that are largely free of the distortions of either refusal or falsification. Furthermore, certain things are revealed by the linking of records that are unknown to either set of records considered singly—premarital pregnancy, for example. Previous research has dealt with premarital pregnancy,[8] but this phenomenon has not until now been related to the intrafaith-interfaith variable. Similarly, previous studies have related interfaith marriage to divorce, but these studies either have been based upon samples where representativeness may be questioned (Bell, Weeks, Landis) or, though upon an entire population, were without the case matching needed for longitudinal analysis (Burchinal and Chancellor).[9]

But the record linkage phase of our study has some shortcomings of its own, mainly due to a narrowing of the search. Because of limited time and facilities, plus the extreme amount of labor involved in the matching processes, it was necessary to greatly reduce the numbers of records handled from what otherwise would have been possible and desirable. The first task was to measure premarital pregnancy by means of linking the marriage records with the birth records. For this we made disproportionate reductions in 1960 marriage cases within each of the religion categories, in the direction of converging the N values; then, to match this smaller sample, we searched Indiana birth records through 1960 and 1961. The second task was to work out divorce rates within each of the religion categories. As background for this, we restricted ourselves to Marion County—the state's largest as to population and its center of government—and then matched all

1960 marriages in that county against divorces recorded in that county up through October 6, 1964. It should be noted again that in these two record-linkage procedures *only* 1960 marriages have been used; though sample size for the Jewish groups would have been improved if later-year marriages had been added, as was done for the first part of our analysis, to have done so here would have distorted the picture, due to differing search spans. (For further details on these sampling and matching procedures, consult the footnotes of Table 3.)

INTRAFAITH-INTERFAITH COMBINATIONS

Before narrowing the analysis to 1960 marriages and to the testing of factors presumed to be associated with the phenomenon under study, it will be well to take an overview of existing patterns. Table 1 presents both frequency and percentage distributions of Indiana marriages over a four-year period, 1960–1963. It will be observed that eight-ninths (88.9 per cent) of the known-religion cases are intrafaith and only one-ninth (11.1 per cent), interfaith.[10]

Furthermore, intrafaith Protestant marriages far outnumber all others, with intrafaith Catholic marriages coming second, though considerably behind; marriages involving Jews and persons of other religions are relatively few in Indiana.[11]

How do Protestants, Catholics, and Jews compare as to percentages who enter an interfaith marriage? To answer this, two kinds of calculations were made from the data of Table 1: interfaith rates for *marriages* and interfaith rates for *individuals*.[12] With the first, it was found that 12.0 per cent of all marriages involving Protestants were interfaith, as were 53.4 per cent of all marriages involving Catholics, and 47.6 per cent of all marriages involving Jews. With the second procedure, percentages for individuals who married across faith lines were found to be 6.4, 36.4, and 31.2, respectively. Interfaith rates based upon marriages are thus seen to be consistently higher than those based upon individuals. Nevertheless, whichever the type, our data show Protestants with the lowest rate and Catholics with the highest. This supports a claimed negative relationship between relative population size and proportion marrying outside the group, which has been reported in other studies. However, if such a relationship were consistent

TABLE 1

Distribution of Religious Combinations of Grooms and Brides
for Total Indiana Marriages Occurring 1960–1963

Religious Combinations*	Number	Per Cent‡
Intrafaith		
PP	123,332	79.5
CC	14,204	9.2
JJ	399	.3
Subtotal	137,935	88.9
Interfaith		
PC	8,033	5.2
CP	7,932	5.1
PJ & JP	270	.2
CJ & JC	82	.1
PO & OP	622	.4
CO & OC	227	.1
JO & OJ	11	.0
Subtotal	17,177	11.1
Unknown†	17,320	
Grand Total	172,432	100.00

* Here, and throughout this paper, P stands for Protestant, C for Catholic, J for Jewish, and O for other religion, with husband's affiliation always shown first. Thus, for example, PC means Protestant husband and Catholic wife.

† Cases in which religion was not stated for one or both of the spouses or in which both groom and bride indicated "other" (801 cases). This latter is included with the "unknown" since, from the punched data, there was no way of distinguishing the interfaith from the intrafaith.

‡ Calculations here exclude the "unknown" category.

among all religions, one would have expected higher interfaith marriage rates for the Jews than for the Catholics (since Jews are fewer in number); the fact that they were not higher in this study suggests that other factors—stronger group cohesiveness perhaps—may be operating among the Jews as counterforces against exogamy.

FACTORS FROM THE MARRIAGE RECORDS

The first column of Table 2 gives the breakdown of cases classified by religious category. The numbers shown represent all Indiana marriages occurring in 1960 (plus 1961, 1962, and 1963 marriages where a Jewish person was involved) wherein both groom and bride were in-state residents, were white, and their religious affiliations and other needed data were shown on the marriage records. These figures are the bases for calculations resulting in the subsequent columns.

Overall (shown on the bottom line), the picture is for slightly less than one-sixth of the weddings to have been by civil ceremony; slightly more than one-fourth of the new spouses to have

TABLE 2

Factors Associated with the Marriage Combinations of Protestants, Catholics, and Jews

(1960 Data for White Indiana Residents with Completed Records)

Religious Combinations	Total Cases†	Per Cent Civil Weddings	Per Cent Previously Married		Median Ages at Marriage		Per Cent High Occupation‡		Per Cent Urban		Per Cent Heterogeneous Residence§
			Grooms	Brides	Grooms	Brides	Grooms	Brides	Grooms	Brides	
Intrafaith											
PP	19,436	14.8	27.6	27.3	23.3	20.7	8.7	5.1	69.4	72.6	20.3
CC	1,952	12.4	11.6	12.3	23.9	21.6	11.4	9.2	79.9	81.4	11.6
JJ	200	7.0	19.5	22.0	25.5	21.7	31.5	13.0	91.5	89.0	17.5
Subtotal	21,588	14.5	26.1	25.8	23.4	20.8	9.2	5.5	70.5	73.6	19.5
Interfaith											
PC	1,156	29.0	22.9	23.3	23.5	20.9	10.3	5.0	76.5	81.0	14.4
CP	922	33.9	29.5	35.6	24.5	21.7	9.0	4.3	81.0	83.5	12.2
Mixed J*	176	50.6	35.8	41.5	27.8	23.7	24.4	9.7	93.8	92.6	11.9
Subtotal	2,254	32.7	26.1	29.4	24.1	21.4	10.8	5.1	79.7	82.9	13.3
Grand Total	23,842	16.3	26.7	26.2	23.5	20.9	9.4	5.5	71.4	74.5	18.9

* The mixed J category combines all interfaith marriages involving a Jew—PJ, CJ, JP, and JC.

† In the two categories where Jews are involved, numbers are for marriages occurring during 1960–1963.

‡ Included in this classification are the following occupational groupings: professional, technical, managerial, officials, and proprietary (except farm).

§ As used here, heterogeneous residence simply means that husband and wife were from different counties at the time of marriage.

been previously married; they married in the early twenties, with the husband averaging nearly three years older; relatively few of them enjoyed high occupational status, especially so for the females; nearly three-fourths of them—relatively more of the females—resided in urban areas; and a little less than one-fifth of these marriages were residentially heterogeneous, as measured by the crossing of county lines.

When the three intrafaith categories are compared (first three lines), we find that Protestants fall at the two extremes—showing highest civil weddings, previous marriages, and heterogeneous residence, but being lowest with respect to all other factors. The Catholics, by way of contrast, showed up lowest on previous marriages and heterogeneous residence and were intermediate on all other factors. Finally, the Jews showed up highest of the three on median age, occupational status, and urban residence and lowest on civil weddings; they were opposite to Protestants on these four factors, and intermediate between Protestants and Catholics on previous marriages and heterogeneous residence.

Interfaith-intrafaith comparisons may be made by observing the two sets of subtotals. When this is done, factor by factor, the interfaith picture appears about as follows: a larger proportion of civil weddings; greater numbers having been married previously (grooms an exception); older ages at marriage; higher occupational status at marriage (brides an exception); more coming from urban areas; but *fewer* of the residential combinations representing heterogeneity. Close examination shows some of these differences to be less than others; furthermore, there are the two exceptions noted. Nevertheless, the crossing of major religious lines in marriage seems to be associated with these factors in *some* degree and in the directions indicated.[13] Future research, with further refinements, may be able to clear up some of the questions remaining.

In the meantime, one can speculate as to reasons that our interfaith couples, in contrast to our intrafaith, tended to select out disproportionately more persons who would turn to a civil wedding, had previously been married, were older, were from relatively high occupational levels, and were residing in urban areas; but to select *fewer* couples who crossed county lines in finding each other. Though explanations are not clear from the available data, following are some hypotheses which seem reasonable:

(1) Both selectivity and causation are involved in explaining the higher incidence of civil weddings—the first because persons with weak or liberal religious convictions are the ones most likely *both* to marry outside their faith and to choose a nonreligious ceremony; the second because, if a couple has already resisted parental and/or church pressure in deciding to marry outside their faith, they then may feel sufficiently rebellious to take the further step, or outside opposition may make a religious wedding more difficult to arrange.

(2) The factors of older age and larger proportions previously married probably fit together, each helping to explain the other. Furthermore, both of these conditions can be presumed to mean greater experience and hence less willingness to yield to outside influence. Also, in some faiths there are strong feelings against permitting a religious ceremony for persons previously married.

(3) Similarly, the larger percentage of grooms with high occupational status may be reciprocally related to the older ages and to the higher percentages of both spouses from urban areas, since prestigeful employment takes time to reach and tends to be concentrated in the cities. In addition, persons within either or both of these categories are likely to be freer from tradition and to experience a larger number of other-faith contacts.

(4) The finding of a lower percentage of heterogeneous-residence marriages in the interfaith category was at first surprising, since the greater emancipation presumed to be with this group might be expected to carry over and to stimulate marital choices spanning greater geographical distances. Nevertheless, our reverse finding may have plausible explanations. It may be, for example, that the urban weighting in the interfaith group has brought its percentage down, since urban persons are apt to experience more of their premarital contacts within the city boundaries and, hence, within the same county. Or, it may be that the intrafaith percentage of out-of-county marriages is high simply because those in this group, being more devout and religiously active, are more apt to search farther afield in order to stay within their faith or are more apt to meet same-faith mate potentials while attending conferences or other church events in distant centers across county lines.

When the three interfaith categories are compared, we find the mixed Jewish to be highest on the first five factors and lowest on the sixth. As a matter of fact, this pattern holds not only for comparisons with other interfaith categories but, with minor exceptions, when the intrafaith categories are taken into account as well. Thus, mixed Jewish marriages show proportionately more civil weddings, more grooms and brides who were previously married, who married at older ages, who engaged in the higher-level occupations, and who resided in urban centers, but *fewer* cases of heterogeneous residence, than any other category (the only exceptions being that the intrafaith Jewish out-distanced this group in occupational status and the intrafaith Catholic had a slightly lower percentage than it regarding heterogeneous residence).

Of particular interest is the comparison of the two interfaith groups PC and CP. In his earlier study, Landis[14] pointed to differing adjustment patterns between marriages involving a Protestant husband and Catholic wife and those involving a Catholic husband and Protestant wife. In the latter, he found higher than average divorce, which he tentatively explained by a presumed tendency for a Catholic father in mixed marriages to monitor his wife's child-rearing practices, making sure she didn't renege on on her antenuptial agreement to rear the children as Catholics— which interference was presumed to make for added conflict. The data of our Table 2, though not directly related to this problem, nevertheless bear on it. It will be noted that CP (Catholic husband with Protestant wife), in comparison with the PC category, shows more civil weddings, more previous marriages, older marriage ages, and greater percentages in urban residence, but smaller proportions in high-level occupations and heterogeneous residences. This discussion will be picked up again in the next section.

LINKAGE WITH THE BIRTH AND DIVORCE RECORDS

As explained earlier, our research was designed to include some longitudinal analysis by means of record linkage. Marriage records were matched with both birth and divorce records to permit measures of premarital pregnancy and of marital breakup, which factors were then related to the intrafaith-interfaith marriage combinations. Because of the amount of labor involved in the matching process, it was necessary to impose rather severe restrictions on both sample size and length of search. Even so—and in spite of the necessarily tentative nature of our generalizations to follow, due to these limitations—this analysis, being among the first of its kind, may add something to existing theory on the problem. Longitudinal analysis, most researchers recognize, has the advantage over cross-sectional analysis of laying bare cause and effect sequences.

To the author's knowledge, the only previous record-linkage research comparing religious groups was one focusing upon the phenomenon of temple marriage in Mormon culture. Christensen and Cannon[15] matched marriage, birth, and divorce records in two Utah counties, with the following results: the temple marriage group (the most religiously orthodox of the Mormons) had lowest rates of both premarital pregnancy and divorce, by considerable amounts; the "Other Church" group came next in both rates; the Mormon non-temple group (some of these eliminated from temple marriage by an official selective process) came third in both rates; and the civil wedding group showed up with the highest rates of both premarital pregnancy and divorce, by considerable amounts. It is to be noted, however, that this study did not deal with the *inter*faith marriage phenomenon.

Table 3 compares premarital pregnancy and divorce among our intrafaith-interfaith categories, with procedures and descriptions of the samples spelled out in the footnotes. Since the search of birth records involved those for only two years and the search of divorce records, those for less than five years, it cannot be presumed that *all* first births or *all* divorces that will eventually occur were tabulated.[16] It is for this reason that we show indices rather than percentages. The latter would not accurately portray a given category, while indices do accurately picture the *relative positions of categories* to each other—which is our concern.[17]

With respect to premarital pregnancy, it will be noted that: (1) among the intrafaith groups, Protestants are highest, Catholics take a middle position, and Jews are lowest; (2) interfaith marriages show a substantially higher rate than do intrafaith marriages, as will be seen from the indices of the two subtotals; (3) among the interfaith, Catholic-husband-with-Protestant-wife is the category with highest premarital pregnancy (in fact, highest of all six categories), the reverse of this is next highest, and mixed Jewish combinations are the lowest.

TABLE 3

Indices of Premarital Pregnancy and Divorce Compared Across
Intrafaith and Interfaith Marriage Combinations

Religious Combinations	Index of Premarital Pregnancy*	Index of Divorce and Annulment†
Intrafaith		
PP	1.08	1.10
CC	.63	.21
JJ	.23	.31
Subtotal	.85	1.00
Interfaith		
PC	1.18	1.11
CP	1.27	.90
Mixed J	.85	1.83
Subtotal	1.22	1.04
Grand Total	1.00	1.00

* Based upon a stratified sample of Indiana marriages occurring in 1960. Random subsamples of 5 per cent of the PP's, 25 per cent of the CC's, 50 per cent of the CP's and PC's, and 100 per cent of all categories involving J's were combined, and the resulting 3,930 cases were checked against the state birth records through the end of 1961. Matchings with the record of first birth to the couple were accomplished for 1,255 cases. Intervals to first birth were calculated and percentages of premarital pregnancy (considered to be those births which occurred within the first 181 days of marriage, plus others up to and including 196 days where the birth weight exceeded 5.5 pounds) were then determined for each religious category. Overall, the percentage of premarital pregnancy in first births found was 26.0. The index values shown in the table are simply premarital pregnancy percentages for each category divided by this total sample percentage. N's for the six religious categories were 390, 345, 17, 270, 224, and 9, respectively.

† Based upon marriages and divorces in Marion County only. Marriages occurring in 1960 amounted to 4,676. These were checked against the county divorce index through August 15, 1964, and against the records showing dispositions through October 6, 1964. Matchings yielded 626 cases of complaints filed, and in 392 of these the divorce or annulment (only 7 cases) had been granted. This latter represents 8.4 per cent of the total marriages. Again, the index values shown are the divorce percentages for each religious category divided by this overall percentage. N's for the six religious categories were 3,712, 440, 39, 247, 225, and 13, respectively.

Though the sample for marriage-birth matching was not a completely random one—and hence the conditions for statistical tests of significance were, strictly speaking, not met—a few such tests were run.[18] Most differences were found to be significant. For present purposes, the most crucial comparison is between the combined intrafaith and combined interfaith categories; here there was obtained a Chi-square value of 11.9 which produced a significance level of .001.

With respect to divorce, it may be observed that: (1) among the intrafaith, Protestants are highest, Jews next, and Catholics lowest (probably because of the Catholic church's anti-divorce position); (2) the slightly higher rate for the combined interfaith group compared with the combined intrafaith group is, though in the expected direction, so small that it probably should be ignored; (3) among the interfaith, mixed Jewish showed the highest incidence of marital breakup (in fact, highest of all six categories) and Catholic-husband-with-Protestant-wife the lowest. This latter finding was especially surprising. Statistical tests of significance have not been run for the comparisons of column two, since generalizations are for Marion County only and the results are parameters: no sampling was involved.

Jewish marriages in comparison with others show up lowest on premarital pregnancy. This is true within both the intrafaith and the interfaith categories, meaning either that Jewish couples have less premarital coitus or that they practice birth control more effectively, or both of these. Furthermore, homogeneous Jewish marriages are very low on divorce, almost as low as Catholics, suggesting the strength of this group's family orientation when the spouses are able to reinforce each other in it. But the highest-of-all divorce index for mixed Jewish marriages suggests either that it is chiefly the more emancipated who marry across religious lines or that mixed marriages involving Jews result in an overdose of tensions, or both of these. In making these comparisons and speculations, however, an important caution must be sounded: small N's make generalization hazardous (see table footnotes).

Returning to our comparisons between the PC's and CP's, earlier we showed that the latter had more civil weddings, more previous marriages, older ages at marriage, and greater proportions residing in urban places. Now, from Table 3, it is seen that CP marriages have more premarital pregnancy but *less divorce* than PC marriages. In just about every factor except the crucial one—divorce—our data support (indirectly, to be sure) the notion promulgated by Landis[19] that mixed Protestant-Catholic marriages experience more problems when the husband is Catholic than when the wife is. But why does this group show less divorce? One reason may be the inadequacy of our sample. It could be, for example, that the husband is the key figure in consenting to divorce and that, when he is Catholic, consent will be longer in coming—which, by our procedure, would eliminate proportionately more of them. Another possibility is that Marion County may not be representative of the larger universe. Finally, it must not be forgotten that the Landis findings may be atypical.[20] More research is called for.

SUMMARY AND CONCLUSIONS

In 1959 Indiana became the second state to include religious affiliation as required information on its marriage forms. This study has taken advantage of the resulting availability of new data by analyzing 1960 marriages of Protestants, Catholics, and Jews within the state. Part of the analysis took the form of replication of earlier studies, but an important innovation went beyond that: by means of record linkage, it was possible to move longitudinally and to involve the variables of premarital pregnancy and divorce.

Approximately one-ninth of all marriages were interfaith (in the sense of crossing major faith lines). Though comparisons among Protestant, Catholic, and Jewish intrafaith marriages, and among several specific interfaith combinations, have been reported above, major attention has been given to the more basic problem of *interfaith versus intrafaith marriage*. Regarding this latter, it was found that interfaith marriage, in comparison with intrafaith, tends more to be by civil ceremony; it tends more to involve individuals who are members of religious minority groups, who have been previously married, who are older, who are in high-status occupations, who reside in urban areas, and who become pregnant before marriage. Interfaith marriages also showed up with a *slightly* higher divorce percentage, but the difference was so slight, and the record search which produced the percentages so short, as to make one wary of the results.

Therefore, the key question—that having to do with relative failure and success potentials of interfaith and intrafaith marriages —is still left in some doubt. It may be that our sampling and procedures are at fault; or it may be that religious differences have become less operative, have perhaps been rendered less important by the intellectual climate of the day. In either case it would seem that future research on this problem will need to refine its conceptualizations and its measuring instruments and procedures. One need is for better control over other variables affecting the marriage while the religious factor is being tested. Another need is for quality control over the religious variable: it is possible, for example, that such things as degree of devoutness or rigidity of belief, and husband-wife combinations thereof, are more important in marital adjustment than is denominational affiliation; that certain intrafaith religious differences may be more disruptive of a relationship than interfaith disparities taken alone.

NOTES

1. See, for example, Lee G. Burchinal and Loren E. Chancellor, "Social Status, Religious Affiliation and Ages at Marriage," *Marriage and Family Living*, 25 (August, 1963), pp. 219–221. Earlier articles are documented in this one.

2. The research was supported by a grant to the authors from the Purdue Research Foundation. The drafting of this report was by Christensen, but it has drawn significantly from Barber's dissertation research. The assistance of Jeffrey K. Hadden and Richard J. Hill, who served as critics of the first draft, is gratefully acknowledged. It is expected that, in due time, additional articles will appear, based upon data not included here and/or not a part of the dissertation.

3. Lee G. Burchinal, "The Premarital Dyad and Love Involvement," chap. 16 in *Handbook of Marriage and the Family*, ed. by Harold T. Christensen, Chicago: Rand-McNally, 1964, pp. 649–653.

4. Howard W. Bell, *Youth Tell Their Story*, Washington, D.C.: American Council on Education, 1938; H. Ashley Weeks, "Differential Divorce Rates by Occupation," *Social Forces*, 21 (1943), pp. 334–337; Judson T. Landis, "Marriages of Mixed and Non-Mixed Religious Faiths," *American Sociological Review*, 14 (June, 1949), pp. 401–407.

5. Glenn M. Vernon, "Bias in Professional Publications Concerning Interfaith Marriages," *Religious Education*, 55 (July-August, 1960), pp. 261–264.

6. Lee G. Burchinal and Loren E. Chancellor, "Survival Rates Among Religiously Homogamous and Interreligious Marriages," *Social Forces*, 41 (May, 1963), pp. 353–362.

7. See D. Jean Pavela, *An Analysis of Mixed and Non-Mixed Religious Marriages in Indiana During 1959*, unpublished M.S. thesis, Purdue University Libraries, 1962. Available for study were 2,302 white marriages occurring during the last four months of 1959. Of these, only 12.5 per cent were interfaith (in the sense of crossing two of the major religious groups—Catholic, Protestant, and Jewish). Analyses of the three most prominent marriage types revealed, among other things, that mixed Catholic-Protestant marriages were highest, homogeneous Protestant marriages in-between, and homogeneous Catholic marriages lowest on the following factors: per cent civil wedding (except that homogeneous Protestants were lowest here), per cent heterogeneous

residence, per cent in older age group, per cent previously divorced (except that differences separating the mixed from the homogeneous Protestants were not statistically significant here), and per cent of grooms in professional occupations.

8. See, for example, Harold T. Christensen, "Child Spacing Analysis Via Record Linkage: New Data Plus a Summing Up from Earlier Reports," *Marriage and Family Living*, 25 (August, 1963), pp. 272–280. Consult reference list at the end.

9. These authors recognized the shortcoming involved in their failure to match marriage and divorce records for identical couples. As a next best they used "marriage- and divorce-linked cohorts of data" which they claimed would approximate longitudinal analysis. For details, see Burchinal and Chancellor, "Survival Rates Among Religiously Homogamous and Interreligious Marriages," *op. cit.*, pp. 354–355.

10. In using these terms, it is only marriages across two of the three broad religious categories—Protestant, Catholic, Jewish—that are considered interfaith. Interdenominational mixtures within Protestantism, for example, do not show up on the marriage records and so cannot be included in our study.

   Furthermore, no account can be taken here of the recent or anticipated conversion of a spouse; that would require supplementary field study.

11. Though of peripheral interest, it is possible to use the data of Table 1 for a rough approximation of overall religious affiliation in Indiana. Tabulations, by religion, of all *persons* (two for each marriage) contracting a marriage during 1960–1963 resulted in 263,521 Protestants, 44,682 Catholics, 1,161 Jews, and 2,462 "other" (latter figure includes the 801 marriages mentioned in second footnote of Table 1). Percentagewise, this is 84.5, 14.3, .4, and .8, respectively.

12. For a discussion of the difference between these two types of rates, and of the need to keep them straight, see Hyman Rodman, "Technical Note on Two Rates of Mixed Marriage," *American Sociological Review*, 30 (October, 1965), pp. 776–778.

13. The reader is invited to extend this interfaith-intrafaith comparison by matching *all* relevant figures within each column; thus, PP compared with PC and then CP, CC compared with PC and then CP, and JJ compared with mixed J. When this is done, minor differences in the interfaith-intrafaith picture are found across the three religious groups; nevertheless, the general outlook is the one reported above.

14. Landis, *loc. cit.*

15. Harold T. Christensen and Kenneth L. Cannon, "Temple Versus Nontemple Marriage in Utah: Some Demographic Considerations," *Social Science*, 39 (January, 1964), pp. 26–33.

16. The truncated nature of our two searches *may* have introduced some bias. Though we know of no differences in timing pattern (timing of first birth or timing of divorce) among the six categories, if such differences do exist this would affect the rates and indices calculated.

17. Should the reader's taste be for indices of "success," rather than the ones shown in Table 3, these can be derived by using percentages *not* premaritally pregnant and *not* divorced and then following the same procedure described in the table footnotes. When this is done, the figures of column one become .97, 1.13, 1.27, 1.05, .94, .91, 1.05, .92, and 1.00, respectively; and those of column two .99, 1.07, 1.06, 1.00, .99, 1.01, .92, 1.00, and 1.00, respectively.

18. In selecting the samples, the computer generated for each category a random number between 1 and 20, then began with that element, and extracted every Nth case. This procedure closely approximates randomness.

19. Landis, *loc. cit.*

20. Cf., Burchinal and Chancellor, "Survival Rates Among Religiously Homogamous and Interreligious Marriages," *op. cit.*, pp. 357–360. These authors reported slightly lower survival rates for mixed marriages involving Catholic husbands, but concluded that the difference was hardly sufficient to support Landis' thesis.

The paradoxical posture of American Jews with regard to religious intermarriage is a well-known and puzzling phenomenon to outside observers. Despite the generally acknowledged Jewish liberal ideology in confronting political and social issues such as the struggle for civil rights and ethnic equality, the typical adult Jewish approach toward involvement in intermarriage by Jews has traditionally been one of resistance if not downright hostility. This stance may be yielding somewhat, however, as American Jews shift preponderantly into the status of native-born parentage. For example, recent sociological research by Marshall Sklare and Joseph Greenblum in "Lakeville," the pseudonym for an affluent Midwestern suburb, showed that although Jewish parents are still anxious about Jewish survival and therefore are opposed to participation in intermarriage by their children, they nevertheless are also committed to the American values of romantic love and freedom of marital choice. Confronted by the researchers with the imagined alternatives for their children of a loved Gentile versus an unloved fellow Jew, the overwhelming majority of adult Jewish respondents in Lakeville, including those vehemently opposed to intermarriage as such, opted for their offspring's romantic intermarriage over a loveless intrafaith match. It requires little imagination to interpret this as signalling ultimate victory for the values threatening Jewish survival over those that support group homogeneity and continuity.

Granted the strategic importance of intermarriage to American Jews as an index of amicable relations and some aspects of assimilation with non-Jews on the one hand, and as a threat to their identity and survival on the other, one would readily assume there is no shortage of comprehensive and detailed scholarly studies of Jewish involvement in the practice. Actually there are no nationwide studies and few books of any consequence on the subject, but one can find instead numerous small-scale community studies and two statewide studies reported in journals, pamphlets, and yearbooks. The author of the two statewide studies, the first in Iowa and the second in Indiana, is Erich Rosenthal, the leading empirical researcher on American Jewish intermarriage. Fully aware of the fact that it would be misleading to generalize about Jewish intermarriage behavior on the basis of findings in two states where the Jewish population is small and scattered, Rosenthal was still attracted there for research purposes for the same reason that attracted Christensen and Barber in their broader study of religious intermarriage in general, namely, pertinent religious data on marriage selection were available only in Iowa and Indiana of all fifty states.

In the following report of his Indiana study, Rosenthal makes clear that his findings, while not representative of an ethnic group which is characteristically distributed in the cities and suburbs of other areas, especially the Northeast, do add weight to his earlier contention in the Iowa study. The current patterns of small-town and midwest Jewish involvement in intermarriage, the absence of large-scale Jewish immigration, and the existence of a low Jewish birth rate, cannot be ignored in calculating the demographic future of the Jewish population in American society.

JEWISH INTERMARRIAGE
IN INDIANA*

Erich Rosenthal

The present study of Jewish inmarriage and intermarriage patterns in Indiana is a continuation of the author's earlier studies of assimilatory tendencies in the American Jewish community. It should however be emphasized at the outset that Indiana as well as Iowa (in the 1963 study) were selected for analysis because pertinent data are available only for them. In no way are they to be considered as samples, representative or otherwise, of Jewish assimilationist tendencies in the United States.

The study analyzes the data in the Indiana marriage record forms for the years 1960 through 1963. The availability of detailed information about the groom's and bride's usual place of residence, the locality where application for the marriage license was made, and the place where the marriage was solemnized made possible an ecological analysis that contributes significantly to our understanding of the formation of Jewish inmarriages and intermarriages. The analysis further reveals the need to reevaluate the relationship between intermarriage and divorce. It has been generally observed that intermarriages were more likely to lead to divorce than inmarriages, and the more frequent failure of intermarriages has been attributed to the religio-cultural differences of the spouses. The Indiana data indicate that many intermarriages occurred after one or both spouses had terminated a *previous* marriage by divorce and that, therefore, this factor will have to be considered in determining the cause of frequent failures of intermarriages.

NATURE OF THE STUDY
The Data

The data to be analyzed here are taken from 785 marriage records, the total number of all marriages involving Jews in Indi-

*Reprinted by permission from *American Jewish Yearbook 1967*, Vol. 68, pp. 243–64. Footnotes omitted.

ana in a four-year-period. The Indiana Marriage Record Form, which is virtually identical with the standard report form developed by the National Vital Statistics Division of the U.S. Public Health Service, contains the standard questions on usual residence, age, birthplace, race, previous marital history, and usual occupation. In addition, however, it also secures information on religion, in compliance with an act of the 1958–1959 Indiana state legislature. This item is pre-coded in a manner that gives each groom and bride one of three choices: "Catholic," "Jewish," or "Protestant." Persons who do not fall within these categories can specify "other." Eleven grooms and 10 brides did not specify their religion, and were classified as "unknown"; six grooms and five brides checked the "other" category. Both categories were included in this study as "non-Jews."

Intermarriage: Definition and Measurement

A couple is considered to be intermarried if one spouse professes a religion different from that of the other. Persons who changed their religion before marriage in order to conform to the religion of their future spouses are considered to be inmarried. The intermarriage rate for Jews is computed by determining the ratio of intermarried couples to the total number of marriages, Jewish marriages, i.e., in which one or both partners are Jewish.

The analysis of the Indiana marriage records measures the *formation* of intermarriages. An average intermarriage rate of x per cent means that of all Jewish marriages that were solemnized during the period studied, x per cent were intermarriages. It does not mean that x per cent of all Jewish families in Indiana are intermarried.

EXTENT OF JEWISH INTERMARRIAGE

In the past we had to be satisfied with few measures of intermarriage. Predominant among them was the overall, or crude, rate showing the frequency of events throughout the entire population, without regard to any of the various smaller groupings that are sometimes used for better observation. The availability of information on the usual residence of groom and bride made it possible to supplement the crude rate with a large number of area-specific rates.

Crude Rate

The listing of all Jewish inmarriages and intermarriages recorded by the Indiana State Board of Health (Table 1) shows that the total number of intermarriages ranged from 175 in 1960 to 232 in 1963, from a low rate of 46.3 per cent in 1960 to a high of 51.7 per cent in 1962, indicating a crude average intermarriage rate of 48.8 per cent. Since the intermarriage rate appeared to fluctuate at random during this period, the further analysis of the data will proceed without regard for the year in which the marriage occurred.

TABLE 1

Total and Jewish Marriages, Indiana, 1960–63

		Jewish Marriages					
			Number			Per Cent	
Year	All Indiana marriages	Total	In-marriages	Inter-marriages	Total	In-marriages	Inter-marriages
1960 ...	42,050	175	94	81	100.0	53.7	46.3
1961 ...	42,302	177	93	84	100.0	52.5	47.5
1962 ...	43,464	201	97	104	100.0	48.3	51.7
1963 ...	45,992	232	118	114	100.0	50.9	49.1
Total ...	173,808	785	402	383	100.0	51.2	48.8

Source: Indiana State Board of Health.

State Specific Rates

Information on the usual residence of groom and bride revealed that within the overall levels of 51.2 per cent of inmarriages and 48.8 per cent of intermarriages three ecological groupings are hidden, each with its own distinct level of inmarriage and intermarriage: 1) extrastate marriages, with both groom and bride usually residing outside Indiana; 2) interstate marriages, with one partner from outside the state; and 3) intrastate marriages, with both partners usually residing within the state. Table 2 shows that extrastate and interstate marriages, each, constitute fully one-fifth of all Indiana marriages; intrastate marriages, slightly less than three-fifths.

TABLE 2

Usual Residence of Holders of Indiana Marriage Records, 1960–1963

Usual Residence	Number	Per cent
Both spouses out-of-state residents	169	21.5
One or both spouses Indiana residents	616	78.5
One spouse	171	21.8
Both spouses	445	56.7
All Indiana marriage records	785	100.0

Source: Indiana State Board of Health.

Table 3 reveals that, among these three groups, the extrastate couples have the highest level of intermarriage (67.4 per cent); the interstate couples the lowest (29.8 per cent), and intrastate couples an intermediate level (49.0 per cent).

TABLE 3

Jewish Marriages by Usual Residence, Indiana, 1960–63

Type of marriage	All Indiana marriage records		INDIANA RESIDENTS				Both spouses out of state residents	
			Both spouses		One spouse			
	Number	Per cent	Number	Per cent	Number	Per cent	Number	Per cent
Inmarriage	402	51.2	227	51.0	120	70.2	55	32.5
Intermarriage	383	48.8	218	49.0	51	29.8	114	67.4
Jewish groom	253	32.2	145	32.6	42	24.5	66	39.0
Jewish bride	130	16.6	73	16.4	9	5.3	48	28.4
Total	785	100.0	445	100.0	171	100.0	169	100.0

Source: Indiana State Board of Health.

INTERMARRIAGE AND EXTRASTATE MARRIAGES

It is obvious that one can no more burden the Jewish population of Indiana with the intermarriage rate of couples usually residing outside the state than one can include out-of-state T.B. patients in computing the morbidity rate of the permanent population of Denver, Colorado. But since these couples constitute one-fifth of all Jewish couples who get married in Indiana, a discussion of why they come into the state for this purpose is to the point.

Licensing Restrictions

Traditionally, couples have crossed state lines to take advantage of more lenient regulations. The absence of a waiting period between the application for a license and its issuance or of a premarital physical examination requirement entices couples to "Gretna Greens" across state lines. At times, also, they get married in the contiguous state because its marriage license bureau is more accessible than that in their home state.

A comparison of the requirements for the issuance of a marriage license in Indiana with those in the contiguous states shows that Indiana offers no advantages to residents of Illinois and Michigan. On the contrary, Indiana has a three-day waiting period, while Illinois has none; Indiana men can marry without parental consent only at the age of 21, as compared with 18 in Michigan. On the other hand, women from Ohio and Kentucky can marry in Indiana without parental consent at the age of 18, while they can do so only at 21 in their home states. In addition, Ohio imposes a five-day waiting period, as compared with three days in Indiana (see Table 4).

TABLE 4

Requirements Governing the Issuance of Marriage Licenses in Indiana and Neighboring States

State	Legal minimum marriage age				Blood test required	Waiting period	
	With parental consent		Without parental consent			Between application for, and issuance of, license	Between issuance of license and performance of marriage
	M	F	M	F			
Indiana	18	16	21	18	Yes	3 days	none
Illinois	18	16	21	18	Yes	none	none
Michigan	18	16	18	18	Yes	3 days	none
Ohio	18	16	21	21	Yes	5 days	none
Kentucky ...	18	16	21	21	Yes	3 days	none

Source: Information Please Almanac *1962* (New York, 1961), p. 239.

An examination of the data reveals that there is no correlation between the strictness of licensing procedures and the crossing of state lines. Although Illinois and Michigan put fewer obstacles in the path of couples who want to get married than does Indiana,

Lake county (contiguous to Chicago, at the northwesternmost border of the state) has the largest number (50) of nonresident marriages; Steuben county (contiguous to Detroit, at the northeasternmost corner of the state) ranks second, with 27. Both are "Gretna Greens" of long standing. At the same time, only 20 nonresident couples were married in Wayne county (contiguous to Dayton, Ohio) and 14 in Dearborn county (near Cincinnati, Ohio), despite the more stringent regulations in Ohio.

Family and Community Pressures

However, young couples may elope and marry in another state for reasons other than licensing restrictions. The considerably higher intermarriage rate for nonresident marriage partners than for inter- or intrastate marriage partners leads to the assumption that the desire to overcome familial and communal pressures against intermarriage may be causally related to elopement. Since we are not in a position to ask the nonresident marriage partners why they crossed state lines to get married in Indiana, we must resort to an operational definition of elopement. For our purposes, a couple has eloped if the following conditions are present: 1) the usual residence of both groom and bride is outside Indiana; 2) the birthplace of both groom and bride is outside Indiana; 3) the marriage license is issued in a border county of Indiana; 4) groom and bride are married in a civil ceremony. (The second and third restrictions are aimed at minimizing any ties to localities in Indiana.) When these restrictions were applied to the data (Table 5), it became apparent that the intermarriage rate rises as one gets closer to the full definition of an eloped couple, pointing to a causal relationship between extrastate marriages and intermarriage.

The exclusion from the total nonresident marriages of partners whose place of birth was Indiana, and therefore may still have had some ties in the state, significantly raised the intermarriage level by 5 points, from 67.4 to 72.4 per cent. By contrast, limitations governing the issuance of marriage licenses raises the percentage by only 1 more point, to 73.5. However, the additional restriction of marriage in a civil ceremony increases the intermarriage rate by another 3 per cent, to 77 per cent. It still remains to be explained why about one-fourth of those who elope marry within their religious faith. Parents may, of course, object to the prospective son- or daughter-in-law on grounds other than re-

TABLE 5

Marriages of Extrastate Residents by Usual Residence, Place of Birth,
County of Issuance of Marriage License, and Type of
Ceremony, Indiana, 1960–63

| | Both groom's and bride's | | | | | | | |
| | Usual residence outside Indiana | | Birth place outside Indiana | | Marriage license issued in border county | | Civil ceremony | |
Type of marriage	Number	Per cent	Number	Per cent	Number	Per cent	Number	Per cent
Inmarriage	55	32.5	37	27.6	31	26.5	23	23.0
Intermarriage	114	67.4	97	72.4	86	73.5	77	77.0
Jewish groom	66	39.0	58	43.3	50	42.7	44	44.0
Jewish bride	48	28.4	39	29.1	36	30.8	33	33.0
Total	169	100.0	134	100.0	117	100.0	100	100.0

Source: Indiana State Board of Health.

ligion. Some elopements may also be spurious: the couple "elopes"
with the parents' knowledge and consent in order to escape a
formal wedding.

For the same or similar reasons, Jewish couples usually residing
in Indiana doubtless elope to neighboring states, and their intermarriage rate is part of the Indiana picture. Although there is no
way to arrive at an estimate of their number, it must be infinites-
imally small compared to the 169 extrastate couples from Chicago,
Detroit, Cincinnati, Louisville, Dayton, and Toledo, with a combined estimated Jewish population of 415,000 (Indiana's Jewish
population is about 23,000).

INTER- AND INTRASTATE MARRIAGES

Allocation of Interstate Marriages

It is clear that marriages of eloped couples from contiguous
states cannot be allocated to the resident population of Indiana. It
is equally clear that marriages in which both partners are usual
residents of the state are generated by its Jewish population. The
question then is to which state should one allocate marriages between instate and out-of-state residents. The fact that, of the total
of 616 intra- and interstate marriages, 171 (or 27.7 per cent) are
interstate would indicate that interstate marriages constitute a significant practice among the Indiana Jewish population.

A closer analysis of interstate marriages reveals that the *recorded* number of interstate marriages understates very considerably the significance of this practice. Table 6 reveals that in 143 of the 171 marriages the groom did not usually reside in Indiana, and that in only 28 cases did an Indiana boy bring home a bride from out of state. The recorded preponderance of pairs with the groom

TABLE 6

Marriage Rates for Couples with One Spouse Instate Resident, Indiana, 1960–63

Type of marriage	Total		Bride instate, groom out		Groom instate, bride out	
	Num-ber	Per cent	Num-ber	Per cent	Num-ber	Per cent
Inmarriage	120	70.2	103	72.0	17	60.7
Intermarriage	51	29.8	40	28.0	11	39.3
Jewish groom ...	42	24.5	35	24.5	7	25.0
Jewish Bride ...	9	5.3	5	3.5	4	14.3
Total	171	100.0	143	100.0	28	100.0

Source: Indiana State Board of Health.

from out-of-state is due to a technicality related to the place where the wedding is held. Since it is customary for the bride's parents to make the wedding and since a wedding requires a license of the state where it is held, most of the marriages between Indiana grooms and out-of-state girls are not recorded by the Indiana State Board of Health. (The marriage of a girl from Fort Wayne to a young man from Elgin, Ill., is recorded in Indiana, although this couple will most likely live in Illinois. But the marriage of the girl's brother, who owns a business in Fort Wayne and imports his bride from Peoria, Ill., will most likely not be recorded in Indiana.) The state licensing procedure, therefore, does not provide for recording the "true" number of interstate marriages by Indiana residents.

Interstate Marriages Are Arranged Marriages

The analysis of extrastate marriages led to the conclusion that most of them were elopements. It was also found that these impulsive marriages produced a very high level of intermarriage. By contrast, it must be assumed that interstate marriages, which have the lowest level of intermarriage, are what might be called "arranged" marriages—the result of the conscious effort to find a Jewish marriage partner. In some instances the marriage may have been arranged in the literal sense of the word. In others, husband and wife may have met in residential colleges or in summer resorts which are often selected with that end in mind.

Table 6 reveals that there is a considerable difference (11.3 per cent) in the levels of intermarriage between couples where the bride is from Indiana (28.0 per cent) and where the bride is from out-of-state (39.3 per cent). To this writer this differential comes as no surprise. It indicates that couples who tend to adhere to tradition in the selection of a marital partner also tend to adhere to convention in the selection of the *place* of marriage, namely the bride's home.

Jewish Population of Indiana

A deeper understanding of the factors contributing to the formation of inmarriages and intermarriages in Indiana will be gained from a knowledge of the size and distribution of the Jewish population of the state. Since the decennial population census does not list the religion of the American people, no official population statistics are available for the Indiana Jewish community. Current estimates vary from a high of 24,700 for 1960 to a low of 23,305 for 1962, representing about .5 per cent of the state's total population.

The general settlement pattern of Indiana Jews, like that of the Jews throughout the United States, is concentration in the large urban centers. Over 80 per cent (Table 7) live in the five largest of the state's eight urbanized areas: Indianapolis, Gary–Hammond, South Bend–Mishawaka, Fort Wayne, and Evansville. It will be noted that, as these areas decrease in size, so does the Jewish population. The largest aggregation is in Indianapolis (approximately 8,500), the smallest number in Evansville (1,225).

County Specific Rates

The intra- and interstate marriage record data for the state are presented here to reflect their relationship to the size of the Jewish communities. They are divided into one set for the five counties where the Jewish population is concentrated—Marion (Indianapolis), Lake (Hammond–Gary), Saint Joseph (South Bend–Mishawaka), Allen (Fort Wayne), and La Porte (Michigan City)

TABLE 7
Jewish Population of Selected Urbanized Areas, Indiana, 1962

Urbanized area	Total popu-lation, 1960	Estimated Jewish population, 1962		
			Cumulative	
		Number	Number	Per cent
Indianapolis	639,340	8,500	8,500	36.5
Gary-Hammond	478,946	5,500	14,000	60.1
South Bend	218,953	3,000	17,000	72.9
Ft. Wayne	179,571	1,225	18,225	78.2
Evansville	143,660	1,225	19,450	83.5
All others	—	3,855	23,305	100.0

—and a second set for the remaining 87 counties. Part A of Table 8 shows that 490 (79.5 per cent) of the 616 intra- and interstate marriages in the state were solemnized in the five counties listed above. The remaining 87 counties generated only 126 such marriages during the same period. A comparison of the county distribution of intrastate marriages and interstate marriages (parts B and C of Table 8) show them to be virtually identical (and confirms the soundness of the decision to treat both types together). Of 445 intrastate marriages, 355, or 79.8 per cent, were solemnized in the five counties; the corresponding percentage for interstate marriages was 78.9 (135 out of 171).

By separating the five major Jewish communities from the minor settlements and the scattered Jewish population we can ascertain their respective marriage levels. According to Part A of Table 8, their intermarriage levels are diametrically opposed: an intermarriage rate of only 38.6 per cent in the five counties, as compared with an inmarriage rate of only 36.5 in the remainder of the state. To express it in different terms: In the five major Jewish communities of Indiana about two-thirds of Jewish marriages recorded were inmarriages, while in the remaining counties two-thirds of Jewish marriages were intermarriages.

What is the significance of these rates for the survival of the small communities? It has been calculated that a random choice of marriage partners by Jews would yield an intermarriage rate of 98 per cent. Therefore it would appear that even among the so-called small-town Jews of Indiana full random selection of mar-

TABLE 8
Intra- and Interstate Marriages by Counties, Indiana, 1960–63

Type of marriage	Total State		Five Counties[a]		Remainder	
	Number	Per cent	Number	Per cent	Number	Per cent
A. All intra- and interstate marriages						
Inmarriages	347	56.3	301	61.4	46	36.5
Intermarriages	269	43.7	189	38.6	80	63.5
Jewish groom ...	187	30.4	129	26.3	58	46.0
Jewish bride	82	13.3	60	12.2	22	17.5
Total	616	100.0	490	100.0	126	100.0
B. Intrastate marriages						
Inmarriages	227	51.0	196	55.2	31	34.4
Intermarriages	218	49.0	159	44.8	59	65.5
Jewish groom ...	145	32.6	105	29.6	40	44.4
Jewish bride	73	16.4	54	15.2	19	21.1
Total	445	100.0	355	100.0	90	100.0
C. Interstate marriages						
Inmarriages	120	70.2	105	77.8	15	41.7
Intermarriages	51	29.8	30	22.2	21	58.3
Jewish groom ...	42	24.5	24	17.8	18	50.0
Jewish bride	9	5.3	6	4.4	3	8.3
Total	171	100.0	135	100.0	36	100.0

Source: Indiana State Board of Health.
[a]Marion, Lake, St. Joseph, Allen and La Porte counties.

riage partners is not practiced. Still, an intermarriage formation rate of 63.5 per cent supports earlier observations about the disappearing small-town Jew. In contrast, an intermarriage level of 38.6 per cent in the five major Jewish settlements suggests a concerted effort toward group survival. One of the devices employed to keep the younger generation within the Jewish group is examined below.

Mobility and Intermarriage

The overall intermarriage rate of 38.6 per cent in the five counties is a combination of two distinctive sets of rates: an interstate intermarriage rate of 22.2 per cent and an intrastate intermarriage rate of 44.8 per cent (Table 8, Parts C and B). The finding that interstate marriages produce only half as many intermarriages as do intrastate marriages leads to the inference that it is the objective of interstate marriages to produce inmarriages. The selection of a partner from across state lines is a conscious effort to find a Jewish spouse.

An examination of the relationship between inter-county and intra-county marriages (Table 9, Part A) showed a tendency similar to that on the state level. In the five-counties area, the inter-county intermarriage rate was 35.2 per cent, as compared with 46.5 per cent for intra-county marriages, with a combined level of 44.8 per cent.

An examination of the effect of the state of the marriage partners' *birth* on intermarriage yielded interesting data. Since inter-

TABLE 9

Intrastate Marriages by Usual Residence and Place of Birth

	USUAL RESIDENCE							
	Both in same county				Both not in same county			
	5 counties		Remainder		5 counties		Remainder	
Type of Marriage	Number	Per cent	Number	Per cent	Number	Per cent	Number	Per cent
A. Total								
Inmarriage ...	161	53.5	27	36.0	35	64.8	4	26.7
Intermarriage .	140	46.5	48	64.0	19	35.2	11	73.3
Jewish groom	95	31.6	31	41.3	10	18.5	9	60.0
Jewish bride	45	15.0	17	22.7	9	16.7	2	13.3
Total	301	100.0	75	100.0	54	100.0	15	100.0
B. Both born in Indiana								
Inmarriage ...	47	63.5	2	18.2	15	83.3	1	50.0
Intermarriage .	27	36.5	9	81.8	3	16.7	1	50.0
Jewish groom	15	20.3	8	72.7	1	5.6	1	50.0
Jewish bride	12	16.2	1	9.1	2	11.1	0	0.0
Total	74	100.0	11	100.0	18	100.0	2	100.0
C. One born in Indiana								
Inmarriage ...	51	43.2	14	37.8	10	71.4	1	14.3
Intermarriage .	67	56.8	23	62.2	4	28.6	6	85.7
Jewish groom	46	39.0	13	35.1	2	14.3	4	57.1
Jewish bride	21	17.8	10	27.0	2	14.3	2	28.6
Total	118	100.0	37	100.0	14	100.0	7	100.0

Source: Indiana State Board of Health.

state and inter-county marriages have lower intermarriage rates than intrastate and intra-county marriages (all based by definition on usual residence) one should expect a lower intermarriage rate for marriages with one partner born outside the state than for marriages with both partners born in the state. A comparison of Parts B and C of Table 9 reveals that this was true of only one of the four groups: of marriages in the remaining counties where both partners' usual residence was in the same county. In all other groups, marriages with one partner born outside the state showed a higher intermarriage rate than those with both partners born in Indiana (56.8 as against 36.5 per cent; 28.6 as against 16.7 per cent; 85.7 as against 50.0 per cent.

Why should individuals who migrate to the five counties and establish usual residence have a higher intermarriage rate than the native-born residing there? There are several explanations for this. Some in-migrants may not want to have ties with the Jewish community, and may even go to some length to avoid them. Others, who would like to establish contacts with the Jewish community may not succeed in doing so. Their age, occupation, or social status may keep them from becoming part of a social set or clique. As the mobility of the American people increases, there will undoubtedly be a greater need for "social engineering," i.e., community organization which would help in-migrants become part of their cultural group.

Jewish Community Characteristics and Intermarriage

An inverse relationship is presumed to exist between intermarriage and the size of the Jewish community (the number of Jews in a given locality); its density (the ratio of the Jewish population to the total—Jewish as well as non-Jewish—population of the area), and the degree of its voluntary segregation (the concentration of Jews in residential neighborhoods). The greater the size, density, and voluntary segregation, the lower will be the level of intermarriage.

The data at our disposal make it possible, for the first time, to demonstrate the overall effect of size upon the extent of intermarriage. Table 10 reveals that the intermarriage rate increases as the size of the Jewish community decreases. In Marion county the intermarriage rate was only 34.5 per cent, while in Allen and

La Porte counties the rate rose to 54.3 and 54.5 respectively. At the same time, the tabulated information demonstrates graphically the abrupt and almost identical decline of vitality in Jewish communities of less than 3,000, in spite of deviations within this range.

The information also reveals in considerable detail the components of the marriage market. It shows that marriages of Indiana brides to out-of-state grooms greatly bolster the inmarriage rate. The fact that this is not the case in La Porte county, the smallest community with a Jewish population of 500, highlights a general condition: with the decreasing size of the Jewish community, the components of the marriage market either fade away or become negative. Here then is the statistical documentation for the depiction of Jewish communal life and of the marriage market in small Jewish communities, as presented by the author in an earlier study.

Religion of Non-Jewish Grooms and Brides

The question arises whether Jewish men and women who intermarry have a preference for spouses of a particular religion. Table 11, which presents data for intrastate marriages, indicates that for every geographic area Protestants constitute at least 70 per cent of all non-Jewish partners in Jewish marriages. It would appear that this ratio reflects the religious affiliation of the state's population, which is estimated at 71.5 per cent Protestant and 28.5 per cent Roman Catholic. Since, however, in three of the five counties where Jews are concentrated (Lake, La Porte, and Saint Joseph) Catholic church members outnumber Protestant, it is most likely that Jews who intermarry show a decided preference for Protestant marriage partners.

REMARRIAGE AND INTERMARRIAGE

Analysis of the Iowa marriage data revealed a considerably higher intermarriage rate for remarriages (54.1 per cent) than for first marriages (36.3 per cent). The higher intermarriage rate for the widowed or divorced was attributed to the limited supply of eligible mates. It was argued that since the Jewish marriage market in general was found to be disorganized in small Jewish

TABLE 10

Inmarriages and Intermarriages in Selected Jewish Communities, Indiana, 1960–63 (Intra- and Interstate Marriages)

USUAL RESIDENCE

Type of marriage	Total		Groom and bride same county		Groom specified county, bride different county		Bride specified county, groom different county		Groom specified county, bride out of state		Bride specified county, groom out of state	
	Number	Per cent	Number	Per cent	Number	Per cent	Number	Per cent	Number	Per cent	Number	Per cent
Marion County (Indianapolis); estimated Jewish population: 8,500												
Inmarriage	169	65.5	97	58.1	9	75.0	11	73.3	8	100.0	44	78.6
Intermarriage	89	34.5	70	41.9	3	25.0	4	26.7	0	0.0	12	21.4
Jewish groom	56	21.7	45	26.9	1	8.3	0	0.0	0	0.0	10	17.9
Jewish bride	33	12.8	25	15.0	2	16.7	4	26.7	0	0.0	2	3.5
Total	258	100.0	167	100.0	12	100.0	15	100.0	8	100.0	56	100.0
Lake County (Hammond and Gary); estimated Jewish population: 5,500												
Inmarriage	72	62.1	37	56.1	6	75.0	4	44.4	7	77.8	18	75.0
Intermarriage	44	37.9	29	43.9	2	25.0	5	55.6	2	22.2	6	25.0
Jewish groom	26	22.4	17	25.7	1	12.5	3	33.3	1	11.1	4	16.7
Jewish bride	18	15.5	12	18.2	1	12.5	2	22.2	1	11.1	2	8.3
Total	116	100.0	66	100.0	8	100.0	9	100.0	9	100.0	24	100.0

Saint Joseph County (South Bend and Mishawaka); estimated Jewish population: 3,000

	N	%	N	%	N	%	N	%	N	%	N	%
Inmarriage	45	60.0	15	44.1	7	77.8	7	63.6	0	0.0	16	94.1
Intermarriage	30	40.0	19	55.9	2	22.2	4	36.4	4	100.0	1	5.9
Jewish groom	23	30.7	15	44.1	1	11.1	3	27.3	3	75.0	1	5.9
Jewish bride	7	9.3	4	11.8	1	11.1	1	9.1	1	25.0	0	0.0
Total	75	100.0	34	100.0	9	100.0	11	100.0	4	100.0	17	100.0

Allen County (Fort Wayne); estimated Jewish population: 1,225

	N	%	N	%	N	%	N	%	N	%	N	%
Inmarriage	16	45.7	7	31.8	0	0.0	0	0.0	0	0.0	9	81.8
Intermarriage	19	54.3	15	68.2	1	100.0	1	100.0	0	0.0	2	18.2
Jewish groom	17	48.6	13	59.1	1	100.0	1	100.0	0	0.0	2	18.2
Jewish bride	2	5.7	2	9.1	0	0.0	0	0.0	0	0.0	0	0.0
Total	35	100.0	22	100.0	1	100.0	1	100.0	0	0.0	11	100.0

La Porte County (Michigan City); estimated Jewish population: 500

	N	%	N	%	N	%	N	%	N	%	N	%
Inmarriage	10	45.5	5	41.6	0	0.0	2	100.0	0	0.0	3	42.9
Intermarriage	12	54.5	7	58.3	1	100.0	0	0.0	0	0.0	4	57.1
Jewish groom	10	45.5	5	41.6	1	100.0	0	0.0	0	0.0	4	57.1
Jewish bride	2	9.1	2	16.7	0	0.0	0	0.0	0	0.0	0	0.0
Total	22	100.0	12	100.0	1	100.0	2	100.0	0	0.0	7	100.0

Source: Indiana State Board of Health.

TABLE 11

Religions of Non-Jewish Brides and Grooms in Jewish
Intermarriages, Indiana, 1960–63
(Intrastate Marriages Only)

Religion	Non-Jewish brides 5 counties		Remainder		Non-Jewish grooms 5 counties		Remainder	
	Number	Per cent	Number	Per cent	Number	Per cent	Number	Per cent
Catholic	21	20.8	3	7.9	7	14.9	3	16.7
Protestant ...	78	77.2	33	86.8	39	83.0	13	72.2
Other	2	2.0	2	5.3	1	2.1	2	11.1
Total	101	100.0	38	100.0	47	100.0	18	100.0
Unknown ...	4		2		7		1	

Source: Indiana State Board of Health.

communities, with a resultant high intermarriage rate, it can be expected that the rate of intermarriage will be even higher for other marriages (i.e., remarriages).

The Indiana findings suggest the need for modifying this interpretation. While the Iowa tabulations had lumped the previously widowed and divorced into one category, the availability of the original Indiana data made it possible to tabulate the precise previous marital status of grooms and brides. Table 12 is arranged to show the intermarriage rates for marriages with neither partner previously married, with one or both previously widowed, and with one or both previously divorced.

Previous Widowhood

The data reveal a marked difference between the intermarriage rates for marriages with one or both spouses previously widowed and for marriages with one or both spouses previously divorced. The intermarriage rate for previously-widowed marriage partners is much closer to the rate for the never-married-before than for the previously divorced. As a matter of fact, the previously-widowed marriage partners have a *lower* intermarriage rate than the never-married-before, indicating that the widowed make a determined effort to remarry within their faith.

Previous Divorce

While previous widowhood generates a high level of inmarriage, previous divorce status produced a high intermarriage rate in all groups analyzed. It will be recalled, for example, that interstate marriages have the lowest intermarriage rate since they were presumably arranged for Jewish group survival. But even among these (Table 12), the previously divorced have a 5 per cent higher intermarriage rate (27.3 per cent) than the previously never married. In the remaining counties where, because of the relative scarcity of eligible Jews, the intermarriage rate is high for the both-never-married-before marriage partners (59.7 per cent for intrastate and 50.0 per cent for interstate), the comparable rates for the previously divorced are 69.2 and 83.3, respectively.

The divorced can be divided into those who obtain a divorce after having met another man or woman whom they would prefer as husband or wife, and those who have been divorced because their marriage failed and have no immediate prospects of remarriage. For the first, divorce is the device through which the exchange of successive marriage partners is accomplished; the second group experience nothing but the pain of the divorce proceedings and its aftermath. For even in societies with a relatively high divorce rate there is no substantial approval of divorce, and, having been forced into a major act of nonconformity, the divorced person may regain his self-respect and respectability within his social circle by remarriage, even to a person of a different faith.

It is widely held that intermarriage leads to desertion and divorce (though this finds scant support in the few scientific studies that have been conducted) because of irreconcilable religio-cultural differences of the spouses. Let us assume, for the moment, that religious intermarriages generate a higher divorce rate than do inmarriages. However, we now know (Table 12) that a considerable number of intermarriages are remarriages. We also know from an early study of marriage and divorce records in Iowa and Missouri that remarriages are not as enduring as first marriages and that the probability of divorce rises with each successive marriage. These findings clearly suggest *"divorce-proneness among divorced persons who remarry."*

SUMMARY

The ecological analysis of the Indiana marriage records revealed the usual residence of groom and bride as a significant factor in the formation of Jewish intermarriages:

TABLE 12
Previous Marital Status and Intermarriage, Indiana, 1960–63

Type of marriage	Both Never Married		One or both Widowed		One or both Divorced	
	Number	Per cent	Number	Per cent	Number	Per cent
A1. Intrastate: 5 Counties						
Inmarriage	139	67.8	12	80.0	46	35.1
Intermarriage	66	32.2	3	20.0	85	64.9
Jewish groom	43	21.0	1	6.7	57	43.5
Jewish bride	23	11.2	2	13.3	28	21.4
Total	205	100.0	15	100.0	131	100.0
A2. Intrastate: Remaining Counties						
Inmarriage	25	40.3	3	50.0	8	30.8
Intermarriage	37	59.7	3	50.0	18	69.2
Jewish groom	26	41.9	2	33.3	12	46.1
Jewish bride	11	17.7	1	16.7	6	23.1
Total	62	100.0	6	100.0	26	100.0
B1. Interstate: 5 Counties						
Inmarriage	81	77.9	5	100.0	16	72.7
Intermarriage	23	22.1	0	0.0	6	27.3
Jewish groom	20	19.2	0	0.0	3	13.6
Jewish bride	3	2.9	0	0.0	3	13.6
Total	104	100.0	5	100.0	22	100.0
B2. Interstate: Remaining Counties						
Inmarriage	14	50.0	0	100.0	1	16.7
Intermarriage	14	50.0	0	0.0	5	83.3
Jewish groom	11	39.3	0	0.0	5	83.3
Jewish bride	3	10.7	0	0.0	0	0.0
Total	28	100.0	0	100.0	6	100.0
C1. Extrastate: Elopees						
Inmarriage	16	30.8	1	100.0	6	13.6
Intermarriage	36	69.2	0	0.0	38	86.4
Jewish groom	15	28.8	0	0.0	27	61.4
Jewish bride	21	40.4	0	0.0	11	25.0
Total	52	100.0	1	100.0	44	100.0
C2. Extrastate: All Others						
Inmarriage	18	52.9	5	100.0	5	20.0
Intermarriage	16	47.1	0	0.0	20	80.0
Jewish groom	7	20.6	0	0.0	14	56.0
Jewish bride	9	26.5	0	0.0	6	24.0
Total	34	100.0	5	100.0	25	100.0

Source: Indiana State Board of Health.

1. Couples who had eloped from contiguous states to Indiana had the highest level of intermarriage (67.4 per cent). A detailed analysis of these extrastate marriages pointed to a causal relationship between elopement and intermarriage.

2. Couples with one partner usually residing in Indiana and the other outside the state had the lowest intermarriage rate (29.9 per cent). It is assumed that these interstate marriages are arranged marriages or the result of a conscious effort to find a Jewish marriage partner.

3. Couples with both spouses residing within the state produce an intermediate level of intermarriage (49.0 per cent). This means that a Jewish young man or woman who relies on finding a spouse close to home has a fifty-fifty chance of inmarriage.

The Indiana data also made it possible to demonstrate empirically the inverse relationship between the size of the Jewish community and the rate of intermarriage. For the individual residing in a Jewish community in the five counties with the highest concentration of Jews, the chances for inmarriage are substantially improved (with an intermarriage rate of 38.6 per cent). In all other counties, where the Jewish population is small, the intermarriage rate is 63.5 per cent.

The marital behavior of individuals who had previously been widowed stands in sharp contrast to that of individuals who had previously been divorced. The former have a high inmarriage rate, higher than that of individuals who were never married before; the latter have a high level of intermarriage, higher than the one observed among the previously-never-married.

THE SIGNIFICANCE OF THE STUDY FOR GROUP SURVIVAL

The finding that interstate marriages have the lowest level of intermarriage led to the inference that they are arranged marriages. The data therefore underline the wisdom of or necessity for the old Jewish tradition of arranged marriages to secure Jewish group survival. Our inference is further strengthened by the findings that elopements, or so-called impulsive marriages, have an intermarriage level of from 67 to 77 per cent, and that dependency on the local marriage market creates a fifty-fifty chance for intermarriage.

Students of Jewish life in America have repeatedly observed that the size of the local Jewish community is a significant factor in the survival of the Jewish group. The larger the Jewish community, the easier it is to organize communal activities, to effect the voluntary concentration of Jewish families in specific residential neighborhoods, and to maintain an organized marriage market. Conversely, the smaller the local community, the more difficult it becomes to maintain an organized community and marriage market. The intermarriage statistics of the 87 Indiana counties with their isolated Jewish families support the oft-told tale of the "disappearing small-town Jew." An earlier study revealed that, in 1957, the fertility of American Jews had been only two-thirds that of American Protestants and Catholics, and more recent local community studies have shown no upswing in the birthrate. On the contrary, there is some evidence that, like the total birthrate, the Jewish birthrate too has declined since then. Studies of intermarriage in the large Jewish communities would make possible a much more exact evaluation of its significance for the American Jew. Such data, however, do not detract from the value of the Indiana study, which adds weight to the author's earlier contention that, in the absence of large-scale immigration and of a substantial rise in the birthrate, the current level of intermarriage formation is going to be of ever increasing significance in the future demographic balance of the Jewish population in the United States.

The most important book-length study of American
Jewish intermarriage behavior to date is Louis A. Berman's
*Jews and Intermarriage: A Study in Personality and Cul-
ture*. The author, a clinical psychologist by training, has
served as psychotherapist and counselor on the faculty at
the University of Illinois, Chicago Circle. Exploiting
the social fact that Jews attend college more than any other
American ethnic group and that his role as college
counselor gave him access to a rich supply of original case
studies and depth interviews on Jewish-Gentile dating and
intermarriage, Berman rounded out his work by bringing
together the major published research findings on the
intermarriage practices of American Jews in social science
literature. Having to rely mainly on scraps and pieces of
data derived from small-scale and local studies as well as
his own clinical evidence, he concluded that Jewish
intermarriage, low as it still is in comparison with the
other principal religio-ethnic groups, is now growing with
each succeeding generation. Principally a product of
urbanization, secularization, mobility, and intergroup
propinquity, he shows in the following summary that
intermarriage is the pivotal mode of exit from the
Jewish community.

JEWS AND INTERMARRIAGE:
SUMMARY, CONCLUSIONS, DISCUSSION*

Louis A. Berman

At first glance, the topic of *Jewish-Gentile* intermarriage may seem too limited in its focus, too parochial in its scope, to provide a framework for scholarly analysis. We have argued that, on the contrary, the scientific approach favors the selection of a specific and identifiable phenomenon—and that reliable knowledge about intermarriage is more likely to flow from a close analysis of Jewish-Gentile intermarriages in the United States (using comparative materials for purposes of contrast or conjecture) than from a study covering everything or anything that can be labelled intermarriage.

Our study began by asking: What do behavioral science theorists, researchers, and counselors say about Jewish-Gentile intermarriage? What factors do they locate in society, or in the individual, to account for attitudes favoring intermarriage? Additionally, we asked: What can the history and culture of the Jews tell us to account for the attitudes of Jews toward their own group, and toward Gentiles—and of the attitudes of Gentiles toward Jews? What of the discrepancy between the Jews' eagerness and aptitude for intimate participation in the life of the majority, and their stern taboo against marrying into the majority group? What of the discrepancy between the Jews' general lack of concern for religious worship and doctrine, and their special concern for observing the rule of endogamy? Does this pose a *dilemma* for the Jews to resolve (for, as the saying goes, "You can't have your cake and eat it too"), or is this a *paradox* for the observer to understand?

These are the questions that have guided our study. If we were looking only for facts, our report could well have been briefer. But we were also looking for better ways of posing the questions, for promising avenues of thought and investigation, for research-

*Chapter 14 of Louis A. Berman, *Jews and Intermarriage: A Study in Personality and Culture* (New York: Thomas Yoseloff, 1968), pp. 547–60. Reprinted with permission. Footnotes omitted.

able hypotheses for future testing, and for enlightened ways of thinking and talking about intermarriage—whether from the standpoint of behavioral science theory, clinical practice, Jewish group survival, or individual guidance.

What have been the results of this study? What facts have been uncovered, what relationships have been drawn, to change the reader's way of thinking about intermarriage, and of the role of Jews in our culture? What facts have been uncovered to enrich the counselor's understanding of the tensions that underlie a client's manifest conflict over cross-ethnic dating or engagement?

As for the facts, Jews who intermarry—compared with those who inmarry—are more likely to have a history of broken homes and lack of contact with extended family (cousins, aunts, uncles, grandparents) than the inmarrying majority. On the other hand, intermarrying Catholics show a history of conflict with parents, and alienation from the Church. Jews attending a prestige private university hold more favorable attitudes toward intermarriage than Jews attending urban state universities. Jewish *men* are more favorably disposed toward intermarriage, and are more likely to intermarry than Jewish women. Intermarrying Jews marry later in life than inmarrying Jews. Oldest children are *least* likely to intermarry; youngest children and only children are most likely to intermarry. Personality traits favoring intermarriage seem to be related to birth order: intermarrieds are venturesome, slightly unconventional persons who see themselves as "exceptions" to the normal rules of society—shading into the hypomanic and manic personality types.

Jews living in rural areas and small towns are more likely to intermarry than Jews living in cities. Children of recent residents of small towns are more likely to intermarry than children of long-established residents. Jews living in new communities are more likely to intermarry than Jews living in older communities. Reform or unaffiliated Jews are more likely to intermarry than Orthodox Jews.

It has been vaguely sensed that college education and socioeconomic advancement somehow increase the probability of intermarriage, and our analysis of available statistics has clarified these relationships somewhat. Intermarriage seems to appeal to Jews whose socio-economic position places them at the periphery of the Jewish community, or outside of it. (This raises, of course, some interesting questions about cause and effect relationships.)

Intermarriage is therefore likely to occur among the highly upward mobile members of the *salaried* professions; Jewish professors and government experts are more likely to intermarry than Jewish physicians, dentists, lawyers, and business owners. Virtually ignored in the intermarriage literature (although published statistics direct attention to this phenomenon) is the relationship between intermarriage and *downward* mobility. The small town Jewish craftsman, foreman, or other blue collar worker is more likely to intermarry than the Jew who holds a position in business or the professions.

The salaried professional must in most cases leave his home community and live in a geographically mobile Gentile world—unlike the doctor, lawyer, and business owner, who are under no such pressure to leave their community of birth. Intermarriage rates may therefore differ strikingly for town and gown—for Jewish academic faculties, and for Jews in the surrounding community. Intermarriage rates likewise differ radically between Jews living in Washington, D.C.—an administrative center peopled by salaried experts—and Jews living in Detroit, Michigan, a hometown community of business owners and independent practitioners. In arriving at an understanding of the intermarriage phenomenon, little is accomplished by calculating the average intermarriage rate for the country as a whole, compared with identifying the characteristics of Jewish communities in which intermarriage is a rarity, and those in which it has become a commonplace.

How shall we interpret the known relationships between occupational choice and intermarriage? Clinical experience and research interview materials point to Jews who feel at odds with the Jewish community. Some feel that they do not fit into business or the independent professions; that they will never earn enough to satisfy a Jewish wife, please Jewish in-laws, or keep up with Jewish neighbors. Others see a world of opportunity that lies far beyond the Jewish community—a world in which they can share the dignity, prestige, power, good manners, and freedom of the majority group—and escape from the burden of anti-Semitism. (To them, Jews live petty, neurotic, insecure, and provincial lives, and do not abide by the rules of polite behavior.) A Gentile spouse is a natural partner for one who addresses himself exclusively to a Gentile status group.

On the other side of the ethnic fence, we encounter Gentiles who see the Jew as a culture hero—steeped in a tradition of learning, sobriety, achievement, and family loyalty. To these Gentiles, Jewish skepticism, liberalism, audacity, and love of life offer a sane alternative to their kind of Christianity—puritanical self-denial, authoritarianism, and other-worldliness. Jewish intimacy in an unfriendly world seems better than Gentile "friendliness without friendship" (as Henry Murray once described the American culture). Clinical experience points to intermarrying Gentiles whose unstable or broken home background lends a special value to the Jewish tradition of family loyalty and group belongingness. While there are undoubtedly many cases in which conversion denotes little more than polite acquiescence to the wishes of Jewish in-laws, there is no shortage of cases (autobiographical and clinical) in which the search for a Jewish spouse was only one aspect of a larger search for entry into the Jewish community.

One finds, on the other hand, mixed marriages in which both partners seem determined to cast their lot with the Gentile elite. Characteristically, the husband is a Jew who has attained a considerable degree of professional success. His wife is a member of the Protestant elite. The husband is likely to hold membership in a Protestant church, or at least attend church services. They live in an elite Gentile neighborhood, orient their social lives mainly around Gentile friends, raise their children as Protestants, and guide them into elite social groups.

SUMMARY, CONCLUSIONS

The intermarriage sex-bias—the preponderance of Jewish husbands and Gentile wives—is analogous to the sex-bias found amongst Negro-white couples and other mixed marriages in American society; the husband is usually a member of a minority group, and the wife a member of the majority group. Traditionally, Negro and foreign-born men of middle class status have been restricted to majority group wives of low status. (Merton accordingly hypothesized a "trading hypothesis"—the minority group male trades his middle class attainment for his wife's majority group status.) To a significantly greater extent, Jews gain access to high status (or even elite status) Gentile wives—or at least this seems to be true for highly talented and achieving Jewish males. We have hypothesized that the sex-bias in Jewish-Gentile intermarriage is also influenced by the fact that Jewish norms of conduct (e.g., aggressiveness, audacity, intellectuality) match up well with the masculine sex role in Western society, and are incongruous—in many respects—with the feminine sex role in Western society. Hence, Jews are regarded as "wonderful husbands" for analogous reasons that Japanese are said to make "perfect wives."

When the choice of a cross-ethnic mate indicates poor judgment at a practical level, or is accompanied by great inner conflict or reluctance, the clinician looks for neurotic drives toward intermarriage. Classically—both in the folk tradition and in clinical lore—the choice of an out-group marriage partner (or pregnancy through an out-group partner) expresses hostility toward parental authority. There is no shortage of clinical evidence to support this formulation.

"Neurotic exogamy"—as Abraham first labelled it in 1913—is described psychoanalytically as a derivative of the affectionate bond between the intermarriage-prone person and his cross-sex parent or sibling, a bond which inhibits his potency with a love object from his own group. Puritanical modesty training, parental seduction, father-son jealousy, and whatever else implants feelings of sexual inhibition, increases tensions toward intermarriage—for "the exotic is erotic," and the attractive stranger arouses more sexual interest than a partner who resembles one's parent or sibling. It may be argued (as the Levinsons do) that preference for a "contrast choice" is an adaptive mechanism for those whose upbringing renders them inhibited to some degree with a partner from their own group. The custom of finding a Jewish mate who grew up in another town was practiced by more affluent members of the Eastern European *shtetl*. Community exogamy has likewise been found to be the prevailing norm among endogamous Jews of American small towns and of at least one kibbutz in Israel.

Problems of the intermarried may be defined so as to include problems of the partners themselves, of their parents, and of their children. Intermarrieds who adopt a Gentile identity must cope with the inner tension of "self-hatred," as Lewin described it—for adopting the Gentile way of looking at the world leads one to look down upon the Jews. They must also face the uncertainty as to whether their children, despite the parents' best efforts to groom them for the Gentile world, will be accepted into Gentile society.

Intermarrieds face a special problem of mutual accommodation when it becomes evident—as it sometimes does—that the partner of Gentile origin is motivated to get *into* Judaism, while the Jewish partner hoped his cross-ethnic mate would help him find a way *out* of the Jewish community.

Jewish wives by conversion must learn to live on indefinite probation, and withstand the skepticism and hostility of the more hidebound members of their adopted community. The serious proselyte often finds a natural ally and protector in the rabbi, drawn into an intermarriage situation by parents who plead with him to break up the match, and a Jewish fiancé who wants as little to do with the rabbi as possible. The Gentile fiancée is often the most cooperative member of the party, the most deferential to the rabbi, and the most appreciative of his primary role—a teacher of Judaism. Intermarriage involves the rabbi with parents and young adults whom the rabbi might otherwise never meet, and confronts the rabbi with a bewildering array of responsibilities, frustrations, temptations, and opportunities.

The impossible demands of distraught Jewish parents, who insist that the rabbi show their offspring the error of his ways, present the rabbi with an enormous temptation to castigate the parents for backsliding in the practice of their faith, for failing to maintain a thoroughly Jewish home, and for having neglected the religious education of their children. To the rabbi who sees intermarriage as a *religious* problem, it may seem absurd to behold such suffering by parents whose religious commitments are nil. The paradox melts away, however, when one views intermarriage *not* as the violation of a religious taboo, but as a threat to the community solidarity of the Jews, and to the emotional security of parents whose status seems to depend upon their contribution to the solidarity of their group. Available data, however limited, indicate that Jewish fathers suffer more deeply and chronically from this status insult than Jewish mothers. This fact may point to the peculiar emotional meaning of intermarriage to the middle-age Jewish male, or to the superior psychological resilience of women in the Jewish group.

After five or fifteen years of marriage, a person may have the same psychological needs but the *priority* of these needs may undergo considerable change, and an ethnic identity which seemed of little worth in young adulthood may assume a new and special value as one assumes the role of parenthood, as one approaches middle age, or as one copes with the crises of living. A regrouping of one's personal loyalties is difficult for the person who has committed himself too deeply to a fixed social position.

What of the children? Clinical materials point to conflicts in identity from which mischlings suffer—and this seems to be especially clear in the case of those boys who feel attracted to the cultural identity of their mothers—as if their choice creates a disturbing ambiguity over their sex-role identity. A study of mischling undergraduates at Harvard University shows widespread and pervasive insecurity over ethnic identity. It appears that a majority of these youths were explicitly indoctrinated at home, in church, and in Sunday school, to regard themselves as Protestants —and were psychologically unprepared to be regarded by their peers as half-Jews. At the high-school-age level, the mischlings seemed to find their Jewish peers friendlier than the Gentile youth for whose company the mischlings had been so carefully groomed. (Ironically, the high school period is a time when Jewish youths begin to make Gentile friends, and when mischlings feel drawn into Jewish friendship groups.)

As college students, Rosten's mischlings may protect themselves against disclosure of their Jewish background, as they circulate among the Protestant elite—uneasy over the risk entailed in their social feint. They are more introspective and more sensitive to their own negative qualities than their Jewish or Gentile classmates. They would like to be both Jewish and Gentile, but this specifies a role for which there seems to be no available model. Compared with mischling boys, adoption of a Gentile identity seems to be easier for mischling girls—especially for those whose father is a born Catholic, who were themselves raised as Catholic, and brought up in a town where anti-Semitism is at a minimum.

Writers on intermarriage who show the widest range of viewpoints—from uncompromisingly anti-intermarriage to uncritically assimilationist—find one issue on which they can agree: *mixed marriages are not well adapted to raising children.* A sizeable percentage of intermarried couples avoid the problem of mixed parenthood by remaining childless.

A review of the textbook literature on acculturation reveals a viewpoint on intermarriage which does not particularly fit the available facts on intermarriage. A sampling of widely-used textbooks on social psychology indicates an uncritical bias in favor of *maximal* assimilation into the dominant group, by every available means. To support this view, current textbooks cite a 1937–1938 interview study of Italian Americans, while many more recent studies in minority group living are ignored. Virtually ignored in the social psychology textbooks are the classic and penetrating essays of Kurt Lewin on the topic of Jewish adaptation to a Gentile world. The pro-intermarriage bias of the behavioral science Establishment is perhaps most wildly evident in Anselm Strauss' interpretation of interview material obtained from a group of Japanese war brides. In a book intended to help close the gap "between research and its utilization by family-serving agencies and organizations," Foote and Cottrell pass along Strauss' conclusion that ". . . heteronomy now seems less likely than was formerly thought to interfere with marital harmony."

What the social psychology textbooks say about intermarriage is largely by implication. What they say explicitly about the Jews revolves almost exclusively around the topic of anti-Semitism, perhaps because that is virtually the only aspect of the Jewish phenomenon that has been subjected to rigorous and extensive behavioral science research (undoubtedly because that is how research funds have been allocated). Accordingly, the college student of social psychology may learn a good deal about the personality structure and values of the tribesmen of New Guinea (thanks to Margaret Mead's indelible portrayal of the Arapesh, Mundugumor, and Tchambuli), but all the student learns about the Jews is that they tend to be disliked, and that social psychologists have devised ingenious ways of measuring the degrees, modes, and sources of this dislike.

What little the behavioral scientists have written about Jewish traits is rather directly related to anti-Semitism, demonstrating how the personality of the Diaspora Jew has been warped and blighted by the insecurity of minority group status, and the insult of anti-Semitism. Perhaps David Riesman deserves a special commendation for the courage to set down explicitly the negative attitude toward Jewish life which his behavioral science colleagues indicate by indirection.

Cahnman and Glazer are probably representative of their behavioral science colleagues in their preference for regarding the Jews as a *religious* group—as "Americans of Jewish faith"—and in explicitly counseling against the perpetuation of social norms which cannot be justified on religious grounds. Their conception of Jewish life in America seems to be governed by what might fit neatly and unproblematically alongside the two major faiths— by what the prevailing American norms seem to "permit," rather than by what the integrity of the Jewish culture would seem to require.

In scientific discussion, *truth is more controversial than opinion.* In the absence of facts, anyone is entitled to whatever opinions he chooses to voice. But when facts are available and they are either distorted or ignored so as to favor certain cherished opinions, the seeds have been sown for a controversy of serious proportions. When all the available facts on intermarriage are assembled, they raise serious questions about how adequately the American behavioral scientist has been dealing with facts that conflict with his social ideology and with the prevailing norms of faculty society.

The Jews, who have survived so many adverse circumstances over past centuries, will also survive the biases of contemporary behavioral scientists. That is not the problem. The problem is this: today's behavioral scientists are asking for (and getting) an increasingly important role in the formulation of social policy at many levels—in the administration of hospitals, schools, and universities; in the training of soldiers, teachers, executives, and other decision-makers; in the fulfillment of the American promise to Negroes and other disadvantaged groups; even in the reduction of international tensions and in the maintenance of world peace. When the academic community embraces a particular social ideology or point of view, what happens to their capacity to deal critically with the entire range of available facts? What happens to their interest in looking at facts that do *not* quite fit their ideology? For the intellectual community, this is probably the most basic and far-reaching question our study can pose.

As for the behavioral scientists' characterization of the Jew as a warped and neurotic creature, the question is not whether this is fair to the Jews (they have put up with worse than that), but whether this is fair to the student, and whether this is fair to the development of social psychology. The Jewish phenomenon is intrinsically too interesting, too rich a source of data on human adaptation, audacity, creativity, and group cohesiveness, to escape the serious and well-rounded study of behavioral scientists indefinitely. What they stand to learn from studying the Jewish phenomenon in depth will certainly be enriching, and may even be useful toward developing a theory of human adaptation to a world of uncertainty and change.

In an age of alienation, when group therapy offers "instant mishpocho," when the task of psychoanalysis has shifted from loosening too rigid an identity to firming up too diffuse an identity, when belongingness seems at least as important as autonomy, when the ability to acquire knowledge is more adaptive than craftsmanship or physical prowess; at such a time in human history, Jewishness is worth something. American novelists and essayists know this, the mass entertainment industry knows this, military historians know this, rabbis know this (from the number of Gentiles who seek access to Judaism without regard to intermarriage). Jews know this too; though they may find it impossible to explain *why* they value their Jewishness, they value it. Sooner or later, behavioral scientists are bound to discover this too.

Those who look hopefully for some signs of progress in behavioral science thinking need not be entirely disappointed. The Leo Srole of 1940 who, with Lloyd Warner, predicted the disappearance of the American Jews in five generations (and reported but was at a loss to explain the unique productivity of Jewish women), is not quite the same as the Leo Srole of 1960, who was willing to conjecture that Jewish family life "often hypothesized by psychiatrists as potentially pathogenic . . . may conceivably be eugenic on balance. . . ." The Nathan Glazer of 1957, who could find no reason why ethnic groups should survive in America, and saw a future for Jewish survival in America only in the form of a religion, is not quite the same as the Nathan Glazer of 1963 who (with Daniel Moynihan) decided that the ethnic group in America is *not* a transitional phenomenon, but has become *a new social form.*

Throughout this work an effort has been made not only to describe what we know about the topic of Jewish identity and intermarriage, but also to sketch out areas of ignorance and ambiguity, and thereby point to various research problems. We need to know more about the prevailing norms of modesty training—the specific behaviors by which the incest taboo is communicated and maintained—and how they influence the individual's attitudes toward the entire gamut of possible sex partners. We need to know more about maternal warmth and maternal seduction, and the conditions under which one form of treatment shades into the other. We need to know more about the extended family—its role in the early socialization process, and in the lives of growing children, adolescents, and young adults. We need to know more about the Jewish "sense of being." We must move up from the anecdotal and clinical level, to a more systematic and empirical level of knowledge concerning life experiences that foster Jewishness as a source of self-actualization, and experiences that make Jewishness a burden and a handicap. We need to better define the "What's wrong with Jewish girls?" problem, and at least identify the prevailing patterns of sex-role adjustment in the Jewish group. We need to know more about intermarriages that lead to good partnerships and successful parentage. We need to know more about mischlings who, unlike the Harvard group, have been brought up as Jews. We need to know something about the influence of these successful families on the attitudes of their Jewish friends and neighbors. We need to know more about the interrelationships between attitude toward intermarriage and a variety of other variables: physical appearance, occupational choice, sexual adjustment, family experience, life goals.

Some of the most fruitful research findings on the Jews have emerged, as we have demonstrated, from larger community studies which describe Jewish life in its natural context—vis-a-vis the larger community. The Lenski study, for example, gave a unique characterization of Jewish group cohesiveness precisely because it compared the Jews of Detroit with their Protestant and Catholic neighbors, on various indices of group solidarity. The reader will recall, however, that some of Lenski's provocative findings lack the stamp of statistical significance because his total sample included fewer than 30 Jews. Veroff's pioneering nationwide sampling of thematic apperception test responses likewise showed provocative differences between Jewish and Gentile fantasy productions, but again (in the opinion of McClelland) Veroff's Jewish sample was quite small. Gurin, Veroff, and Feld conducted a nationwide interview study to assess the mental health of American adults. When they turned to religious group differences, in the analysis of their data, they compared Protestants and Catholics —and simply set aside all those who did not belong to either of the "two major religious groups": Jews, Buddhists, atheists, and others.

In each of the above three studies the populations were obtained through probability sampling methods, and the number of Jews drawn into the sample was roughly proportional to their representation in the population sampled. To double the number of Jewish respondents, however, would *not* necessitate doubling the entire study group; this could be accomplished through the established and familiar survey research procedure of over-sampling. If the investigators were interested in collecting data on Jewish attitudes and adjustment patterns, this could have been done without adding significantly to the cost of the research project. Entirely apart from what could be learned through special research projects, much more could be learned about the Jewish ethos from prevailing community studies—if behavioral scientists were interested in doing so.

The Jewish reader who hoped to find in this work a battle plan for fighting intermarriage, or a program for safeguarding the Jewish tradition of endogamy, may be dismayed that the author calls for research on good and successful intermarriages. It is the viewpoint of this author that intermarriage *per se* is not a threat to Jewish survival, though some of the conditions that lead to intermarriage are disruptive of Jewish group life. Throughout this work an effort has been made to identify those underlying conditions, so that the Jewish community can address itself more deliberately to its problems.

Jews who worry about intermarriage probably make too much of the fact that those Jews upon whose heads fell the worst blows of anti-Semitic savagery—the Jews of Germany—were a highly intermarried group. Simplism and uncritical moralizing have no place in the analysis of this complex and tragic phenomenon of our times. It should at least be borne in mind that the Jews of Poland, who adhered much more faithfully to the tradition of endogamy, were long subjected to a virulent brand of domestic anti-Semitism before Hitler introduced Nazi efficiency into the black art of persecution. And it may also be borne in mind that there have been highly intermarrying communities, like Italy, where anti-Semitism never really flourished.

What Rabbi Mordecai Kaplan once said about the Jewish view on restrictive real estate covenants must also apply to a sane view on intermarriage, or even mixed marriage. No Jew takes pride in a fellow Jew's preference for living in an all-Gentile neighborhood, but a Jew's right to live where he wishes (and with the marriage partner of his choice) cannot be denied in an open society. An open society where ethnic boundaries survive because they serve the individual's need for variety, for belongingness, for continuity, for identity, for authenticity—where ethnic boundaries are not prison walls—where those Jews who would rather be Gentiles and Gentiles who would rather be Jews are equally free to cross the boundary and find a more congenial ethnic home—that, in this writer's opinion, is a good society.

PART SIX

Postmarital Consequences of Intermarriage

The postmarital consequences of intermarriage are among the most hotly debated and, at the same time, least understood aspects of the phenomenon from a scientific point of view. Conservatives, particularly those with vested interests in ethnic groups, are usually quick to claim that there is nothing but maladjustment and unhappiness in store for intermarried couples and their children. Social and cultural differences, they claim, generate marital and family discord rather than harmony. Isolated from both sets of relatives and the community, the couple is likely to lack social support in achieving interpersonal adjustment, and the children of intermarriages allegedly suffer from marginality and ambiguous identification. But, we may ask, how representative are the cases that are pointed to in illustrating these and other alleged deleterious consequences of intermarriage?

To shed some light systematically on this problem, Biesanz and Smith decided to study the adjustment of intermarriage between Panamanians and Americans on the Isthmus of Panama. Cross-cultural studies of this type are useful because they are based upon ethnic intergroup relations different from those normally found in American society. They show that adjustment depends, in addition to the general factors in all marital adjustment, upon the ethnic intergroup situation, especially the three variables: prestige, informal-primary organization, and formal-secondary organization for each ethnic group represented in the intermarriage.

ADJUSTMENT OF INTERETHNIC MARRIAGES ON THE ISTHMUS OF PANAMA*

John Biesanz and *Luke M. Smith*

An interethnic situation makes it possible and necessary to view marriages as points of contact and adjustment between groups rather than—the usual approach—between the spouses as individuals. Therefore along with factors general to marriage, such as age at time of marriage and number of children, there are two situational factors specific to interethnic marriage: the intergroup situation, and the diverse ethnic norms of the two groups.

The intergroup situation involving native Americans and an ethnic minority in the United States is different from the intergroup situation involving Panamanians and Americans on the Isthmus. The native Panamanian ingroup has relatively low prestige, but is well organized on both informal-primary and formal-secondary levels, e.g., has long-established kinship and friendship groups and also its own government; whereas the American outgroup is poorly organized on informal-primary but well organized on formal-secondary levels, e.g., has few long-established kinship and friendship groups but separate government and a high degree of industrial discipline. Ownership and operation of the canal, achievements in tropical sanitation, military and naval establishments, and consequent domination of Panamanian economy all give the American outgroup high prestige and require a high degree of formal-secondary organization.

Thus the constants in any intergroup situation are the ingroup and the outgroup; the variables are the relative degrees of prestige, relative degrees of organization on the informal-primary level, and relative degrees of organization on the formal-secondary level.

American Sociological Review, Vol. 16, No. 6 (December 1951), pp. 814–22. Reprinted by permission.

EFFECT OF THE INTERGROUP SITUATION UPON
GENERAL FACTORS IN MARITAL ADJUSTMENT[1]

Some of the general factors in marital adjustment operate in the same way as they do in ethnically homogeneous marriages in the United States; others are affected by the intergroup situation; while still others operate differently because of specific differences between Panamanian and American cultures rather than because of the intergroup situation.

1. *Age at Marriage; Socioeconomic Status; Education.* These general factors operate in approximately the same way as they do in ethnically homogeneous marriages in the United States[2] and therefore are not clearly affected by the intergroup situation on the Isthmus. Happiness tends to increase with age at marriage,[3] with socioeconomic status,[4] and with education.

2. *Length of Courtship; Time Married; Number of Children.* Contrary to general marriage findings (those dealing with factors general to marriage) in the United States, comparatively short courtships do not result in adjustment difficulties. Couples commenced courtship almost as soon as they met; most of them married within a year.[5] Panamanian women are predisposed in favor of the high prestige American husband, while the American male migrant to the Zone is socially unorganized at first and hence more likely to marry outside of his ethnic group. The longer he waits the more he is likely to establish social relationships with his ethnic group; and the more he learns that Americans look down upon Panamanians and resist their attempts to break into the monopoly of American positions and possessions. It may be deduced that if he marries early upon arrival, later relationships with his compatriots will not greatly affect the happiness of his Panamanian marriage. *When the outgroup spouse is socially unorganized on the informal-primary level, marriage into an organized ingroup tends to restructure the situation for him and to prevent unhappiness in marriage,* even though later he becomes more integrated into his own group.

As would be expected, then, there is no significant decrease of unhappiness with length of time married.[6] This is contrary to some general marriage findings in the United States.

Happiness increases with the number of children.[7] General marriage studies in the United States show that the number of children does not increase marital happiness unless they are wanted. Since Panamanian women normatively desire a number of children, it may be concluded that the presence of children keeps the social situation of the husband structured toward the wife's ethnic group and in this way aids marital adjustment.

3. *Rural-Urban Origin; Previous Marital Status.* Contrary to general marriage findings in the United States, which show the greatest marital adjustment when the spouses are of rural origin, the Isthmian data show Panamanian-American spouses to be happiest when the Panamanian wives are from urban areas. The two large cities of Panama are contiguous to the urban areas of the Zone and therefore allow a greater degree of assimilation than would be true of rural areas, while Panama's rural culture is little removed from its primitive Indian background. Mere urban origin in itself, however, is not the important factor, but rather the degree of assimilation to the group of the high prestige spouse. Thus when racial background and education are held constant, there are no significant rural-urban differences.

Previous marital status findings are incomplete. The mores do not sanction divorce;[8] and in addition to legalized marriage there is the consensual union, where couples live together without civil or religious ceremony, and the mistress system. These patterns being only semi-institutionalized, it is difficult to obtain intimate data about them.

DIVERSE ETHNIC NORMS AND THEIR OPERATION WITHIN THE MARRIAGE

Because spouses are culture bearers, diverse ethnic norms operate within the marriage as well as through pressure of culture bearers outside the marriage.

1. *Language.* Wives are more often bilingual than husbands. Americans usually reveal disdain for Panamanians by refusing to learn Spanish; Panamanians who desire to profit by contacts with Americans must learn English. Panamanians feel sensitive over such concessions, which define them as the low prestige group on their own soil. Bilingual spouses have the highest marital adjustment. Where only one language is spoken higher adjustment

occurs when that language is Spanish, because the American husband is able to participate with his wife's well-established circle of friends and relatives, who desire contact with him; whereas he has few friends and relatives of his own on the Isthmus, and these do not desire contact with the low prestige group.[9]

2. *Cuisine.* Adjustment problems do not arise. Urban Panamanian diet includes many high prestige American foods, and the privilege of buying at low cost Zone commissaries reinforces this tendency.

3. *Religion.* Such differences also produce few problems.[10] Marriages of Catholics are only a little happier than mixed marriages. The explanation may lie in the socially unorganized position of the Protestant spouse. On the Isthmus, away from the controls of his family of orientation, there is little pressure from Protestant in-laws. Furthermore, Panamanian men are rarely expected to go to church except for family rituals such as weddings and funerals.

4. *Institutionalized Roles of Husband and Wife.* Norms in each ethnic group relieve the strains caused by parallel norms in the other. American husbands typically give their wives more liberty, attention, and faithfulness than do Panamanian husbands; and Panamanian women often admittedly prefer American husbands for these reasons. Panamanian wives typically are more passionate, home loving, and submissive than American wives, and are willing to grant their husbands greater liberty. Marital happiness is positively correlated with sharing activities, husband's help about the house, and wife's participation in management of income.[11]

Where a Panamanian man marries an American woman, the different institutionalized roles increase marital strain. It is generally agreed that these marriages have a far smaller chance of success than the former type. Furthermore, in the comparatively few intermarriages of this type on the Isthmus, the courtship and wedding usually occurred in the States, the American wives entering the marriage with little understanding of Panamanian culture.

5. *Attitudes of the Spouses toward the Ethnic Differences.* Happy as well as unhappy wives tend to attribute their happiness or unhappiness to the fact that their husbands are American, and husbands do the same with respect to their Panamanian wives.[12] One American says his wife is neat, another complains his is

slovenly; both say, "Panamanians are like that." The same is true of thrift and extravagance, jealousy and understanding, diligence and laziness.

ADJUSTMENT OF THE INTERMARRIED COUPLES TO THE
INTERGROUP SITUATION

On the Isthmus, the most important extraneous factor interfering with adjustment of Panamanian-American couples is American prejudice against other nationalities and races, and the tendency to categorize all Panamanians as colored "Spiggotties." The high prestige American outgroup, of course, desires to keep its relationships and possessions for its own members, and therefore strongly disapproves of any move to break into this monopoly. Hence the rationality of the prejudice. Panamanians, on the other hand, not only desire the prestige of relationships and things American, but also as members of the ingroup feel entitled to greater consideration.

1. *Kinship Relations*. In the intergroup situation in the United States, marital adjustment may be difficult because the families of orientation exert pressure upon mixed couples to swing them over to one ethnic group or the other. On the Isthmus the intergroup situation may actually aid adjustment. American in-laws are usually far away, and if they disapprove—as they are very likely to do where racial mixture is involved—they can do little about it. However, they often make their disapproval felt when the husband takes his bride home for a visit or tries to settle in the States—where she looks darker than she did on the Isthmus. Wives are seldom taken back to the States on visits to in-laws.[13] Indirect relationships through correspondence, however, are positively correlated with marital happiness.[14]

As for the husband's relationships with his Panamanian in-laws, nearly all husbands visit them and receive them at home. They usually approve of him,[15] and change to disapproval only in distinctly unhappy cases. In view of the advantages of obtaining relationships with the high prestige Americans, one would expect this tolerant behavior.

2. *Friendships*. Shared friendships are positively correlated with happiness.[16] Yet, most wives also say they and their husbands have most of their friends among their respective national-

ities. Apparently sharing friends is less important to adjustment than is liking and respect for the other spouse's nationality.

3. *Status in the Community.* These marriages carry little or no stigma in the Republic, whereas in the Zone they are condemned and the couples snubbed. A man may find a job promotion blocked by his marriage to a Panamanian. Wives who are rated as "colored" tend to be unhappier than those rated as "white."[17]

In view of these manifestations of prejudice, would it not seem likely that marital adjustment would be more difficult in the Zone? Yet the sample shows the opposite to be true: Zone dwellers are rated as happier. Also, nearly half the wives (18 out of 41) living in the Republic prefer the Zone from the standpoint of economy, quiet, and convenience. It may be concluded that Panamanian women prefer the Zone, in spite of the prejudice against them there, because it is the territory of the high prestige group, and residence there is a symbol that the Panamanian woman is successful in achieving the ends for which she married an American.

Furthermore, it is easy for the Panamanian wife to retain her kinship and friendship relations in the Republic, which is just across the street from Zone territory. On the other hand, even if the couple lives in the Republic, the American husband usually works in the Zone, retains his ties with compatriots, and feels the pressure of their prejudices.

SUMMARY

Adjustment of interethnic marriages depends, in addition to general factors in marital adjustment, upon the intergroup situation and the diverse norms of the two ethnic groups. The intergroup (ingroup-outgroup) situation comprises three variables for each group: relative degrees of (1) prestige, (2) informal-primary organization, and (3) formal-secondary organization.

In one combination of these variables, the high prestige group is the outgroup and relatively unorganized on the informal-primary level, whereas the low prestige group is the ingroup and well organized. In this combination strong prejudice is exhibited against the intermarried couple by outgroup members wishing to retain their monopoly of high prestige positions and possessions. The ingroup wife is able to obtain prestige symbols of her husband's group without losing security in her own—because *her* group has stronger informal-primary organization. Prejudice of the high prestige group, then, has little effect upon marital adjustment. The husband is able to use the relationships in his wife's group to restructure his situation, and his resultant feeling of respect for his wife's group contributes to her security there. It is these attitudes toward the other spouse's ethnic status as a *total* status which are basic to adjustment.

Diverse norms of the two ethnic groups are important only when they symbolize this total status, happiness as well as unhappiness being attributed to the other spouse as a typical bearer of his ethnic norms. Even those norms which relieve or heighten strains caused by parallel norms in the other culture are effective mainly because of the total status meaning given to them.

Reduction of these ethnic differences through assimilation is successful chiefly if it is in the direction of preserving the wife's security with her relatives and friends (e.g., *husband's* linguistic and religious assimilation), while on the other hand allowing her to obtain some of the prestige of the outgroup to which her husband belongs (e.g., outgroup norms giving the wife greater liberty and respect than afforded by ingroup norms).

NOTES

1. This analysis is based primarily on schedule interviews of 66 Panamanian women married to Americans, 41 of whom reside in Panama City or its suburbs and 25 in the adjacent Canal Zone. For method, and social data on the spouses, see John Biesanz, "Inter-American Marriages on the Isthmus of Panama," *Social Forces*, 29 (December, 1950), 159–163.

   Inasmuch as the study is focused upon interethnic relations rather than marital relations *per se*, it was not useful to have a representative sample of all Panamanian-American marriages. Therefore the sample was not enlarged beyond the relatively stable unions which happened to be selected by the middle class students who did the interviewing. Thus the specific effects of the interethnic marriages could be studied in isolation from other factors. Cases of desertion were omitted as abnormalities.

   Happiness ratings: (1) *By interviewer:* very happy, 9; happy, 36; average, 14; unhappy, 3; very unhappy, 2; no answer, 2. (2) *By interviewee:* very happy, 23; happy, 30; average, 10; unhappy, 2; very unhappy, 1. Where there is a discrepancy, the *interviewer* rating is used, as it is more conservative by one point in the scale and possibly more objective. *Computations are based on the 64 interviewer happiness ratings.*

2. Ernest W. Burgess and Leonard S. Cottrell, Jr., *Predicting Success or Failure in Marriage*, New York: Prentice-Hall, 1939; Lewis M. Ter-

man *et al., Psychological Factors in Marital Happiness,* New York: McGraw-Hill, 1938; Clifford Kirkpatrick, *What Science Says about Happiness in Marriage,* Minneapolis: Burgess Publishing Company, 1947; Harvey J. Locke, *Predicting Adjustment in Marriage,* New York: Henry Holt and Company, 1951.

3. Happiest, above 30; less happy than majority, below 20; least happy, 26–30.

4. Couples with servants show greatest marital happiness. Only half the wives of skilled workers are happy or very happy. Nine-tenths of the professionals are in happy categories, the white collar group almost as high.

5. Largest group—the happy—typically courted about a year, all others about 8 months (range: 2 weeks to an atypical case of 6 years).

6. Couples were married from less than one up to 26 years (average 4.2; median 5.3 years).

7. Very happy: 0.45 children per year of marriage; happy 0.30; average 0.28; unhappy 0.18; very unhappy 1.0 (each couple with one child and married only a year). Children per couple: very happy, 1.6; happy, 1.4; average, 1.0; unhappy 2.3 (these 3 couples include one married 26 years with 4 children); very unhappy, 1.0.

8. Only 6 Panamanian wives were divorcees. None was very happy, none very unhappy; only one was unhappy, 2 average, and 3 happy.

9. While 7 out of 10 happy husbands know Spanish, only 4 out of 10 average and unhappy do. Nine out of 10 happy wives and 8 out of 10 average and unhappy ones know English. Children are more likely to be bilingual in the happier homes.

10. In 40 cases both spouses are Catholic; in 3 both Protestant; in 20 husband is Protestant, wife Catholic; no data on religion and happiness in 3 cases. It may be that many couples do not marry because of these differences, so that those who do are not typical adherents of their respective faiths. Cf. Burgess and Cottrell, *op. cit.,* 87–88.

   Arrival of children makes adjustment more difficult, although the sample is too small to warrant generalization. More Protestant husbands disapprove of Catholic baptism for their children in average than in happy homes.

11. All except unhappy wives share much leisure time, more so in happier cases. In 39 cases husbands share household tasks. In the happy categories, 4 out of 5 help their wives, only half in the less happy categories. Fourteen of the 15 who plan expenditures jointly, and 21 of the 30 in which the wife holds the purse strings, are happy or very happy, but only 2 of the 17 whose husbands manage the money are so rated; no data on 2 cases.

12. Only 5 wives (2 of them unhappy) say that Panamanians make better husbands.

13. Only 14 of the wives report such visits.

14. All but one of the very happy wives correspond regularly with in-laws; two-thirds of the happy, one-sixth of the average, and none of the unhappy wives.

15. He has won over all but 3 of the 9 disapproving families in the happier marriages and 2 of the 4 in the average.

16. Seven of the 9 very happy report mutual friendships, 22 of 36 happy, 6 of 14 average, 1 of 3 unhappy, and neither of the 2 very unhappy.

17. Of the 21 "white," 19 are happy or very happy, but only 26 of the 41 "mixed"; no data on race or happiness in 4 cases.

Another research approach to understanding the
postmarital consequences of intermarriage in terms of the
intensity and quality of the alleged strain and disharmony
between husband and wife is available in the study of
war-bride marriages. Anselm Strauss, the author of the
following essay on American-Japanese intermarriages
involving servicemen who were among the occupying
forces in Japan at the conclusion of World War II, sought
to test the assumption that racial intermarriage is
particularly conducive to such strain and disharmony.
Among other things, his findings show that this assumption
represents a gross oversimplification. Indeed, some
Oriental-Caucasian intermarriages he studied were so
stable and harmonious that they revealed greater
compatibility than many racially endogamous marriages.

STRAIN AND HARMONY
IN AMERICAN-JAPANESE
WAR-BRIDE MARRIAGES*

Anselm L. Strauss

Several days after the surrender of Japan, American occupation
troops landed on the alien shore expecting hostile, if controlled,
responses from the conquered population. As everyone now
knows, this expectation proved quite unwarranted: the Americans
—according to fiction and fact—winning hearts by politeness,
gifts, and democratic ways, and the Japanese displaying cooperation, charm, real or feigned lack of resentment, and other unantici-

*Reprinted by permission from *Marriage and Family Living* (now
Journal of Marriage and the Family), Vol. 16, No. 2 (May 1954), pp.
99–106.

pated virtues. Within a short time the Americans with customary forthrightness, and often in disregard of official regulations, were establishing various kinds of relations with Japanese women. Sooner or later they wished to marry and to bring their wives home. Although Public Law 271 was passed in December, 1945, to permit servicemen's brides to enter the United States, the law made no provision for Japanese or other oriental war-brides. Not until July, 1947, was the law amended; and only then, and for a very short period, were soldiers in Japan allowed legally to marry Japanese in American ceremony. After August, 1950, marriage was again permitted.[1]

It was official army policy for several years to discourage inter-marriage in Japan. Aside from informal pressures, the policy was implemented by placing a series of formal barriers in the way of marriage. To get married a man had to obtain the permission of his commanding officer, had to go through an interview with his chaplain who usually tried to dissuade him, had to produce proof of his single status and his ability to support his wife; while her record in turn was checked by the Japanese authorities to screen out known prostitutes and criminals.

Pessimistic predictions were made about these marriages on the grounds of what the couples would experience in America in the way of race prejudice and in-law reception. Differences in religion, in language, and in East-West mentality were foreseen as disruptive factors. In the words of two rather sympathetic journalists, "Nothing much but time and bitter experience can overcome great hazards like language difficulties, racial question marks, and the separation of truth about America from dreams of America as expounded by home-sick soldiers and distorted movies."[2]

There was and is made a ready assumption that Oriental-Caucasian marriages are subject to greater strains than the ordinary marriage. Students of the family and of social structure also make this assumption about interracial and other types of in-termarriage since exogamy is viewed as presenting additional stresses and fewer institutional bulwarks than does endogamy. In this paper I wish, on the basis of data gathered on war-bride marriages, to challenge this assumption, which though often true in general, does represent a substantial oversimplification. My contention is that, as in other unions, the strains that occur in

Japanese-American marriages are patterned and relatively predictable. These strains are related to the ways that husband and wife have been socialized during their respective premarital years, and to the ways that they handle their respective conceptions of personal identity both with regard to each other and to significant other persons. Hence some Japanese-American marriages are likely to be quite "stable," and to involve fewer major stresses than a great many marriages between native Americans.

The materials that will be presented in support of these assertions are drawn from a study being carried on at the University of Chicago under the joint sponsorship of the Family Study Center and the Race Relations Center. . . . The data at hand are adequate to challenge the customary assumption about intermarriage discussed above.[3]

SELECTION: WHO MARRIED WHOM

The conditions under which interracial contact and intermarriage take place are probably highly important for the outcomes of these marriages. There is always social selection of those who meet and those who marry. In postwar Japan, American troops followed customary American practices of dating, picking-up, and propositioning women. Many men eventually lived with their paramours. For monetary, romantic, and other reasons, Japanese women responded to American advances: and possibly those sectors of the Japanese population who dated and "shacked up" were more specially selected than the American side of the equation. Of those who dated, visited, and lived together, relatively few married. Much contact was casual or expedient. Furthermore soldiers broke marital promises, changed their minds, deserted their girls before and after marriage, and undoubtedly some Japanese girls did likewise. From both sides pressure against marriage was brought to bear. All this points to a severe selective process for those who did marry in the end.

The couples interviewed in the Chicago study are further distinguished by the fact that they are living in Chicago—generally for one of three reasons. They come to Chicago because the husband is a professional soldier and must go where he is stationed; or because they wish to live near the husband's parents; or they have come to Chicago to be near other war-brides, sometimes after living in the husband's small town. Couples usually live, therefore, at or near army installations, and with or near parents or other war-bride couples. We have interviewed hardly any suburban couples, because they are difficult to locate. We do not have among the couples any who have made their homes under rural or small town conditions; nor of course do we have couples who have returned to Japan to live or who have never left Japan. We would assume that under all those different conditions the strains incurred in living with an interracial partner would be correspondingly different, rather than that interracial marriage is relatively homogeneous.

Consider now some of the distinguishing characteristics of the Chicago couples: for these characteristics are clearly related to their becoming wed. The median age of brides at the time of formal American wedding was twenty-two years, which is a little less than the average age of marriage for Japanese females.[4] This was, then, a group of girls which was ready to marry. Few of the women were older than twenty-four—so these were not the desperate moves of very over-aged women. Some are from small towns, though most are urban; but almost all met their husbands in cities where the men were quartered. Usually the women were working so that they were easily available for GI approach. Frequently they went out with the men on dates, and often lived with them, without parental knowledge or sanction. Generally speaking these were girls who no longer lived at home, and were away working for their own support. Although of respectable social standing,[5] economic conditions in postwar Japan made it easy for women to get work and to receive parental permission for doing so. Few parents, however, encouraged marriage with Americans and a great many at first opposed it; but none of the families were actively seeking mates for their daughters in the well-known Japanese style. The girls were therefore uncommitted to Japanese males either by contract or understanding; and few had any courting contact with Japanese men. As for relations with their families, with hardly an exception the women had no real obligations to support their families financially (they would have to be only daughters to bear this responsibility); nor were they heavily emotionally dependent upon their parents. None was committed to an occupational career; nor were they deeply committed to any Japanese institution or organization whose representatives might have exerted pressure against intermarriage.[6]

The American husbands at time of marriage tended either to be young, having entered the army at an early age, or above the average age of American husbands at marriage. (Their average age at marriage is twenty-four.) A few men married considerably younger women than themselves, and sometimes these constituted second marriages. Their fathers are almost all skilled or semi-skilled laborers, and their own occupations are mainly professional soldiering, semi-skilled or skilled labor, or white collar (which is not surprising since we are studying only large-city residents). These are not career-men or upwardly mobile aspirants. Their average education is correspondingly low: high school or partial high school. Like their wives they were at time of marriage uncommitted by previous marital agreements. Not one man broke an engagement or a firm understanding with an American girl. They had no strong institutional affiliations that acted to block marriage: their church attendance, for instance, is spotty or non-existent; they belong to few organizations; and their ethnic allegiances are generally nil or weak. Sometimes the men married before announcing the *fait accompli* to parents; but more often they wrote home before hand, receiving enthusiastic or grudging approval. But there was little direct or strong family interference. If the man was strongly attached to his family he expected no real opposition to his bride upon her appearance in America. If he was not particularly close to his family he was apparently willing to take his chances with their responses. None of the men were responsible for more than partial financial support to their parents.

Granting that the selection profile for another group of war-bride marriages (residing, say, in the state of Kentucky) would be somewhat different, the picture that emerges is this: these are persons who have no obligations—to family, to other institutions, or to an occupational career—strong enough to block mixed marriage. There was, presumably, terrific pressure both externally (from institutional representatives) and internally (from conscience and allegiance) to prevent intermarriage when men had considerable career aspirations and/or were receiving strong opposition from parents to whom they were obligated or upon whom they were in some deep sense dependent.[7]

It is generally several years after the couples first meet that they get to America. During the period of courtship and first living together, before or after marriage, a great many problems typical of courtship and early marriage were faced and handled. These included matters of content and timing having to do with food, sex, play, work, finances; also the handling of argument, of learning mood, temperament, and marital tactic. In addition there were such matters, in this intercultural situation, of learning how to communicate, of handling the women's parents, of making the shift from dating to housekeeping and from simple housekeeping to becoming parents. By the time these couples are interviewed by us the differences of age, class, religion, and education apparently do not make for great marital strain. It is very probable, however, that these differences operated overseas to prevent initial contact, to prevent the development of strong affectional relations; and undoubtedly helped prevent passage from merely living together to getting married. None of the areas noted above appear to be central foci of strain in the marital relations of our subjects.

During the early years of marriage there are a series of potential stressful areas or points other than those just discussed. These have not so much to do with personality or temperamental characteristics, as with such structural matters as making transitions of allegiance and identity from one family to another or setting up obligations to both or neither branches; of separation from former peer-groups or realignment of relations with them; and the like. In a certain sense these are universal issues that must be handled—institutionally or otherwise.[8] Without detailing a great number of these stress points, around them we can organize discussion of strains and lack of strains in war-bride marriages.

TYPES OF STRAINS

Certain kinds of strains—at least for this period of the ever-evolving marital relationship—appear to be relatively infrequent and relatively mild. This is of theoretical as well as practical importance, for it signifies that mixed marriages may avoid certain strains that are operative in many endogamous marriages. The point is, however, not so much their infrequency as the fact that such strains do not appear in some mixed marriages for good and determinable reasons, while they appear in many American-American marriages. Other strains appear in interracial marriages but they are in no way specific to such marriages. They represent an inability to solve precisely the same kinds of relational problems that confront many non-interracial unions.

1. *Strain attendant upon symbolic separation from one's family.* The relations of marital partners to their respective families is a universal problem and must be handled. In some societies the transfer of one partner away from his own family and into the family of his or her mate is institutionally arranged and facilitated. In other societies there exist traditional modes for adopting the new member without requiring him to leave his own family. And, of course, elsewhere the marital couple may be expected or allowed to form a new family unit without much obligation or allegiance to parents or relatives. In America, the prevalence of in-law conflict indicates a certain lack of institutionalization and considerable indecision concerning which family will claim or win major loyalty, the man's family or the woman's.

In Japan, girls are socialized in such a fashion that they expect to leave their families with requisite transfer of obligation and allegiance to husband, and to husband's family if he has one. Furthermore, the postwar period was such that our Japanese subjects made the symbolic move away from their families through such experiences as living away from parents, working away from home, and through living with their prospective husbands before asking parental permission. Parental opposition to marriage seems not to have left much residue of guilt, shame, or stress that shows up in desire to return to Japan, restiveness at being half a world away, or in unfulfilled obligations to parents. Many of the brides would like to go back to Japan to visit, to show their children to their families: but their motivation is to see Japan once again, to let parents see the children, or even to visit with an elderly parent once more before death intervenes.

Two unusual cases involving much marital strain will serve to highlight the mechanics of the more usual transfer of family allegiance. One girl was unusually dependent upon her mother, was in her own words a spoiled child who had only a minimum of household duties. After marriage she and her husband lived in her parents' house, and the husband often complained that instead of sleeping with him she often slept in the mother's room.

This is, for our Japanese subjects, an extremely unusual child-parent relation; and it shows up in the post-American period in fantasies of return to Japan and in transfer of the load of affect to the husband's father—whom she would like to take for a visit through Japan sans husband! Another woman is an only child, hence responsible for carrying on the support and name of her family. Her guilt at having come to America is extreme. A major part of her marital strategy is to persuade her husband to return to Japan and take up the support and name of her parents' family. She tells her husband that his parents have a number of children but that her parents have none, and that it is only fair therefore that they return to Japan. Our interviewer witnessed a family drama when the husband returned to the house from work and was instantly and without ado attacked by the wife who demanded that they return to Japan and that he adopt the family name of her father.

2. *Strains deriving from strong institutional loyalties.* Institutional pressure on these highly selected interracial couples was never severe in Japan and it seems not to cause much strain in America. For instance, suppose that the woman were a devout Buddhist and that the husband was highly antagonistic to her remaining that much of a Japanese, or to her being Japanese in quite that way. Or suppose that he were a devout Catholic and that his wife was antagonistic or openly indifferent; or that she were a member of certain Japanese organizations that warranted her spending a great deal of time among non-war-bride Japanese. A notable omission in the lives of these couples is organizational affiliation of any kind. Some wives belong to the local war-bride club, but this is hardly a vigorous or absorbing preoccupation for most. A few brides have become Catholics, thus avoiding possible sharp institutional differences between themselves and their husbands. Since a great many of the recreational activities of both partners take place in the home or in the homes of other war-bride friends, not many outcroppings of organizational tendency are, as yet, appearing. Thus a considerable potential source of strain in the marriages of native Americans is almost automatically eliminated.

3. *Strains attendant upon career and mobility aspirations.* The Japanese wives sometimes work, either because they are childless and hence bored or because extra income is desired; but they

are not career minded. Neither do the women exert much pressure upon their husbands to improve themselves occupationally or in status. Although some women come from a higher comparable class than their men, the American standard of living is generally so much superior that the class difference does not cause the women to make great material demands of their husbands. Unlike many American wives, they do not seem to make great demands, or successively increasing ones, upon their husbands to supply them with money for clothes and other status symbols. Occasionally when such changes in consumption habits do occur —as with one wife who learned from her mother-in-law—husbands will complain that "she is becoming too Americanized in some ways." The war-bride, associating as she does frequently with other war-brides, is rather protected against major changes in consumption tastes and status aspirations, although army-husbands sometimes complain of competition for household goods among their wives. The lack of demand is reciprocal, for husbands do not require their wives to take up a career or to become mobility-conscious; nor do the husbands puzzle their wives and strain their loyalty by themselves changing in midstream. In a very few marriages where the men are pursuing more long-range occupational plans there is evidence that the wives go along without quite understanding the sustained drive; but great marital strain does not yet occur, as it may someday, because the pursuit of status has not yet made excessive consumption demands of her. A related point is that there is, in these mixed marriages, a divorce of job and wife. Hence no great requirements are laid upon the wife for occupational purposes, such as developing skill in social relations. Occasionally, among those couples who have mobility plans, there is tension of the kind that occurs among American couples: the wife does not keep up with current events, does not quite hold her own in public gatherings, does not quite fulfill intellectual requirements.

4. *Strains attendant upon separation from, and formation of, peer group relations.* Like separation and entry into families, peer group relations must be handled. In some societies the marital couple is given institutional aid with this set of problems. In America, of course, a marriage can be prevented by the failure of a prospective mate to win the approval of the other's close friends —or vice versa; and after marriage the marital union can falter

and founder on peer group allegiances. But with our Chicago war-bride couples there is no competition among rival sets of pre-marriage friends; neither does the wife confront the problem of how to get her husband accepted and liked by her old friends. Unlike the practice in many American marriages, there seems not to be very much introducing of wives to men's friends either, although this of course does happen. The problem, in a sense, is avoided by the male who quite often pays the price of associating solely with a clique of other interracial couples. This association is facilitated by residence near or at army installations, or by residence near other war-bride couples. The problem of fitting in the wife with the husband's peer group is avoided also when small town men yield and move into Chicago so that their wives may have Japanese companionship. The willingness of husbands to find their friends almost solely among other mixed couples bespeaks a readiness to go along with, or be concerned with, their wives' need for Japanese gesture and conversation. Only very occasionally are there clearly visible strains stemming from peer group loyalties. The most prevalent, although usually not very severe, are found in the army group where the husbands —following occupational as well as class custom—would like a fair amount of purely male conviviality. When the men's friends are part of an occupational world that the wife cannot easily penetrate (such as the world of popular musicians), then, quite as in American marriages, stressful relations are abetted. There is one instance, among our interviews, which by its very unusualness highlights the relative simplicity of peer group realignment necessitated by most of the marriages. A middle class male married a Japanese girl of good status: previous to marriage she had dated and established very friendly relations with several American officers now living as civilians in Chicago. The husband chose his wife with his own college friends in mind, but since he now lives in Chicago where none of them reside, he has succumbed to his wife's interest in her American male friends; so that their friends are neither his own friends nor other war-bride couples, but his wife's American friends and their wives.

5. *Strains arising from the occupational transition of the male.* The Japanese brides do not aspire to much, occupationally speaking, but they do require "steadiness." When their husbands remain in the army, and the women are satisfied with this status, then

there is no particular strain deriving from occupation. Likewise if the man has a job or occupation to return to after being overseas, then there is little strain. But quite as in other marriages the husband may feel constrained to, or be pressured to, change his occupation. Japanese wives sometimes do not wish to face the prospect of having their husbands sent overseas, or do not wish to have to make the adjustments of living in still another country, so they force their husbands out of the army. The man may never have been anything other than a professional soldier, either because he had been in the army for a long while or because he went in as a youngster—so that he feels insecure in the civilian world and incompetent at non-army work. One husband had been a professional jazz musician since he was fourteen, and had toured all through Japan playing with bands while he was a soldier; but on his return home was pressured both by mother and wife to abandon "that kind of life." Yet he feels he knows no other.

6. *Strains arising from relations with the husband's family.* The picture given by interviewees is that the husband's parents generally greeted their daughters-in-law warmly at first and without visible racial prejudice or ethnocentric manifestations. Almost without exception, the first few months after return to the United States were spent with or near the husband's parents. Many in-laws appear to have played an important part in the acculturation of the bride, teaching her about shopping, about kitchen equipment, and the like. This relatively open-armed policy of greeting the Japanese bride is interesting in view of what might ordinarily be expected to happen if a son announced that he was going to wed a Nisei. However the problem of the initial reception is rather different than setting up satisfying and enduring relations. The wife of the professional serviceman does not particularly face this problem, partly because the couple do not live near the parents and partly because the husband would not remain in the army if he were not already rather independent of his family. Some of the husbands are small town boys who have moved to Chicago mainly because the wife needed Japanese companionship, and we take this to mean that enduring and satisfying relations were not consummated with the husband's family.

Failure successfully to enter the male's family is especially stressful when the husband is very devoted to his parents. Even when the wife tolerates his family or is fond of it, her husband—as in any marriage—may experience conflicts of loyalty. If wife and in-laws virtually reject one another, and the male is unwilling to give up his parents, then strain is at a maximum. Quite as in non-interracial marriages, some war-bride couples experience this kind of severe strain. Three cases will serve as illustration. The first illustrates the role of strong ethnic affiliation. A husband who has been reared in an Italian immigrant family has not been able to make a proper bridge between both sides of his family equation: especially as his parents speak no English and view his wife as a great disappointment because she is not Italian. The husband has worked out unstable compromises around scheduled family visits and his wife is currently maneuvering to get him to return to Japan. Another husband married his wife believing that because her family had treated him warmly, had indeed almost adopted him, that his Japanese wife would sink readily into the bosom of his own warmhearted family. This has not happened, and his wife, who furthermore feels guilty about abandoning her own parents, is demanding that they return to Japan. In a third and more tragic marriage, a Japanese woman killed her child and attempted suicide. Here the interviews revealed an almost complete lack of understanding between parents and daughter-in-law, compounded by the son's allegiance to his parents and a limited ability to empathize with his wife. The wife was staying at the time of her attempted suicide with the parents while the husband was overseas. Another possible outcome of in-law reception—one that sometimes occurs in American marriages—is that the wife may be so well received by her in-laws that this close relationship will cause stresses between herself and her husband. Although there are occasional signs of this in the mixed marriages, they are rare and the resulting stresses are mild.

SUMMARY AND CONCLUSIONS

Contrary to the usual assumption that interracial marriages, like other exogamous unions, are peculiarly subject to strains and instability, we have argued that the strains incurred in war-bride marriages are much like those in more endogamous marriages. We have further suggested that many strains indeed are less likely to occur in mixed marriage than in many non-mixed marriages.

The occurrence or lack of occurrence of these stressful issues is complexly determined. It is not merely a matter of gross cultural differences necessarily leading to domestic clash. This is not to go overboard and claim that homogamy between husband and wife is of no importance in marital selection or in the evolvement of domestic fates. However the easy assumptions that interracial marriages are doomed to destruction or that the couples must have something extra special to make a successful go of the marriage are much oversimplified notions. Romanzo Adams' fine volume *Interracial Marriage in Hawaii*,[9] although it promulgates the special ability notion, inadvertently presents suggestive support for our conclusion. In a table contrasting divorce rates for endogamous and exogamous racial marriages for each group in Honolulu County (1927), it appears that for some groups the divorce rates are much higher for the endogamous marriages.[10] His table and our study make clear the need for reevaluation and restudy of exogamous marriages with particular attention paid to the special conditions of contact, selection, and group structure.

NOTES

1. "Between June 22, 1947, and December 31, 1952, 10,517 American citizens, principally Armed Service Personnel, married Japanese women. Over 75 per cent of the total Americans are Caucasian." (Private communication, February 1953, from J. B. Pilcher, American Consul General.)

2. J. E. Smith and W. L. Worden, "They're Bringing Home Japanese Wives," *Saturday Evening Post*, 224: 29, January 19, 1952.

3. About 45 Caucasian servicemen and their Japanese wives have been located in the Chicago area. Thirty of the men and fifteen of the women have been interviewed: the men by a Caucasian ex-GI (Boyd Peyton) and the wives by a Nisei woman (Mrs. T. Mukoyama) who speaks fluent Japanese. Some background data were also gathered from wives by a Japanese-born woman, Miss Y. Kimura. Several Nisei-war-bride and Negro-war-bride couples have been interviewed for contrast. Interviews were conducted at the couples' homes, husband and wife being interviewed separately as far as was possible. Interviews took between two and three hours and were of a relatively unstructured form.

4. The median period of time intervening between first meeting and marriage was 1½ years.

5. Father's occupations: 2 farmers, 7 laborers, 5 white collar workers, 4 professionals, 8 proprietors.

6. Many girls were pregnant before date of legal American marriage, although often an agreement to get wed seemed to exist before preg-

nancy. Pregnancy ought not to be overstressed as a selective pressure since many children were born of unions that never eventuated in marriage.

7. *McCalls* magazine recently published a full length novel by James Michener (*Sayonara*) which deals with the romance of a middle class army career officer, the son of a General, and a Japanese career woman, a dancer. The rhetoric of dissuasion employed by the hero's father—in terms of the difficulties of intermarriage, of security versus romance, of harm to career—is beautifully calculated to appeal to the son; and the motives appealed to presumably are very well understood and sympathized with by the readers of the magazine.

8. Cf. R. Merton, "Intermarriage and the Social Structure; Fact and Theory," *Psychiatry*, 4: 361–74, 1941.

9. New York: The Macmillan Company, 1937.

10. *Ibid.*, p. 224.

One of the traditional and commonsense techniques
to avoid strain and promote harmony in religious
intermarriage is for one of the mates to convert to the
faith of the other. We have already noted that the orthodox
and conservative branches of Judaism insist on the
premarital conversion of the non-Jew to Judaism
before they will recognize and officiate at the ceremony.
Although the Christian religions do not make conversion
obligatory in intermarriage cases, there is nevertheless
pressure of varying intensity by church authorities and
family members to bring about the conversion of the
outgroup partner for the sake of marital harmony and the
proper socialization and clearcut identity of the marriage's
offspring.

Conversion may also be an aftermath of the intermarriage. In the essay that follows, Lazerwitz presents
data and generalizations about the Chicago metropolitan
area comparing the identity characteristics of those who
intermarry and who are converted on the one hand,
with those who intermarry but fail to convert, and finally
those who merely change denominations within their faiths.

INTERMARRIAGE AND CONVERSION:
A GUIDE FOR FUTURE RESEARCH

Bernard Lazerwitz

BACKGROUND

The characteristics and consequences of intermarriage and conversion have been long-standing major concerns and "scare"

Excerpt from *The Jewish Journal of Sociology,* Vol. 13, No. 1 (June
1971), pp. 41–63. Footnotes omitted.

topics among both Jews and Christians. In turn, these concerns have stimulated a large number of research endeavors. Among the very recently published works are the studies by Goldstein (1968) of Springfield, Massachusetts and, with Goldscheider (1968), of the Providence, Rhode Island, Jewish Communities; Axelrod *et al.* (1967) on Boston Jewry; Sklare and Greenblum's (1967) study of a contemporary Jewish suburb; Gordon's (1967) case studies of conversion; and Rosenthal's (1963) investigation into intermarriages in Washington, D. C., and the small Jewish communities of Iowa. Elsewhere, research is becoming equally productive, intermarriage data being developed for the Jews of Australia by Lippmann (1969), for Italy by Pergola (1969), for Canada's Jews and Christians by Heer (1962), and even for Israel by Cohen (1969). The characteristics of intermarriages and conversions amongst United States Protestants and Catholics have been recently investigated by Greeley (1964); Croog and Teele (1967); and Salisbury (1964 and 1969).

Collectively the studies of Jewish intermarriages have revealed the following demographic information:

a) Low, but increasing, intermarriage levels. The United States Census Bureau's (1958) Current Population Survey, taken in March 1957, reports that 7 per cent of existing Jewish marriages were with non-Jews. However, all researchers agree that in this century the percentage of Jews married to non-Jews rises considerably with the number of generations in an industrial diaspora country. For example, the Springfield and Providence surveys by Goldstein (1968: 145–48) and Goldstein and Goldscheider (1968: 155–57) report that 4.4 and 4.5 per cent of Jewish households were based on intermarriages but that the children of respondents have intermarriage rates of 9 per cent and 6 per cent, respectively.

b) Intermarriage rates appear to be highest in large growing Jewish communities and in the very small ones. For instance, Rosenthal (1963: 16) reports that a substantial (for the United States) 13 per cent of Washington, D.C., Jewish marriages were intermarriages, and that the small Jewish communities of the state of Iowa averaged a 42 per cent intermarriage rate between 1953 and 1959.

c) Many more Jewish men intermarry than do Jewish women.

d) The intermarried have a higher proportion who are in their second, or more, marriage. For example, Goldstein and Goldscheider (1968: 164–65) report an intermarriage rate of 24 per cent among those 40 to 59 years old who have married more than once but one of only 4 per cent among those of this same age group married just once.

e) The typical convert to Judaism is a non-Jewish woman marrying a Jewish man. Furthermore, according to Goldstein and Goldscheider (1968: 157) the conversion rate is on the increase. Among their intermarried couples 60 years old or older, none of the non-Jews had been converted to Judaism. Among those intermarried couples under 40 years, 70 per cent of the non-Jews had been so converted.

f) All students of intermarriage agree that very few Jews are converted to other faiths.

g) Goldstein and Goldscheider (1968: 164), Goldstein (1968: 150), and Rosenthal (1963: 30) report less intermarriage with increasing amounts of Jewish education.

Students of Protestant-Catholic intermarriages have found:

a) Rather sizable Catholic intermarriage rates. For example, Greeley (1964: 3) reports that 12 per cent of his respondents in a national sample of Catholics were intermarried. The Current Population Survey of March 1957 reported that 21 per cent of married Catholics had non-Catholic spouses and 9 per cent of married Protestants had non-Protestant spouses.

b) As in the case of the Jews, Greeley (1964: 8) finds that the intermarriage rate increases as the proportion of the Catholic population declines.

c) Unlike the case of the Jews, Greeley (1964: 6) finds that Catholic women are considerably more likely to intermarry than are Catholic men. Salisbury (1964: 420) also states that more Protestant women intermarry than do their men.

d) As among Jewish intermarriages, Salisbury (1964: 424–25) reports a divorce rate of 14 per cent for Protestant-Catholic marriages in contrast to 5 per cent for marriages in which both spouses are Catholics and 8 per cent when both are Protestants.

e) As with Jews, most conversions to Catholicism or Protestantism are results of intermarriages. After examining the available research literature, Salisbury (1964: 420–22) concludes that there are about equal conversion rates among the Protestant and Catholic religious communities.

f) Salisbury (1969: 126–27) observes that Protestant women are converted at a higher rate than Protestant men and Catholic men and women.

g) Both Greeley and Salisbury report that those who intermarry become less involved with their religions. Those in Catholic "invalid" intermarriages are the least likely to raise their children as Catholics or to send them to Catholic parochial schools. Finally, Catholic women who marry higher social status Protestant men are converted at a higher rate than are Catholic women who marry equal or lower status Protestant men.

h) Salisbury (1964: 421) reports a greater likelihood that children of intermarriages who have Catholic mothers will be reared as Catholics. Croog and Teele (1967: 97–98) qualify this by saying that Catholic upbringing is likely for the children of low status intermarriages who have Catholic mothers, while Catholic women married to high status Protestants are more inclined to rear Protestant children.

The research literature on the intermarried, then, does an excellent job of presenting their demographic and social status characteristics. By way of contrast, information on the group identity factors among the intermarried is rather scarce. This article seeks to narrow this gap in our knowledge in the following two ways:

a) Presenting data on the group identity characteristics of those who are converted and those who intermarry without being converted.

b) Contrasting converts and those couples who intermarry without conversion with Jewish and Protestant denomination changers, with third generation American Jews, and with white Protestants and Catholics.

The final goal is to present a set of generalizations to be tested on the large quantity of intermarriage data now being gathered by the United States national Jewish population survey.

Source of data

The intermarriage data to be presented were gathered as part of a survey of religio-ethnic identification in the Chicago, Illinois, metropolitan area. The survey involved 572 Jewish, 464 white Protestant, and 257 white Catholic interviews. All respondents resided in Cook County (including Chicago) or contiguous areas in eastern DuPage and southern Lake counties in Illinois during 1966 and 1967. A disproportionately selected and multistage area probability sample was used to pick respondent housing units within each religio-ethnic community. Then, within sample housing units one respondent 20 years old or older was selected for interview by the use of the Kish adult selection tables (1965: 398–401).

This survey yielded merely 63 Jewish intermarriages, consisting of 11 conversions to Judaism, 3 conversions from Judaism, 29 marriages with Protestants, and 20 with Catholics. There were 138 Protestant-Catholic intermarriages including 35 conversions *to* Protestantism from Catholicism and 25 conversions *from* Protestantism to Catholicism.

It is clear that the small number of interviews with those who had intermarried or been converted requires us to handle the data with considerable awareness of their limitations. Despite this, in the judgment of the author, the quality of the data is adequate for the task of contrasting those who marry within and without their religio-ethnic communities and for reaching conclusions to be tested by more ample data.

The conceptual scheme

The previous analyses of these data from the Chicago area survey have been the exploration of the components and consequences of religio-ethnic identification. By the use of similar research upon religious and ethnic identification, such as is found in Glock and Stark (1965) and Lazerwitz (1953), together with concepts developed during the survey's design stage, eight theoretical dimensions of religio-ethnic identification were developed and measured by a set of equivalent indices.

These identity dimensions and their measurements are:

1) Religious behavior: this component is measured by an index of religious behavior formed from such standard items as

church and synagogue attendance on the sabbaths and the yearly religious holidays, etc.

2) Pietism: this dimension is concerned with the more intense religious experiences and practices, and is equivalent to Lenski's (1961: 22–24) concept of devotionalism and the Glock and Stark (1965: 20) experiential component. It is measured by an index formed of items such as private prayer, religious fasts and abstinences, etc.

3) The intellectual: this covers a respondent's formal religious education and knowledge together with participation in less structured learning situations such as religious summer camps and adult religious study classes. Hence, an index of religious education is formed from all these items.

4) Religious organizational activity: this consists of an index measuring activity in religious and ethnic voluntary associations and charities.

5) Ideological: this dimension covers both traditional beliefs and those beliefs now current among the better educated and informed members of a religious grouping. For this survey only a traditional beliefs index has been formed.

6) Attitudes towards and concern about co-religionists in the rest of the world. For the survey this was confined to Jewish concern about Israel and has been measured by a Zionism index.

7) The parental role: this dimension covers what a respondent's parents do for him religiously and what a respondent, in his turn, does as a parent. Children's religious education and parental concern over religious intermarriage are included. This dimension has been established by two indices. The first index covers childhood religious memories, childhood attendance at services, and parental religiosity; the second index covers the actual religious education given, or intended to be given, to their children by respondents.

8) The ethnic element: this covers the concentration of friends and courtship within one's religious and ethnic grouping and is measured by an ethnic index based upon such question items.

The basis of the operational indices involves our viewing people as relating to their religious community in one of the following ways:

a) Involving themselves in both an active and consistent manner. For example, this means that such people relate to churches or synagogues by going to weekly services *and* observing the various yearly religious festivals *and* observing the several religious fasts and acts of self-denial.
b) Involving themselves in a somewhat active but inconsistent manner. For example, such people, if Jewish, might eat on Yom Kippur but not eat bread during Passover.
c) Involving themselves in an infrequent manner. This could consist of going to religious services just a few times a year.
d) Involving themselves not at all.

The use of these four categories frees one of too great a concern over which particular question to ask in any of the eight identity dimensions. Any series of questions which cover the behavioral and attitudinal aspects of an identity dimension in a way which permits expression of varying amounts of activity and consistency will furnish adequate operational categories.

In order to get enough survey cases into the analytical categories, each of these eight identity indices had to be divided into a high level composed of respondents who were consistently involved on the various items forming an index; a low level composed of respondents who were slightly or not at all involved on the various items of an index; and a medium level composed of the remaining respondents.

Intermarried respondents have been separated from the other respondents by a series of questions which ascertain the religious preferences of past or present spouses in contrast to the religion in which respondents have been reared. Anyone who reported now being married, or having been married, to someone of a faith different from that of his childhood has been considered intermarried. Converts were separated out by a series of additional questions about the faiths in which respondents had been reared in contrast to their present faiths. Those who reported being reared as Jews, Protestants, or Catholics but were now members of another one of these three faiths have been considered converts. Such converts were asked extra questions about their childhood homes and early religious experiences and education. In Jewish housing units with intermarriages or converts, both spouses were interviewed. In such Christian households only one adult was interviewed.

Jewish and Protestant denomination changes were ascertained by asking in which denominations respondents who had not been converted had been reared and what their present denomination affiliations or preferences were. Where childhood and present denominations did not match, respondents were classified as denomination changers. For example, Jews who were reared in the Orthodox denomination but are now Conservative or Reform Jews have been put into the denomination change category.

SUMMARY OF FINDINGS

A. Converts

1) Converts usually melt successfully into their new religio-ethnic community.
2) They are often religiously and organizationally more active than those born into a religio-ethnic community.
3) They come of parents who were marginally attached to their childhood faiths.
4) Converts have received less religious training and education than other members of their childhood faiths.

B. Spouses of converts

1) The spouses of converts, too, are quite active religiously and organizationally in their faiths.
2) They have received considerable religious training and education.
3) They have a childhood and adolescent history of activity in their religio-ethnic communities.
4) Hence, as fairly solid members of their religio-ethnic community, it is to be expected that they would only intermarry with marginal members of other faiths,
5) and that such marginal members would regard it as "the natural thing" to be converted.
6) Typically, it is the men who become spouses of converts and the women who are the converts. This applies to all groups. Hence, even among intermarried Jews, it is expected that intermarried Jewish women will often be more remote from Judaism and more frequently converted to other faiths than intermarried Jewish men.

C. *Religiously heterogeneous marriages*

1) Those who intermarry without conversion will frequently be marginal religio-ethnic members marrying marginal members of other religio-ethnic groups.
2) They will frequently come of parents who had reduced, or marginal, religio-ethnic attachments.
3) They will have had less religious training and education than most members of their childhood faiths.
4) After marriage, they and their spouses will frequently further reduce, if not fully eliminate, any involvement with both their childhood faiths.
5) Such people often deliberately seek out marital partners from other religio-ethnic groups. In contrast to the more accidental set of factors which result in a "core" member of a religio-ethnic group intermarrying (and which often produce a convert), the people falling into this type frequently seek intermarriage or are highly indifferent to religio-ethnic backgrounds.
6) If a marginal man marries a not-so-marginal woman, their children will be brought up in the wife's faith, but usually the man will not be converted.
7) Typically, the presence of different, and marginal, faith backgrounds in the same family will neutralize any tendencies towards religio-ethnic activities. If such a situation becomes intolerable with regard to the rearing of children, such a couple will seek out a mutually "neutral" faith such as Unitarianism in the United States.

D. *Denomination changers*

1) This group differs little from most members of their faith.
2) In all probability their change of denomination is frequently a function of geographical or socioeconomic mobility rather than meaningful religious change.
3) More traditional denominations will find that members change to those less traditional denominations which better facilitate adjustment to and activity in modern urban industrial society. Hence, the children of Orthodox Jews become Reform or Conservative Jews; children of fundamentalist Protestants become members of mainline Protestant denominations. Since the changes from the eastern European orthodox milieu have

been so great and abrupt, such denominational changes are considerably more frequent among Jews than among fundamentalist Protestants, who have undergone a lesser and slower rate of social change.

E. A Typology

Slotkin (1942: 35–39), in a case study of Chicago Jewish intermarriages, proposed eight types of intermarried person: a) the unorganized or demoralized; b) the promiscuous; c) the adventurous; d) the detached or isolated; e) the rebellious; f) the marginal; g) the acculturated; and h) the emancipated. This early characterization of the intermarriage process stressed the destructive effects of immigration and poverty upon Chicago's Jews which resulted in, according to Slotkin, 30 per cent of the intermarriages involving deviant personalities. The other 70 per cent of the intermarriages were of people who had little part in Jewish communal life.

It is now suggested that contemporary intermarriages in all three religious communities show a greatly reduced percentage of deviants, a moderate reduction in the percentage of those marginal to their religio-ethnic community, and the appearance of a substantial minority of intermarried people who have and maintain religio-ethnic involvement. It is this last group whose spouses are converted.

The data permit one to contrast the small Jewish intermarriage group with a much larger all-Jewish marriage group whose family members typically rank low on the identification indices. The contrast shows that the basic threat to Jewish continuity does not stem from intermarriage. Rather, intermarriage (without conversion) is but a symptom of diaspora Jewry's growing dissatisfaction with contemporary Jewish institutions and cultural forms.

These generalizations, as they apply to Jews, will soon be fully tested on the much larger number of interviews with Jews, intermarried and not, to be obtained by the forthcoming national survey of the United States Jewish population. Most importantly, the prior statement of many of the identity concepts and generalizations guiding this major Jewish survey ensures that the basic advantage of concept testing will be obtained and post hoc formulations reduced.

BIBLIOGRAPHY

AXELROD, MORRIS, FLOYD FOWLER, and ARNOLD GURIN. 1967. *A Community Survey for Long Range Planning: A Study of the Jewish Population of Greater Boston*, Boston: Combined Jewish Philanthropies of Greater Boston.

BARNETT, LARRY. 1962. "Research in Interreligious Dating and Marriage," *Marriage and Family Living* 24 (May): 191–95.

BARRON, MILTON. 1946a. *People Who Intermarry*. New York.

—— 1946b. "The Incidence of Jewish Intermarriage in Europe and America," *American Sociological Review* 11 (February): 6–13.

—— 1951. "Research on Intermarriage," *American Journal of Sociology* 57 (July): 249–55.

BERMAN, LOUIS. 1968. *Jews and Intermarriage: A Study in Personality and Culture*, New York.

BESANCENEY, PAUL. 1965. "On Reporting Rates of Intermarriage," *American Journal of Sociology* 70 (May): 717–21.

BOSSARD, JAMES and HAROLD LETTS. 1956. "Mixed Marriages involving Lutherans," *Marriage and Family Living* 18 (November): 308–10.

BOSSARD, JAMES and ELEANOR BOLL. 1957. *One Marriage, Two Faiths*, New York.

BURCHINAL, LEE and LOREN CHANCELLOR. 1962a. *Factors Related to Interreligious Marriages in Iowa, 1953–1957*, Ames, Iowa: Iowa State University Research Bulletin: 510.

—— 1962b. "Proportions of Catholics, Urbanism, and Mixed Catholic Marriage Rates Among Iowa Counties," *Social Problems* 9 (Spring): 359–65.

—— 1963. "Survival Rates Among Religiously Homogeneous and Interreligious Marriages," *Social Forces* 41 (May): 353–62.

CAPLOVITZ, DAVID and HARRY LEVY. 1965. *Interreligious Dating Among College Students*, New York: American Jewish Congress.

CHANCELLOR, LOREN and THOMAS MONAHAN. 1955. "Religious Preference and Interreligious Mixtures in Marriages and Divorces in Iowa," *American Journal of Sociology* 61 (November): 233–39.

COHEN, ERIK. 1969. "Mixed Marriage in an Israeli Town," *The Jewish Journal of Sociology* 11 (June): 41–50.

CROOG, SYDNEY and JAMES TEELE. 1967. "Religious Identity and Church Attendance of Sons of Religious Intermarriages," *American Sociological Review* 32 (February): 93–103.

DAVIS, MOSHE. 1968. "Mixed Marriage in Western Jewry: Historical Background to the Jewish Response," *The Jewish Journal of Sociology* 10 (December): 177–220.

EICHORN, DAVID. 1954. "Conversions to Judaism by Reform and Conservative Rabbis," *Jewish Social Studies* 16 (October): 299–318.

GLICK, PAUL. 1960. "Intermarriage and Fertility Patterns Among Persons in Major Religious Groups," *Eugenics Quarterly* 7 (March): 31–38.

GLOCK, CHARLES and RODNEY STARK. 1965. *Religion and Society in Tension*, Chicago.

GOLDSTEIN, SIDNEY. 1968. *A Population Survey of the Greater Springfield Jewish Community*, Springfield, Mass.

GOLDSTEIN, SIDNEY and CALVIN GOLDSCHEIDER. 1968. *Jewish Americans*, Englewood Cliffs, N.J.

GORDON, ALBERT. 1967. *The Nature of Conversion*, Boston.

GREELEY, ANDREW. 1964. *Mixed Marriages in the United States*, Chicago: National Opinion Research Center (mimeograph report).

HARRÉ, JOHN. 1966. *Maori and Pakeha*, London.

HEER, DAVID. 1962. "The Trend to Interfaith Marriages in Canada," *American Sociological Review* 27 (April): 245–50.

HEISS, J. 1960. "Premarital Characteristics of the Religiously Intermarried in an Urban Area," *American Sociological Review* 25 (February): 47–55.

KISH, LESLIE. 1965. *Survey Sampling*, New York.

LAZERWITZ, BERNARD. 1953. "Some Factors in Jewish Identification," *Jewish Social Studies* 15 (Winter): 301–309.

—— 1969. *The Components and Consequences of Jewish and Christian Religio-Ethnic Identification: An Integrative Approach*, Mimeographed Paper, Columbia, Mo.: Department of Sociology, University of Missouri.

—— 1970a. "An Investigation into the Associations Between Fertility and Religio-Ethnic Identification Among Protestants and Jews," *Sociological Quarterly* (in press).

—— 1970b. "Contrasting the Effects of Generation, Class, Sex, and Age on Group Identification in the Jewish and Protestant Communities," *Social Forces* (in press).

LENSKI, GERHARD. 1961. *The Religious Factor*, Garden City, N.Y.

LEVINSON, MARIA and DANIEL LEVINSON. 1958. "Jews Who Intermarry: Socio-Psychological Bases of Ethnic Identity and Change," *YIVO Annual of Jewish Social Science* 12 (Winter): 106–28.

LIPPMANN, WALTER. 1969. "Australian Jewry in 1966," *The Jewish Journal of Sociology* 11 (June): 67–73.

LOCKE, HARVEY. 1957. "Interfaith Marriages," *Social Problems* 4 (April): 329–33.

MALLER, ALLEN. 1969. "New Facts About Mixed Marriage," *Reconstructionist* 34 (March): 26–29.

MONAHAN, THOMAS and WILLIAM KEPHART. 1954. "Divorce and Desertion by Religious and Mixed Religious Groups," *American Journal of Sociology* 59 (March): 454–65.

PERGOLA, SERGIO DELLA. 1969. *Marriages and Mixed Marriages Among the Jews of Milano, Italy*. Paper given at the Fifth World Congress of Jewish Studies, Jerusalem; available from the Institute of Contemporary Jewry, Hebrew University, Jerusalem, Israel.

PRICE, CHARLES and JERZY ZUBRZYCKI. 1962. "The Use of Inter-Marriage Statistics as an Index of Assimilation," *Population Studies* 16 (July): 58–69.

REISS, PAUL. 1965. "The Trend in Inter-faith Marriages," *Journal for the Scientific Study of Religion* 5 (Fall): 64–67.

RODMAN, HYMAN. 1965. "Technical Note on Two Rates of Mixed Marriages," *American Sociological Review* 30 (October): 776–78.

ROSENTHAL, ERICH. 1963. "Studies of Jewish Intermarriage in the United States," New York: *American Jewish Year Book* 64: 3–53.

SALISBURY, W. SEWARD. 1964. *Religion in American Culture*, Homewood, Illinois.

—— 1969. "Religious Identification, Mixed Marriages, and Conversion," *Journal for the Scientific Study of Religion* 8 (Spring): 125–29.

SKLARE, MARSHALL and JOSEPH GREENBLUM. 1967. *Jewish Identity on the Suburban Frontier,* New York.

SLOTKIN, J. S. 1942. "Jewish-Gentile Intermarriage in Chicago," *American Sociological Review* 7 (February): 34–39.

United States Bureau of the Census. 1958. "Religion Reported by the Civilian Population of the United States: March, 1957," Current Population Reports. Washington, D.C.: Series P-20, No. 79.

In marked contrast to the generally optimistic findings in the Biesanz and Smith and the Strauss studies of the consequences of intermarriage, Bossard and Boll's study of religious intermarriage tends to support the position that such marriage is particularly risky, for it involves "the union of two differing ways of living and thinking in life's most intimate relationship." Their monograph, *One Marriage, Two Faiths,* was the culmination of more than a quarter of a century spent in gathering data on the problem. The stated purpose of their book was to consider how religious differences between husband and wife tend to affect family relationships and child development. Utilizing numerous case histories, the research findings of others, and statements of church policy, the implications drawn by Bossard and Boll are overwhelmingly conservative: They maintain that persistent and pervasive problems are more likely to be found in religious intermarriage than are personal and social adjustment.

There is justification in asking how representative their case histories are, for it is to be expected that intermarriage maladjustments have a higher visibility. Inasmuch as we are not informed by the authors how they gathered their cases, it is not safe to assume they are a cross section of religious intermarriages in American society. The following excerpt of the Bossard and Boll study considers the problems they found concerning the children born of these intermarriages.

WHEN THE CHILDREN COME
IN INTERFAITH MARRIAGES*

James H. S. Bossard and *Eleanor Stoker Boll*

Marriage, it has been suggested, is considered by most young people to be strictly their own affair: a union between the two of them. About five out of every six marriages in the United States, however, produce children. Once married, people who make interfaith marriages seem to come to an understanding of what their marriage may mean for the children. Evidences of it appear in studies of childlessness and the birth rates of these families. A study made in Indianapolis, by Drs. Kiser and Whelpton, of couples who were almost past their childbearing years, showed that Protestant-Catholic couples had a higher rate of childlessness than either Protestant or Catholic couples. In the same city, the Protestant-Catholic birth rate was lower than the Catholic or the Protestant birth rate. There are a number of possible reasons for these low rates other than a conscious agreement between the couple on family limitation; but the rates do indicate some serious concern over the special problems of children, and because of children, that such marriages create. This chapter is concerned with some of those problems.

WHAT IS THE PURPOSE OF THE FAMILY?

Every human society has some kind of family system. Though the forms of these systems vary widely, they have universally two functions. They are the perpetuation of the group physically and culturally. In other words, every group desires to extend itself into the future by bearing children and caring for them so that they may live to grow up and produce other children. Just as important is the desire to rear those children in the ways of doing and thinking of the particular group. If this is not done,

*Excerpt of Chapter Seven of James H. S. Bossard and Eleanor Stoker Boll, *One Marriage, Two Faiths* (New York: The Ronald Press Company, 1957), pp. 123–49. Copyright © 1957. Reprinted by permission.

the society loses its identity. . . . It wants to pass its cultural heritage down to its children so that it will survive and so that the children will have the best possible heritage.

A religious group, as well as a nation, is a cultural group. A family in which parents are of different faiths cannot easily fulfill the function of cultural transmission. Which culture is to be handed down? Shall it be a mixture? Or both? Or neither? Presumably each parent has some feelings about his own heritage.

WHAT IS A FAMILY FROM THE CHILD'S POINT OF VIEW?

A child does not define his family in terms of its functions, but rather of his own feelings. It is, to him, a given number of people who do things to him and for him, and who tell him things. He is utterly dependent upon their acts for his survival and upon their love for his security and feelings of worth. As a matter of fact, some sociologists also define the family, not by its functions, but as a group of people who act with and upon each other. This sort of definition is, perhaps, more true to the child's eye than to society's. Recently, the family has been described as an "emotional organization." . . . Within this emotional organization of the family the child does not react emotionally the same way to all his family members—nor to outsiders, either. Some are warm, some pleasant, helpful, understanding, glamorous to him; others are the opposite of one or all of these things. Being relatively unaware of, and disinterested in, moral values, the small child tends to identify with the people to whom he is drawn because they are "nice" to him and he "likes" them, and to be repelled by those who are not and whom he does not like. He wants to be like the former (though from a moral point of view that person may be a jolly renegade) and avoids taking on the characteristics of the latter (who may be a veritable pillar of the community).

This is the case in all families. Where there is a cultural way, or a philosophy of life, that is common to all members of the family and kin groups, the differences that the child sees among them will be mainly in terms of personality traits and gross behavior variances. He can adopt some and reject others in becoming himself, and yet stand as a person in unity with his whole family's cultural consensus. He is sure of the general route he must follow, and is only being selective of the particular roads he takes.

PERSONALITY IN A MIXED RELIGIOUS HOME

With the child of a mixed religious marriage, the case is different. His parents and their families represent two ways of life, often two opposing ways. He sees them being lived by people who are not equally attractive to him. Perhaps the following quotation will serve to illustrate how great a burden this can be to a child:

My Jewish grandmother was the sweetest, most self-effacing woman I have ever known. She had a way with children and we all loved her. She never tried to force her religion on us, she never mentioned it, but I could see how strong and wholesome it was. I don't think she deserved the daughter she go because my mother was a shrill and demanding shrew, if there ever was one, hard and calculating, too. My father (Catholic) was the soul of gentleness and kindness and patience. My heart bled for him. The only times that he ever became firm were when his sisters tried to make good Catholics out of us children (which they were always doing chiefly by the method of denouncing anything and everything that was Jewish). Father insisted that we must be allowed to make up our own minds. Make up our own minds, indeed! I was so confused by the sweetness of my father and grandmother and the harshness of Mother and the aunts about everything that the others stood for that I had to grow up, go overseas, and be away from them all for five years before I could get any idea of what I wanted to be, or what life was really all about. Both my brother and sister had much the same experience.

A unified cultural training, it is often said, leads to narrow-mindedness and bigotry in social relationships. Will not a Catholic, who has been taught Catholicism by his whole family and church, sent to a parochial school, a Catholic college, and kept in a circle of Catholic social relationships, be "intolerant" of the attitudes and behavior of non-Catholics? One wonders, though, about the individual's personality integration. Neuroses come from inner conflicts, that is, from having more than one idea of how to behave, of what to be, of what is right and wrong, of what one believes, and having to choose between them. A child whose parents, school, and church all teach him "the one way," may seem narrow to those of another way, but he has no conflict within himself for he is certain and sure, has no decisions to make, and no pangs of conscience if he follows "the straight and narrow path." For the child, however, whose own parents represent two ways of life, who argue about the right way of living, and who attempt to pull him back and forth between them there is no such certainty. This is quite a burden for a young child to carry. He has no background of experience on which to base a decision. It often happens that such a child cannot make one. He sways back and forth, seeing first the "truth" of what Mother says and then the equal "truth" of what Father says. When they are both good to him and live up to the ideal of each of their religions, it is difficult for him to choose a side. When they are unkind and show evidences of hypocrisy in their faith (which children are very quick to see), the child may become bitter against each religion in turn. Whatever the case may be, he has conflicts about what to do. No matter which way he goes, a haunting pang of conscience follows him for deserting the other way that, after all, is characteristic of one of his own parents. Conflict and guilt feelings are the essence of the neurotic personality, and like the bigoted person, the neurotic is not always successful in his social relationships. These two types may be at opposite ends of a pole, but the child with a unicultural training is at least more comfortable within himself than was the girl in the following case:

My Mother was a Catholic and my Dad a Protestant. She had been very devout, was the only person in her family who married outside her religion, and she never got over the feeling of guilt about it. Dad didn't go to church himself, but he hated the Catholic religion and he was a stern and domineering man. Mother told us never to mention her religion when his family was around. We kids were sent, not taken, to the Methodist Church and Sunday school. Often I persuaded my little sisters to play hooky. No one ever knew. It wasn't a very good example for them but I hate to be told what to do against my will. Later, I fell in love with a Catholic boy. Father was beside himself and insisted upon breaking it up. So we eloped. Dad was right in this one thing, though. My husband was a lazy ne'er-do-well, who ran off four months after we were married. I never got anything out of my marriage except a baby. All of this preyed on Mother's mind so much that she had a breakdown and is in a hospital. Now, I want to have my son christened in the Catholic faith; but Mother isn't here to support me in it, and I know just what would happen with Dad. After my marriage, I don't know whether I should defy Dad, anyway. I just don't seem to know what is right and it's easier just to let things slide.

SOME FORMS OF INTRAFAMILY ARRANGEMENTS

The manner in which the families in our case records operated in the acculturation of their children is quite varied, but certain general patterns did emerge.

1. A frequent form is the "taking over" of the children by a dominating parent, and silent submission by the other. The results, as voiced by the children, were not too successful. For one thing, one parent always seemed not really to belong to the family. This apparently mattered less if the father was the outsider and the mother was considered a "good mother" by her children. It was much less satisfactory if those roles were reversed. If the dominating parent was not considered a "good parent," however, sympathy went out to the submissive one, resulting in a break with the family head, and the religion, at the first possible moment.

2. Another pattern shows both parents to be relatively ineffective, or uninterested, in the face of the pressures from their respective kinsfolk. Children feel especially helpless and bitter in such cases. One girl, who lived for periods of time alternately with her father's and mother's people, wrote:

I went to live with my maternal grandmother . . . and was used as a whipping boy for my uncle to pour out his hatred for the Vatican, the Pope, Archbishops, Bishops, and "scheming" priests of Catholicism. My father's visits there were unwelcome. . . .They attempted to destroy my affection for him by stripping him to ribbons after each of his departures. In the eyes of a small child, it was most cruel, but I clung madly to my belief that my father was a good father. I went to live with my father's people. That side of the house immediately went to work to criticize my upbringing in the family of my mother. They accused them of spoiling me and making me ashamed of my Catholic "blood"—and inferred we were all born out of wedlock.

3. In some families, when one parent appears to dominate, the other parent is not actually submissive. There is a continuous planned program of subversion for the benefit of the children, though one member of the family is unaware of it. This usually results in children having little respect for either parent when they become fully aware of what has been going on and how one parent has been fooled.

4. There are the cases in which the family is divided by parental prearrangement. "You can have the girls and I'll take the boys," or "You take the first, I'll take the second, and so on." This has its problem aspects, too. First, the children do not always agree, and reassort themselves when they are able, with the result in one family that a father forbade his daughter his home when she changed her religion in mid-adolescence, and he did not see nor speak to her for eleven years. Her comment was that he spoke to her again only when he "needed" her. A choice by sexes, then, appears to be dangerously divisive, separating the male and female loyalties and activities into two camps, with a firm line between them. Sex hostility, as well as religious hostility, was marked in a number of these families, and the children remained divided, changing their religions less frequently than in the former pattern.

5. There is a pattern of complete lack of decision. Both the mother and the father fight continuously for all of the children, or for certain of the children. In some cases, even where a plan has been decided upon, the parents change their minds, and this pattern results.

6. Some parents agree to attend to different aspects of their children's lives. One has his say in the religious training; the other, in the educational or social training. There is less conflict in these homes, provided the parents mean what they promise, are happy in it and do not interfere with each other, the children agree, and the religious and educational training are not completely incompatible. There is less conflict, but there is no picture of strong family cohesiveness.

7. Finally, there are the parents, usually not practicing members of their own faiths, who take a "hands off" policy, and manage to maintain it. Their children can go to whatever churches they care to or they can go to none; they may attend a "neutral" school, and make their own religious choice. The picture that emerges of children wandering from church to church, trying to find a religious faith, is rather pathetic. Some never can. When they do, they usually choose because of pleasant social relations rather than because of one set of religious values. If a change in relationships or locale comes about, the search begins all over again. When they are successful, however, their concern usually tends in the direction of their parents, like the little boy, who,

finding himself happy in the Friends Meeting, came home one
First Day from the service to say, "I wish I had a good Mummy
and Daddy like the other kids." Fortunately, in a few of the cases,
this attitude in their children had a strong effect upon the parents,
and ended with the family uniting religiously, after the children
had paid a high price to obtain that end.

In all these forms of intrafamily arrangements, two factors are
constant. One is the lack of "certainties" for children to hold onto
when family relationships are strained. It is not only interfaith
families that have troubles. Many parents are ineffective or dominating. Many marital parents have conflicts, and when they do,
the conflicts affect the children and make them uneasy. If their
parents are at odds, how can the children be secure, and on whom
can they depend? A youngster whose parents were in the process
of divorce reported that when she felt most "scared" she found
complete assurance in singing her favorite hymn very loudly: "Be
not dismayed whate'er betide. God will take care of you." She
knew that if she pleased God, as her parents and Sunday school
teachers had shown her, everything would turn out all right for
her. The child of an interfaith marriage, who is not sure how to
please one personal God, lacks this incomparable support to help
him carry his problems with confidence. The second constant
factor is that, even though the family tensions may spring from
the same kind of personality differences that exist in a one-religion
family, it is religion that is used as a tool and an epithet. Children
not only have no firm religious conviction, but religion has been
stressed for them as the cause of their troubles and a divisive
influence.

BROTHER-SISTER RELATIONSHIPS

Although most of the books dealing with child development
speak of the relationships between brothers and sisters in terms
of hostility and jealousy, and how to avoid them, there is some
evidence that these relationships may be just as important and
constructive as parent-child relationships. If so, some attention
to brother-sister interaction is a meaningful part of the story of
interfaith families.

The evidences just referred to come from sources of varying
degrees of scientific authenticity. In a study of large families,

which the authors have made, it was discovered that children thought of their sense of security as coming from their brothers and sisters, the people who were closest to them in age and interests. Even when their parents were bickering or brutal or alcoholic, there were enough children around to present a solid front. Small families do not have this advantage. Yet the father who began early in the life of his two children to stop their quarrels by impressing them with the fact that their family was small, and that they should keep close to each other because the time would come when they had only each other as family, understood the need for family blood ties even after adulthood, marriage, and the establishment of a new family. The third bit of evidence has been suggested elsewhere. There is a point in life at which one strikes off the family. It is short lived, and one begins increasingly to take interest in one's roots. The remaining family may then consist of a brother or a sister. It is then that barriers often begin to crumble, and brothers and sisters come closer together again.

It was a very persistent story, in the case records of children of interfaith marriages, that religion had been a barrier between them, and one that was difficult to span. Instead of the feelings of the brothers and sisters becoming less hostile with time, the advent of their own children increased awareness of religious differences and made the siblings even more wary of each other and of social communication with each other.

One aspect of early sibling relationships was that the children used religion as a tool in their rivalry with each other for the affections of a preferred parent. There was little that either a mother or father could do to force a particular religion upon a child after a certain age, and especially since one parent was receptive to a change in the child's religion or was actually trying to woo him into it. From this situation came the cases of youngsters weaving back and forth from one religion to another for the sole purpose of gaining favor. Another aspect was that the siblings of one religion used religious epithets for those of the other religion, even in their childhood play, in order to establish superior and inferior statuses. Needless to say, this does not lead to healthy attitudes about any religion, nor to good family relationships. In other cases, the separation was less vocal—in fact, it was non-vocal. There was a firm dividing line as far as religion and observances were concerned. In other areas of family living, they joined together, but the moment religion entered in any way they silently drew apart, as if a wall had suddenly been erected between them. There were instances in which the father and mother did everything in their power to keep one brood of children from "infecting" the other. This was especially marked in one family where it had been decided that the Protestant father would rear all the boys in his faith and the Catholic mother could do the same with all the girls. When the family was completed, it was composed of four boys and one girl. The bargain was kept, but the little girl was reared almost as if she had no brothers. Her mother, feeling very badly that she had defied the laws of her church, was determined to rear her one daughter to be the best possible Catholic, and would brook no possible anti-Catholic influences from the Protestant side of the family.

The continuation of this kind of separation in later life was voiced by a childless married woman of thirty-six: "I love my nephews and nieces and I need their companionship. There are so many things I could do for them, too. But my brother is afraid to let us get friendly because of the differences in our religious beliefs. . . ."

TO WHOM DO I BELONG?

Human beings seem to have a need to be accepted completely and as they are, without pretenses or defenses, by other human beings. It is not enough to be loved partially, so that one has to pretend something or hide something in order to be accepted. That is a great effort and a nervous strain. For peace of mind and body, it is necessary to have someone with whom one can relax and be one's self. The most obvious source of such relaxation and acceptance is the members of the family. The many children who go through "adoption fantasy" show the truth of this. They have somehow gotten a notion that their parents love them only partially, that there is something about them that their parents do not accept. So they decide that they do not really belong to those parents, but have been adopted; and they press their parents hard. These children want assurance that, no matter what they are, their family likes them that way, or that there is another family that will. This feeling extends beyond childhood, however, as witnessed by many mature (and unhappy) people who actually have been adopted and who spend much effort and time to trace their own origins.

Children of interfaith marriages, in cases where the parents cannot come to full and sincere agreement about their rearing, have to cope with the problem of total acceptance. They know full well that there is something about them that one or both parents do not like. . . . Human beings not only need to be accepted as they are, but to be so accepted by someone whom they respect. It is of little value to be loved by anyone else. In the cases where children loved both the mother and the father equally, and yet had to deal with a religious difference between them and their families, the burden was heavy and bitter. To whom should he belong? It might be decided for him for awhile, but eventually he had to make his own choice. He could decide on one or the other, or neither. . . .

THE CHILDREN'S FRIENDSHIPS

Apparently some of the difficulties of the marital partners of a mixed marriage in forming friendships become a part of the inheritance of the younger generation. Our records show several problems in this respect, some of them caused by the family and others by the friends. They will be mentioned only briefly, to avoid repetition.

First, children when very young are not aware of social distinctions such as religions unless adults make the children aware. They like some children just because they like them, and dislike others because they do not. A family that is religiously divided, however, is very conscious of differences in faith because they are highlights in their lives, and their children realize there are these differences before they are old enough to understand them. As one girl, with very keen insight, commented: "Families who have had children marry outside their religion have the same reaction to one thing, I have noticed. Upon discussing or upon meeting someone new, the first question asked about said person is his religion. It suddenly seems quite important to them, even to those members of the family who only attend church once a year. Religion becomes the issue of issues." Something that started early in the lives of children in our records was the family's sizing up of playmates on the basis of their faiths, and this kept up even more emphatically during adolescence, when children's loyalties to their friends are so strong. For instance:

In my friendships I find my mother's people accepting readily my Protestant friends and defending them if I do any fault finding. However, my Catholic friends never reach the sanctum sanctorum of my family. They are always politely received, little is said about them or to them and there is never an invitation for them to return. I am generally cautious when I invite my Catholic friends, for the reaction to such an invitation is one of general annoyance when they are discussed and not too complimentary remarks are made following their departure. When the friends are Protestant they are immediately accepted and after their departure they most always say, "Jane . . . well, now, there's a fine girl! Why don't you bring more like her home?" This entire difficulty became so disturbing to me that, in order to keep my friends, I moved to a small apartment of my own as soon as I was able, where I entertain anyone I choose to.

In a few families where the house was firmly divided against itself, the children of one faith were permitted one set of friends and the children of the other faith, another set. It need scarcely be described how unsatisfactory this was in terms of both friendships and sibling relationships.

THE FAMILY THROUGH THE YEARS

Just as marriages age, change, and meet with crises, so do families. Perhaps it will prove helpful in this connection to speak of the family cycle, which many students of the family have emphasized in recent years. The idea is that family histories consist of a series of stages, each of which presents its own interests, activities, tensions, and problems. Some writers speak of the founding, the expanding, and the contracting stages of a family. Others elaborate the central idea in greater detail. . . . Each stage in the cycle is characterized by its own specific problems for the parents and children in a mixed religious family. In the earliest stages the difficulties may be minor, for man and wife are concerned first with themselves and then with the physical care and habit training of babies—and not very much with the babies' ideas. It is later that uncertainties about education and relations outside the family arise; still later that the sorts of young people with whom children date, court, and marry come into focus; and even later when the married couple find themselves alone again, deprived of the children who were their chief common interest, faced with beginning together again pretty much as they did when they were first married, and wondering just how their grandchildren are going to be reared. The fact is that such families do not ordinarily face and solve once and for all, early in life, the decisions necessitated by their kind of marriage. New ones arise throughout the whole cycle of family life to disturb and create a need for readjustments.

THE CHILDREN'S DECISIONS

Quite apart from parent's intentions for children and the pressures upon them as they grow up, the children ultimately decide for themselves. Many studies of the second generation in these families state what happens. Children keep to the religion in which they were reared; they choose the religion of one parent or the other; they choose a "neutral" church; or they become nonpracticing or agnostics or atheists.

A very careful analysis of our data suggests that all these ways are taken, but that this is too simple a story. The very great majority of the children never did make one certain decision to which they clung throughout life. They turned from, they turned back, they tried another, they gave it up. This was the general pattern, but in endless variations. Of these variations, the major portion ended, at the date of recording, with "nonpracticing." Many indicated that they were not happy about this decision, but had been unable to find a church in which they felt comfortable.

A part of their decision about religion was evidenced by their own marriages. It is widely accepted as fact that children of mixed marriages themselves mix-marry more frequently than do children from one-faith families. Our analysis showed clearly that the majority of the children did marry outside of the faith in which they had been reared. Where our records included a third generation, definite patterns again emerged. About half of the second-generation parents who had turned from their faith and married outside of it let their spouses take over the religious training of the children. The other half made strong attempts to turn their children back to the religion of their own childhood. This was sometimes successful, and sometimes it was not. . . .

SUMMARY AND CONCLUSION

It has been pointed out that people who make interfaith marriages apparently realize that children will cause problems or will have problems. The lower birth rate and the higher rate of childlessness among such couples suggest this. A part of the difficulty is caused by a primary function of the family—to pass down the cultural heritage. When the parents are of different religions, the family is a cultural mixture and the child is torn, in choosing his religion and philosophy of life, between two sides of the family. This results not only in "taking sides" within the family, but in inner conflict for the child. The divisiveness extends to brothers and sisters as well as to parents and tends to separate them even when they grow up, marry, and have their own children who are reared in various faiths. Children of an interfaith marriage find some of the same problems in making friends that their parents had, with the additional difficulty of having their parents bicker about which friends are suitable. Apparently, all of this causes a certain amount of restlessness, for many of the cases under study never could choose a religion once and for all. They changed back and forth and most of them ended by being nonpracticing. Because of the recent revival of religious feeling among young people, the parents' nonpracticing status may become an added problem to them if their children reject their parents' secularism and turn again to religion for comfort and direction.

One of the important questions concerning the long-range consequences of religious intermarriage has to do with the religious identification and church attendance of the children who are offspring of these intermarriages. Are there any underlying principles giving direction to the ultimate identity and religious behavior of people whose parents differed in religion prior to their marriages? Studying a sample of young army inductees who were the products of Roman Catholics married to Protestants, Croog and Teele were able to provide some answers to this question. They inform us that patterns of these young men's religious identification are significantly related to whether the parental intermarriage combined a Protestant father and a Catholic mother, or the combination was that of a Catholic father and a Protestant mother. Mediating the patterns of religious identification is the social status of the family as crudely measured by the father's educational status. Furthermore, Croog and Teele found that differential patterns of church attendance depend upon whether the sons are Protestant or Catholic and upon the educational level and religious identities of their parents.

RELIGIOUS IDENTITY AND CHURCH ATTENDANCE OF SONS OF RELIGIOUS INTERMARRIAGES*

Sydney H. Croog and
James E. Teele

INTRODUCTION

Although there are powerful pressures toward homogamy in choice of marital partner, numerous marriages are formed in which partners come from disparate backgrounds, such as differing class, ethnic, religious, and racial origins. Recent empirical research and numerous theoretical observations have focused on the relative stability of such intermarriages, on social and personal characteristics of intermarriers, and on the kinds of problems they meet.[1] However, many questions in the area of long-term consequences remain for empirical examination. For example, in instances of intermarriage, what factors determine the social identity of offspring? In what dimensions of social behavior, if any, do offspring of intermarriages differ from persons whose parents come from homogeneous social and cultural backgrounds? Principles underlying the patterning of social identity and the social behavior of children of intermarriage remain still to be clarified through both national and cross-national research.

The present paper is a report on the (a) religious identification and (b) church attendance of a population of young men who are the products of exogamous religious marriages. First, it presents data in regard to differential patterns of association between religious affiliation of offspring and social variables. These data are oriented to the following series of questions:

Is the religious affiliation of the son a simple pattern of conformity to the religion of the parent of one sex rather than another? Does one religion tend to be dominant, in the sense that regardless of parental affiliation, the son tends to adopt that religion? Does pattern of choice of religion vary by social status of the family of orientation?

American Sociological Review, Vol. 32, No. 1 (February 1967), pp. 93–103. Reprinted by permission.

A second issue refers to the problem of possible relationship of types of religious intermarriage to one dimension of religious behavior of their offspring, i.e., church attendance. We are dealing here with one kind of atypical marriage pattern, often one in which two people have undertaken marriage in the face of pressures toward conformity to the principle of religious endogamy. In such cases, does the church attendance of male offspring of intermarriage differ from that of men who are the product of religiously homogeneous marriages? An associated issue is also examined. In the case of sons of religious exogamous marriages, how are social status variables and type of intermarriage related to church attendance? This approach, in sum, constitutes an exploratory effort at delineating some basic patterns and identifying relationships in an area which has been little explored empirically.

The issue of determinants of religious identity of offspring of religious intermarriage is not a simple one. As has often been noted, in American society affiliation with a particular religious group is an important element of social identity.[2] Further, persons engaging in exogamous marriages, as Cavan and others have noted, tend to be marginal in orientation to their own social groups.[3] In the case of religious intermarriage they must usually proceed in the face of powerful sanctions which encourage marriage within their own religious group. The children of these intermarriages, as they mature, may be influenced in various ways in choice of religion. First, they may identify with the religion of one parent on the basis of personal choice of theology, dogma, and set of practices. Or their identity may be determined by a program of deliberate training by parents in one religion rather than another. Third, in situations where offspring are permitted free choice, one parent may serve as a role model, exerting through the power of example and personality a determining influence upon the child.

In the case of religious intermarriage, there have been numerous speculations and observations concerning identity patterning and behavior of offspring. For example, Landis has suggested on the basis of data from a study of midwestern Americans that a child tends to follow the religion of his mother.[4] Leiffer has maintained similarly on the basis of analysis of an urban sample of intermarriages that "the mother is more important than the denomination" in determining the religious affiliation of the children.[5] On the other hand, recent research on differential patterns of power and influence in the family indicates that the roles of father and mother in decision-making vary in relation to specific issues and in terms of social status and situational variables.[6] Although evidence is contradictory in such studies, they offer ample reasons to suspect that the matter of parental influence over choice of religion by a child is not simply patterned. The fact that only a meager number of studies of offspring of intermarriages are reported in the literature has thus far been a handicap to clarification of speculation and contradictory observations regarding religious affiliation and church behavior of such persons. Further, minimal information is available concerning these offspring when they reach adult status.

METHOD

The data for the present report were collected in connection with a large-scale study of Army inductees.[7] Two thousand three hundred inductees were chosen by a random selection technique as they were processed through the induction center at Fort Dix, New Jersey. As participants in the research, all completed a sociological questionnaire, in addition to carrying out other procedures required by the study design.

For the purpose of this report, two groups of men were identified: (1) sons of parents who engaged in religious intermarriage and (2) sons of parents who married within their own religion. Two criteria for differentiation were used: reported religion of each parent at birth and reported religion of the parent at the time of the study. Those men who identified their parents as being of different religions at present were classified as sons of interreligious marriages providing that the present religion of each parent was the same as the reported religion at birth. Similarly, those men whose parents were reported as being of the same religion currently were classified as sons of religious endogamous marriages provided the parent's current religion was the same as at birth. This technique for isolating two study populations was designed to eliminate from each group those men who were the sons of parents who converted to religions other than the ones into which they were born. In addition, converted respondents, i.e., sons of religious endogamous parents who reported their own religion to be different from that of the parents, were also eliminated. Negro and foreign-born inductees were not included on the basis of insufficient numbers of religious intermarriages and small representation in the original study population.

After procedures for isolating the study populations had been carried out, it was discovered that only Catholic-Protestant intermarriages were present in sufficient number to permit statistical analysis.[8] Hence, this report deals solely with this type of religious intermarriage. The final intermarriage study group consists of 281 men. A total of 1,066 Catholic and Protestant men who were the sons of religious endogamous parents were isolated on the basis of study criteria. This group consisted of 790 Catholic and 276 Protestant inductees.

The religious composition of the study populations examined in this report owes its special characteristics in considerable part to the fact that the locus of the research was Fort Dix, New Jersey. The induction and training center is located in an industrialized, urban area with a large Catholic population. Because of the special characteristics of the inductees and the region from which they come, caution should be exercised in generalization of findings from the present study.

For purposes of brevity, the two types of religious intermarriage patterns are referred to in this report as follows:

FcMp = Father Catholic, Mother Protestant
FpMc = Father Protestant, Mother Catholic

Similar usage of letter symbols is made in regard to religious ingroup marriages, with FcMc referring to Catholic and FpMp to Protestant marital combinations.

Traits of the Inductees

By virtue of their having been inducted into the Army, the respondents constitute a special group in several respects. Since all had met the physical and mental health requirements for military service, the possibility that physical or mental handicaps impeded opportunities for attendance at church services in civilian life was minimal. Further, the respondents were relatively homogeneous in age, with a mean age of 21.1 years. They are primarily urban in origins, with approximately 40 per cent designating their home city as New York City. Less than 2 per cent were from rural, farm backgrounds. About 80 per cent came from two states,

New York and New Jersey, while the remainder came primarily from the New England states.

Judging on the basis of the age of the inductee respondents at the time of the study, it can be estimated that the marriages of their parents were formed during the latter years of the 1920's and the early years of the 1930's. Since norms regarding religious intermarriage and principles of child-rearing in religious traditions cannot be assumed to be constant over time, it must be emphasized that the patterns reported here cannot necessarily be generalized as predictive of outcome in marriages currently being formed.[9]

FINDINGS

Among those men whose parents entered into an exogamous Protestant-Catholic marriage, what is the pattern of their current formal religious identification? In the study population the Catholic religion clearly was dominant, in terms of reported identification by the inductees. Of the 281 men, nearly two-thirds, or 63 per cent, identified themselves as Catholics, while 35 per cent described themselves as Protestant. The remaining 2 per cent cited their religion as being "none."

In view of the nature of Catholic norms regarding religious intermarriage, this finding at first impression would appear to support common stereotypes regarding general effects of Catholicism in intermarriages. Powerful influences are customarily exerted within the Catholic subcultural group toward assuring that the children of such marriages will be raised as Catholics. In fact, if a Catholic intends to form a religious exogamous marriage which will be considered valid by his church, the Protestant partner must sign an Ante-Nuptial agreement. The agreement specifies that all children of the marriage will be baptized and educated as Catholics, even in the event of the death of the Catholic spouse. While we do not have information on the numbers of Protestant parents of the inductees who made the formal Ante-Nuptial agreement, the existence of this regulation is but one indication of the forces in such marriages turned toward assuring that offspring of the marriages will be adherents to Catholicism.

However, further consideration of the data reveals that there is no simple general effect of Catholicism in the intermarriages.

Indeed, it is notable that over one-third of the men did not become Catholics. Obviously, factors are at work which reduce the influence of one religion over another, insofar as the upbringing of offspring of intermarriage is concerned. Two of these which can be examined here are (1) the relative degree of influence of the maternal and paternal affiliations on the religion of the son and (2) a variation in religious identification by social status level.

Variation in Terms of Parental Religious Affiliation

One factor commonly associated with choice of religion by offspring of religious intermarriage is the influence of a mother. This view has been supported in part by empirical evidence from studies noted earlier and in part by assumptions concerning the primary role of the mother in the socialization of the child.[10] Our data indicate that the relationship of maternal religious affiliation to that of the son is not a simple one. Of the 281 respondents identified as the offspring of religious intermarriages, 60.5 per cent adopted the religion of the mother. However, an examination of the relationship between marriage pattern of the parents and the religion of the offspring indicates that the weight of maternal influence is greatly affected by whether the mother's religion is Catholicism or Protestantism.

As indicated in Table 1, in marriages in which the mother is Catholic and the father Protestant, 70 per cent of the inductees identified themselves as Catholics. In those cases where the mother is Protestant, and father Catholic, a slight majority of men follow the religion of the father, rather than that of the mother. However, the percentages are so similar that it seems clear that the likelihood in such marriages is about equal that the son will follow the

TABLE 1

Protestant-Catholic Intermarriage Type and
Respondent's Religion (N = 281)

Respondent's Religion	Father Protestant Mother Catholic		Father Catholic Mother Protestant		Total
	N	%	N	%	
Catholic	115	70.2	62	53.0	177
Protestant	44	26.8	55	47.0	99
None	5	3.0	—	—	5
100% =	164		117		281

religion of either mother or father. In the Chi-square test the parental religious identification pattern in the intermarriages was found to be a statistically significant variable in regard to the religious identification of the inductees. In brief, although previous writers have contended that offspring of religious intermarriages follow the religion of the mother, regardless of her religious identity, we find that the particular religion of the mother makes a considerable difference. It is possible that the strength of the Ante-Nuptial agreement, i.e., the influence of the Catholic church, operates most markedly when the *female* partner in interreligious marriage is a Catholic.

Obviously, other variables may help to explain the patterning of religious affiliation of the offspring of the intermarriages. Although we have only limited data on other possible factors, information on social status was available. One measure of status—educational level of the father—was employed as a control variable in the exploration of the relationship between religion of the respondent and the intermarriage pattern of his parents.[11]

As may be seen in Table 2, in families where the father is either a high school graduate or where he has completed three years of high school or less, the pattern is similar to that reported in Table 1. In both instances, where the mother is Catholic, the majority of inductees are Catholic. Where mother is Protestant, the distribution of Catholics and Protestants among the sons of such families is about equal.

An exception, however, is found in the families in which the father has had at least one year of college. Here the influence of the Catholic mother is distinctively less. In fact, as may be seen in the first column, two-thirds of the sons of Catholic mothers identify their own religion as either Protestant or None. In contrast to the families of men with "high school" and "less than high school educations," no statistically significant difference was found between the two types of marriages in which female Catholics were married to college-educated male Protestants and those in which college-educated Catholic males were married to female Protestants, insofar as the religious identification of the sons was concerned. In sum, it would appear that in at least one group, cases in which women married college educated men, neither parental role nor any single religious group was significantly associated statistically with the choice of religion made by the sons.

TABLE 2

Protestant-Catholic Intermarriage Type and Respondent's Religion,
Controlling Education of Father (N = 264)*

Marriage Pattern

Respondent's Religion	Father Protestant Mother Catholic		Father Catholic Mother Protestant	
	N	%	N	%
	Less than High School			
I				
Catholic	71	74.0	33	54.0
Protestant	25	26.0	28	46.0
None	0		0	
100% =	96		61	
	High School Graduate			
II				
Catholic	34	74.0	14	50.0
Protestant	12	26.0	14	50.0
None	0		0	
100% =	46		28	
	College Plus			
III				
Catholic	5	33.3	9	50.0
Protestant	5	33.3	9	50.0
None	5	33.3	0	
100% =	15		18	

* 17 cases with insufficient data on father's education.

As previously noted, other studies dealing with areas of decision-making, personal dominance, and power have reported differences between families of varying social levels. The findings here raise questions about differential patterns of influence and marital interaction, particularly in those cases in which Catholic women marry comparatively well-educated Protestant men. Although we have no data on attitudes or feelings of partners in the intermarriages, one might hypothesize that when Catholic women engage in intermarriage with college-educated Protestant men, they may feel only minimally compelled to carry out the normative requirements of their religion and to raise their children as Catholics. Indeed, our evidence indicates that those Catholic women who marry college-educated men tend to be better educated themselves than their Catholic sisters who marry non-college men. Instead of molding their marriages along lines of Catholic cultural traditions, such women may in fact feel emancipated and inclined toward adopting the Protestant cultural system of their husbands. The fact that all of the soldiers who claimed they had no religion were the offspring of this category of intermarriage may be an indication of the relative disinterest of both mother and father in their own religious traditions.

Another possibility is that in these marriages a proportion of the Catholic women are upwardly mobile. In adapting to the way of life of their husbands, they may reduce their own religious ties and affiliations, accepting in part at least the dominance of their Protestant upper-status spouse. Certainly empirical findings of this order suggest the need for further, more intensive research into religious intermarriage patterns at differing social status levels and into the psychological and social characteristics of persons who enter such marriages.

Religious Intermarriage and Church Attendance of Male Offspring

Although the religious practices of the children of religious intermarriages has only rarely been the object of empirical research, many speculations and assumptions in this area are current.[12] However, systematic knowledge is limited concerning the degree to which mixed marriage influences beliefs and practices of offspring and the ways in which these patterns differ from those held by children of religious inmarriages. An assessment of the relationship between intermarriage and one dimension of the religious behavior of offspring—church attendance—is possible from the Fort Dix data. The research questions which interest us here concern (a) the degree to which the church attendance of sons of intermarried couples differs from the attendance of the sons of couples in homogeneous religious marriages and (b) differences between the offspring of the various types of intermarriage. In Table 3, the church attendance reported by respondents identifying themselves as Protestants and as Catholics are recorded separately.

Some notable differences in church attendance patterns of Catholic and Protestant respondents can be seen. Parenthetically, the Catholic respondents attend church much more frequently than Protestant respondents, a finding consistent with those in other studies. With respect to the Catholic soldiers, the church attendance of sons of intermarriers is similar to that of the sons of ingroup marriers. No statistically significant differences were found

(1) when the sons of intermarriages were compared with the sons of non-intermarriers and (2) when the sons of different types of intermarriages were compared with each other.

TABLE 3

Marriage Pattern and Respondent's Church Attendance,
Controlling Religion of Respondent (N = 1312)*

Frequency of Church Attendance

Marriage Pattern	0-11 per year		1-3 per month		weekly or more		100% =
	N	%	N	%	N	%	
Respondent Catholic							
(A) Fc, Mc	90	11.4	124	15.7	576	72.9	790
(B) Fp, Mc	16	15.8	15	14.9	70	69.3	101
(C) Fc, Mp	10	17.0	12	20.3	37	62.7	59
Respondent Protestant							
(D) Fp, Mp	100	36.2	105	38.1	71	25.7	276
(E) Fp, Mc	9	23.1	22	56.4	8	20.5	39
(F) Fc, Mp	25	53.2	20	42.6	2	4.2	47

* 35 cases with insufficient data

In the case of Protestant soldiers, however, the situation is different. In that group of men from FpMc families, the church attendance pattern is similar to that of Protestant men whose parents were religious ingroup marriers (FpMp). However, the attendance pattern of men from FcMp families is markedly different from those of the sons of homogeneous marriages and the sons of FpMc intermarriages. Only about 4 per cent of the sons of these FcMp intermarriages attend church at least once weekly, while over 50 per cent are either non-attenders or irregular attenders. The church attendance pattern of men in this latter FcMp group differs significantly from (a) the sons of parents with Protestant homogeneous marriages and (b) from the sons of intermarriages of FpMc type. In brief, the results show that when the son in an intermarriage is Protestant, he is much more likely to attend church when the father is the Protestant than when the mother is the Protestant. Or to put it another way, when the mother is Catholic in an intermarriage, a Protestant son is more likely to attend church than when the mother in the interreligious marriage is Protestant.

In the case of the Protestant sons of intermarriers, two possible interpretations of effects of the intermarriage can be noted. First, given the acknowledged key role of a mother in the training of her offspring, it would appear that Catholic mothers in the FpMc marriages may possibly instill norms of regular attendance in their offspring, even though their sons are being raised in another religion. Catholic emphasis on regularity of church attendance may be given expression through the mother despite the fact of intermarriage. Or it is possible that Protestant fathers with the support of their Catholic wives exert an influence upon their sons which leads them to accept and follow through on Protestant norms regarding church attendance. Second, looking once again at the role of the mother, it appears that in instances of FcMp type marriages, traditional ties to religious norms may be weakened. Being married to a man whose religion emphasizes that the children should be raised as Catholics, both she and her husband may have come to a compromise in which minor emphasis is placed on religious training. An alternative explanation, looking at the role of the Catholic father in such FcMp marriages, may be that the Catholic men are rebels against their religion. Leaving the major tasks of religious training to the mother, the Catholic father is assigning a responsibility to a woman whose ties to her own religion may be weak and who is unlikely to stimulate her son to conform to the Protestant pattern.

In the absence of detailed evidence on interpersonal relations and religious beliefs among intermarried parents, only tentative interpretations of these data have been possible. Whatever the explanation, however, it appears that the two types of intermarriage patterns (Father Catholic–Mother Protestant, and Father Protestant–Mother Catholic) are distinctive and that differing kinds of forces may be operating within each, insofar as adaptation to the fact of religio-cultural differences is concerned.

Church Attendance Patterns with Educational Level Controlled

The positive relationships between church attendance patterns and educational level has often been reported in studies of Protestant and Catholic denominations in American and European settings. In addition, variation by educational level has been found in the present population.[13] In view of the evidence for an

distinctive way from that of men in the other two educational categories. Thus, 30 per cent of the men whose parents are both Protestants report attending church at least once weekly. In contrast to their counterparts in the "high school graduate" and "less than high school graduate" categories, however, respondents in the FpMc category are the *least likely* to attend church weekly and the *most likely* to attend infrequently.

Indeed, a further examination of the relationships involving the four variables (respondent's education, marriage pattern of parents, religion of respondent, and church attendance) was suggested to us, since it appeared that, in contrast to the other types of marriages, an inverse relationship existed between education and church attendance for the Protestant respondents from the FpMc type of marriage.

Thus, Pearsonian coefficients were computed between respondent's education and church attendance, controlling marriage pattern and religion of respondents (Table 5). The results confirm the appearance of the inverse relationship for the FpMc group.

TABLE 5

Pearsonian Coefficients Between Respondents' Education and Church Attendance, Controlling Marriage Pattern and Religion of Respondent (N = 1297) **

	Pearsonian Coefficient	N
Respondents Catholic		
Father Catholic, Mother Catholic	.27*	776
Father Protestant, Mother Catholic	.29*	100
Father Catholic, Mother Protestant	.43*	59
Respondents Protestant		
Father Protestant, Mother Protestant	.21*	276
Father Catholic, Mother Protestant	.38*	47
Father Protestant, Mother Catholic	—.45*	39

* p < .01, two-tailed test
** 50 cases with insufficient data

The data presented in Tables 4 and 5 raise some issues which can be at least noted here briefly. In particular, data on the church attendance of college graduates may, in combination with data in Table 2, be pointing in the direction of a special relationship of education to dominance-submission patterns and religious practices in families originating in religious intermarriage. Thus, as noted in Table 2, when Catholic women married Protestant men who completed four years of high school or less, a significant proportion of the sons were themselves Catholic. On the other hand, when Catholic women married Protestant men with college educations, the chances that the son would be non-Catholic were considerably enhanced. Moreover, among the Protestant sons of FpMc marriages, an inverse relationship between church attendance and the education of the respondent is found. This pattern is in distinct contrast to the church attendance patterns of sons of homogeneous Protestant marriages and of FcMp types of intermarriages, for in these the higher the educational level of the respondent, the higher is the church attendance level. Since this church attendance pattern varies so markedly from that of sons of other types of marital combinations, the basis for this difference certainly merits further empirical investigation, possibly along lines of variations in family religious belief systems and the associated intrafamily relationships.

CONCLUSION

This paper has set forth empirical findings regarding relationships between religious intermarriage of Catholic and Protestant parents and the religious identities and church attendance of their sons. Briefly, it has been shown that differing patterns of religious identity of the sons are evident, depending upon whether the parental marriage involves Protestant father–Catholic mother or Catholic father–Protestant mother. In addition, it was seen that patterns of religious identity of the sons are mediated by social status of the family, as indicated in rough form by educational status of the father. In particular, having a Catholic mother tended to result in a predominantly Catholic identity among the sons in the lower status levels, while in the families of college educated fathers, presence of a Catholic mother was associated more with non-Catholic identity in the sons. Further, differential patterns of church attendance were found, depending upon whether the son was Protestant or Catholic and depending upon his educational level and the religious identities of his parents. As has been seen, there are dramatic differences in church attendance patterns between (a) all Catholic and Protestant respondents and

(b) between Protestant soldiers who are the sons of differing types of marital combinations.

These data are, of course, only one manifestation of complex phenomena at work in the family settings from which the respondents come. To understand the basis for these findings, further empirical research might be followed through in a number of areas. At one level, for example, these data may constitute outcomes of (a) the situation of the triad and (b) of the rational and nonrational elements which enter into the decision-making process. They bear on problems of factors associated with power relationships and dominance-submission patterns within the family. At another level these data bear on matters which are only rarely the subject of sociological research, such as the rational and mystical elements which underlie choice of the religion through which one will worship and the factors which comprise the religious ethos of an individual family. Finally, the issues raised by religious intermarriage are linked also to larger questions of (a) the social, psychological, and institutional consequences of exogamous and endogamous marriages in general and (b) outcome in situations of interpersonal contact between individuals from differing cultures.

This paper is based upon data collected in connection with research carried out by the Neuropsychiatry Division, Walter Reed Army Institute of Research, Walter Reed Army Medical Center, Washington, D.C. The authors are particularly indebted to Dr. David McK. Rioch, Director of the Neuropsychiatry Division, and to Dr. Albert J. Glass, Colonel, U.S. Army (ret.), formerly Deputy Director, for the opportunity to make use of these data.

NOTES

1. See, for example, James Bossard and Eleanor Boll, *One Marriage, Two Faiths*, New York: Ronald Press, 1957; Lee G. Burchinal and Loren E. Chancellor, "Ages at Marriage, Occupations of Grooms and Interreligious Marriage Rates," *Social Forces*, 40 (May, 1962), pp. 348–54; "Factors Related to Interreligious Marriages in Iowa, 1953–57," Iowa Agricultural and Home Economics Experiment Station, Iowa State University, Ames, Iowa, Research Bulletin 510, November 1962; "Survival Rates Among Religiously Homogamous and Interreligious Marriages," *Social Forces*, 41 (May, 1963), pp. 353–62; Loren E. Chancellor and Thomas P. Monahan, "Religious Preference and Interreligious Mixtures in Marriages and Divorces in Iowa," *American Journal of Sociology*, 61 (November, 1955), pp. 233–39; Joseph Golden, "Patterns of Negro-White Intermarriage," *American Socio-*

logical Review, 19 (1954), pp. 144–47; Jerold S. Heiss, "Premarital Characteristics of the Religiously Intermarried in an Urban Area," *American Sociological Review*, 25 (February, 1960), pp. 47–55; August B. Hollingshead, "Cultural Factors in the Selection of Marriage Mates," *American Sociological Review*, 15 (1950), pp. 619–27; Ruby J. R. Kennedy, "Single or Triple Melting Pot? Intermarriage Trends in New Haven, 1870–1950," *American Journal of Sociology*, 58 (1952), pp. 56–59; Judson T. Landis, "Marriages of Mixed and Non-Mixed Religious Faiths," *American Sociological Review*, 14 (June, 1949), pp. 401–07; Murray H. Leiffer, "Mixed Marriages and Church Loyalty," *The Christian Century*, 66 (January 19, 1949), pp. 78–80; Harvey Locke, *et al.*, "Interfaith Marriages," *Social Problems*, 4 (April, 1957), pp. 329–33; Simon Marcson, "A Theory of Intermarriage and Assimilation," *Social Forces*, 29 (January, 1950), pp. 75–78; J. L. Thomas, "The Factor of Religion in the Selection of Marriage Mates," *American Sociological Review*, 16 (1951), pp. 487–91.

2. See the exposition of this point, for example, in Will Herberg, *Protestant-Catholic-Jew*, Garden City, New York: Anchor Books, Doubleday & Co., Inc., 1960, Chapter 3, esp. pp. 36–41.

3. See the discussion in Ruth S. Cavan, "Subcultural Variations and Mobility," in Harold T. Christensen (ed.), *Handbook of Marriage and the Family*, Chicago: Rand McNally & Co., 1964, pp. 353–62.

4. Landis, *op. cit.*

5. Leiffer, *op. cit.*, p. 107.

6. For example, see Robert O. Blood, "The Husband-Wife Relationship," in F. I. Nye and Lois W. Hoffman (eds.), *The Employed Mother in America*, Chicago: Rand McNally, 1963, pp. 282–305; Robert O. Blood and R. L. Hamblin, "The Effect of the Wife's Employment on the Family Power Structure," *Social Forces*, 36 (1958), pp. 347–52; Robert O. Blood and D. M. Wolfe, *Husbands and Wives: The Dynamics of Married Living*, Glencoe: The Free Press, 1960; David M. Heer, "Dominance and the Working Wife," *Social Forces*, 36 (1958), pp. 341–47; "The Measurement and Basis of Family Power," *Marriage and Family Living*, 25 (1963), pp. 133–39; Lois W. Hoffman, "Parental Power Relations and the Division of Household Tasks," *Marriage and Family Living*, 22 (1960), pp. 27–35; R. Middleton and S. Putney, "Dominance in Decisions in the Family: Race and Class Differences," *American Journal of Sociology*, 65 (1960), pp. 605–09; Jesse R. Pitts, "The Structural-Functional Approach," in H. T. Christensen (ed.), *Handbook of Marriage and the Family*, Chicago: Rand McNally & Co., 1964, Chapter 3, pp. 51–124.

7. The study was undertaken in 1954 by the Neuropsychiatry Division of Walter Reed Army Institute of Research, Washington, D.C., and it was designed to explore methods of prediction of the incidence of peptic ulcer. For examples of other publications reporting research on the inductee study population, see S. H. Croog, "Ethnic Origins, Educational Level, and Responses to a Health Questionnaire," *Human Organization*, 20 (Summer, 1961), pp. 65–69; "Relations of Plasma Pepsinogen Levels to Ethnic Origins: Implications in Duodenal Ulcer," *United States Armed Forces Medical Journal*, 8 (June, 1957), pp. 795–801; S. H. Croog and Peter Kong-Ming New, "Knowledge of Grandfather's Occupation: Clues to American Kinship Structure," *Journal of Marriage and the Family*, 27 (February, 1965), pp. 69–77;

H. Weiner, *et al.*, "Etiology of Duodenal Ulcer. I. Relation of Specific Psychological Characteristics to Rate of Gastric Secretion (Serum Pepsinogen)," *Psychosomatic Medicine*, 19 (January-February, 1957), pp. 1–10; P. G. Yesler, M. F. Reiser, and D. M. Rioch, "Etiology of Duodenal Ulcer. II. Serum Pepsinogen and Peptic Ulcer in Inductees," *Journal of the American Medical Association*, 169 (January, 1959), pp. 451–56.

8. The frequency of mention of Jewish-Protestant and Jewish-Catholic parental intermarriages as well as intermarriages involving Greek Orthodox and Armenian Orthodox parents was minimal, and these cases were accordingly omitted from the analysis.

9. For reports on historical variation in patterns of intermarriage, see Milton L. Barron, "The Incidence of Jewish Intermarriage in Europe and America," *American Sociological Review*, 11 (1946), pp. 6–13; R. J. R. Kennedy, *op. cit.*; Claris E. Silcox and Galen M. Fisher, *Catholics, Jews, and Protestants*, New York: Harper and Brothers, 1934; and J. L. Thomas, *op. cit.*

10. For specific discussion of this point, see Landis, *op. cit.* and Leiffer, *op. cit.* For more general commentary on maternal roles in child development, see, for example, John Bowlby, *Maternal Care and Mental Health*, New York: World Health Organization, 1951; E. Z. Dager, "Socialization and Personality Development in the Child," in H. T. Christensen (ed.), *Handbook of Marriage and the Family*, Chicago: Rand-McNally Co., 1964, pp. 740–781; D. R. Peterson, *et al.*, "Child Behavior and Parental Attitudes," *Child Development*, 32 (1961), pp. 151–162; Robert F. Winch, *Identification and its Familial Determinants*, Indianapolis: Bobbs-Merrill, 1962.

11. Other measures such as occupational level of the father, social class of the father, and education of the mother were also employed in our analysis, and all yielded results essentially similar to those obtained when educational level alone was employed.

12. For example, see Joseph H. Fichter, *Southern Parish: Dynamics of a City Church*, Vol. 1, Chicago: University of Chicago Press, 1951; Landis, *op. cit.*; Leiffer, *op. cit.*; Joseph B. Schuyler, *Northern Parish: A Sociological and Pastoral Study*, Chicago: Loyola University Press, 1960, p. 294.

13. Finding reported in Sydney H. Croog and David E. Lavin, "Church Attendance and Associated Sociological Variables," unpublished manuscript.

What does it mean to grow up "between two worlds,"
as in the case, for example, of the child of a Jewish father
and a Roman Catholic mother? For the final selection
in this part of the book on the postmarital consequences
of intermarriage, we have the unusual, sensitive insights
of a participant observer. Richard Goldhurst (the
pseudonym of a young man who grew up in New York
City) tells us how he found himself "adrift between two
religious communities" and unable to make a compromise
between the two. He concludes that, in his own case,
an adjustment to any one religious community could not
be made, but he hopes to make an adjustment to the
American tradition of absorbing the immigrant and
reproducing the pioneer.

GROWING UP BETWEEN
TWO WORLDS*

Reflections of the Child of a Mixed Marriage

Richard Goldhurst

When we reached high school age, my mother wanted to finance
our education at a Catholic prep school. My mother's brother
tried to convince my father, a Jew, that the plan was sensible,
beneficial, and beautiful. The whole house rocked.

"Thou shalt not proselyte another man's child!" shouted my
father and shook his finger in my uncle's face. The fight left my
brothers and me with the feeling that we didn't want to go to *any*

*Reprinted by permission from *Commentary,* Vol. 16, No. 1 (July
1953), pp. 30–35, copyright © 1953 by the American Jewish Committee.

school. But the family compromised. My brothers went to parochial school and I went to public school. It will never seem to
me to have been an intelligent compromise. It is as if we, as
brothers, changed our names, but bore no name commonly. . . .

In the past three decades a mountain of literature has been
built up about the mixed marriage, the marriage between Gentile
and Jew. Leopold Bloom, Robert Cohn, Noah Ackerman were
all Jews married to Gentiles. And there have been a plethora of
articles, statistical studies, and essays by well-informed laymen
and prominent clergymen. Unfortunately, the mixed marriage has
been investigated mainly by nonparticipants, who understand
the issue in a general sense, but with little immediate knowledge
of the feelings and motivations of the individuals involved.

I have myself been very much a participant in a mixed marriage
—as one of its products. This will be a case history, as it were,
and at firsthand.

Basically, what can the child know of his parents? In the
deepest sense, perhaps very little. But he can report what he has
seen and felt.

Harry G. was a fairly successful stock-broker in his early
twenties when he hired a young secretary named Jenny N. Seven
years from the first day of her employment they were married.
They spent their courtship in the best New York restaurants,
applauded the most sophisticated plays, and went to every Army
and Navy football game.

Jenny had grown up in Scranton, Pennsylvania, the daughter
of an Irish Catholic ward-heeler. Her primary and high-school
education she got in parochial schools; then she went to a teachers'
college, after which she came to New York City to make her way.
Harry was the son of an immigrant Jew who had come here in
one of the tidal waves of immigration in the 1900's. From Stuy-
vesant High School, Harry went to Columbia College, and from
there to a brokerage house.

At their wedding reception Harry asked the orchestra to play
"My Wild Irish Rose" and Jenny requested "I'm Just Wild About
Harry."

Despite the enthusiasm of the couple and the approval of their
friends, the match met with vigorous opposition from both families. Jenny's mother asked her to think the matter over carefully,
and was finally won over only by the calm words of Jenny's

uncle, appropriately enough a judge. He said, "Is there anything you can do about it? No? Then I suggest you follow propriety and let your daughter lead her own life. God knows, there's a lot of Catholic Irishmen who will make her a bad husband, the Jew might make her a very good one."

Other of Jenny's relatives were not as reasonable, and she bore them resentment. After all, Harry had signed the *Lex Canulia,* and Catholic doctrine, if it would not urge, would at least sanction, and Catholic clergy perform, the marriage. Among her brothers and sisters, however, Jenny did find encouragement. In fact, three of her many brothers and sisters were later to marry Protestants.

Harry's immediate family was in despair. One of his brothers told him, "You're going to kill your poor father and you know it." They cried at Harry's stubbornness, scolded him for his decision, and then threw up their hands in resignation. They would not attend the marriage, which took place in the vestry of a Catholic church, or the reception afterwards. It is true that one of Harry's inveterately curious sisters wanted to come, but the others prevented her by the simple expedient of hiding all her clothes. While they were on their honeymoon, Harry's father had a heart attack as simulated as it was obvious.

Time improved everybody's manners—until the depression came along.

Harry lost his money as suddenly as he had made it. He had three children to feed. For the first time since her marriage Jenny went to work. Life became a siege of despair without hope. Money, often the ultimate factor in the success of a marriage, changed the relation between Harry and Jenny, and the complexion of their children's lives.

Much later, when the happiness of his youth had been irrevocably lost, Harry said to me: "Jews should never marry Christians. Christians always condescend to them. When they marry Jews they explain it to themselves on the ground that the Jew in question is a poet or a millionaire. You never hear of a Gentile marrying a poor, mediocre Jew. No, when Jews marry Gentiles they have all the furniture paid for!"

Jenny did little to contribute to this bitterness. She did not chronically complain about finances. Still, when my maternal aunts and uncles were present, or when my mother talked of them, complaint hung in the air. Success had come to them, and stayed. Socially ambitious, they were uncomfortable about my father. And Harry was prone to suspect that unintelligent conservatives were necessarily unintelligent bigots. The worst her family thought of Jenny was that she had bet on the wrong horse: that the wrong horse happened to be Jewish was only a contingent objection. But if his Irish relatives-in-law caused my father unhappiness, and he them, it was because there are basic values that Catholics and Jews do not, will not, and cannot hold together.

Still other things contributed to my father's bitterness. Hitler was in the ascendant in Germany and anti-Semites in the country were making the Jew more and more conscious of his Jewishness. My brother came home one day with a copy of *Social Justice* that he had bought from a woman hawking the magazine outside his parochial high school. The impotent rage of my father when he found *Social Justice* in his son's hands created a thunderous scene. Mother wanted no part of *Social Justice* or anti-Semitic prejudice—at least not consciously. To us children it always seemed that my father was trying to make her responsible for the sins of every Catholic bigot and Grand Inquisitor. Jenny read the copy of *Social Justice*, and tearfully she promised Harry, "I'll write the Bishop about this and ask him why he's letting it go on."

In a way, Harry had dug his own grave. Jews were finding this a time in which to remember and consolidate their traditional consciousness of themselves. Harry felt this need as much as any other Jew. Yet his children were making their first Catholic communion. He had no religious ties with his family. His brothers, in fact, resented him secretly, for they themselves had no sons and therefore no Bar Mitzvah to celebrate.

Perhaps this was the first time my brothers and I came to understand our own uniqueness. On both sides of the family we were the only sons. The interest my Jewish relatives took in us was slight; but let one of our paternal cousins fall ill and the whole family was at the bedside. Let a paternal cousin marry, choose a college, fail, succeed—it demanded a family decision and family encouragement. Not so in our case.

Our Irish relatives took a completely different tack. They were too interested. We had a prescribed course of conduct to which we were to adhere. No sins on our part were ever forgiven —and they looked for sins. The petty selfishness of children was a crime magnified by Jenny to the proportions of incest. We went to every social gathering of our maternal relatives, and while we were there we were the best behaved, quietest Lord Fauntleroys possible, which was an awful lot of silence for three boys to bear. On one occasion my mother told us that because we were Jewish we had to be that much better than other children.

The indifference we received from one side, and the strain of perfect behavior in the presence of the other, made my brothers and me viciously anti-family on every conceivable level. One brother later told me, in jest supposedly, that the reason he married his wife was because she was one girl with whom he could keep a distance of 500 miles between themselves and all relatives.

As well-behaved as we were, my brothers and I created a great deal of trouble. Trouble for our parents most of all. My father's religious convictions in his youth had been nothing. Himself emancipated, he came, he considered, from a long line of superstitious ancestors, and superstition in others frightened him. That his children could relapse, if only outwardly, into a modern form of primitive superstition—so he termed Roman Catholicism—he felt as an affliction. Actually, however, my mother's efforts to make Catholics of us failed completely. We grew up as Jews. True, we went to Mass every Sunday, but society at large understood us best as Jews. And society's decision provoked strange hostilities in Jenny.

It is to be doubted if anyone in our society escapes anti-Semitism altogether. Surely Jenny hadn't. She had been reared in an environment that considered Jews "subterranean." After all, many Christians hold that the Jews killed Jesus and have remained guilty of that crime ever since. During the 1930's this idea was being dug up from its religious grave and given a new political life. It created a climate impossible to ignore.

My mother's anti-Semitism manifested itself in two ways: the first was the distinction she would make between "classy" Jews and "cheap" Jews. Harry's family was "cheap" and deserving of evil; her children were warned they had damned well better be "classy." And then she had a long-standing feud with my father's sister, Clair. Clair was a vulgar, stupid, dishonest, and undignified woman who couldn't do anything right even when her motives were good. People with judgment would have nothing to do with her. Nevertheless my mother kept up relations with her for years, primarily in order to vent on Clair the anti-Semitism she never directly released against Harry. To be sure, my mother's sentiments when she took the trouble to think them out were not illiberal, and her anti-Semitism was minimal compared to what we usually call that.

In the early years of her marriage she had been punctiliously religious, going to Mass with clocklike precision. Her perseverance was more Christian than Christianity itself, for she had three sons and a husband who saw it all as the sheerest futility. What happens rarely to people of genuinely religious impulses happened to my mother. Over a period of years she was subjected to a constant barrage of skepticism and she began to think about the possible errors of her faith. Her religion and her ardor became tempered. Mass was no longer important to her as before and she neglected her Confessional.

On the other hand, as Harry struggled against his wife's faith, he came to rely, not on reason and logic, but on the early patterns and instincts he had acquired as a Jew. Today the change is almost complete, and Harry is a "progressively" religious Jew. But not so in a ritualistic sense as much as in a tribal and nationalistic one. In most things my father is a rationalist of the literal kind, but not in religion. Today he is omnivorous for any and everything Jewish.

Were it only ethical values he sought, Catholicism might have supplied them, but what he wanted, and maybe what he found, was that thread of reason in Judaism which began when someone in the Near East five thousand years ago found it hard to believe that God was like an animal. His anti-Catholicism became, in the end, only another way of justifying his religious feelings— which may have been kindled originally and subconsciously as a way of doing penance for having married a Gentile. Why these feelings asserted themselves explicitly only after the tension about religion between him and Jenny had relaxed, is something I can't answer here.

As a little boy I remember fortnightly visits to Grandpa's. He was a gray little man with a small round *yarmelke* covering his bald pate. He used to stand in the door of his apartment and greet us with, *"Vos machstu,* boys?"

"Vos machstu, Grandpa?"

"Are you all well? Have you been good boys?"

"Yes, Grandpa."

"That's fine. And how is the *shikse*?"

I was fifteen before I discovered that *shikse* did not mean "mother."

Then there was an Irish aunt, full-throated and belligerent, who used to warn that if we didn't go to church and love Jesus dearly, our mother would be fed to the flames in Hell. "The worst of all sins, boys," she'd yipe, "is for a Catholic to renege on his religion. You don't want your mother to go to Hell and burn because you don't go to Mass, do you?"

And so my brothers and I grew up conceiving of God as a split personality. Children exposed to warring religious faiths will respond with metaphysical skepticism—literally. They will also decide that the truly good people of this world are those who mind their own business. My mother and father were far better at convincing me of each other's mistakes than they were at correcting their own. Some parents, when they have nothing to say, tell stories to their children. Mine used to darken the day with God.

I made my first Communion, shuddering at my father's bitterness and blinking at my mother's tears. Supposedly, this is an hour of triumphant joy for Catholic children. I was too young to know at that time the exact mechanics of divorce but it looked like it was going to come at any minute. None of us dared ask a question at home about the importance or significance of the ritual because we knew a fight between our parents would be inevitable. As a consequence, I knew no more of the meaning of the whole thing than our Baptist elevator boy did.

Mother thought there was nothing unseemly in our being brought up and educated as Catholics. Before marriage my father had willingly conceded this to her, and she could not understand why he opposed her now.

Father never forbade us to go to Mass, but he told us we betrayed him by doing so. Mother tried to dispel our doubts by telling us that Father had no business in the matter. With my playmates I was sometimes ashamed of him; not only did he not want his children to go to Mass but he never went himself. Once

I lied to some friends who asked if he *never* went to Mass at all. "He *might* go around Easter," I said.

A little later I found out why he didn't go. It was brand-new to me that there was a possibility either of having more than one God for the universe, or that my mother might be wrong, and that there weren't any Gods at all.

Catholics did little to convince me that my mother was right; all they could say was that my father, because a Jew, was *a priori* wrong. Most of the time Catholics acted as though they were doing me and my brothers a favor when they let us attend Mass. All of my prayer and piety did not make me fulfilled in their eyes. I know now that I did not particularly want their acceptance, but that did not make church any the less uncomfortable for me when I was young.

My brothers and I were privileged to hear a lot more anti-Semitism than most other Jews ever do. Very little of it was serious or vicious. But what I did hear taught me this: the majority of Roman Catholics have no understanding of the true heart of Catholicism. They approach its poetic edges, but the shining ideal of a worldwide house for all men is alien to them.

All in all, the children I knew were just tactless; it takes a lot of energy and more of cleverness to be downright rude. They felt it was perfectly all right for someone to be a Jew, but he was still a Jew and there's something a little bit more different about being a Jew than there is about being left-handed. As they grow older, their ideas change, often for the worse. It has been argued that all children are essentially the same, that they tend to accept their contemporaries for what their contemporaries are worth. This is a mistake. Children are as sophisticated and as cruel as the most advanced of their elders. They have their own conception of society and they can smell the heretic as quickly as any Babbitt can.

Over and over again I have identified myself as a Jew, primarily because society did, and does. But there is an inner belonging that I know I lack. One born half-Catholic and half-Jew does not face the problem of whether to be Jewish or Catholic, but the problem of what sort of Jew to be. In any ritualistic sense my brothers and I are no more Jews than Caesar was a Laplander. Jewishness in general remains for us something peripheral to our lives. Unfortunately this has provoked the antagonism of a great many Jews. There have been Jews who envied my meed of Gentile blood and yet worried about my welfare; no good, they warned me, could come of posturing as a Gentile.

Other Jews have felt I was, and would remain, neurotic and repressed until I repudiated the influence of my mother. Still others insisted that my youth must have been a chronicle of supreme torture. None of this is true. My youth knew its frustrations, but there is no need to suppose these still dangle in front of me like a carrot in front of a mule. The fact is, my Jewishness is casual, not thoroughgoing, and exists only in an ethnic sense—and that for convenience. I find it hard to be militant about it.

The instability of my youth has given way to the compromise of adulthood. One never forgets such instability and it is remembered with a certain self-pity. The question "Where do I belong?" is one that few adult minds can resolve. To thrust the question upon a child at an age when he is not at all equipped to answer it was unfair.

By themselves, Catholics and Jews may be noble and understanding, possessed of every elemental decency. The world around them is not. Too many contingencies cannot be foreseen. Politics, for instance. Had my parents known in advance of Hitler's effect upon the world, it might have altered their marital plans. Had my mother known of the effect my father and her children were to have on her, certainly she would have hesitated. With a Catholic education behind me I did not belong to the Jews; having been to the "nether" world, I did not belong to the Catholics either. So I could not belong to the society of children. For children know two criteria of right and wrong—home and their playmates. If these two are not kept in constant balance, the child may live in half-doubt and confusion, until his age permits him to think things out for himself.

Yet the story of the half-Jewish child is not only tears and homelessness; it also has a positive side, one that it is important to take into account. His "exposure" can give him something more of sight and sound and sensibility than is bestowed on other children. And there is this that he can know: as the child of a mixed marriage he is probably the best example—and exponent —of the *immigrant tradition*—that masterpiece of the vivid extremes that have come together to give America her promise and her vitality.

Whenever I've been asked about my ancestry, and I've explained it, whatever other feelings my interrogator has experienced, he has still shown the smile of one who glimpses romance. The Catholic-Jew is a symbol of reshuffling and expansions. The romance is there because the Catholic-Jew is so *typically* an American product. . . .

Jews themselves, as well as Americans generally, all too often conceive that Jews have somehow a special problem in achieving dignity. The Jew, they feel, needs sympathy because of the social and psychological problems society engenders for him. The assumption is even made that the problem of gaining dignity and self-acceptance will prove too big for him to master. If this is true, it should be too terrible to admit.

The Jew is an American settler, and it might be some reassurance to him to realize that countless settlers before him have been unique, too. The Pilgrims were white in a land of red men; until long after the Civil War the Irish were a strange, unfathomable lot. The Italians formed a new and special group, just as special as Jewish children or children of a mixed marriage. The capacity and the chance to adjust are more or less equal. True, the Jews have behind them a history of pogroms and persecutions, but anti-Semitism in America will probably never be *respectable* as it was on the continent of Europe. And that makes a big difference.

Every man finds society in some way "structured" against him. Actually, a child who lives straddled between the Jewish and Catholic hemispheres has problems no more cruel than those of a child born into poverty or to a crippling infirmity. The chief problem of the child of mixed marriage is that he wants to be more than a "Catholic-Jew," that he does not want forever to live on the margins of heresy, adrift between two religious communities.

But America is still composed largely of such communities; the separation between state, religion, and politics has not yet been completely effected. It would have been better had either the split been more pronounced, or the unification through religion more binding. The division, so-called, between secular and clerical has been more theoretical than practical. God stalks America like an angry bloodhound. Everyone is presumed religious in a churchgoing sense until the contrary becomes embarrassingly obvious.

Catholics and Jews like Jenny and Harry cannot adjust to each other, and their children find it impossible to adjust to either of their parents, because there is no tradition of adjustment to grasp. The child of mixed marriage may identify himself with Jewishness if only in order to keep society quiet—but from then on he is on his own, and must pick and choose for himself. No path is open except metaphysical skepticism, naturalism, heroic secularism. Yet this is peculiarly American. The Catholic-Jew is America in miniature, he is a child without tradition and much of his energies must be spent in testing hypotheses on the way to the discovery or creation of a tradition of his own. In 1830 de Tocqueville wrote of America that ". . . it is one of the countries where the precepts of Descartes are least studied and best applied. Men living in this state of society cannot derive their belief from the opinions of the class to which they belong; every man there readily loses all trace of the ideals of his forefathers or takes no care of them."

Out of his unhappiness, the child of mixed marriage can find a way of life that is no compromise. The adjustment to a religious community may not be made, but the adjustment to an American tradition may. America is constantly absorbing the immigrant only to reproduce the pioneer. Perhaps the child of mixed marriage will live to know himself one.

BIBLIOGRAPHY

The following works on intermarriage are selective of the literature rather than exhaustive. They are offered as a resource whereby readers may supplement their knowledge and pursue their interests beyond the limits of this volume. In preparing this bibliography, it seemed most practical to assume that the mother-tongue of the book's audience would be so overwhelmingly English that it would be fruitless to suggest further readings in other languages. Thus, a rather extensive literature on the subject, especially that prepared by German scholars, was eliminated from consideration. It was further assumed that social science analyses of intermarriage would be more enlightening than fictional, hortatory, and entertainment motivated approaches to the problem.

The classification scheme used in this bibliography calls for a brief explanation. Some books and articles are comprehensive or general in scope, limited to no single ethnic aspect of intermarriage. Others dwell on either racial, nationality, or religious intermarriage and are most easily discernible under separate classification in each instance. Finally, by the very nature of the unyielding posture of Jews to any arbitrary categorization as a race, religious group, or nationality, and by virtue of an unusually prolific flow of scholarship on the subject, the final classification is devoted to suggested further readings on Jewish-Gentile intermarriage.

GENERAL

Barron, Milton L., *People Who Intermarry,* Syracuse, Syracuse University Press, 1946, 389 pp.
———, "Race, Religion and Nationality in Mate Selection," in Fishbein, Morris and Kennedy, Ruby Jo Reeves, eds., *Modern Marriage and Family Living,* New York, Oxford University Press, 1957, pp. 60–73.
Bugelski, B. R., "Assimilation Through Intermarriage," *Social Forces,* Vol. 40 (1961), pp. 148–53.
Drachsler, Julius, *Democracy and Assimilation,* New York, Macmillan, 1920, 275 pp.
———, *Intermarriage in New York City*: Studies in History, Economics and Public Law, No. 213, New York, Columbia University Press, 1921, 204 pp.
Freeman, Linton, "Homogamy in Interethnic Mate Selection," *Sociology and Social Research,* Vol. 39 (1954–5), pp. 369–77.
Gordon, Albert I., *Intermarriage: Interfaith, Interracial, Interethnic,* Boston, Beacon Press, 1964, 420 pp. (Paperback, 1966).

Hollingshead, August B., "Cultural Factors in the Selection of Marriage Mates," *American Sociological Review*, Vol. 15 (October 1950), pp. 619–27.

Kennedy, Ruby Jo Reeves, "Single or Triple Melting Pot? Intermarriage Trends in New Haven, 1870–1940," *American Journal of Sociology*, Vol. 49 (January 1944), pp. 331–9.

———, "Single or Triple Melting Pot? Intermarriage Trends in New Haven, 1870–1950," *American Journal of Sociology*, Vol. 58 (July 1952), pp. 56–9.

Macormick, Thomas C., and Macrory, B. E., "Group Value in Mate Selection in a Sample of College Girls," *Social Forces*, Vol. 22 (1944), pp. 315–7.

Marcson, Simon, "A Theory of Intermarriage and Assimilation," *Social Forces*, Vol. 29, No. 1 (October 1950), pp. 75–8.

———, "Intermarriage and Generational Status," *Phylon*, Vol. 12 (1951), pp. 357–63.

———, "Predicting Intermarriage," *Sociology and Social Research*, Vol. 37 (Jan.–Feb. 1953), pp. 151–6.

Price, C., and Zubrzycki, J., "The Use of Intermarriage Statistics as an Index of Assimilation," *Population Studies*, Vol. 16 (July 1963), pp. 58–69.

Sanua, Victor D., "Intermarriage and Psychological Adjustment," in Silverman, Hirsch Lazar, ed., *Marital Counseling*, Springfield, Ill., Charles C. Thomas, 1967, pp. 423–42.

Simpson, George E., and Yinger, J. Milton, "Intermarriage: Interracial, Interfaith, and Internationality," *Racial and Cultural Minorities*, New York, Harper and Brothers, 1958, pp. 540–73.

Stern, Bernhard J., "Intermarriage," *Encyclopedia of the Social Sciences*, Vol. 8, pp. 151–4.

RACIAL

Adams, Romanzo, *Interracial Marriage in Hawaii*, New York, Macmillan, 1937.

Berry, Brewton, *Almost White*, New York, Macmillan, 1963. (Paperback, Collier Books, 1969)

Burma, John H., "Research Note on the Measurement of Interracial Marriage," *American Journal of Sociology*, Vol. 57 (May 1952), pp. 587–9.

Cheng, C. K., and Yamamura, D., "Interracial Marriage and Divorce in Hawaii," *Social Forces*, Vol. 36 (1957), pp. 77–84.

Collins, Sydney F., "The Social Position of White and 'Half-Caste' Women in Colored Groupings in Britain," *American Sociological Review*, Vol. 16 (December 1951), pp. 796–802.

Golden, Joseph, "Characteristics of the Negro-White Intermarried in Philadelphia," *American Sociological Review*, Vol. 18 (April 1953), pp. 177–83.

————, "Patterns of Negro-White Intermarriage," *American Sociological Review,* Vol. 19 (April 1954), pp. 144–7.

————, "Social Control of Negro-White Intermarriage," *Social Forces,* Vol. 36 (March 1958), pp. 267–9.

Harre, John, *Maori and Pakeha: A Study of Mixed Marriages in New Zealand,* New York, Frederick A. Praeger, 1966, 158 pp.

Larsson, Clotye Murdock, ed., *Marriage Across the Color Line,* Chicago, Johnson Publishing Co., 1965, 204 pp.

Lynn, Sister Annella, *Interracial Marriages in Washington, D. C., 1940–7,* Washington, D. C., Catholic University of America Press, 1953.

Monahan, Thomas P., "Interracial Marriages," *Social Forces,* Vol. 48 (1970), pp. 461–73.

Schmitt, Robert C., "Interracial Marriage and Occupational Status in Hawaii," *American Sociological Review,* Vol. 28 (October 1963), pp. 809–10.

Schnepp, Gerald J., and Yui, Agnes Masako, "Cultural and Marital Adjustment of Japanese War Brides," *American Journal of Sociology,* Vol. 61 (1955), pp. 48–50.

Smith, Charles Edward, "Negro-White Intermarriage in Metropolitan New York," unpublished Ph.D. Thesis, Columbia University, 1960.

Washington, Joseph R., Jr., *Marriage in Black and White,* Boston, Beacon Press, 1970, 358 pp.

NATIONALITY

Bossard, James H. S., "Nationality and Nativity as Factors in Marriage," *American Sociological Review,* Vol. 4 (1939), pp. 792–8.

Catapusan, Benicio T., "Filipino Intermarriage Problems in the United States," *Sociology and Social Research,* Vol. 22 (Jan.–Feb. 1938), pp. 265–72.

Hunt, C., and Colley, R., "Intermarriage and Cultural Change: A Study of Filipino-American Marriages," *Social Forces,* Vol. 35 (1957), pp. 223–30.

Johnson, Hildegard Binder, "Intermarriages Between German Pioneers and Other Nationalities in Minnesota in 1860 and 1870," *American Journal of Sociology,* Vol. 51 (January 1946), pp. 299–304.

Mittelbach, Frank G. *et al., Intermarriage of Mexican-Americans,* Los Angeles, University of California, 1966, 84 pp.

Wessel, Bessie Bloom, "Comparative Rates of Intermarriage Among Different Nationalities in the United States," *Eugenical News,* Vol. 15 (1930), pp. 105–7.

RELIGIOUS

Allred, Vincent C., *The Legal Status of the Ante-Nuptial Promise Before Mixed Marriage,* Washington, D. C., National Catholic Welfare Conference (1952), 45 pp.

Baber, Ray E., "A Study of 325 Mixed Marriages," *American Sociological Review,* Vol. 2 (1937), pp. 705–16.

Barnett, Larry D., "Research in Interreligious Dating and Marriage," *Marriage and Family Living,* Vol. 24 (May 1962), pp. 191–4.

Bealer, R. C. *et al.,* "Religious Exogamy: A Study of Social Distance," *Sociology and Social Research,* Vol. 48 (1963), pp. 69–79.

Besanceney, Paul H., *Interfaith Marriages: Who and Why,* New Haven, College and University Press Services, 1971, 223 pp.

Bishop's Committee on Mixed Marriages, *A Factual Study of Mixed Marriages,* Washington, D. C., National Catholic Welfare Conference, 1943.

Black, Algernon D., *If I Marry Outside My Religion,* New York, Public Affairs Committee, 1954, 28 pp.

Bossard, James H. S., and Letts, Harold C., "Mixed Marriages Involving Lutherans," *Marriage and Family Living,* Vol. 18 (Nov. 1956), pp. 308–10.

Bossard, James H. S., and Boll, Eleanor Stoker, *One Marriage: Two Faiths,* New York, The Ronald Press Co., 1957, 180 pp.

Brown, James Stephen, "Social Class, Intermarriage, and Church Membership in a Kentucky Community," *American Journal of Sociology,* Vol. 57 (1951–2), pp. 232–42.

Burchinal, Lee G., "Membership Groups and Attitudes Toward Cross-Religious Dating and Marriages," *Marriage and Family Living,* Vol. 22 (August 1960), pp. 248–53.

Burchinal, Lee G., and Chancellor, Loren E., "Ages at Marriage, Occupations of Grooms and Interreligious Marriage Rates," *Social Forces,* Vol. 40 (May 1962), pp. 348–54.

———, "Proportions of Catholics, Urbanism and Mixed Catholic Marriage Rates Among Iowa Counties," *Social Problems,* Vol. 9 (1962), pp. 359–65.

———, "Survival Rates Among Religiously Homogamous and Interreligious Marriages," *Social Forces,* Vol. 41 (May 1963), pp. 353–62.

Chancellor, Loren E., and Monahan, Thomas P., "Religious Preferences and Interreligious Mixtures in Marriages and Divorces in Iowa," *American Journal of Sociology,* Vol. 61 (Nov. 1955), pp. 233–9.

Dekker, G., *Mixed Marriages in the Netherlands,* Meppel, J. A. Boom en Zoon, 1965, 205 pp.

Duvall, Evelyn Millis, *In-Laws Pro and Con,* New York, Association Press, 1954 (Chapter 5: Mother-in-Law Roles in Mixed Marriages, pp. 70–88).

Glick, Paul C., "Intermarriage and Fertility Among Persons in Major Religious Groups," *Eugenics Quarterly,* Vol. 7 (March 1960), pp. 31–8.

Greeley, Andrew M., "Religious Intermarriage in a Denominational Society," *American Journal of Sociology,* Vol. 75 (May 1970), pp. 949–52.

Hairle, Rudolf K., Jr., "A Survey of Literature on Religious Intermarriage," unpublished M.A. Thesis, University of Chicago, 1962.

Harris, Monford, "On Marrying Outside One's Existence," *Conservative Judaism*, Vol. 30 (Winter 1966), pp. 61–4.

Heer, David M., "The Trend of Interfaith Marriages in Canada: 1922–1957," *American Sociological Review*, Vol. 27 (April 1962), pp. 245–50.

Heiss, Jerold S., "Interfaith Marriage and Marital Outcome," *Marriage and Family Living*, Vol. 23 (August 1961), pp. 228–33.

Herberg, Will, "The Triple Melting Pot," *Commentary*, Vol. 20 (1955), pp. 101–8.

Landis, Judson T., "Marriages of Mixed and Non-Mixed Religious Faith," *American Sociological Review*, Vol. 14 (June 1949), pp. 401–7.

Lazerwitz, Bernard, "Intermarriage and Conversion," *The Jewish Journal of Sociology*, Vol. 13 (June 1971), pp. 41–63.

Leiffer, Murray, "Mixed Marriages and the Children," *The Christian Century*, Vol. 66 (January 26, 1948), pp. 106–8.

Little, George, "Analytic Reflections of Mixed Marriages," *Psychoanalytic Review*, Vol. 29 (1942), pp. 20–5.

Locke, Harvey J., Sabagh, G., and Thomas, M. M., "Interfaith Marriages," *Social Problems*, Vol. 4 (April 1957), pp. 329–33.

Monahan, Thomas P., and Kephart, W. M., "Divorce and Desertion by Religious and Mixed Marriage Groups," *American Journal of Sociology*, Vol. 59 (1954), pp. 454–65.

Pike, James A., *If You Marry Outside Your Faith*, New York, Harper and Brothers, 1962 (rev. ed.), 159 pp.

Prince, Alfred J., "Attitudes of College Students Toward Interfaith Marriage," *Coordinator*, Vol. 5 (September 1956), pp. 11–23.

Rodman, Hyman, "Technical Note on Two Rates of Mixed Marriage," *American Sociological Review*, Vol. 30 (October 1965), pp. 776–8.

Rosenthal, Erich, "Divorce and Religious Intermarriage: The Effect of Previous Marital Status upon Subsequent Marital Behavior," *Journal of Marriage and the Family* (August 1970), pp. 435–40.

Salisbury, W. Seward, "Religious Identification, Mixed Marriages, and Conversion," *Journal for the Scientific Study of Religion*, Vol. 8 (Spring 1969), pp. 125–9.

Schnepp, Gerald J., *Leakage from a Catholic Parish*, Washington, D.C., Catholic University of America Press, 1942.

Schnepp, Gerald J., and Roberts, Louis A., "Residential Propinquity and Mate Selection on a Parish Basis," *American Journal of Sociology*, Vol. 58 (July 1952), pp 45–50.

Silcox, Claris E., and Fisher, Galen M., *Catholics, Jews and Protestants*, New York, Harper, 1934 (Chapter 7, pp. 239–72).

Smith, John D., "Why They Marry Others and Subsequent Results," *The Catholic World*, Vol. 176 (October 1952), pp. 46–50.

Thomas, John L., *The American Catholic Family,* Englewood Cliffs, Prentice-Hall, 1956 (Chapter 6, pp. 148–64).

Traynor, Victor J., "Urban and Rural Mixed Marriage," *Social Order,* Vol. 6 (April 1956), 154–8.

JEWISH-GENTILE

Angoff, Charles, "In the Margin: Intermarriage," *Jewish Spectator,* September 1959, pp. 21–4.

Barron, Milton L., "The Incidence of Jewish Intermarriage in Europe and America," *American Sociological Review,* Vol. 11 (February 1946), pp. 6–13.

———, "Jewish Husbands and Gentile Wives," *Congress Bi-Weekly,* Vol. 36 (Dec. 19, 1969), pp. 11–15.

Berman, Louis A., *Jews and Intermarriage: A Study in Personality and Culture,* New York, Thomas Yoseloff, 1968, 707 pp.

Bigman, Stanley, *The Jewish Population of Greater Washington in 1956,* Washington, D.C., Jewish Community Council of Greater Washington (Chapter 8, pp. 123–39).

Cahnman, Werner J., "New Intermarriage Studies: A Critical Survey," *Reconstructionist,* Vol. 33 (March 17, 1967), pp. 7–13.

———, ed., *Intermarriage and Jewish Life: A Symposium,* New York, The Herzl Press and the Jewish Reconstructionist Press, 1963, 212 pp.

Cohen, Erik, "Mixed Marriage in an Israeli Town," *The Jewish Journal of Sociology,* Vol. 11 (June 1969), pp. 41–50.

Davis, Moshe, "Mixed Marriage in Western Jewry: Historical Background to the Jewish Response," *Jewish Journal of Sociology,* Vol. 10 (December 1968), pp. 177–220.

Dean, John P., "Patterns of Association Between Jews and Non-Jews," *Jewish Social Studies,* Vol. 17 (1955), pp. 247–68.

Eisenstein, Ira, *Intermarriage,* New York, Burning Bush Press, 1964, 23 pp.

Fein, Leonard J., "Some Consequences of Jewish Intermarriage," *Jewish Social Studies,* Vol. 33 (1971), pp. 44–58.

Felder, Eleanor, "My Child: Jew or Christian?" *Commentary,* Vol. 14 (1952), pp. 231–6.

Fishberg, Maurice, *The Jews: A Study of Race and Environment,* New York, Walter Scott Publishing Co., 1911 (Chapters 8 and 9).

Freehof, S. B., "Report on Mixed Marriages and Intermarriage," *57th Yearbook of the Central Conference of American Rabbis,* 1947, pp. 158–84.

Goldstein, Sidney, and Goldscheider, Calvin, "Social and Demographic Aspects of Jewish Intermarriages," *Social Problems,* Vol. 13 (Spring 1966), pp. 386–99.

Jospe, Alfred, "Intermarriage and the Jewish College Student," *Jewish Heritage,* Spring 1965, pp. 5–13.

Kirschenbaum, David, *Mixed Marriages and the Jewish Future,* New York, Bloch Publishing Co., 1958, 144 pp.

Kligfeld, Bernard, "A Review of the Literature on the Subject of Mixed Marriages," *70th Yearbook of the Central Conference of American Rabbis*, 1961, pp. 135–6.

Lestschinsky, Jacob, "Mixed Marriages: United States, Australia and Argentina," *Current Events*, Series 6, January–March 1953, pp. 14–19.

Levinson, M. H., and Levinson, D. J., "Jews Who Intermarry: Sociopsychological Bases of Ethnic Identity and Change," *Yivo Annual of Jewish Social Science*, Vol. 12 (1958–9), pp. 103–30.

Litvinoff, Emanuel, "Children of Two Inheritances," *Commentary*, Vol. 15 (March 1953), pp. 272–9.

Maller, Allen Stephen, "New Facts About Mixed Marriage," *Reconstructionist*, Vol. 35 (March 21, 1969), pp. 26–9.

Mayer, John E., *Jewish-Gentile Courtships*, New York, Free Press of Glencoe, 1961, 240 pp.

———, "Jewish-Gentile Intermarriage Patterns: A Hypothesis," *Sociology and Social Research*, Vol. 45 (1960), pp. 188–95.

Resnick, Reuben B., "Some Sociological Aspects of Intermarriage of Jews and Non-Jews," *Social Forces*, Vol. 12 (1933), pp. 94–102.

Rosenthal, Erich, "Acculturation Without Assimilation? The Jewish Community of Chicago, Illinois," *American Journal of Sociology*, Vol. 66 (November 1960), pp. 275–88.

———, "Studies of Jewish Intermarriage in the United States," *American Jewish Year Book: 1963*, Vol. 64, Jewish Publication Society of America, Philadelphia, 53 pp.

Schwartz, Arnold, "Intermarriage in the United States," *American Jewish Textbook: 1970*, Vol. 71, Philadelphia and New York, Jewish Publication Society of America and American Jewish Committee, 1970, pp. 101–21.

Shanks, Herschel, "Jewish-Gentile Intermarriage: Facts and Trends," *Commentary*, Vol. 16 (October 1953), pp. 370–5.

Sklare, Marshall, "Intermarriage and the Jewish Future," *Commentary*, Vol. 37 (April 1964), pp. 46–52.

———, "Intermarriage and Jewish Survival," *Commentary*, Vol. 49 (March 1970), pp. 51–8.

Slater, Eliot, "A Note on Jewish-Christian Intermarriage," *Eugenics Review*, Vol. 39 (1947), pp. 17–21.

Slotkin, J. S., "Jewish-Gentile Intermarriage in Chicago," *American Sociological Review*, Vol. 7 (February 1942), pp. 34–9.

———, "Adjustment in Jewish-Gentile Intermarriages," *Social Forces*, Vol. 21 (December 1942), pp. 226–30.

Wolff, G., "Social Significance of Jewish-Christian Intermarriage," *Scientific Monthly*, January 1946, pp. 95–8.

INDEX

CONTRIBUTING AUTHORS

Kenneth E. Barber was born in 1933. Both his bachelor's and master's degrees were earned at Brigham Young University, and he was awarded the Ph.D. at Purdue University in 1967. A member of the sociology department at Washington State University, Professor Barber's special fields are marriage and the family and social psychology.

Milton L. Barron was born in 1918 and received all his higher education at Yale University. After the B.A. and M.A. degrees, he was awarded the Ph.D. in 1945. Professor of sociology at the City College of the City University of New York, he has concentrated primarily in race and ethnic relations and the problems of the juvenile and the aged. His doctoral dissertation was on intermarriage in a New England industrial community.

Louis A. Berman, born in 1921, was educated at Wayne State University for his B.A. and received his Ph.D. at the University of Michigan. A psychologist specializing in the confluence of psychology and religion, Dr. Berman is a member of the faculty at the University of Illinois, Chicago Circle. His book, *Jews and Intermarriage* (1968), is one of the most sophisticated and comprehensive monographs on the topic.

Paul H. Besanceney was born in 1924 and has been study director of the Sociological Study of the Society of Jesus and its Apostolates, Detroit Province, since 1966. He received undergraduate degrees from Xavier University and West Baden College, and the M.A. degree from St. Louis University. After returning to West Baden for his theological degree, he attended the University of Michigan and received his Ph.D. at Michigan State University in 1964. Professor Besanceney, chairman of the sociology department at John Carroll University, is the author of *Interfaith Marriages: Who and Why* (1970).

John Berry Biesanz was born in 1913. He earned his B.A. at the University of Chicago, and the University of Iowa awarded him his Ph.D. in 1941. Professor Biesanz is a member of Wayne State University's department of sociology where he specializes in sociological theory and social change.

Eleanor Stoker Boll was formerly associate director of the University of Pennsylvania's William T. Carter Foundation for Child Development. For many years she collaborated with Bossard on many research projects in the field of family relationships. In recent years she has lived in Woodbury, Connecticut.

James H. S. Bossard, who was born in 1888, died in 1960. A graduate of Muhlenberg College, he took his master's degree and the Ph.D. (1917) at the University of Pennsylvania. Director of the William T.

Carter Foundation for Child Development for many years, Professor Bossard's central interests were in family relationships and social problems. His book in collaboration with Mrs. Boll, *One Marriage: Two Faiths* (1957), enjoyed a wide audience among laymen and clergymen.

John H. Burma was born in 1913. Educated at Trinity University for the B.A. and the University of Texas for the M.A., he received the Ph.D. degree from the University of Nebraska in 1941. A sociologist with special interests in race and ethnic relations and delinquency and crime, Dr. Burma teaches at Grinnell College.

Harold T. Christensen, who was born in 1909, received his bachelor's and master's degrees from Brigham Young University, and his doctorate in 1941 from the University of Wisconsin. Now a professor of sociology at Purdue University, he concentrates in the fields of comparative social systems and marriage and the family.

Sydney H. Croog was born in 1926 and took all his university training and degrees at Yale University, culminating in the Ph.D. in 1954. A sociologist specializing in marriage and the family and medical sociology, Professor Croog is a member of the Department of Behavioral Sciences and Community Health at the University of Connecticut's Health Center in Hartford, Connecticut.

Joseph P. Fitzpatrick was born in 1913. He received his B.A. from Georgetown University, his M.A. from Fordham University, and in 1949 Harvard awarded him his Ph.D. A specialist in delinquency and crime and in race and ethnic relations, he is a member of Fordham's department of sociology.

William Barry Furlong is a free-lance writer who makes his home in Chicago. He is a frequent contributor to the *New York Times Magazine.*

Richard Goldhurst is the pseudonym of a New Yorker whose first published work was the autobiographical account of his parents' intermarriage and its influence upon him as it appears in this volume.

Albert I. Gordon was born in 1903 and died in 1968. Educated at New York University for his bachelor's and master's degrees, he was awarded his doctorate in anthropology in 1949 at the University of Minnesota. A rabbi in Massachusetts for many years, Dr. Gordon also served as a labor arbitrator and executive director of the United Synagogue of America. After his book on intermarriage was published in 1964; his work on *The Nature of Conversion* appeared in 1967.

Andrew M. Greeley was born in 1928. He was awarded his bachelor's degree by St. Mary of the Lake Seminary, and his M.A. and Ph.D. (1962) degrees by the University of Chicago. Program director at the University of Illinois, Chicago Circle, Dr. Greeley's specialties are the sociology of religion and education.

Bernard Lazerwitz, who was born in 1926, was educated at Washington University (B.A., 1950), the University of Chicago (M.A., 1952), and the University of Michigan (Ph.D., 1959). Now a professor of sociology at the University of Missouri, his key fields are methodology and statistics and urban sociology.

Robert K. Merton was born in 1910 and did his undergraduate work at Temple University. Trained subsequently at Harvard for his master's degree, he received his Ph.D. from that university in 1936. He is professor of sociology at Columbia University, and he is best known for his teaching and writings in sociological theory and the sociology of science and knowledge.

Erich Rosenthal, who was born in 1912, received both his master's and doctor's degrees at the University of Chicago, the latter in 1948. Professor of sociology at Queens College of the City University of New York, his special fields are urban sociology and race and ethnic relations. Dr. Rosenthal's studies of Jewish intermarriage in Indiana and Iowa have been widely acclaimed as the best of their kind.

Luke M. Smith was born in 1912 and died in 1968. After receiving his bachelor's degree at UCLA in 1938, he earned his M.A. and Ph.D. (1948) at Harvard University. His last academic position was the chairmanship of Alfred University's sociology department where he concentrated in political and occupational sociology, penology, and race relations.

Anselm L. Strauss, who was born in 1916, took his B.S. at the University of Virginia and his M.A. and Ph.D. (1945) at the University of Chicago. He is now at the University of California in San Francisco where he specializes in social psychology and medical sociology.

John L. Thomas was born in 1910 and was educated at St. Louis University for the B.A., the University of Montreal for the M.A., and the University of Chicago for the Ph.D. (1949). A sociologist whose fields of concentration are marriage and the family and the sociology of science and knowledge, Dr. Thomas is a member of the Cambridge Center for Social Studies.

James E. Teele was born in 1927. He earned his bachelor's degree at Virginia Union University and his master's and doctor's degrees at New York University, the latter in 1961. Professor Teele is currently in the department of sociology at Boston University where his special interests are medical sociology and deviant behavior.

Clark E. Vincent, who was born in 1923, was university-educated entirely at the University of California, Berkeley. He received his Ph.D. there in 1952. His present affiliation is with the Bowman Gray School of Medicine and his fields are medical sociology and marriage and the family.